THE CONGRESSIONAL PARTY

New York · *John Wiley & Sons, Inc.*

London · *Chapman & Hall, Ltd.*

David B. Truman

COLUMBIA UNIVERSITY

THE CONGRESSIONAL

PARTY

A Case Study

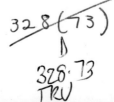

PREFACE

Although the fortunes of men and institutions are not turned toward triumph or disaster by any single factor, poets and politicians long have known that some one practice or quality may so reflect the strengths and weaknesses of a whole range of influences that it may be taken as critical. In the gallant gamble of contemporary democracy the representative assembly, the legislature, is such a crucial element. The fate of a nation is not hinged on it alone; especially in the American scheme of things the national legislature cannot be regarded as the sole or, from most points of view, even the most important determinant of the country's future. Yet the Congress of the United States so mirrors the nation in all its complexities and so intimately affects the other elements in the political system that without distortion one may regard its operations as setting limits upon the effectiveness of the whole.

In keeping with its political importance, the Congress has been much written about. Its activities stimulate a large fraction of the outpourings of the daily press, and the books devoted to it would fill a sizable library. Yet the Congress, however well known, is but little understood. The reasons for this paradox are many. Certainly one is the difficulty of finding a reliable pattern in the welter of discrete events and in the words of more than half a thousand men that constitute a Congressional session. Although much that occurs in the vicinity of Capitol Hill is not visible even to the close observer, the activities of no major political body in the world are as completely open to public view as are those of the Congress. Not only its debates, its votes, and its committee hearings, but also even its corridor conferences and its cloakroom confidences are remarkably accessible to the citizen or his surrogates in the press corps. Its accomplishments and perhaps especially its failures—given the psychological mechanism of projection—are public property to an extraordinary degree. Critic and champion alike, inside of the Congress and out, easily can find in this mass of material ample illustrations for whatever prejudgments he brings to his task.

A second major reason for the Congress appearing as a well-known stranger is that it is both old and forever new. Allowing for differences in style, a student of the legislature of the 1840's needs no completely fresh introduction to the materials of the 1880's, the 1920's, or the 1950's. The operations of the legislature, especially in their more obvious forms, have changed but not so extensively that they seem unfamiliar. At the same time one can reasonably expect and on some matters easily show that the national legislature in the middle years of the twentieth century is not the institution of even three decades ago. Neither its preoccupations nor its operating structure have escaped the changes that, for example, have given the national government its new domestic and international responsibilities and have produced the institution of the modern Presidency. But, even after the point is acknowledged, it still is difficult to determine whether and in what respects the Congress one sees is the same institution as the Congress one has known.

The principal object of this book is to contribute to an understanding of the legislature on both of these counts, that is, to suggest the nature of some reliable patterns in Congressional behavior and to indicate the peculiarly contemporary functions of the national legislature in our political system.

The book approaches this objective by analyzing the legislative parties in the House and Senate and particularly the roles of their designated leaders in the Eighty-first Congress. The study was not designed to determine the relative importance of party affiliation among the influences affecting the behavior of senators and representatives. Ample evidence already exists to support the proposition that, at least in the act of voting, the party label is consistently the most reliable predictor of a legislator's actions. It is not a perfect indicator, as the evidence of the study clearly shows, but it is sufficiently central in the operation of the legislature that an examination of the Congressional parties and their leaders is both feasible and instructive.

The book thus builds upon and only incidentally supplements the evidence concerning the importance of party in the behavior of individual legislators. It asks what can be learned of the nature and contemporary features of the Congress through an examination of the parties and their leaders as they reveal themselves in legislative behavior and particularly in voting on the floor of the two chambers. If one seeks a reliable understanding of the Congress, it is likely to be found most readily in those complexes, the legislative parties, that are the most prominent elements in its operations. And, if one seeks indications of the tendencies that are distinctive in our national legislature at mid-century, they are almost immediately found in the flexible, largely uncodified, and highly personalized roles of the Congressional party's leaders.

Congress is, of course, much more than its votes. The voting data therefore have been supplemented by an examination of the whole formal record of the two sessions chosen for study. This evidence was further amplified through personal interviews with senators and representatives, including most of the leaders of the Eighty-first Congress, with legislative and executive staff, and with press observers. The yea-and-nay votes, nevertheless, though often enigmatic, are a public record of choices made among measures and men. Their number and regularity make them significant composite indicators of roles. Properly used, they are a protection against an easy tendency to find in the many-faceted Congressional institution illustrations of one's prejudices rather than answers to one's objective questions.

Of the many problems encountered in presenting the results of a study of this sort the most troublesome is that of offering the inferences that seem warranted by the evidence without doing violence to the data in all their unruly variability and without at the same time keeping so close to the descriptive material that the main lines of the analysis are obscured. The operation of the Congressional party and the key roles within it can be described in terms of broad tendency and general pattern, and it is important that these be identified, but the diverse factors affecting these tendencies and patterns confront the analyst with risks of oversimplification. Under the watchful eye of a careful publisher, I have attempted to deal with this problem by relegating much of the supporting material to the footnotes and by retaining in the body of the text enough detail to indicate the basis of the argument without submerging the major interpretations.

No study that is limited to a single two-year period and is focused upon one set of primary data can produce unqualified conclusions. It can, however, in accounting for the events within its compass, offer interpretations of potentially longer reach. This is both the opportunity and the obligation of an author of a case study. If the following pages not only help to explain the legislative events of 1949 and 1950 but also contribute to an understanding of the Congress and its leadership in the years at mid-century, I shall have met my intention and discharged my obligation.

An enterprise of this sort, inevitably one man's responsibility, nevertheless reflects the contributions of many others. The original research for the book was made possible by a grant from the Carnegie Corporation of New York. Though I must disclaim any implication that the Corporation approves the views or opinions contained in the resulting study, I gratefully acknowledge its support. The months of interviewing in Washington and the completion of the statistical analysis were made possible by a fellowship from the John Simon Guggenheim Memorial Foundation, and the book was written in final form while I held a Ford Research Professorship in American Government granted by Columbia University. To both foundations and to the University I express my grateful appreciation.

The extensive machine computations on which the study is based were made possible through the facilities of the Watson Scientific Computing Laboratory, maintained by the International Business Machines Corporation in cooperation with Columbia University. I am deeply indebted to Dr. Wallace J. Eckert, Professor of Celestial Mechanics and Director of the Watson Laboratory, to Dr. David Mace, Research Associate in the Laboratory, and to their staff for invaluable help and encouragement. I also wish to thank Mr. Stanley Poley, then a graduate student in the Department of Civil Engineering, Columbia University, for his design of the original machine procedure.

As so often happens, the research underlying this book involved exploring many blind alleys as well as a few open roads. On some of these journeys I have had the companionship of several present and former graduate students at Columbia: Merton L. Reichler, R. Deane Postlethwaite, Eve Glassberg, and James S. Young. Though they may not recognize their efforts in the results, their loyal assistance contributed mightily to the final product.

During my stay in Washington I was extended innumerable courtesies by current and former members of Congress, by staff people in both House and Senate, by members of the press corps, and by my patient friends. I agreed at the time that those who served as my informants would not be identified in these pages; I honor those commitments reluctantly, since doing so prevents my publicly expressing my appreciation to each of them individually. It is not inconsistent with the obligation of anonymity, however, to record my respect for the willingness of busy men in public life to discuss their activities with a curious investigator to whom they normally have no ties other than a common interest in the institutions of government.

For permission to quote extensively from his two books, *The Taft Story* and *Citadel: The Story of the U. S. Senate,* both published by Harper and Brothers, I am indebted to William S. White. I am also grateful to the *American Political Science Review* for permission to reprint portions of Chapter 7, which first appeared in the pages of that journal.

A number of colleagues have generously accepted the task of reading and commenting on the manuscript at various stages: Herbert A. Deane, Richard E. Neustadt, and Wallace S. Sayre of Columbia; Robert A. Dahl of Yale; V. O. Key, Jr., of Harvard; and Duncan MacRae, Jr., of the University of Chicago, who also generously shared the materials of his research on the House in the Eighty-first Congress. I gladly absolve them all of any blame for the book's deficiencies and gratefully acknowledge their contributions to whatever merits it displays.

Finally, these lines would be seriously incomplete if they did not record my profound debt to my principal assistant, Elinor G. Truman, whose imaginative collaboration at all phases of the enterprise—library delving, coding, card-punching, machine operation, analysis, and typing—far exceeded the obligations of the marriage contract and in a very real sense made this a joint project.

DAVID B. TRUMAN

Scrub Hill
Hillsdale, New York
July, 1959

CONTENTS

one · THE CONGRESS AND THE CONGRESSIONAL PARTY   1
Factors in the Shift of Initiative   2
The Problem   7
The Method   10

two · THE CONTEXT: *The Story of the Eighty-First Congress*   15
The First Session, 1949   16
The Second Session, 1950   28

three · DIVISION AND COHESION: *The Structure of Party Voting in the Senate*   42
A Few Matters of Technique   45
Sources of Cleavage   49
The Democrats Disunited   50
The Democrats in Harmony   63
Republican Structural Cleavages   72
The Republicans United   82
Summary   89

xi

four · PARTY LEADERSHIP ROLES IN THE SENATE   94
The Positions   99
The Floor Leaders   104
The Whips   117
Other Elective Leaders   122
The Policy Committees   126
The Seniority Leaders   133

five · DIVISION AND COHESION: *The Structure of Party
Voting in the House of Representatives*   145
Sources of Cleavage   147
The Structure of Democratic Cleavage   150
The Democrats in Harmony   167
Republican Structural Cleavages   172
The Republicans United   186
Summary   190

six · PARTY LEADERSHIP ROLES IN THE HOUSE OF REPRE-
SENTATIVES   193
The Positions   197
The Floor Leaders   202
The Whips   226
Other Elective Leaders   230
*The Committees on Policy, on Rules, and on
Committees   231*
The Seniority Leaders   237
Summary   245

seven · INTRAPARTY GROUPS AND VOTING STRUCTURE IN THE
HOUSE: *The State Delegations and the Standing
Committees*   247
The State Party Delegations   249
The Standing Committee Delegations   269

eight · FUNCTIONAL INTERDEPENDENCE: *The Elective
Leaders, The White House, and the Congres-
sional Party*   279
Emergent Patterns and Their Implications   280
Leadership of the President's Majority   289
Perplexed Minorities and Truncated Majorities   308
Cases and Trends   316

appendix · THE ANALYSIS PROCEDURE   320

index   331

chapter one

THE CONGRESS
AND
THE CONGRESSIONAL PARTY

The twentieth century has been hard on national legislatures. The Congress of the United States, along with other representative assemblies, has not been spared the thrust of change that has reached into every corner of the world. More often than not that thrust has implied a threat of eclipse rather than a promise of new vigor. With increasing frequency events have called into wavering question the place and powers of representative assemblies. Doubt and apprehension have been perhaps more often implied than expressly stated, but from within as well as from outside the legislatures of the democratic nations have emerged questions about not only the proper, but even the actual, role of these bodies in the political scheme of things.

During these years the volume of demands upon governmental institutions has, of course, grown tremendously. Contemporary demands, however—such as those loosely referred to by the term "welfare state" and those reflected in the *de facto* responsibility for managing the national economy—are different from the demands of a century ago not only in number and in substance but also in other and more important respects. Many, indeed probably most, of these responsibilities deal

1

with problems that appear and change with great speed; they call upon a high order of technical knowledge and skill; they require assessment not only on their merits but also in terms of their relations to the whole corpus of governmental actions; and they need both flexibility and specificity of choice and guidance.

These familiar but not fully assimilated facts of political life have been accompanied by a general shift in the function of legislating, of making new rules and new law, a shift toward the executive, toward civilian and military bureaucracies and toward those directing them. This change, involving less a loss of function by the legislature than a growth of responsibilities in the executive, has in most democratic countries gradually acquired legitimacy, but in many it has not been fully or explicitly acknowledged. In the United States as compared, for example, with Great Britain, the shift toward the executive and the bureaucracies has been a tendency rather than a consummated fact, and its acknowledgment has been correspondingly limited. For reasons peculiar to the American scene, it may never be more than a tendency. But, in a world that not only has become smaller but also has been so polarized as to place in American hands the survival of free institutions everywhere, the special urgency of foreign relations and security policy is not likely to permit a reversal of the tendency, though its open justification may be long delayed.

FACTORS IN THE SHIFT OF INITIATIVE

The shift of function away from the Congress, though a clear tendency, has been discontinuous and especially controverted, and, partly on this account, it has not been fully rationalized. The probable reasons for this halting discontinuity involve a tremendous complex of factors, including the forms and myths of the Constitution, the federal system and the facts underlying it. This is not the place to attempt a detailed explanation of the complex, but, at the risk of oversimplification, one can assume the validity of the proposition that for most of their first century and one-half our politics were largely domestic and essentially simple. Continental expansion, the discovery and exploitation of virgin resources, and the initially decentralized development of the industrial revolution, made relatively modest demands upon national politics. The interests needing adjustment, economic and basically sectional, required a minimum of governmental activity in Washington. The accommodation of these interests, to the extent that it was done through political channels, took place appropriately and, with the major exception of the Civil War, easily. The principal governmental channel of accommodation was not legislation alone, but legislation generated primarily by way of the representative assembly, the Congress. Moreover, the whole process—conquest of the continent, industrialization, and particularly political adjustment of competing interests through a loosely integrated government—was fostered by what has since been recognized as the hundred years' peace, from 1815 to 1914.[1]

That this political setting, domestic and international, has changed is a commonplace, but nevertheless the fact has not been fully accepted in all its implications. Our politics are no longer simple. They have by no means lost their sectional character, but the issues that have been cast up or are constantly on the verge of making their appearance on the domestic scene rest on a complicated structure of interests, major and minor, produced by specialization and the urban-industrial complex. The inducements for oil exploration in North Dakota, the profits from a wheat farm in Nebraska, the pension of a clerk in Los Angeles, the supply of electricity in Vermont, the education of a Negro youngster in Alabama, the business of a contractor in Philadelphia, the volume of freight traffic on a New York railroad, and the housing prospects of a Harlem slum-dweller—all depend in varying degrees on decisions taken in the Federal Government. And in varying degrees all those immediately affected know it. On the international scene the United States has had to take on the burden of preventing the horrors of world war. This responsibility has replaced the almost unchallenged opportunities of the hundred years' peace, for which the American government was not even a nominal trustee. Hence, the "constituents" upon whose consent the fortunes of the Federal Government depend today are not just the voters from Maine to California, nor are they confined to Ottawa, London, Paris, and Rome. They are in Delhi, in Bangkok, in Djakarta, and Kabul, in Osaka, and Baghdad, and Lusaka, and Lagos. It may not be true that a depression in the United States means disaster for its allies, but if half the world thinks so, the opinion is important.

In partial consequence of this politics of international complexity, it has become accepted that the President and the executive branch generally not only should make recommendations to the Congress, but recommendations in detail. Detailed recommendations, however, whether upon projects originating in the executive or on many of those first reaching the government through the legislature, have involved the drafting of proposed legislation and, in turn, executive ef-

---

[1] Karl Polanyi, *The Great Transformation: The Political and Economic Origins of Our Time,* New York: Rinehart, 1944.

forts at securing enactment. In practice this represents a major change from what was the expected pattern even a few short decades ago.

Along with some related shifts that need not be detailed here, the change toward an extended executive initiative has not been consistently acceptable to all segments of the Congress. Strictly partisan motives aside, the central reason for the legislators' reaction is not hard to find. For the natural implication of the change is that it narrows the range, not of what the Congress *can* do, for the constitutional forms remain unaltered, but of what it is *likely* to do, what its members feel that it can do. The matters about which the Congress acts today are far more important, as senior members of both House and Senate readily acknowledge, than those that occupied most of its time prior to the Wilson Administration or even during the 1920's. Increasingly the classic preoccupations with rivers and harbors legislation, with roads and post offices, with pension bills, and with periodic revisions in the tariff have been crowded aside. Most of them are still on the agenda, but in a less prominent position, befitting their lesser consequence. The center of the stage now tends to be occupied by the military program, by foreign policy, and by problems concerned with management of the domestic economy. These more important matters, however, permit less room for the free play of the legislators' initiatives. They involve remote "constituencies" and technical secondary consequences for which the executive tends to be the spokesman.

Congressional discretion with respect to both the initiation and the declaration of policy is, of course, in practice still very wide, and narrowing of the range has not been uniform over all fields of public policy. Yet the tendency toward a *de facto* encroachment on the discretion of the legislators, especially in "newer" policy areas, has been clear enough both to produce recurrent demands that the Congress recapture the initiative and to encourage some fairly ambitious attempts in that direction. Restoration of legislative initiative was one of the issues close to the surface of the debate over the so-called Bricker Amendment, which proposed to restrict the reach of the treaty power; it has appeared repeatedly in the testimony of members of Congress in connection with proposals to alter the internal organization of the House and Senate;[2] and it has been expressed frequently in

---

[2] See, for example, *Organization of Congress*, Hearings, Joint Committee on the Organization of Congress, 79th Cong., 1st sess., Washington: 1945, and *Organization and Operation of Congress*, Hearings, U. S. Senate Committee on Expenditures in the Executive Departments, 82d Cong., 1st sess., Washington: 1951. William S. White sees the Senate, in the ten years following World War II, dedicated to the effort to recapture its independence from the Presidency. *Citadel: The Story of the U. S. Senate*, New York: Harper, 1957, pp. 98–9 and *passim*.

a variety of other connections. In an interchange concerning proposed amendments to the Federal Regulation of Lobbying Act in 1956, Senator Goldwater of Arizona stated his concern over the influence of the executive on the voting decisions of members of the Congress, especially the Representatives. "My fear," he said, "is that . . . the legislative becomes nothing but a mill the crank of which is turned by the other end of the street . . . , and the laws become automatic."[3]

Demands such as these for a restoration of legislative initiative are not mere rhetoric. They represent a variety of factors deeply rooted in the structure of American politics and in the attitudes associated with that structure. These attitudes, held by members of the Congress as well as in the electorate generally, cannot be expected to change as rapidly as governmental practices. In this connection it is worth noting that the average member of the Congress that assembled for its first session in January 1949 had passed his twenty-first birthday during Wilson's second term. He was thirty during the summer of 1927, when Coolidge laconically announced that he "did not choose to run" again for the Presidency.[4] In other words, he had reached maturity in a period when it was still assumed, and with considerable accuracy, that the initiation of general rules and the setting of particular policies were, and properly should be, concentrated in the legislature. It is not strange that such a man should feel uneasy about apparent shifts in the legislature's role in the political scheme of things. His attitudes, moreover, unquestionably are matched by similar ones within the constituencies. Here, however, there may be less consistency, for while a candidate for re-election may be damaged by the charge that he has been a "rubber stamp" for the Executive, he may also be penalized for not "going along" with the requests of a popular President. On balance, however, a candidate probably would be prudent, if he could not avoid the question, to assert that it is up to the Congress to write the laws and to declare policy and that the executive branch should be confined to suggestion and enforcement.

These attitudes, as part of the mythology of the Constitution, are reinforced by institutional forms, both legal and conventional, of which the separation of powers is only one. The fact of federalism and the existence of the diversities that underlie its continued vitality

---

[3] *Oil and Gas Lobby Investigation*, Hearings, U. S. Senate Special Committee to Investigate Political Activities, Lobbying, and Campaign Contributions, 84th Cong., 2d sess., Washington: 1956, p. 585.

[4] The ages of members of the Eighty-first Congress are tabulated in the *Congressional Quarterly Almanac*, Vol. 5, Washington: Congressional Quarterly News Features, 1949, pp. 20–4.

almost inevitably demand resistance to standardizing solutions in the political sphere, including those emerging from the national executive. The corresponding structure of the electoral parties and the hard necessities involved in carving out a political career, despite tendencies within the electorate toward division along national cleavage lines, similarly encourage a degree of independence at least sufficient to permit the assertion of parochial dissent and opposition.[5] Moreover, these facts of structure, both constitutional and electoral, provide a leverage for interest groups that reinforces protests against executive expansion. Groups that feel themselves in jeopardy in consequence of secular changes in the society as well as those tactically disadvantaged normally find championship of legislative initiative and independence a worthy object of their energies. "The American system," as William Anderson has aptly suggested, "provides a series of appeals from one center of power to another, to another, to another, over a wide range."[6]

In consequence many, perhaps most, demands from within the Congress for a restoration of legislative initiative represent interest claims couched in the language of constitutional debate. Many, however, also reflect a genuine institutional concern, an almost guilty perplexity over the role of the legislature in the contemporary setting. What, they seem to ask, is a representative assembly that is not the prime initiator of rules, the principal decider of policy? If it is no longer, or only in reduced degree, a legislature in this sense, what is it? Illustrative is a comment by former Representative Jerry Voorhis shortly after his defeat in 1946. Though he was not conspicuously hostile to the executive branch during his ten years in the House, in explaining why the Congress did not enact what he regarded as an adequate fiscal program during World War II he said, "It took the weak and futile position that its own legislative action had to wait upon Executive recommendation."[7] No matter that this was a practice as old as the Republic. The conscientious anxiety revealed in the criticism is its significance.

The institutional concern running through many congressional protests has some warrant. The question of how the Congress does and

---

[5] See Herbert Wechsler, "The Political Safeguards of Federalism," and David B. Truman, "Federalism and the Party System," in Arthur W. Macmahon, editor, *Federalism Mature and Emergent,* Garden City: Doubleday, 1955, pp. 97–136. For an analysis of the impact of national issues on state politics, see V. O. Key, Jr., *American State Politics,* New York: Knopf, 1956, chap. 2.

[6] Quoted in Macmahon, *Federalism Mature and Emergent,* p. 86, from discussion at the Columbia University Bicentennial Conference on Federalism.

[7] Jerry Voorhis, *Confessions of a Congressman,* New York: Doubleday, 1947, p. **307.**

should fit into the political scheme of things in the midtwentieth century is not idle. Important values underlie the institution of the representative assembly, values concerned with the worth of human diversity and political values, not less important for being primarily instrumental. From the standpoint of domestic stability, a Congress that never legislated, never initiated or decided policy, whose function was only to criticize and to ratify, could mean shutting off from the central political councils troublesome, perhaps small, but explosive interests in the society whose expression could be justified as a technical political necessity if not as a moral right. On the other hand, if a line ever existed between "domestic" and "foreign" policy, it has now all but disappeared. Budgetary choices between the claims of American and foreign "constituents," policies on the handling of agricultural surpluses, and decisions concerning racial discrimination are as important to American influence in the world as the forging of alliances and the development of military strength. From the standpoint of the role of the United States in the leadership of the free world, therefore, a role it cannot escape but may easily neglect, a Congress that never relinquished or, in response to parochial interests, fitfully reclaimed the whole power of legislation could produce disaster. These statements somewhat oversimplify the matter by putting it in extreme terms, but the consequences they imply need not be fully realized to be destructive.

THE PROBLEM

The shift of initiative toward the executive, which has come about because it has had to, has thus been halting and often inconsistent. Unwelcome in many quarters and regarded as insufficient in others, outside of the government it has been the focus of a debate that has recurred with increasing frequency at least since the time of Woodrow Wilson. In this debate the proponents of executive influence, perhaps largely because of their identification with interests demanding innovation, have been more conspicuous than those who might be classified as the defenders of the representative assembly. Among the friends of the Congress are some who, though not greatly alarmed about executive encroachment, are strongly disposed to accept the Congress as it stands, to argue that the effectiveness of the Federal Government is in no important degree threatened by the existing patterns of congressional performance.[8] Others, including such distinguished scholars as

[8] See, for example, the moderate views presented in Ernest S. Griffith, *Congress: Its Contemporary Role*, New York: New York University Press, 1951.

Edward S. Corwin, are less concerned with the Congress as such than with the potentialities of the legislature for reducing what in this modern Whig view are regarded as dangerous tendencies toward autocracy in the modern Presidency.[9]

On the other side of the debate, some responsible critics have advocated a basic, and probably unattainable, alteration in the Constitution that would attempt to recast it more nearly in the mold of party government as it is thought to operate under the British cabinet sysem.[10] A more radical, though less concrete, view has been urged by Walter Lippmann. His criticisms, though they include this country, are not confined to the United States and they are not easily summarized. To the extent that his position can be put in institutional terms, he sees usurpation, not by the executive, but by the representative assembly. "The power of the executive," he argues, "has become enfeebled, often to the verge of impotence." [11] Less extreme, and less pessimistic, are those who acknowledge a relative decline in Congress but attribute it to "congressional abdication and obstruction, not presidential usurpation." [12] They would welcome a presidential influence that had grown from leadership to rule through the mechanisms of a centralized electoral and legislative party.

For many of the legislature's critics—as well as for some of its defenders—the party, both in the electorate and within the Congress, is the chief point of attention. Characteristically their view is toward revision of congressional practices and toward alterations, some of them fairly basic, in the electoral system. Their central target, however, is the legislative party. They expect by their proposed changes to produce "more responsible" parties based on adherence to agreed policy programs.[13]

In the opinion of most critics of the national legislature, especially

---

[9] Edward S. Corwin, *The President: Office and Powers,* 4th edition, New York: New York University Press, 1957, chap. 7 and *passim.*

[10] Different in detail but similar in tendency are William Y. Elliott, *The Need for Constitutional Reform,* New York: McGraw-Hill, 1935, and Thomas K. Finletter, *Can Representative Government Do the Job?* New York: Reynal and Hitchcock, 1945. Substitution of a parliamentary system after the French pattern that would subordinate the President has been advocated by Henry Hazlitt in *A New Constitution Now,* New York: McGraw-Hill, 1942.

[11] Walter Lippmann, *Essays in the Public Philosophy,* Boston: Little, Brown, 1955, p. 55. For a less consistent but somewhat similar view, based on a fear of congressional investigations, see Alan Barth, *Government by Investigation,* New York: Viking, 1955.

[12] James M. Burns, *Congress on Trial,* New York: Harper, 1949, p. 181.

[13] Committee on Political Parties, American Political Science Association, "Toward a More Responsible Two-Party System," *American Political Science Review,* Vol. 44, no. 3 (September, 1950), Supplement.

those who are not part of it, the Congress is what the legislative parties are. With this view there can be little quarrel, but the range of opinion among the critics indicates wide disagreement not only on what the Congress and the legislative parties ought to be, but also on what in fact the Congress is and on what the legislative parties within its chambers are. These questions of fact constitute the problem to which this study is directed. Before one can arrive at a defensible judgment of the proper place of the Congress in the political scheme of things and before one can estimate with any degree of confidence the probable consequences of various proposals for change, a clear conception of the actual place of the legislature and of the roles of the congressional parties is essential. In the realm of politics, as in other complex phases of the society, what might be is inevitably, if only in part, a function of what is.

The analysis starts from the cardinal fact of maturing American federalism in the twentieth century, a fact agreed to almost unanimously: the pivotal position achieved for the Presidency under a series of "strong" Chief Executives dealing with an almost unbroken series of domestic and world crises. If this development can be taken for granted, may it not be the case that changes have occurred in the functioning of the Congress, changes more subtle than those suggested by words like "usurpation" and "abdication"? It is entirely possible that many Americans hold a view of Congress not sharply different from that ascribed by a perceptive English scholar to most Europeans, who in his judgment, even when they are friendly and informed, ". . . look on Congress much as most Americans view the French National Assembly—as a chaotic, incoherent aggregation of small-minded and shortsighted individualists, whose incomprehensible behavior is predictable only in that, on matters of international concern, they so often seem 'like inverted Micawbers waiting for something to turn down.'" [14]

How close to reality is this impression of the national legislature? How much of pattern and regularity can be found beneath an appearance of unpredictability or even of chaos? Is there any evidence, in particular, that in a system whose pivot increasingly is the White House the congressional party is a valuable or significant instrument of governing? Party affiliation does have reality as a factor in the behavior of individual legislators.[15] But what is the congressional party's

---

[14] Philip Williams, "Political Compromise in France and America," *The American Scholar,* Vol. 26, no. 3 (Summer, 1957), p. 274.

[15] Julius Turner, *Party and Constituency: Pressures on Congress,* Baltimore: The Johns Hopkins Press, 1951; V. O. Key, Jr., *Parties, Politics, and Pressure Groups,* 4th edition, New York: Crowell, 1958, pp. 727 ff.

appearance on either side of the aisle in both Senate and House? What is its role in relation to the White House? Does it operate to enhance or to diminish the recurrent conflicts between the two branches, and under what conditions does it function in these respects?

If the legislative party shows any coherent pattern as a stable organizational element in the political system, what of the structure, or structures, through which it is led? Specifically, what are the roles of its designated leaders? What functions are they expected to perform? How free are they to choose for themselves the range of duties they will assume? How narrowly are they limited by convention or explicit restriction? What influence do they exercise? What are the sources of such influence? How do they operate with their colleagues and, in particular, with the President, whether he is of their own party or of the opposition?

THE METHOD

Final answers to questions such as these are not likely to be produced by any method of inquiry. The importance of the problem to which the questions relate, namely, the place and prospects of the national legislature, is grave enough, however, to demand that answers be attempted by such tools of inquiry as can be devised.

The chief difficulty faced by any form of investigation in this area is that the Congress and the legislative parties are institutions with many facets. They present a quite different appearance at various times in their evolution, even within a relatively short period. Differences of view on what the Congress is in fact, on what the legislative parties are and how they operate, are thus almost inevitable. Examined through the history of a single piece of legislation, both the Congress and the parties may give a quite different impression of their functioning from that produced by the analysis of another bill. If one describes them by examining the official rules and procedures, the manifest forms, or if one views them from a single vantage point such as one of the standing committees, or if one looks at them through the biography of a prominent senator or representative, one may arrive at a series of rather contradictory impressions. None of these approaches is inherently wrong, of course, and, since the institutions do have many facets, none is without value. Each, however, has its limitations, in time and scope.

The method underlying this book also has limitations, but its value is that it seems peculiarly well adapted to providing at least tentative answers to questions such as those raised in the foregoing paragraphs, questions important to understanding the national legislature and the congressional parties. This method has two basic features: First, it is a cross-section case analysis covering the two years of a single Congress, the Eighty-first, which met during the years 1949 and 1950; second, it relies primarily upon the formal record of that Congress and, more particularly, upon the roll call votes, on which the preferences of the individual senators and representatives are recorded. The evidence from the record votes was supplemented extensively by interviews with senators and representatives who were active in the Eighty-first and subsequent Congresses, with staff people in both houses, and with journalists. In addition, the documentary record, official and unofficial, was examined with care. These sources of information were invaluable in providing insights and in checking on inferences drawn from the voting analysis. They were, nevertheless, only supplementary to the evidence from the roll calls.

Intensive study of a whole Congress through this sort of case analysis has the general advantage of approximating an account of the full pattern of activity in the House and Senate for a two-year period. In this respect, therefore, it is more representative than an investigation of a single piece of legislation or a series of such items, since these kinds of cases permit no reliable inference concerning whether the items selected are typical, are characteristic of congressional behavior even in the particular session or sessions in which the legislation was developed. They may reflect the legislature in an extreme situation, but it is impossible to determine objectively whether they do or not. A two-year case involves no subjective judgment of what is important or typical, since all measures on which roll calls have been taken are included. Moreover, since its boundaries are set by time rather than by a subjective definition, it has advantages over the study of legislative behavior in a particular area of substantive policy, such as agriculture or foreign policy, since the boundaries of such areas in almost all cases must be set arbitrarily or, at best, conventionally.

The limitations involved in studying a single Congress are, first, those of any case. In contrast to a representative sample, a single case provides no scientific basis for generalizing to the whole category or universe of which the case is one element, for example, all Congresses after World War II. As later chapters will demonstrate, the use of a variety of comparisons—between sessions, between parties, and between the two chambers—somewhat reduces the seriousness of this limitation, but does not eliminate it. In the same way, though study of a single Congress may provide significant clues to trends that have occurred over a longer period of time, it does not permit firm conclusions about such changes. A single case, in other words, even one covering the events of twenty-four months, is essentially exploratory. Finally, a study that takes a whole Congress as its focus almost inevitably must lack the richness of detail that is possible when a single measure is examined intensively. Since its target is the identification of general patterns, those evident over a two-year period, the more subtle details and revealing nuances are deliberately neglected except as occasional illustrations of a broad tendency.

Roll call votes, the principal source of the patterns found in this study, have the great advantage of being "hard" data. Like statistics on elections, they represent discrete acts the fact of whose occurrence is not subject to dispute. They do not depend for their validity as data upon verbal reports of action or upon the impressions of fallible observers. Taken in quantity, therefore, they can be examined statistically with more confidence than can be granted to data whose reliability depends upon the objectivity of visual observation or verbal reporting. In the Congress, moreover, the "yeas and nays" closely approximate a record of the principal actions of the two houses. Not all votes are taken by roll call, of course, but it is rarely the case that a matter of real controversy, or one of importance in other respects, is disposed of in either chamber without at least one vote recording the preferences of the individual senators and representatives.

Interpretation of the "yeas and nays," determining the "meaning" of the roll calls, presents difficulties, of course. The act of a voting choice is a matter of record, but the reasons for it and the consequences intended by the legislator are a good deal less evident. The ambiguity of the legislator's vote, however, is not greatly different, in kind or degree, from that of the choice recorded by an elector in a polling booth. Analysis of election returns, though often fruitfully supplemented by methods such as opinion surveys, has long been relied upon in the study of politics. Congressional roll calls have been less consistently exploited, but they contain no inherent weakness that renders them less satisfactory as evidence.

Reservations properly can and should be registered, however, against an uncritical reliance upon roll calls as indicators of the full range of legislative behavior. They are unmistakably a record of decisions taken, of choices made, but they are evidence of only the most public choices. Ordinarily they indicate nothing about measures that never reach the floor of the House or Senate, and they directly reveal nothing about what has occurred behind the scenes. In the Congress, as in most American legislatures, the choices made in committees, both standing legislative committees and the *ad hoc* conference groups authorized to resolve differences in measures passed by the two houses, are of great consequence. The roll calls occasionally permit inferences concerning events in committee, and other materials can be used to supplement these, but alone the record votes reflect only the most conspicuous features of legislative action.

The public character of the choices recorded in the roll calls in other respects considerably enhances their value as data. In particular it narrows somewhat the problem of attaching meaning or intent to the vote. The registered choice is one the senator or representative is willing to have shown beside his name in the *Congressional Record,* available for whatever use both opponents and supporters may wish to make of it. The importance attached to this public performance is evident, for example, from the precautions that are taken in both House and Senate to give advance notice of voting on all major measures and to avoid record votes on days when many members are likely to be absent. The function of such notice in some cases, of course, may be to permit senators and representatives who would prefer not to state their positions on a difficult vote to make their plans accordingly. But whether this is the result or whether, as is usually the case, members make an effort to have their preferences recorded, the significance attached to the public character of the roll call is acknowledged. Therefore, although examining a large number of these public choices in series and in combination may miss some subtleties of meaning, it can be a reliable procedure for identifying patterns of intent—general tendencies of behavior that may lead to a clearer understanding of the congressional party, of its utility as an instrument of governing, and of the representative body in which it operates.

To inform, or remind, the reader of the setting in which the data of the study were generated, the pages immediately following tell the story of the Eighty-first Congress in straight chronological terms, with little or no attempt at interpretation. Voting within the Senate parties is then examined in some detail in order to identify patterns of voting agreement among senators both when party unity was relatively high and when the legislative parties were internally divided. The various formal elements of leadership are then located within this structure, and an estimate is made of the roles of the Senate party leaders, their relative importance, their interconnections, and the differences between the leaders of the majority and those of the minority. The parties and the party leaders in the House are then analyzed in essentially the same terms. In addition, an assessment is made of the importance for congressional voting of two influences that exist within the legislature but are in varying degrees independent of the mechanisms of party, namely, affiliation with the delegations from the various states and membership on the standing legislative committees. The detailed findings on the parties in both Senate and House are then drawn together in a concluding synthesis that attempts to answer the book's two basic questions: What is the significance of the congressional party as a governing instrument? What meaning has this estimate for an understanding of the place of the national legislature in the political scheme of things at midcentury?

chapter two

THE CONTEXT:

The Story
of the Eighty-First Congress

No Congress is typical. Each has its own combination of leaders, and in each the membership differs, sometimes slightly, sometimes drastically, from all the others. The deliberations that take place and the decisions that are made during the two years of its constitutional life reflect not only the issues and events of that period, but also the circumstances under which the Congress was chosen and the expectations its members entertain concerning the future. Although the objective of the present inquiry is not history, not description of the unique elements in a stream of events, but identification of the features of the Eighty-first Congress that are basic and persistent, an awareness of at least the major outlines of the circumstances under which these occurred is nevertheless essential. Such an account is important not only to understanding what was taking place, but also to estimating the extent to which inferences drawn from the material are indeed matters of general tendency or are primarily reflections of a unique set of circumstances. The nature of a single case is such that one cannot determine with precision what is peculiar to it and what is common to all instances in the same class of phenomena. One must, therefore, be particularly careful to keep in mind the events and circumstances of the case in order to judge how far one may have confidence in the general tendencies inferred from it.

THE FIRST SESSION, 1949

Repercussions of 1948. Perhaps the most important single influence upon the Congress that assembled on the third day of January, 1949, certainly for at least the first 18 months of its existence, was the election of 1948. Since the midterm elections of 1946, which had given the Republicans a majority in both House and Senate, the assumption had been general throughout the country that President Truman had in effect been repudiated by the electorate and that, almost regardless of the nominees they selected, the Republicans would recapture the White House in 1948. The events of the spring and summer prior to the presidential election did nothing to reduce Republican confidence. The Democratic party seemed hopelessly split, with the candidacy of Henry Wallace on the Progressive ticket likely to draw off an important fraction of the left-wing support in the North and the States Rights party under Strom Thurmond and Fielding Wright certain to deny the Democrats some Southern electoral votes. Almost without exception the experts, pundits and pollsters alike, assumed the victory of the Dewey-Warren slate and, of course, the return of a Republican congressional majority.

The Democratic sweep which became apparent in the early hours of Wednesday, November 3, 1948, inevitably produced accusations and recriminations among the Republicans.[1] Partisans of Senator Taft blamed Governor Dewey and his campaign strategy for converting certain victory into humiliating defeat, and the "Dewey wing" of the party ascribed the failure to the ineptness of the Republican congressional leadership in the Eightieth Congress. This dissension, which certainly affected Republican legislative behavior throughout much of 1949 and 1950, was particularly evident in the Senate. A small group of rebels, led by Senator Ives of New York, went so far as to attempt to force a change in the party's leadership. When the Senate Republi-

---

[1] The partisan division of the Eighty-first Congress when it assembled in January, 1949, was: in the Senate, 54 Democrats and 42 Republicans; in the House, 262 Democrats, 171 Republicans, one member from the American Labor Party, and one vacancy.

can Conference met on the opening day of the Congress, this group supported Senator Knowland of California against Senator Wherry of Nebraska for the post of Minority Leader, which the latter had held during the previous Congress, and nominated Senator Lodge of Massachusetts to replace Senator Taft as Chairman of the Senate Republican Policy Committee. These moves were both defeated, by votes of 28 to 14.[2] Senator Millikin of Colorado was unopposed for re-election as Chairman of the Conference, and, as a gesture to the rebels, Senator Saltonstall of Massachusetts was chosen as Minority Whip. In the House there were no overt repercussions among the Republicans. Representative Halleck vacated the position of Floor Leader, to which Representative Martin, the retiring Speaker, was duly elected, and Representative Arends of Illinois was rechosen as the Minority Whip.

The Democrats had no serious organizational problems. In the Senate they designated Senator Lucas of Illinois to move up from Whip to Floor Leader to succeed Senator Barkley when the latter took the oath as Vice President on January 20. Senator Myers of Pennsylvania was chosen for the post of Whip. In the House the Democratic leadership was placed in familiar hands. The caucus nominated Representative Rayburn to serve his fourth term as Speaker and elected Representative McCormack as Majority Leader. Representative Priest was chosen as Majority Whip.

The November victory nevertheless left the Democrats, and especially the Administration, a legacy of other problems. During the campaign, including the special session of the Congress in the summer of 1948, President Truman had in effect committed himself to a program of legislation that was not only extensive but also heterogeneous and at a good many points highly controversial. Truman was almost inevitably a prisoner of the kind of campaign he had conducted. Following the "coup" at the Philadelphia convention he had embraced the civil rights program with renewed vigor, and his attacks on the Republicans had all but obliged him to seek repeal of the Taft-Hartley Act and passage of legislation on public housing, rent and price controls, education, and farm prices, to list only the most conspicuous domestic matters. The diversity and controversiality of these commitments were a standing threat to the solidarity of an already divided

[2] *New York Times,* January 4, 1949. Except as otherwise indicated, the account in this chapter is based upon the *Congressional Record,* 81st Cong., 1st and 2d sess., Vols. 95 and 96, and upon reports in the *New York Times,* supplemented by materials in the *Congressional Quarterly Almanac,* Washington: Congressional Quarterly News Features, 1949 and 1950.

party, and the size of the program meant that the most favorable conditions would be required if legislative action were to be taken on any considerable number of the items.

Rules controversies. The Democrats' difficulties were evident when efforts were undertaken in both chambers to alter the rules. In their House caucus on January first, after prolonged debate, a decision was taken to support an amendment to the House rules that would reduce the power of the Rules Committee to block legislation. Originally sponsored by Representative Eberharter of Pennsylvania, it was put forward because its supporters feared that the Administration's program otherwise might be indefinitely delayed or emasculated by a coalition majority on the Rules Committee. The amendment, which came to be known as the "21-day rule," provided that on the second and fourth Mondays in the month it should be in order for the chairman of a committee that had reported a public bill, the proposed rule for which had been before the Rules Committee for 21 days, to call up for immediate consideration by the House the rule not granted by the Committee on Rules. In the caucus Eberharter had the strong support of Representative Rayburn, who, when the resolution was offered on the floor of the House by Rules Committee Chairman Sabath, effectively guided it to adoption.[3]

The proposed change in the Senate rules provided the first major battle of the 1949 session. Rule XXII, or those provisions of it dealing with the limitation of debate, had been adopted in 1917. Infrequently used, it had been so riddled with exceptions over the years as to be almost meaningless. Strengthening it was essential if the Senate were to take any positive action on civil rights measures. After lengthy hearings before the Committee on Rules and Administration, Senator Lucas moved on February 28 to take up the resolution. This immediately set off a filibuster, which continued until it was voluntarily halted on March 15. After three days of debate and voting, in which various proposals concerning the rule were rejected, the Senate on March 17 adopted a version sponsored by Senator Wherry on behalf of a coalition of Republicans and Southern Democrats. The new rule was in most respects less usable than the one it replaced.

---

[3] There are indications that neither Sabath nor Rayburn relished this change, the former because it threatened the prestige of his committee and the latter because it might either put too much control in the hands of the committee chairmen or place responsibility with unwanted clarity upon the Speaker. Both apparently regarded the change as involving a lesser handicap than obstruction by an unchecked Rules Committee. For a good discussion of the rule and its use, see Lewis J. Lapham, "Party Leadership and the House Committee on Rules," unpublished doctoral dissertation, Harvard University, 1953, pp. 191 ff., 280, and *passim*.

The President's program. This controversy was an inauspicious beginning on the long list of legislative proposals that the President had presented in four major installments during the month of January. Most of the Administration program was covered in the first of these, the State of the Union message, delivered on January 5. Among its most important recommendations, in addition to the civil rights measures, were repeal of the Taft-Hartley Act, universal military training, a 75-cent minimum wage, extension of the reciprocal trade agreements program, a tax increase of approximately four billion dollars, and an eight-point program of controls over prices and production. Less novel proposals covered farm, power, and resource programs, aid to education, extension of social security, low-rent public housing, and medical insurance. The economic report on January 7 and the budget message on January 10 elaborated on some of these. The economic message, despite increasing signs of recession, presented a detailed justification for the anti-inflation and tax recommendations and specifically asked for repeal of the tax on oleomargarine. The budget anticipated a deficit of nearly one billion dollars without additional taxation.

The last of these documents, the Inaugural Address of January 20, dealt almost entirely with foreign affairs. In this area the President set out a four-point policy involving continued support for the United Nations, renewal of our economic aid programs, strengthening the free nations against aggression (referring to the North Atlantic Treaty, which was about to be submitted to the Senate), and what came to be known as "Point 4." This last was presented as a "bold new program" for making scientific and industrial advances available to underdeveloped areas.

February and March: reorganization, reciprocity, and rent. The House, as usual, moved fairly rapidly on a number of these items. Early in February it passed requested legislation reauthorizing the President, subject to congressional veto, to reorganize the executive along the lines recommended by the Hoover Commission. (Delayed in the Senate, this measure was not finally approved until late in June.) It then passed, in substantially the form requested by the President, a three-year extension of the reciprocal trade program, the votes being cast almost entirely along party lines. A few days later it voted to extend the President's authority to control exports, and by mid-March it was ready to take up the controversial matter of extending rent controls. After three days of intense debate, it passed a bill extending controls for 15 months, but allowing states and localities to decontrol particular areas and guaranteeing landlords, "in so far as practicable," a "reasonable return" on their property.

The Senate, having meanwhile disposed of the cloture issue, took up the rent measure on March 21. It debated much the same issues as the House and with equal heat, eventually passing a similar bill after rejecting a series of more restrictive amendments, most of which were sponsored by Senators Bricker, Capehart, and Cordon.

April: economic aid and housing. The debate on renewal of the European Recovery Program, which opened in the Senate on March 24, extended well beyond the terminal date of the 1948 legislation. With little effective opposition to the general policy, the debate had many of the earmarks of old-fashioned tariff controversies. Some foreign-policy "hobbies" were supported, such as the special provision for aid to those areas of China "not under Communist domination," but more were rejected. Much of the debate, however, concerned the granting of special advantages to particular American interests, such as ship owners, writers of marine insurance, producers of agricultural surpluses, food processors, and small businesses. Although House consideration of the measure centered upon the same kinds of issues, no significant changes were made in the committee bill, and the President signed the act on April 19.

Most of the remaining time of the Senate in April was devoted to the legislation that eventually became the National Housing Act of 1949, authorizing programs of slum clearance, low-rent public housing, and farm-housing grants and loans, which had been before the Congress in one form or another since the end of World War II. The strenuous opposition was spearheaded by Senators Bricker and Cain, but only a small fraction of their amendments was adopted. Most votes on amendments found a majority of Democrats opposing a majority of Republicans, but, with such minority influentials as Senator Taft supporting the legislation, Republican unity on the roll calls was generally low.

May: Taft-Hartley, education, economy, defense, and grain storage. In the last days of April and the first week of May the attention of the country was focused on the House, where the first attempt to alter the Taft-Hartley Act was being staged.[4] The bill reported by the House

---

[4] The House was somewhat distracted by the opening scenes of a classic battle among the military services. This was touched off by the resignation on April 26 of Navy Secretary Sullivan in protest against Secretary of Defense Johnson's cancellation of work on the first "super" aircraft carrier. As a result of this incident the House Armed Services Committee in June held hearings on charges of improper conduct in connection with the procurement of B-36 bombers. These unsubstantiated charges were traced to the Navy. After they were rejected by the Committee, the underlying issue was raised even more explicitly in a note endorsed by top Navy officers, including Admiral Denfeld, Chief of Naval Operations, that was

Education and Labor Committee proposed a largely symbolic repeal of Taft-Hartley and a reinstitution of the Wagner Act with changes that would have made it differ from Taft-Hartley in two major respects. It would have withdrawn authority to issue injunctions in strikes involving national emergencies and in unfair labor practice cases, and it would have legitimized the closed shop and preferential hiring practices. Since the House was operating under an "open" rule permitting extensive debate, a great many amendments were offered and debated. But the key issues were provided by two substitutes for the committee bill, one sponsored by Representative Wood of Georgia, who proposed to alter Taft-Hartley in only minor respects and in particular included no change in the provision for injunctions in emergency disputes; and one offered by Representative Sims of South Carolina that differed significantly from the committee bill only in retention of the emergency strike injunction, which thus became the pivotal point of controversy. Inability to compromise on this point was evident when the Sims substitute was defeated on May 3 by a vote on which several conspicuous labor supporters were recorded among the opposition. The Wood substitute was then adopted by a narrow margin. The next day, however, the bill was recommitted, the Majority Leader and the chairman of the committee voting for the motion whose adoption ended consideration of the measure in the House.

At the same time the Senate was debating and passing a bill for federal aid to elementary and secondary education, essentially like one it passed in the Eightieth Congress. The proposed measure reflected skillful negotiation of a compromise formula for dividing funds between the richer and poorer states, for avoiding the hot religious issue, and for side-stepping the racial question. When the new bill was taken up on April 29, half a dozen amendments which would have upset these arrangements were defeated, and the measure was passed in the Senate by a substantial majority. In the House committee the measure foundered when Representative Barden of North Carolina, chairman of the subcommittee, insisted on confining support to public schools. The deadlock produced charges of bigotry, which were echoed by Cardinal Spellman of New York. These were criticized by Methodist Bishop Oxnam, and by Mrs. Franklin D. Roosevelt who was in turn denounced by the Cardinal.

The annual appropriation bills, which began to move through the legislature in the early spring, contained the normal number of contro-

---

given to the press. It charged that Defense Department policies concerning budget allocations and the assignment of missions were jeopardizing the Navy's efficiency. The resulting hearings ran through most of October, ending on the 21st. Six days later Admiral Denfeld was dismissed.

versies. In the Senate, however, most of them encountered a novel device for effecting reductions. Avoiding assault on particular items, this tactic involved amendments directing the President or the heads of agencies to cut expenditures 5 per cent below the amounts voted in the appropriations. Sponsored in most instances by Republicans, these attempts were uniformly unsuccessful. The appropriation bills throughout the spring and summer produced some spectacular contests over substantive policy in both houses, notably in connection with foreign economic aid, including a strenuous effort to require aid to Spain, and over public electric power facilities.

Toward the end of May the Senate considered and passed legislation significantly changing the National Security Act of 1947. The measure created little controversy, although there was debate over whether the bill went too far or not far enough in giving power to the Defense Secretary, over the powers of the new Chairman of the Joint Chiefs of Staff, and over whether the measure gave sufficient protection to the Marine Corps and the Navy. Some of these matters reflected the B-36 controversy, then at an early peak,[5] and they threatened to color the House debates in July. However, the Senate version, substantially unchanged, was eventually accepted.

A portion of the 1948 campaign was re-argued in April and May in both chambers, when action was taken to amend the charter of the Commodity Credit Corporation, the provisions of which, as passed by the Eightieth Congress, were regarded by Democrats as having caused losses to grain-growers and an increase of votes for the Democrats in 1948 by limiting the government's acquisition of grain storage facilities. Though debate was partisan, voting was not, and the measure was enacted without major difficulty.

June: health, Taft-Hartley, and housing. Perhaps the most spectacular legislative performance of late May and early June took place not on the floor of either house but before the Senate Committee on Labor and Public Welfare, which was holding hearings on the President's controversial health program. Truman had reopened this matter on April 22 with a special message. The bill incorporating the Administration program had four provisions that were a necessary foundation for the explosive compulsory health insurance proposal. The Administration had no serious expectation that more than these four would be enacted in 1949 or 1950,[6] but witnesses at the hearings concentrated

---

[5] See above, note 4.

[6] See Richard E. Neustadt, "Congress and the Fair Deal: A Legislative Balance Sheet," *Public Policy*, Vol. 5, Cambridge: Harvard University Press, 1954, pp. 367–8.

on the insurance program. Bills dealing with the four preliminary features were passed by the Senate, and one of these, increasing the hospital construction program, became law in October. The other three were bottled up in the House, partly in consequence of the massive opposition of the organized medical profession, whose campaign against "socialized medicine" was then approaching a crescendo. But the American Medical Association's efforts may have been assisted by a developing climate of distrust in which all innovations from the political "left" were regarded with suspicion. The Smith Act trial of the top leaders of the American Communist Party had been going on before Judge Medina since mid-January; in March Judith Coplon was arrested and indicted on espionage charges; in May Gerhard Eisler, under indictment for contempt of Congress and passport fraud, fled to Europe on a Polish liner; and in June the first trial of Alger Hiss got under way in New York.

Most of the month of June was taken up in the Senate proper by the attempt there to repeal the Taft-Hartley Act. Debate on the Administration proposal, sponsored by Thomas of Utah, began on June 6. By mid-June it became apparent that the principal point in dispute, as in the House, was the authority for injunction and seizure powers in national emergency strikes. (The Thomas bill authorized neither.) The crucial vote in a complicated series was on a Taft amendment in the form of a substitute for the entire section dealing with national emergency strikes. The amendment authorized injunctions as well as seizure and nominal control. When this was adopted on June 28 with a ten-vote majority, Taft moved to substitute his own bill for the remainder of the Thomas proposal. This in effect re-enacted Taft-Hartley with a few alterations. Passage of what was now the Taft bill followed promptly, and the measure shortly joined the recommitted House version in the inactive files of the House Labor Committee.

During the same period in June the bitterness of this Senate fight was at times exceeded by the eruptions in the House over the new housing legislation. The House bill differed from the measure passed by the Senate in April only in minor degree. When the Rules Committee, with the active support of Minority Leader Martin, refused to grant a rule for the bill in early June, Speaker Rayburn gave open support to the use of the 21-day rule and even went so far as to schedule a Democratic caucus for shortly before the time when the bill would be called up. On June 14, however, three members of the Rules Committee unaccountably changed their positions, and the rule was reported out. The opening skirmish on June 22 was literally that, as Rules Chairman Sabath and his regular adversary on the committee,

Cox of Georgia, engaged in brief physical combat during debate in the House on the adoption of the rule. Thereafter matters proceeded more smoothly. The measure was reported out of the Committee of the Whole, however, with one amendment which would have removed the entire public housing section. In the House proper this amendment, sponsored by Rees of Kansas, was defeated by a narrow margin, and the measure was passed on June 29 and signed by the President on July 15.

July: farm prices, poll taxes, and NATO. July was also marked by considerable controversy in the House. In the context of the 1948 election results the perennial problem of a general agricultural price policy generated more than the usual amount of heat. An early occasion for dispute was supplied by the Secretary of Agriculture on April 17, when he presented to a joint session of the agriculture committees of the two chambers a long list of proposals which quickly became known as the "Brannan Plan." The most controversial item in this complex scheme was a system of direct subsidies to producers of perishable commodities to make up the difference between an average price in the free market and that calculated under the parity formula.

Action on the farm price program in the first session was imperative because there was widespread dissatisfaction with the statute passed in 1948, which was to take effect at the end of 1949. On July 20 the House took up the Pace bill, which included authority for a trial run of the subsidy plan for three perishable commodities. Through a majority that included most of the Republicans and a sizable minority of Democrats, the House on July 21 substituted the Gore bill, in effect continuing the existing program for one year, which was then passed by a large bipartisan vote.

The anti-poll-tax bill reported to the House on June 24 acquired heat not only from its substance but also from the fact that is was the first measure taken up by the House under the 21-day rule. This occurred on July 25, to the accompaniment of a display of parliamentary maneuvering unusual in the lower chamber. Before the House could vote on the rule for consideration of the bill, no less than six roll calls were forced, producing a warning from Speaker Rayburn against dilatory tactics. The minority on these votes included up to one-fifth of the Republicans and two-fifths of the Democrats. After the roll call adopting the rule, debate became fairly heated, and three unsuccessful attempts, settled by teller votes, were made to weaken the bill. On July 26 a motion to recommit, on which the opposition registered its maximum strength, was lost by a margin of 144 votes, and passage of the bill followed. The Senate took no action on this proposal.

Throughout most of July the Senate was engaged in a historic debate on approval of the North Atlantic Treaty, which the President had transmitted in April and had followed with several public requests for early and unconditional acceptance. There was no conspicuous Democratic opposition; among the Republicans Vandenberg led the supporters, and Wherry, Taft, and Watkins guided the opponents. The pivotal vote was taken on a reservation sponsored by these three that rejected any obligation to supply arms to the other signatories. It was defeated on July 21 by a margin of 53 votes. Two further reservations by Watkins were then disposed of, and the Senate proceeded to give its unconditional consent to the treaty, only 13 votes being registered in the negative out of 95 recorded.

August: reorganization, gas, wages, and military aid. In August occurred final disposition of seven plans for reorganizing portions of the executive branch, submitted by the President in June after approval of the authorizing legislation. Six of these were not seriously challenged in either house. But Plan Number 1, creating a new Department of Welfare, became entangled with the "socialized medicine" excitement and was disapproved by a wide margin in the Senate.

The House in early August passed a version of what since 1947 had become one of the hardy perennials of the congressional scene, a bill amending the Natural Gas Act of 1938 to exempt from the regulatory authority of the Federal Power Commission the "independent producers" selling to interstate pipelines. The explosive quality of the bill was reflected in the submission of four separate reports from the committee, in a vigorous debate on adoption of the rule for considering the measure, and in Speaker Rayburn's making one of his rare appeals from the floor, this time in support of the measure. In the voting on August 5 the Democrats were badly divided, though a small majority were opposed to the bill on final passage. Since among the Republicans supporters of the legislation outnumbered opponents by about three to one, it was passed by a comfortable margin. A similar measure was reported to the Senate in June, but it was not debated during the first session. The issue boiled over, however, into the consideration in October of the President's nomination of Leland Olds to a third term on the Federal Power Commission, which was rejected in a bipartisan vote, 15 to 53.

Both chambers in August considered one of the key Administration measures, amendment of the minimum wage sections of the Fair Labor Standards Act of 1938. Early proposals included not only an increase in the minimum wage from 40 to 75 cents an hour but also an increase in coverage, and these two became the focus of controversy.

Attempts on the floor to weaken the minimum wage provisions were successfully resisted, but a number of exemptions from coverage were adopted.

Efforts in the Senate committee to increase the coverage of the act were also abandoned at an early date, and almost the only positive provision in the bill as reported was the 75-cent minimum. In that form it had the support of the ranking minority member of the committee, Senator Taft. Restrictions on coverage were added, but four attempts to alter the wage provisions were rejected. In consequence the measure signed by the President on October 26 raised the minimum wage to 75 cents but reduced by several thousand the number of affected employees.

On August 17 the House began the final stages of legislative action on the Mutual Defense Assistance Act, popularly known as the military aid program. Debate was concentrated on the financial provisions of the bill. Authorized appropriations were cut in half, and a provision for contract authority, which would have guaranteed continuance of the program beyond one year, was eliminated entirely. Aside from a familiar requirement that half of all shipments be in American-flag vessels, the bill was adopted without further significant change, a majority of the Democrats favoring it and a majority of the Republicans in opposition.

September: reciprocity and military aid. Senate consideration of the military assistance program did not take place until late in September, after the upper chamber had dealt with renewal of the reciprocal trade agreements statute. Debate on the tariff measure ranged widely, but the focus of controversy was the bill's omission of the so-called "peril point" restriction by repealing the 1948 legislation, in which it had been included. An amendment to retain peril points was rejected on September 15, with all Republicans supporting it and all but two Democrats voting in the negative.

Senate hearings on the military assistance bill were held jointly by the Foreign Relations and Armed Services Committees. The bill they reported to the floor differed from that adopted in the House primarily in that it restored most of the House cuts in funds and provided for a program of aid to China. No changes of consequence were made on the floor, and efforts by George and Knowland to cut the funds authorization were easily defeated. Passage came on September 22, and the bill was approved by the President on October 6. This dispatch may have reflected the impact of the President's announcement on September 23 that an atomic explosion had recently occurred in the Soviet Union.

October: farm prices and social security. Early in October the Senate began debate on a new farm program, on which the House had reached its decision in July. The bill considered in the Senate, after the committee had considered and then abandoned all provisions of the Brannan Plan in nine months of maneuvering, had as its chief features a new parity formula and a revised version of the flexible price supports of the 1948 legislation. The House bill had re-enacted high rigid price supports, and this became the key issue in the Senate. After a complicated series of parliamentary maneuvers, a Young-Russell amendment providing for mandatory supports at 90 per cent of parity was decisively rejected. Most proposals for special treatment of particular commodities were also defeated. The conferences that followed Senate passage produced a compromise by which high rigid supports on basic commodities were extended through 1950, to be followed by gradual adoption of flexible supports.

The House acted in October on the Administration's recommendations for increasing both coverage and benefits under the social security system. The Democratic majority on the Ways and Means Committee reported a bill on August 22 that went half way with the Administration's requests for extended coverage and supported some of the increased benefits requested, especially with respect to disability, but it languished in the Rules Committee for several weeks. At the end of September Speaker Rayburn called for its release and threatened use of the 21-day rule if the Committee did not act. When the Rules Committee acceded, considerable objection was registered. In fact, the vote on ending debate on adoption of the rule was closer than any taken on the bill proper (175 to 154). Opposition to the measure on the final vote was negligible. The Senate took no action on it in this session.

Portents of 1950. There were a number of other measures on which the House acted in the first session that did not reach a final vote in the Senate prior to adjournment on October 19. Two of these were certain to produce controversy during 1950: the so-called basing-point bill, and that amending the Displaced Persons Act of 1948. The former had its origin in the 1948 decision of the Supreme Court in the Cement Institute Case, in which the cement industry's system of eliminating transportation differentials as a factor in pricing—widely used in a number of industries—was held to be contrary to the antitrust laws.[7] Following this decision, an investigating committee recommended a moratorium on prosecutions and eventually permanent remedial legislation. The debate, which showed almost no consensus

---

[7] Federal Trade Commission *v.* Cement Institute, 333 U. S. 683 (1948).

on the economic effects of basing-point pricing and its alternatives, began in the Senate on May 31 and ended with the adoption of a permanent moratorium bill sponsored by Senator O'Mahoney. The House version differed somewhat from that passed by the Senate, and the conference reported a bill that differed from both. It was accepted in the House on October 14. In the Senate a Douglas motion to postpone further action until January 20, 1950, was agreed to.

The movement for displaced persons legislation grew out of criticisms of the statute passed in 1948, specifically condemned as "inadequate and bigoted" in the Democratic platform of 1948 and attacked repeatedly by Truman during the campaign. A House bill, considerably compromised in committee, was passed without significant change on June 2. In the Senate, however, the chairman of the Judiciary Committee, McCarran of Nevada, refused to advance the legislation. Despite a threat from the Majority Leader to call up a resolution discharging the committee from further consideration of the bill, McCarran left for Europe on September 14 to look into the displaced persons situation. As a result of a revolt within the Judiciary Committee, the House bill was reported to the Senate, where debate dealt not only with the merits of the bill but also with the propriety of going over the head of a committee chairman in his absence. A motion to recommit the bill with instructions to report back by January 25, 1950, was eventually carried by a vote on which both parties were deeply divided.[8]

In the eleven weeks after the adjournment of the first session on October 19, various developments pointed to some of the major lines of controversy that were likely to appear in the second session. It became apparent that the country was undergoing an economic recession; on November 11 a strike in the steel industry was settled after several weeks; and on December 8 the Chinese Nationalist government moved its capital to Formosa, ending effective resistance to the Communist forces on the mainland.

THE SECOND SESSION, 1950

The program and political turbulence. The contents of President Truman's three major messages to the Congress in January were for the most part familiar. His State of the Union message on January 4 called for the maintenance of strong defenses, continued support of the

---

[8] Stephen K. Bailey and Howard D. Samuel, *Congress at Work*, New York: Henry Holt and Company, 1952, pp. 236–67, give an excellent account of the history of this legislation.

free nations' resistance to Communism, repeal of the Taft-Hartley Act, and enactment of the civil rights program. He emphasized the dangers of a renewed isolationism in threatened cuts in foreign aid, asked for moderate tax increases, and recommended the extension of rent controls. For the first time he used language indicating complete endorsement of the Brannan Plan for agriculture, urged passage of a housing program for middle-income families, and recommended revision of the Displaced Persons Act. The economic report two days later announced a five-year goal of 64 million jobs, repeated some earlier recommendations on domestic matters, and elaborated on others. In the foreign affairs field it asked for approval of the charter of the International Trade Organization, enactment of a technical assistance program, and provision of guarantees for private investment in underdeveloped areas. A deficit of five billion dollars was anticipated in the budget submitted on January 9. Tentative approval was given in the budget and in the special tax message on January 23 to cuts in certain wartime excise taxes on condition that compensating increases were provided elsewhere in the revenue legislation.

The political atmosphere was turbulent during the first month of the session and it became no less so as the year went on. Indictments were coming from the "five percenter" inquiry of the previous fall, the slowdown in the coal mines as a result of unsuccessful contract negotiations was reaching a critical stage, early in the month Senator Taft charged that the Department of State was being guided by "leftists" who defied the wishes of Congress, and before the month was out Secretary of State Acheson had added to his problems on Capitol Hill by publicly declining to condemn Alger Hiss after his second trial resulted in conviction.

January: oleo and F.E.P.C. The Senate's first business in January was the bill repealing the excise tax on oleomargarine, which had been passed by the House the preceding April. Debate in the Senate was complicated by efforts to entangle the bill with proposals for action on other excise taxes and on civil rights, but the measure was passed without major change on January 18.

Meanwhile the first major controversy in the House occurred over an attempt to repeal the 21-day rule. A repeal resolution voted in the Rules Committee on January 13 was taken up in the House on Friday, January 20. The Republican leadership favored repeal but wished to avoid appearing to oppose establishment of a Fair Employment Practices Commission, which was to be debated under the 21-day rule on Monday, January 23. Accordingly, on Friday Minority Leader Martin at the opening of the session moved adjournment. His motion was defeated in an almost perfect party vote.[9] In the following debate on the resolution, which was defeated by a comfortable margin, Speaker Rayburn appealed from the floor for negative votes on the ground that retention of the rule was essential to the Administration's legislative program. Rayburn, asserting that the circumstances were not appropriate, declined on January 23 to recognize Lesinski for the purpose of calling up F.E.P.C.

Supporters of F.E.P.C. subsequently relied on the Calendar Wednesday device, but, with the Education and Labor Committee standing fifth on the alphabetical list and with opponents in both parties dragging out the proceedings so that no more than one committee could call up a bill on any Wednesday, their chance did not arrive until February 22. Immediately following the annual reading of Washington's Farewell Address, Cox moved adjournment "as a further mark of respect to George Washington," and this was followed by a long succession of similar dilatory moves, so that Lesinski did not get the floor until late in the afternoon. Debate and delay continued until the early hours of the morning of February 23, when the House substituted a version of the bill that lacked enforcement powers.

February: electoral votes, strikes, and McCarthy. Meanwhile on February 1 the Senate considered and passed a proposed amendment to the Constitution, sponsored by Senator Lodge of Massachusetts and Representative Gossett of Texas, whose central provision would have abolished the electoral college system of electing the President and Vice President. It would have substituted a procedure whereby candidates would share the electoral vote of a state in proportion to their percentage of its popular vote. Debate on the proposal was not extended, and it was approved with three votes over the necessary two-thirds majority. (In the House a companion measure was defeated when the chamber in July declined by a vote of 134 to 210 to suspend its rules and take up the proposal.)

February 1950, however, was perhaps less important for strictly legislative developments than for a series of political events only partly legislative in character. On the sixth the long-simmering coal strike suddenly became a reality, and the President at once invoked the Taft-Hartley Act and asked the Congress for authority to seize the mines. Although a settlement was finally reached on March 4 without further legislation, the President was accused by Senator Taft and others of

---

[9] There were some strange bedfellows among the 5 Republicans and the 4 Democrats who dissented from their parties, the strangest among the latter being Adam Clayton Powell of New York and Howard Smith of Virginia.

having tried to discredit the labor relations statute, and his handling of the strike was not uniformly approved in the ranks of labor.

The impact of these events, however, was dwarfed by the repercussions from the opening of the McCarthy "era." In Wheeling, West Virginia, on February 9 and in several other cities on succeeding days Senator McCarthy charged that there were variable numbers of known Communists employed in the State Department. The effect of these accusations may have been increased by the news a few days before of the espionage case involving Dr. K. E. J. Fuchs, English scientist who had been privy to the mysteries of the atomic bomb. In any case, McCarthy's charges, repeated in a six-hour speech in the Senate on February 20, were startling enough so that the Senate, on the initiative of the Majority Leader, at once authorized an investigation by a subcommittee of the Foreign Relations Committee. Its hearings, chaired by Senator Tydings, and McCarthy's activities in the Senate provided ample press copy through the month of June. They and the committee's July report, which over Republican protests branded the charges as false, figured prominently in the fall congressional campaign.

March: science, housing, and gas. Despite these distractions, the House gave its approval on March 1 to a bill establishing the National Science Foundation. The Administration had pressed for such legislation for nearly five years. The Senate had adopted a revised measure during 1949 without much debate. In the House it had been blocked by the Rules Committee. On February 27, 1950, it was called up under the 21-day rule and, although complicated by amendments, it passed after three days of debate.

In mid-March both Senate and House were concerned with housing for middle-income families. The bills considered in both chambers contained a new program of long-term, low-interest loans to housing co-operatives. This new feature enjoyed the almost unanimous opposition of real estate, building, and home-financing groups, and was the principal focus of debate. Senate decision on this point came on a motion by Senator Bricker to eliminate the entire section dealing with co-operatives from the bill, which was adopted on March 15 by a majority composed of 13 Democrats, principally from the South, and most of the Republicans. The key vote in the House came a week later on essentially the same motion, sponsored by Wolcott of Michigan, and with the same result. Democratic support of the Wolcott amendment, though it included a minority of the party, was not so completely Southern as it was in the Senate.

From housing the Senate turned to natural gas. The chief supporters of the bill of course were Senators from the principal gas-producing states, and the major opponents were from states at the ends of the pipelines, but the lines of cleavage were not entirely sectional, and both parties were badly split. After the defeat of three amendments designed to effect a compromise, the Senate accepted a substitute sponsored by the two Oklahoma Senators, which gave the Federal Power Commission investigatory but no regulative power. In the House the Senate version was accepted, but only by a two-vote margin and only after Speaker Rayburn had appealed from the floor for passage. Given the close votes in both houses, no effort was made to override the President's veto, which was forthcoming on April 15.

April: displaced persons, pork, foreign aid, and crime. In accordance with the Senate's instructions of the previous October, the Judiciary Committee had on January 25 reported out the bill for revision of the Displaced Persons Act. A minority report, submitting a substitute bill bearing Senator Kilgore's name, was brought in on February 14. Debate began on February 28 and continued for over a week, when it was postponed for nearly a month. In a 12-hour period on April 5 the Senate took approximately 80 votes, 20 of them roll calls. It had to dispose of a large number of amendments proposed by McCarran and others before the Kilgore substitute could be voted upon and action completed. The bipartisan coalition opposing McCarran was in effective control of the situation, however, and the Kilgore substitute, whose provisions were fairly close to those of the House bill, was eventually adopted, 49 to 25, with small majorities of both parties in favor.

During April the Senate also disposed of an omnibus rivers, harbors, and flood control authorization that late in the first session had passed the House without important change and without controversy—once it was forced to the floor under the 21-day rule. Senate consideration was interesting chiefly for its demonstration that a Public Works Committee package of projects to be carried on by the Army Engineers was impervious to attempts at alteration deriving from the Administration, from the interests of other agencies in the executive branch, or, of course, from individual senators. The chief matter at issue was an effort, approved by the Administration as an acceptable substitute for development of the Columbia River valley on T.V.A. lines, to establish a coordinated Army-Interior plan for the valley. Jurisdictional rivalries between Senate committees assisted in defeat of the effort, but its failure probably was as certain in any case as were Douglas's attempts in the course of two days of debate to cut "pork" from the bill. The measure was passed on April 17, unchanged except in details acceptable to the committee.

Passage of the 1950 Foreign Economic Assistance Act was relatively uneventful in the House, where it was debated during the last week of March. One of the two matters in major dispute was an effort to require that approximately one-third of authorized funds be spent for surplus agricultural products. With the assistance of a letter from the President, read on the floor by the committee chairman, the attempt was defeated. The new technical assistance program ("Point 4") was also the object of unsuccessful attack, and among those who appealed for support of "Point 4" was Speaker Rayburn.

The Senate's action on foreign aid was slower and stormier. Its principal Republican champion, Senator Vandenberg, was hospitalized, and its critics were vocal and resourceful. The Foreign Relations Committee reported a bill that was substantially identical with Administration requests. Various attempts were made to cut the funds authorized, and a Bridges amendment cutting one-quarter billion dollars was finally passed. Attempts to bring Spain into the program and to impose a number of new restrictions were defeated. The principal focus of debate, however, was the "Point 4" provision. Motions to remove this feature were twice proposed and defeated, but the Senate engaged in three more days of debate, largely over "Point 4," before agreeing in a party vote to a House-approved conference compromise.

The Senate's foreign aid debate was frequently interrupted by repercussions of the Tydings committee investigation into McCarthy's charges against the State Department and by debate on a resolution authorizing Kefauver's peripatetic investigations into interstate crime. Though the set-up of the Kefauver committee was bitterly fought by the minority, its hearings, which went on throughout the year and provided extensive television material, caused a good deal of embarrassment to the Democrats in states such as Illinois and Missouri and may have adversely affected the fortunes of some of their candidates in the November elections.

May: F.E.P.C., reorganization, and omnibus appropriations. The Senate Majority Leader on May 8 moved to take up the F.E.P.C. bill, despite threats of a filibuster. Ten days later Lucas filed a cloture petition. When he called for a vote on it on May 19, a majority supported the motion, but it still lacked 12 votes of the 64 necessary to shut off debate. Lucas made another attempt on July 12. This time the cloture motion failed for lack of nine votes, and no further effort was made on the subject.

During 1950 the President submitted 27 plans for reorganization of various portions of the executive branch. Of these, 7 were disapproved, 6 of them by the Senate. The most controversial of the President's proposals was that concerning the National Labor Relations Board, which would have increased the powers of the board's chairman and altered those of its general counsel specified in the Taft-Hartley Act. Although a majority of Democrats supported the President, the resolution of disapproval was adopted on May 11. On the same date the plan for the Treasury Department was also rejected, primarily because it threatened the "independence" of the Comptroller of the Currency, whose supervision of the national banks was vigorously defended by bankers' groups and by Treasury Secretary Snyder. The other disapproved plans dealt with the Interstate Commerce Commission, the Federal Communications Commission, the Department of Agriculture, the Reconstruction Finance Corporation, and the Federal Security Agency, whose elevation to the status of a cabinet-rank department met the opposition of the organized medical profession, which again successfully conjured up the threat of "socialized medicine."

Under the leadership of Representative Cannon, head of the House Appropriations Committee, and Senator Byrd, the Congress in 1950 tried a one-time experiment with an omnibus appropriation bill, in place of the usual 10 or 12 individual measures. Designed to achieve speed and integrated examination of appropriation requests, the procedure resulted in a bill that was passed in May by the House with few substantial changes in the committee's proposals, except that two "economy" requirements were added, one directing the President to reduce the nonmilitary expenditures authorized in the bill by 600 million dollars and one prohibiting the filling of more than 10 per cent of the personnel vacancies occurring in Federal agencies during the next year.

June: basing-point prices, rents, and social security. The controversial basing-point pricing bill was finally disposed of during June after a complicated series of maneuvers during the first five months of the session. Most Republicans voted to approve the final version of the much-debated conference report, and, though the party was badly split, a majority of Democrats were in opposition. In mid-June the President vetoed the measure, and no attempt was made to override.

In the second session, as in the first, the issue of rent control renewal produced considerable heat. Debated in a number of different contexts almost from the beginning of the session, it became the pending business in both chambers early in June. Senate voting on a bill extending controls to the end of the year was delayed by a one-man filibuster by Senator Cain of Washington. Passage was finally secured, however, with a majority of the Democrats on the prevailing side and a majority of the Republicans opposed. The House bill, which differed only slightly from the Senate version, was adopted without major changes. As in the Senate, voting followed party lines fairly closely. The bill was signed by the President on June 23, but this did not end the matter for the session, as early in December an extension through March 31, 1951, was enacted.

More than eight months after the House had approved its version of the bill amending the social security law, the Senate began debate on a bill that was considerably narrower in scope. Attempts, for the most part unsuccessful, were made on the floor to broaden the measure. The most hotly debated change in the bill was an amendment, sponsored by Senator Knowland, to restrict the power of the Federal authorities to withhold their contributions to the state unemployment insurance funds as a penalty for failure to comply with Federal regulations. This insertion was in response to a 1949 case in which the states of California and Washington had been obliged to alter their policies concerning eligibles as a consequence of a threat to withhold Federal funds. This amendment was adopted by a vote on which 12 Southern and Border State Democrats joined all but 3 of the Republicans in support. The President signed the measure in August, with a request that the Knowland provision be reconsidered in a later bill.

June: the impact of Korea on the draft, military aid, and taxes. These were the major developments in the Congress up to June 25, 1950, the date of the outbreak of hostilities in Korea, after which legislative activities occurred in a wholly different context. American and United Nations intervention smoothed the way for some Administration proposals but handicapped or completely sidetracked others. An example of the first sort was the bill extending Selective Service. As passed by the House in late May, the measure prevented the President from inducting draftees or members of the reserves and the National Guard into the regular army without a concurrent resolution from Congress declaring a national emergency. The Senate version was somewhat less extreme. Most controversy on its bill was over an amendment requiring optional assignment to racially segregated units, which was finally defeated on a pair of roll calls on which more than half of the Democrats opposed both the Majority Leader and the Administration. The conference committee, which met after the Korean invasion, in effect rewrote the measure to extend the law of 1948 without significant change.

The one-year renewal of the Mutual Defense Assistance Act, requested by the President on June 1, had a somewhat similar history. Debate on the extension bill had begun in the Senate two days before Korea was invaded, and the prospects then were that it might be considerably modified. Most of the restrictive amendments were abandoned, however, and the bill passed the Senate on June 30 without a dissenting vote. In July the House approved the Senate bill with only one negative vote.

Tax legislation also showed the effects of the Korean war. In the House the Committee on Ways and Means had been working on a new revenue act since early in the session. Reported on June 22, the bill bore only slight resemblances to the recommendations of the President. It lowered or repealed most excise taxes, increased rather than decreased depletion allowances on oil and minerals, and closed certain alleged "loopholes." Although the bill was passed as reported on June 29, with few votes recorded in the negative, it was obvious that reductions of the sort contemplated in this legislation were not likely to reach the statute books in 1950. Late in July the President asked that the excise tax reductions in the bill be dropped and that individual and corporate income taxes be increased, and the Senate substitute for the House bill went a long way in these directions. Debate on the measure, however, concentrated on the question of immediate enactment of an excess profits tax. Sentiment for such legislation, which was also strong in the House, was led by Senator O'Mahoney, but the preferences of Senator George, which also corresponded with those of the President, were for a delay. Accordingly the Senate on September 1 adopted an amendment directing the House and Senate committees to report as early as possible in 1951 a retroactive excess profits measure. Conference on the bill was delayed by the same controversy, the final compromise directing the committees to have a profits tax bill ready as soon as possible after November 15 or, if the Congress were not in session, in 1951.

July: appropriations and rearmament, with interruptions. Meanwhile the Senate had spent the better part of four weeks, beginning July 11, on the omnibus appropriation bill. It was interrupted in these proceedings from time to time, most spectacularly on July 20 by a heated controversy over the adoption of the Tydings committee's report on the McCarthy charges against the State Department, a controversy that blocked even the appearance of closing ranks following the outbreak of war. Following a Republican Policy Committee statement which declared that the Tydings committee had "failed" and that its report was "derogatory and insulting to Senator McCarthy," Senator Wherry provoked four straight party votes in efforts to prevent the filing of the report. These events, incidentally, coincided with the arrest of Julius Rosenberg on charges of operating as a spy for the Soviet Union.

The appropriation bill reported to the Senate differed from the

House version chiefly in its omission of the two "economy" provisions inserted in the lower chamber and in its inclusion of funds for the economic and military aid programs, which had not been authorized at the time of the House debate. Voting in the Senate was prolonged, but the principal changes were a requirement that the executive branch make a 10 per cent cut in the funds appropriated, increases in the economic aid and "Point 4" appropriations, and authorization for an Export-Import Bank loan to Spain. Senator Douglas spent days on a series of fruitless attempts to get the Senate to adopt some of his dozen amendments aimed at cutting approximately one billion dollars from nondefense appropriations. A conference report on the complicated measure did not appear for some time, and the law was not finally signed by the President until September 6.

This omnibus appropriation bill, which during the spring looked as if it would indeed cover all authorizations in a single measure, in fact, because of the outbreak of the Korean war, included less than half the funds authorized during the second session.

August: economic controls. Funds for rearmament were somewhat more readily forthcoming after the Korean war began than were authorizations for controls over the economy. In his message of July 19 the President asked the Congress to provide statutory authority to establish a system of priorities and allocations for defense production, to requisition plants and materials, to set up a system of loans and related devices for encouraging production, and to control credit and commodity speculation. For various reasons he did not request authority to establish price controls and, by attempting to avoid controversy, in this instance rather succeeded in creating it.[10] Reflecting the rapid increase in prices after June 25, demands were made in both houses for adding wage and price controls to the legislation that was to become the Defense Production Act.

The House bill followed the lines of the President's recommendations and contained nothing on wage and price controls. After several days of confused debate and maneuver an amended bill was adopted which authorized stand-by wage and price controls, provided no authority for controls on commodity speculation, and restricted credit controls on real estate to new construction. A majority of the Democrats opposed the more restrictive of these amendments but were defeated by a coalition of Republicans and Southerners.

The measure reported in the upper chamber was essentially the same as that in the House, with authority for price and wage controls

---

[10] Neustadt, "Congress and the Fair Deal," pp. 372–3.

added. Criticism in the Senate followed the line that the powers granted in the bill were more extensive than circumstances warranted. General attempts to restrict them were supplemented, as in the House, by efforts to achieve privileged standing for particular industries. Attempts to remove all wage and price controls from the bill were unsuccessful. Efforts to delete the machinery for settling labor disputes also failed, perhaps in part because a succession of strikes had made this aspect of the mobilization effort peculiarly conspicuous. The conference compromise restored most of the powers asked by the President and omitted some special protections for particular industries.

September: internal security. These legislative developments took place in an atmosphere of increasing anxiety about the activities of Soviet agents and alleged Communists and their sympathizers within the country and especially within the executive branch of the government. During July and August both houses had approved legislation granting the heads of eleven government agencies summary dismissal powers over civilian employees deemed security risks and authorizing the President to extend such authority to other segments of the executive.

More sweeping was the Internal Security Act of 1950, which was placed on the statute books at the end of September. This complicated measure was approved by the lower chamber in a one-sided vote after the failure of a substitute, introduced in response to a presidential message, that would have dealt almost exclusively with strengthening existing laws on sabotage and espionage. Support for the legislation was equally strong in the Senate, strong enough to produce a threat to attach one version of it as a rider on the Defense Production Act. After defeating attempts, led by Lucas and Kilgore, to pass a more acceptable substitute, the Senate approved the act by a vote of 70 to 7 on September 12. The President vetoed it on September 22, declaring that it would hinder rather than help the government's efforts to deal with subversion and would put the United States into "the thought-control business." The House immediately voted to override, 286 to 48, and the Senate followed suit the next day by a vote of 57 to 10.

Election recess. When the Congress recessed on September 23, to reassemble on November 27, three weeks after the midterm elections, the military situation in the Far East looked somewhat less desperate than it had during the summer. Shortly before recessing the Senate had confirmed the appointment of General Marshall as Secretary of Defense. Marshall's assignment was greeted favorably, despite criticism from some opponents, such as Senator Jenner, who described him as "a front man for traitors" and "a living lie." In mid-September the United Nations forces in Korea had started their counter-offensive with the dramatic landings at Inchon, by October 7 American forces had crossed the 38th parallel, and on October 13 MacArthur outlined his occupation policy. In mid-October President Truman and General MacArthur held their conference on Wake Island, on which the President reported confidently in a speech on October 17. The next day it was announced that American forces were in Pyongyang, the North Korean capital.

Despite the favorable military news, somewhat qualified by reports of Chinese "volunteers" in North Korea, the results of the election on November 7 were decidedly unfavorable to the Democrats. In the Senate they suffered a net loss of five seats. Among those defeated were Lucas, the Majority Leader, Myers, the Majority Whip, Tydings of Maryland, and Thomas of Utah. Taft was re-elected in Ohio by an impressive margin, and among his new colleagues on the Republican side of the aisle was Richard M. Nixon of California. In the House the Democratic majority was reduced by 27 seats.

December: retreat and controversy, domestic and foreign. By the time the Eighty-first Congress resumed its second session on November 27 matters in Korea had become decidedly worse. On the 20th, American troops had reached the Manchurian border, and three days later a "final" offensive was launched. With the massive intervention of the Chinese on the 27th, however, the attack was first halted and then turned into a humiliating, if not disastrous, retreat. General Mac-Arthur declared on November 28 that the United Nations forces faced an entirely new war, and on December 4 the U. N. forces abandoned Pyongyang. On December 15 the President addressed the nation by radio and television and announced his proclamation of a national emergency.

The December deliberations were inevitably stormy, but they were not without substantial results. Both houses by December 11 had agreed on a measure extending rent control for 90 days. As contemplated in the earlier revenue legislation, the proposed excess profits tax was an item for urgent consideration. House debate on the bill, which was somewhat more lenient than the Administration proposal, was colored by the threatening Korean situation. However, a Republican move to substitute a version sponsored by the Minority Policy Committee was defeated in a party-line vote, and the measure on December 5 was passed as reported, with only 20 votes recorded in the negative. A considerably milder Senate bill was passed after perfunctory debate on December 20, and it was the principal model for the agreement reached in conference.

Also passed before the end of the session was an amendment to the Railway Labor Act, desired by the affected unions, permitting railroad unions the same right to the union shop and the check-off that was permitted other unions under the Taft-Hartley Act. The Senate approved the bill on December 11. The House version of this measure had languished before the Rules Committee since midsummer, but passage of the Senate bill after the other had been reported in substantially the same form permitted the House managers to bypass the Rules Committee by moving to take the Senate bill directly from the Speaker's table. Efforts to prevent consideration at an unusual New Year's Day session were defeated, and the bill was passed without opposition.

As a result of Senate action in mid-December a long-standing gap in the Clayton Act was closed. The amendment forbade mergers by acquisition of the assets of one corporation by another if the effect would be substantially to lessen competition. Presidents had recommended this legislation for nearly 25 years, but without success until the Senate on December 13 approved a bill to this effect that had been passed by the House in 1949.

Most controversy during December, however, occurred in the field of foreign policy. The President on November 29 asked appropriation of funds for the relief of famine in Yugoslavia. The bill incorporating this request encountered a movement, led by Knowland, to make the authorization contingent upon the President's prior expenditure of an equivalent amount previously set aside for Nationalist China. This effort was narrowly defeated on a vote almost completely along party lines. In the House the proposal produced an unusually stormy debate in which matters of religious freedom and ideology were conspicuous. The bill was passed without major alteration, however.

More spectacular were the Republican efforts growing out of the talks between Prime Minister Attlee and the President in Washington, December 4 through 8. While the talks were proceeding, 24 Republican senators signed a resolution proposed by Kem of Missouri calling for a full report of the conference and demanding that any agreements reached be submitted to the Senate in the form of a treaty. The temper of this demand was reflected in a resolution adopted by the Senate Republican Conference on December 15 that called for the dismissal of Secretary of State Acheson. On December 14 Kem attempted to call up his resolution, and Majority Leader Lucas immediately moved that the Senate recess until the next day. Although the Lucas motion was carried by only one vote, no Democrat opposed it and no Republican supported it. Four days later the Kem resolution was in effect pigeonholed by referring it to the Committee on Foreign Relations. On neither of the votes concerning Kem's resolution did any Democratic senator leave the ranks of his party colleagues, and on both of them only three Republicans lined up with the Democratic majority, Smith of Maine, Saltonstall of Massachusetts, and Gurney of South Dakota.

.   .   .

These, then, were the principal events of the Eighty-first Congress. They do not constitute a representative sample of legislative behavior at midcentury, but, when it adjourned *sine die* on January 2, 1951, this Congress had encountered almost the full range of issues likely to confront the Federal Government in the years after World War II. Its setting, its composition, and in many respects, therefore, its responses were unique. If, however, examination of its formal record reveals any consistent patterns in the two sessions and any stable characteristics of its parties, it may lead to a more adequate understanding of the nature of this protean but crucially important representative institution.

chapter three

DIVISION AND COHESION:

The Structure of Party Voting in the Senate

A curious feature of the congressional party is that its existence is so familiar to any layman that no newscaster need define it in the course of a five-minute summary of the day's events, and yet its essential character—how (or even whether) it operates, what it means not only to the functioning of the Congress but also to the political life of the country—is at best only vaguely understood. Apparently it makes a difference to someone—to most of the contestants in an election, to the incumbent President, to various groups and individuals throughout the country—whether the Democrats or the Republicans "control" the Congress. The Speaker of the House and the chairmen of the standing committees in both chambers will bear the label of the party that wins a majority, and a President is expected to get on less well with a legislative majority that is not of his party than with one that is. But what other political differences follow from the outcome of a Congressional election? The reports of a legislative session may say less about party than about various blocs and coalitions, and when the parties' names do appear, as often as not the reference is to some segment or fraction—"Southern" or "Northern" Democrats, "internationalist" or "isolationist" Republicans, "liberals" or "conservatives," "Administration supporters" or "anti-Administration" legislators. Where is the congressional party in all this?

The underlying reason for this paradoxical mixture of clarity and confusion is that the legislative parties and the Congress itself are indeed protean. Examined closely at one point in time they present one appearance, and at another they seem quite different. It is much easier, therefore, to say what the congressional party is not than to arrive at a valid understanding of what it is. As much of the scholarly literature on the Congress demonstrates, the party is not a highly disciplined group like the party in the British House of Commons or like the parties in some American state legislatures. Reflecting the diversities of attitude and preoccupation in a continental nation and in turn the complexity and diffusion of power characteristic of American electoral parties, the congressional party is not a tightly knit grouping of highly predictable form.

But the positive question remains. What is the nature of the congressional party? Is its name no more than a meaningless label? Or are there, underlying its apparently continuous changes, persistent elements that give it some stable definition? Is the behavior of congressional partisans, Republicans and Democrats alike, apparently haphazard or continuously shifting, so that over a period of time the only order it displays is that of the kaleidoscope, an endless grouping and re-grouping in response to the demands of local constituencies and organized interest groups? Or are there continuing patterns of association and cleavage within the parties? What lines do they follow? How stable are they? And between the parties are there identifiable differences of tendency and preference? If so, how can these be accounted for? Are they traceable primarily to influences from within the Congress? What relevance, if any, have the activities of the President for the functioning of the parties on Capitol Hill?

Questions such as these have to do with structure, in the sense of a continuing pattern of relationships among a collection of individuals. How can this be examined? In a natural or experimental grouping small enough to permit fairly continuous observation of all relationships within it, one can identify structure with considerable precision, indicating who generally sides with whom when a choice is to be made, which members characteristically take the initiative, which serve to reconcile differences of view, and so on.[1] Alternatively one

---

[1] For examples of this sort of technique see William F. Whyte, *Street Corner Society*, Chicago: University of Chicago Press, 1943, and Robert F. Bales, *Inter-*

can ask the members of such a group to rank their associates on such criteria as their desirability as companions, their influence in the group, and these responses in turn can be analyzed so as to reveal the structure of the group.[2]

The record votes in a legislative body are not wholly unlike the data used in these examples. They do not provide the range of observations that can be made upon a small group, and hence they do not on their face indicate the sources of initiative and other aspects of the internal composition of the segments into which the legislature or its parties divide. The choices they record, aside from the fact that they are not made at the behest of the observer, are not, at least manifestly, expressions of preference among their colleagues but choices between alternative lines of public policy. And yet, in making such choices among "externals," those members of the legislative body who characteristically choose the same side of a series of policy issues are in a sense both choosing each other and at the same time revealing the possibility of some degree of association prior to the announcement of their votes. That is, a succession of identical or markedly similar divisions within a legislative party or comparable grouping reveals its gross structural tendencies; moreover, to the extent that they are persistent, these divisions lead to the entirely reasonable assumption that their members not only are aware of their similarity of view but also may have been actively associated with one another prior to or in consequence of these choices.[3] Even in a legislative body as large as the

action *Process Analysis,* Cambridge, Mass.: Addison-Wesley, 1951. Compare Ralph K. Huitt, "The Congressional Committee: A Case Study," *American Political Science Review,* Vol. 48, no. 2 (June 1954), pp. 340–65.

[2] For illustrations see Helen H. Jennings, *Leadership or Isolation,* 2d ed., New York: Longmans, Green, 1950; Theodore M. Newcomb, *Personality and Social Change,* New York: The Dryden Press, 1943; Leon Festinger, et al., *Social Pressures in Informal Groups,* New York: Harper and Brothers, 1950; Gardner Lindzey and Edgar F. Borgotta, "Sociometric Measurement," in Gardner Lindzey, editor, *Handbook of Social Psychology,* Cambridge, Mass.: Addison-Wesley, 1954, pp. 405–48; Muzafer Sherif and Carolyn W. Sherif, *Groups in Harmony and Tension,* New York: Harper and Brothers, 1953; and Robert S. Weiss, *Processes of Organization,* Ann Arbor, Mich.: Survey Research Center, 1956.

[3] For the technically inclined it may be noted that indirect support for this assumption, if that be needed, can be found in the experience of those who have analyzed legislative roll calls by means of the Guttman scaling techniques originally developed for the analysis of data from opinion surveys. These investigators have found that scales developed from legislative votes show a higher degree of consistency than those based on questionnaire data, suggesting the influence of face-to-face contact upon legislators' choices. See Duncan MacRae, Jr., "Some Underlying Variables in Legislative Roll Call Votes," *Public Opinion Quarterly,* Vol. 18, no. 2 (Summer 1954), p. 194.

United States House of Representatives or one of its constituent party groups, it is unlikely that persistent divisions occur without some measure of prior contact among at least the most consistent of their members. The analysis of a large number of record votes thus can reveal the major structural outlines of the chamber or of its constituent parties, and, though it will provide no conclusive evidence on the leader-follower relationships within these blocs, it will also permit, as later chapters will demonstrate, some inferences concerning the behavior of the formally designated leaders within the party.

A FEW MATTERS OF TECHNIQUE

A general idea of the procedures that were followed to arrive at a description of the structure of the parties in the Senate and the House of Representatives is necessary to understand the findings and their limitations.[4] The first step was to divide the roll calls into sets that would be considered in this phase of the study. The votes of each member of the party on each of these sets were punched on cards, and the cards in turn were processed through a machine that compared each member of the party with every other and recorded the number of agreements between each such pair, "agreements" covering not only actual votes but all recorded preferences as well.[5]

The number of agreements between pairs of party members thus constituted the basic data of the analysis. This number hereafter will

---

[4] A more technical account of the procedures will be found in the Appendix. The basic technique was developed more than thirty years ago by Stuart A. Rice, *Quantitative Methods in Politics,* New York: Alfred A. Knopf, 1928, chap. 16, and extended by the late Herman C. Beyle, *Identification and Analysis of Attribute-Cluster Blocs,* Chicago: University of Chicago Press, 1931, chaps. 1–3.

[5] Since it is rare for all members of the Senate or House to vote on any roll call, nonvoting introduces problems in an investigation of this sort. To minimize these and to have the positions of every legislator as complete as possible, any declared preference recorded in the permanent edition of the *Congressional Record* was included along with the "yeas and nays." Thus a member who voted "nay" on a roll call and one who was paired or announced against would be counted as in agreement on that vote. "Absences" thus cover all unrecorded preferences, including general pairs in which neither partner announces his position. The unavailability of mechanical means for handling this step in the analysis is largely responsible for the limited use of the Rice-Beyle technique since its development. Some idea of the prohibitively complex task involved in analyzing manually a body of more than a dozen or two members is indicated by the fact that on a single roll call the number of possible agreements among the 262 Democrats in the House in 1949, taken two at a time, is 34,191.

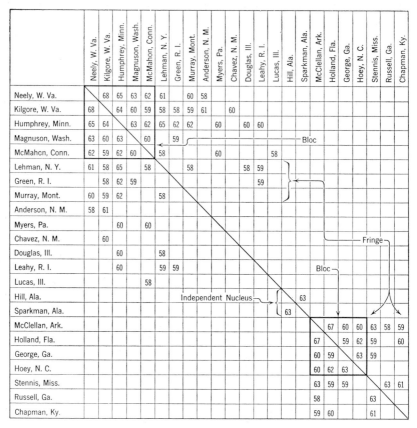

Figure 1. Portion of a matrix, showing 23 Democratic senators with scores of 59 or higher on 74 selected roll calls, 81st Congress, 2nd session. (These are low-cohesion roll calls. See text, p. 48.)

be called a "score," representing the actual number of agreements rather than a percentage. These scores, beginning with the highest and proceeding as far down the list as was profitable, were then entered on a matrix on the top and left-hand margins of which the names of the members were inserted. (See Figure 1.) Each score was entered twice, in the appropriate cells on either side of a diagonal running from the upper left-hand to the lower right-hand corner of the matrix. As these successive scores were entered, adjacent cells became filled and clusters of agreements appeared as squares bisected by the diagonal. Thus, in the example in Figure 1, when all pairs involving scores of 59 or higher had been entered on the matrix, two such clusters had appeared. One included Senators Neely, Kilgore, Humphrey,

Magnuson, and McMahon, and the other, Senators McClellan, Holland, George, and Hoey.[6]

These clusters are blocs, the structural elements of the party, as reflected in the record votes. It is important to bear in mind, however, that these blocs strictly speaking are clusters of interrelated pairs. In the illustration in Figure 1, although each member of the blocs evident at that stage agreed with each of the others on at least 59 of the 74 selected roll calls, this does not mean that all were agreed on the same 59 votes. In the five-man bloc in the upper corner of this incomplete matrix there were no dissenting votes on 52 of the 74 roll calls. For reasons to be given later, no scores of less than 38 were added to the matrix, and at this stage the same bloc had grown to include 18 members, all of whom were agreed on 24 of the votes. The number of agreements among all members of a bloc, as this illustration suggests, is almost always somewhat smaller than the lowest score among the constituent pairs.[7] The particular votes on which all members of a bloc are agreed nevertheless indicate the policy tendencies of the group and differentiate it from others, even though they do not describe each of the constituent pairs in full detail.

Since it is not feasible to reproduce a complete matrix in these pages, even for a single party in the Senate, it is worth noting that a matrix provides a good deal of detail that can be summarized in words. Thus inspection of Figure 1 reveals that each of the completely distinct blocs has associated with it a number of men who have scores with one or more members of the bloc but not with all. These will be referred to arbitrarily as composing a "fringe" if they have scores of a designated minimum magnitude with at least half the members of the bloc. The remainder will be described as "isolates." Thus Senators Lehman, Green, and Murray composed the "fringe" of the bloc in the upper corner of Figure 1, Senators Stennis and Chapman the "fringe" of the other bloc. At this stage the remaining nine senators—and all those Democrats not listed—were among the "isolates." It is evident also that Senators Hill and Sparkman of Alabama at this stage of the analysis differed from the other isolates in that they constituted an independent nucleus. As is often the case with senators from the same

---

[6] This process is not quite as automatic as the description suggests or as appears from the illustration in Figure 1. A number of matrixes is usually necessary before all the principal clusters are identified, and detecting the emerging clusters requires some practice.

[7] The technical reasons for working from pairs rather than from groupings of larger size need not be dealt with in detail here. It is enough to say that the number of possible combinations of three or more in even a small legislative body is so large as to make any other procedure prohibitively complicated.

state (and the same party), they voted the same way on approximately six roll calls out of seven, but neither agreed with any other member of the party on as many as 59 votes. Only as additional scores are added to a matrix is it possible to determine whether such a pair remains isolated, becomes the nucleus of a separate bloc, or eventually becomes a part of one of the existing blocs.

The matrixes developed in this way were based, as was noted above, upon a selection of roll calls. Since in the Eighty-first Congress the Senate took 227 roll-call votes in the first session and 229 in the second, it was necessary to adopt a relevant but objective criterion for choosing among them.[8] The purpose of the study at this stage being to identify party structure, the most appropriate criterion was one which would reflect the degree of cleavage within each party on each of the votes. Accordingly on each roll call an index of cohesion for each party was calculated, the zero value indicating a 50–50 split, or complete disunity, and 100 indicating unanimity within the party.[9] Taking each session separately, the roll calls of each party were arranged in ascending order of cohesion. A set of votes with the lowest indexes of cohesion was selected from each list for treatment as a unit, making two such sets for each party. In the same way an equal number of votes, beginning where the first set left off, was selected from the roll calls in each session.[10] Thus for each party four sets of votes were available for the structural analysis, two "low-cohesion" sets and two "high-cohesion" sets. As Table 1 suggests, on the votes excluded by this procedure the party was unanimous or so nearly so that these roll calls would be of almost no value in describing party structure, though they were significant for other phases of the analysis.

---

[8] The corresponding figures for the House are: first session, 121; second session, 154.

[9] This is the Rice Index of Cohesion (*Quantitative Methods*, chap. 15). Arithmetically it is the difference between the per cent favoring and the per cent opposing a motion. Thus an index of 50 indicates a 75-25 split in the party, 60 an 80-20 split, 80 a 90-10 division, and so on. Note that only actual votes, not including paired or announced positions, are used in this calculation. Votes on private bills were not considered, and, in those few instances where the Senate explicitly reversed itself on successive votes, only the final decision was included.

[10] The tabulating procedure devised for the analysis would not permit efficient handling of more than 74 roll calls at one time. Thus each set, with one exception, contains 74 roll calls, chosen as described in the text. The exception was the Democratic high-cohesion set of the second session. Only 73 votes were included in this set because the party's cohesion indexes on the next two votes were identical.

SOURCES OF CLEAVAGE

The Republicans, as Table 1 demonstrates, were a good deal less unified than the Democrats in both sessions.[11] This circumstance, which will have to be taken into account in comparing the structures of the two parties, presumably in part reflects the demoralization of the mi-

Table 1

DISTRIBUTION OF PARTY COHESION INDEXES ON EIGHT SELECTED SETS OF ROLL CALLS, 81ST CONGRESS, SENATE

	Republican	Democratic
FIRST SESSION		
High-cohesion set		
Number of roll calls	74	74
Range of indexes	39.4–68.8	57.9–87.0
Mean of indexes	54.7	73.1
Median of indexes	55.2	73.7
Low-cohesion set		
Number of roll calls	74	74
Range of indexes	0.0–37.5	0.0–56.9
Mean of indexes	19.3	26.3
Median of indexes	18.95	25.6
SECOND SESSION		
High-cohesion set		
Number of roll calls	74	73
Range of indexes	29.4–68.0	47.0–77.8
Mean of indexes	47.6	62.6
Median of indexes	47.4	63.2
Low-cohesion set		
Number of roll calls	74	74
Range of indexes	0.0–28.6	0.0–46.6
Mean of indexes	14.9	25.2
Median of indexes	13.55	25.9

---

[11] The Democrats' votes showed a high degree of consistency between the sessions in at least one other respect. The incidence of votes on which a majority of one party opposed a majority of the other, "party votes," was a little under two-thirds in each of the Democrats' low-cohesion sets and a little over that proportion in their two high-cohesion sets. Among the Republicans slightly over half the votes were party votes in each set except the high-cohesion set of the second session, where they were a little over two-thirds.

nority party following the upset of 1948, but, especially in view of the lower indexes of the second session, it would seem also to have some connection with the particular issues that characterized the Eighty-first Congress.

Some idea of the sources of unity and disunity within each of the parties may be had by classifying the roll calls into subject-matter categories and comparing the incidence of these substantive classes in the low- and high-cohesion sets with that in a whole session.[12] The five patterns into which these topics can be arranged are shown in Table 2. Despite the crudity of the classification, it is apparent, as one would have expected, that on issues concerning labor and on civil rights and matters of internal security the Republicans were relatively united and the Democrats as consistently split. The greater unity of the Democrats on votes concerning the confirmation of presidential appointments, foreign aid, foreign policy, and public housing, matters central in the Administration program, is one indication of the significance of the White House in the voting of the majority party. On agricultural questions, which normally reflect a maximum of trading between regions and among the representatives of constituencies in which particular commodities are important, neither party was particularly cohesive, the Republicans even less so than the Democrats.

THE DEMOCRATS DISUNITED

The voting of the Senate Democrats on the low-cohesion roll calls was patterned and stable. That is, on both sets of low-cohesion votes the party was split into distinctive blocs, and the composition of these blocs was virtually identical in both sessions. Had the cleavages on one or both of these sets of 74 votes occurred haphazardly, with each vote or series of votes reflecting a different combination of senators, the sharply differentiated blocs in Tables 3 and 4 would not have appeared.[13]

---

[12] Consistently high incidence of a category in the low-cohesion sets indicates the disruptive tendencies of this type of issue. Uniformly low incidence in these sets reflects a unifying characteristic of the issues. Low incidence in both low and high sets reveals a very marked degree of unity within the party on the sort of question included in that category, since it means that on a high proportion of the votes of that type the party cohesion indexes were too high for inclusion in either of the sets. The substantive categories are necessarily crude since there are few roll calls that cannot be assigned to more than one category no matter how sharply the latter are defined.

[13] Tables 3 and 4 are based on matrixes that recorded all instances in which pairs of Democrats agreed on more than half (38 or more) of the 74 votes in

Table 2

THE SUBSTANCE OF PARTY UNITY AND DISUNITY IN THE SENATE: DISTRI-
BUTION OF ROLL CALLS, CLASSIFIED BY SUBJECT, AMONG HIGH- AND LOW-
COHESION SETS AS COMPARED WITH INCIDENCE IN SESSIONS AS A WHOLE,
81ST CONGRESS

Voting Pattern	Subject	
	Republicans	Democrats
1. Very high unity (subjects under-represented* among both low- and high-cohesion sets of both sessions)	1. Civil rights and internal security	1. Presidential appointments
2. High unity (subjects markedly over-represented† in high-cohesion sets and under-represented in low-cohesion sets)	1. Labor 2. Public power	1. Foreign aid 2. Housing 3. Public power
3. Unity (subjects slightly over-represented in high-cohesion sets and under-represented in low-cohesion sets)	1. Economic controls 2. Foreign aid 3. Taxation and general appropriation cuts 4. Presidential appointments 5. Housing	1. Foreign policy 2. Economic controls 3. Public works
4. Disunity (subjects under-represented in high-cohesion sets and and over-represented in low-cohesion sets)	1. Agriculture 2. Foreign policy 3. Public works	1. Civil rights and internal security 2. Labor 3. Miscellaneous
5. Ambiguous (subjects showing no consistent pattern of incidence)	1. General government organization 2. Miscellaneous	1. Agriculture 2. Taxation and general appropriation cuts 3. General government organization

* UNDER-REPRESENTED: proportionately fewer votes on the subject in the set specified than in the session as a whole.

† OVER-REPRESENTED: proportionately more votes on the subject in the set specified than in the session as a whole.

Despite the existence of the overlapping Bloc II in the first-session structure, which is partly a consequence of the fact that the cohesion indexes of this set were somewhat higher than those of the second session, the most striking feature of the party structure in the two sets of votes is the similarity in size and composition of the corresponding major blocs.[14] Given the fact that the issues at stake in these two sets of votes were on their face far from identical, the structural stability evident in these tables clearly indicates a marked consistency of underlying attitude. When the Senate Democrats were divided, they typically split along the same line of cleavage almost regardless of the substantive content of the vote.

The stability of this structure demonstrates that the behavior of the Senate Democrats on these low-cohesion votes was highly patterned rather than haphazard, but this stability was not perfect. In the first place, the ranking of the members within the blocs in Tables 3 and 4 was not the same on both sets of roll calls. To some extent these differences in rank are a function of variations in the member's "absence" rate, that is, in the proportion of the roll calls on which he registered

---

the set. This cutting point is an arbitrary one. Selection of a higher figure would permit a more detailed description of the resulting blocs, since each would be agreed on a larger proportion of the votes, but it would place fewer members in the blocs and thus account less completely for the structure. A lower figure would place more members in blocs, but it would also tend to obscure the major cleavages and would handicap description, since the number of agreed votes within the resulting blocs would be considerably smaller. For a discussion of Beyle's attempt to establish a cutting point on the basis of probability, see the Appendix.

While the full detail of a matrix cannot be recorded in tables such as these, the ranking of bloc members according to their mean scores with others in the bloc suggests something of the internal structure of the bloc. Further, those members of the blocs and of their fringes who had scores of 38 or higher with one or more but less than half the members of other bloc systems are identified on the tables by the symbol X opposite their names. These scattered scores suggest in a rough way who were the more moderate elements in the various blocs. Members of the blocs or fringes who lacked such occasional scores with members of other blocs clearly were among the extremists in the party structure. Finally, the mean scores among all members of a bloc, as shown in Tables 3 and 4, constitute a rough measure of the cohesion of the bloc in comparison with others.

[14] There were 49 Democratic senators who were included in the analyses of both sessions; 37 of these were in the same wing (bloc plus fringe) in both sets. Among the remaining 12 none appeared in the "left" wing in one session (Bloc I) and in the "right" wing in the other. Of the 4 senators whose only membership in the first session was in Bloc II (Table 3), one, Johnston of South Carolina, appeared in the "right" wing in the second session (Table 4). The other 3, Johnson of Texas, Kerr of Oklahoma, and Long of Louisiana, in the second session were in the "isolates" category, to be discussed in more detail below. Like these 3, the remaining 8 changes were shifts into or out of the list of isolates.

Table 3

DEMOCRATIC CLEAVAGE: BLOC STRUCTURE OF SENATE DEMOCRATS ON 74 LOW-COHESION ROLL CALLS, 81ST CONGRESS, 1ST SESSION

Bloc I		Bloc II		Bloc III	
Members: 18		**Members: 9**		**Members: 10**	
Mean Score: 49.2		**Mean Score: 45.8**		**Mean Score: 47.7**	
RANK		RANK		RANK	
18	Downey, Cal.				
17	Anderson, N. M. (e)		X		
15	Hayden, Ariz. (e)		X		
13	Murray, Mont.				
12	Taylor, Ida.				
11	Myers, Pa. (e)		X		
10	McMahon, Conn. (s)				
7	Lucas, Ill. (e)		X		
4	Green, R. I.		X		
9	Douglas, Ill.		X		
8	Thomas, Utah (s)		X		
6	Kilgore, W. Va.		X		
5	Magnuson, Wash.		X		
1	Neely, W. Va. (s)	2	Neely (s)		
2	Humphrey, Minn.	4	Humphrey		
3	Pepper, Fla.	3	Pepper		
16	Hill, Ala.	5	Hill		
14	Sparkman, Ala.	1	Sparkman		
		6	Johnston, S. C. (s)		X
	X	7	Long, La.		X
	X	8	Kerr, Okla.		
	X	9	Johnson, Tex.		
			X	10	Chapman, Ky.
			X	9	Stennis, Miss.
			X	8	Fulbright, Ark.
			X	7	Russell, Ga.
				6	Byrd, Va.
				5	McClellan, Ark. (s)
			X	4	Holland, Fla.
				3	Robertson, Va.
			X	2	Hoey, N. C.
				1	George, Ga. (s)
FRINGE: 3		FRINGE: 6		FRINGE: 3	
O'Mahoney, Wyo. (s)		O'Mahoney (s)			
Kefauver, Tenn.		Kefauver			
Graham, N. C.		Graham			
	X	McFarland, Ariz.			
	X	Withers, Ky.			
	X	McKellar, Tenn. (e)		McKellar (e)	
	X		X	Connally, Tex. (s)	
			X	Ellender, La.	

LEGEND: Each *bloc* member agreed with each other bloc member on 38 or more of the 74 votes in the set. *Mean score* of the bloc: the mean of the number of agreements between all pairs of bloc members. *Rank:* the rank of each bloc member according to the mean of his scores with all other bloc members, 1 designating the highest average number of agreements. *Fringe:* nonmember having scores of 38 or higher with at least half of the blocs members. X: member of a bloc or fringe who had scores of 38 or higher with some but less than half the members of another bloc. (e): elective leader (see text, pp. 99–103). (s): seniority leader (see text, pp. 99–100).

no preference. But they also reflect the tendency of these senators, though voting regularly enough with a particular group of party colleagues to form an identifiable bloc, to agree on a number of issues with other groupings in the party and in the Senate. The voting showed a pattern, but one that did not preclude diversity and dissent.

In the second place, the internal structure of the blocs was not identical in all cases. In the development of a bloc matrix one of two general types of structure may appear: (1) the binuclear or multinuclear type, in which, at the higher score levels, two or more separate groupings of three or four men may emerge and subsequently combine to form a larger bloc at the lower levels; (2) the uninuclear type, in which a single small grouping appears on the matrix at the higher score levels and gradually expands through the adherence of additional men at the lower levels of agreement.[15]

Bloc I in the first-session set is the only one in Tables 3 and 4 that is binuclear. It grew from the merger of two nuclear groupings, one composed of Neely, Humphrey, Kilgore, and Magnuson and the other made up of McMahon, Myers, Green, and Lucas. These groupings merged at a fairly early stage, and the differences between them were neither numerous nor particularly important. But the appearance of this binuclear bloc indicates that, though the structure of the party as a whole was rather highly polarized and was remarkably stable, within this general pattern there was some shifting and divergence.

The positions of some of those who were in the "isolate" category on these two sets of votes also indicate divergence from the general pattern.[16] There were 12 isolates on the low-cohesion set of the first

---

[15] The first of these types, the multinuclear, reflects opposed or divergent views on the part of the several nuclear groupings on a limited number of issues, although the members of the bloc are in agreement on a larger number of votes. The divergences may or may not represent significant or persistent tendencies, but they may be evident even among the later adherents to the bloc, some of whom may score more strongly with one nucleus than with the other. The second, or uninuclear, type indicates the existence of a rough continuum of attitude scaling down from the single nuclear group through an increasing number of dissents from it, dissents which are nevertheless not so concentrated as to produce an alternative nucleus or bloc. Both blocs shown in the incomplete matrix in Figure 1 are uninuclear.

[16] An "isolate" may be defined somewhat more precisely as a member of the party who, though holding his seat for all or most of a session, has scores of the minimum magnitude (here 38) with less than half the members of any bloc. In addition to these, some senators were omitted from this analysis because they were in the Senate for only a small portion of the session. In the first session: Wagner of New York and Miller of Idaho. (McGrath of Rhode Island might have been added to this list, since he resigned in August 1949, to become Attorney General, and only 51 of the 74 votes were taken while he held his seat.) In the second session: Downey of California and Withers and Clements of Kentucky.

Table 4

DEMOCRATIC CLEAVAGE: BLOC STRUCTURE OF SENATE DEMOCRATS ON 74 LOW-COHESION ROLL CALLS, 81ST CONGRESS, 2ND SESSION

	Bloc I		Bloc II	
	Members: 18 Mean Score: 52.6		Members: 14 Mean Score: 50.7	
	RANK		RANK	
	1 Humphrey, Minn.			
	2 Neely, W. Va. (s)			
	3 Kilgore, W. Va.			
	4 Magnuson, Wash.			
	5 McMahon, Conn. (s)			
	6 Lehman, N. Y.			
	7 Green, R. I.			
	8 Murray, Mont.			
	9 Leahy, R. I.			
	10 Anderson, N. M. (e)	X		
	11 Lucas, Ill. (e)			
	12 Myers, Pa. (e)			
	13 Douglas, Ill.			
	14 O'Mahoney, Wyo. (s)			
	15 Chavez, N. M. (s)			
	16 Hill, Ala.	X		
	17 Benton, Conn.			
	18 Taylor, Ida.			
			1 McClellan, Ark. (s)	
			2 Stennis, Miss.	
			3 Holland, Fla.	
			4 Hoey, N. C.	
			5 George, Ga. (s)	
			6 Chapman, Ky.	
X			7 Russell, Ga.	
			8 Ellender, La.	
			9 Eastland, Miss.	
			10 Byrd, Va.	
X			11 Connally, Tex. (s)	
			12 Robertson, Va.	
X			13 McKellar, Tenn. (e)	
			14 Maybank, S. C. (s)	
	FRINGE: 9		FRINGE: 3	
	Sparkman, Ala.			X
	Graham, N. C.			
	McFarland, Ariz.			X
	Hunt, Wyo.			
	Pepper, Fla.			
	Hayden, Ariz. (e)			X
	Thomas, Utah (s)			X
	O'Conor, Md.			
	Kefauver, Tenn.			
X			McCarran, Nev. (s)	
X			Johnson, Colo. (s)	
			Johnston, S. C. (s)	

LEGEND: Each *bloc* member agreed with each other bloc member on 38 or more of the 74 votes in the set. *Mean score* of the bloc: the mean of the number of agreements between all pairs of bloc members. *Rank:* the rank of each bloc member according to the mean of his scores with all other bloc members, 1 designating the highest average number of agreements. *Fringe:* non-member having scores of 38 or higher with at least half of the bloc members. X: member of a bloc or fringe who had scores of 38 or higher with some but less than half the members of another bloc. (e): elective leader (see text, pp. 99–103). (s): seniority leader (see text, pp. 99–100).

session and 8 on that of the second session. Their names are listed in
Table 5, along with the number of their "absences," the number of
scores of 38 or higher which they had, and the blocs in which these
scores appeared.

Some of these men were "isolates" simply because they were "absent"—that is, their preferences were unrecorded—too often.[17] The vot-

Table 5

DEMOCRATIC ISOLATES: SENATORS NOT INCLUDED IN IDENTIFIED BLOCS
OR FRINGES, LOW-COHESION ROLL CALLS, 81ST CONGRESS

Senator	Number of "Absences"*	Number of Scores 38 or Higher	Blocs in Which Scores Occur
First Session			
Johnson, Colo. (s)	9	2	III
Gillette, Ia.	12	4	II
O'Conor, Md.	15	2	– – –
Maybank, S. C. (s)	17	5	III
Frear, Del.	17	0	– – –
Hunt, Wyo.	18	6	I, II
Tydings, Md. (s)	19	2	III
Thomas, Okla. (s)	20	1	– – –
McCarran, Nev. (s)	21	1	– – –
Eastland, Miss.	25	3	III
Chavez, N. M. (s)	29	0	– – –
McGrath,† R. I. (s)	30	2	I
Second Session			
Gillette, Ia.	11	2	– – –
Tydings, Md. (s)	13	7	I
Long, La.	14	5	I, II
Johnson, Tex.	16	3	II
Kerr, Okla.	17	6	II
Frear, Del.	17	0	– – –
Fulbright, Ark.	18	5	II
Thomas, Okla. (s)	32	0	– – –

* "Absences" cover those roll calls in the set on which the senator did not
vote and did not record his preference in any other way.

† Senator not seated for whole session.

(s) Seniority leader.

[17] A close analysis of "absences" can sometimes be informative, but for present
purposes those with high rates may be ignored. These would probably include
the 9 men in the first-session set with 17 or more "absences" and the one in the

ing of the remaining isolates deviated from the generally stable pattern in two ways. First, some of them distributed their support so evenly between the two major blocs that they became affiliated with neither.[18] The other reason for a man's appearing among the isolates involves deviant voting of another sort, namely, agreement *as an isolated individual* or one of a small and uncohesive cluster with a Republican faction so frequently as to remain unaffiliated with any Democratic bloc.[19]

The gross features of the Democratic structure are those that were to be expected. The most obvious and least astonishing of these is the decidedly sectional character of the smaller of the two major blocs in each set (Table 3, Bloc III, and Table 4, Bloc II).[20] By way of con-

---

second-session set with more than 22 (Table 5), since these were unrecorded more frequently than any member of the identified blocs.

[18] O'Conor of Maryland in the first-session set and Tydings of Maryland in the second seem to have been in this position, apparently a fairly common one for legislators from the Border States. (Note that on each of these sets 4 of the 9 Democrats from the Border States were in the isolate category.) Fairly even support of both major blocs is almost certainly the explanation for Long, Kerr, and Johnson of Texas on the second-session set, especially since they were the lowest-ranking members of Bloc II in the first session (Table 3), which as a group was intermediate between the two major blocs.

[19] Of course, if several Democrats joined in voting consistently with a Republican faction, they would appear as another Democratic bloc. This was characteristic of Bloc III in Table 3 and Bloc II in Table 4. Though it is impossible to say with certainty, it seems likely that Johnson of Colorado in the first session and Gillette in both should be explained as isolated adherents to a Republican bloc. Frear of Delaware almost certainly was deviating in this way in the second session. Note that although he and Kerr had the same number of "absences," Frear agreed with no Democrat on as many as 38 votes while Kerr had 6 scores of 38 or higher within the party. In the set of the second session Fulbright of Arkansas cannot be classified with confidence. Along with the other "isolates," however, he illustrates the point that there were a number of individual exceptions to the generally stable Democratic voting pattern on these roll calls.

[20] Some explanation of the designation of blocs is in order. To have given names to the blocs in these tables would have been to indulge in misleading simplification. Therefore, in the chapters on both the Senate and the House, the various blocs are given Roman numbers. Since some consistent procedure had to be followed in assigning these numbers and in arranging the blocs in the tables, they are arranged on a crude and fairly subjective left-right dimension, the lower numbers indicating the blocs that seemed to be on the political "left" of the party. In the text sectional labels are occasionally attached to the blocs where no violence is thereby done to the evidence, and more rarely the terms "left" and "right" are also employed. The reader may find it convenient to use the bloc numbers in the same way, but this should be done with caution, especially as in some structures, particularly among the Republicans, it is almost impossible to say, even in the crudest fashion, which blocs are "left" and which "right."

trast, the other blocs were in varying degrees intersectional in their composition.

Looking at the roll calls on which the members of Bloc I were in complete agreement,[21] one is not surprised to discover that there is a strong "Fair Deal" tone to their votes. These Democrats rather consistently took an "internationalist" position on the foreign aid program and on other features of foreign policy, including the votes on amending the Displaced Persons Act in the second session. On the domestic scene they were usually on the "liberal" side on votes concerning labor, rent control, housing, public power, and social security. Though not united on those civil rights issues involving matters of race, a reflection of the intersectional composition of the bloc, they tended to support the unsuccessful efforts to moderate the provisions of the 1950 Internal Security Act.

The members of Bloc III in the first session, who were agreed on 28 votes, and the members of Bloc II in the second, who were agreed on 24, consistently took the restrictive or "conservative" position on all the votes classified under the heading of civil rights and internal security in these two sets, as would be expected, but they also took a comparable position—typically in opposition to Bloc I—on an astonishingly wide range of other issues. These others included most of the labor votes in the two sets, those on public power, rent control, and several dealing with taxation and spending policy. The Southern bloc tended to oppose liberalization of the Displaced Persons Act and to favor restricting the authority of the Federal Power Commission to regulate the production and distribution of natural gas, an interesting agreement considering that by no means all of the bloc came from gas-producing states.

A striking aspect of these agreements within the Southern bloc thus is the range of issues that they cover. Roll calls dealing with racial questions were a relatively small proportion of those on which these senators agreed. The larger fraction dealt rather with most of the more controversial issues of contemporary foreign and domestic policy. This evidence does not controvert the accepted proposition that Southern Democrats in the Congress are as a whole genuinely cohesive only on

---

[21] "Complete agreement" within a bloc refers not only to those roll calls on which all members of a bloc recorded the same preference but also to those on which less than half the bloc were unrecorded ("absent") and the remainder voted the same way. This convention broadens the base for describing a bloc, especially in the case of relatively large groupings, and does no violence to the tendencies evident in the cluster. In the first-session set the members of Bloc I were agreed on 17 votes, in the second-session set on 24.

issues involving the race question. Nor does it disagree with Key's conclusion that other sorts of issues tend to split Southern senators.[22] What it does seem to indicate is that within the Senate Democratic party, collective dissent from the majority, as distinguished from random individual deviation, was a peculiarly Southern characteristic and one not confined to matters of race.

The Southern bloc, consistently the smaller of the two major groupings, was a dissenting element of a particular sort. It did not as a unit offer continuous, unremitting opposition to the remainder of the party. Rather the composition of the bloc showed a good deal of variation from issue to issue.[23] Members of the Southern bloc, in other words, were more likely than those in the larger grouping to break away and vote with the other bloc. Dissent was relatively unstable, and its very instability revealed that the central tendency of the party was reflected in the position of Bloc I.

In the first-session set Bloc II, as the discussion of "isolates" has suggested, was on all counts intermediate between the extremes represented by the other two (Table 3). Like the "isolates," its existence somewhat qualified the polarization evident in the general structural pattern, though only on a limited number of questions. It was the least cohesive of the three blocs, and its members were in agreement with one another on relatively few votes (15), considering the small size of the bloc. Although there were enough of these to give the group identity, its low cohesion indicates the tendency on the remaining votes for some of its members to side with Bloc I while a smaller number agreed with the Southern dissenters. Among its 15 agreements none was shared with Bloc III. It took the same position as Bloc I on 4 votes—dealing with foreign aid, public housing, and public power—but typically not those that were most controversial within the party.[24] Aside from these votes, the most distinctive characteristic of the agreements within this bloc was a tendency to oppose the much debated, and largely ineffectual, "economy drive" of the first session.

These statements describe the composition and the general preferences of the various blocs, but they indicate little of their relative im-

---

[22] V. O. Key, Jr., *Southern Politics,* New York: Alfred A. Knopf, 1949, chap. 16, especially pp. 355–9.

[23] This is indicated by its lower mean agreement scores in the two sets of votes (Tables 3 and 4). The cohesion of Bloc I, as measured by the mean scores, was in both sets higher than that of the Southern bloc. This was the case in spite of the larger size of Bloc I and the higher mean "absence" rate of its members, both of which normally are associated with lower mean scores.

[24] The mean index of cohesion of the 17 votes on which Bloc I agreed was 38.4, that of the 4 votes on which both I and II were agreed was 52.6.

portance in the party or in the Senate. How frequently did a particular bloc or one of its members support the Administration position? How frequently did they form a portion of the party majority? How often was their position the prevailing one in the Senate? To answer the first of these questions those votes on which the record indicated a presidential preference were separated from the others and designated Administration support votes. For each session the votes and declared preferences of each senator were scored on a scale from 1 to 5, the latter value indicating a vote in support of the President. The arithmetic means of these values for an individual senator or for a group or bloc provide an index of Administration support for the entire session.[25] Twenty-seven of these votes fell into the low-cohesion set of the first session and 32 into the comparable set of the second session. To indicate the tendencies of each bloc within the set, the proportion of these on which each was agreed in support of the President was also calculated.

A similar procedure was followed in dealing with the question of a bloc's relation to the party majority. For each session an index of party orthodoxy was set up, also on a scale of 1 to 5, with the latter value indicating a vote in support of the party majority, and covering all the roll calls of the session. For each set the proportion of a bloc's agreements that were on the side of the party majority was also calculated.

Finally, to deal with the question of a bloc's disposition toward the winning side in the Senate as a whole, the percentage of its agreements which were on the prevailing side in the Senate was calculated.

These calculations for each of the major blocs in the two low-cohesion sets confirm some interpretations already made and suggest some others. Figure 2, which compares the proportion of each bloc's agreements on the side of the party majority with the proportion on the prevailing side in the Senate, reveals the central position in the party occupied by Block II in the first-session set. Though frequently in the minority in the Senate, its members were invariably agreed on the side of the party majority. Clearly these were middlemen who were not agreed among themselves on a wide range of issues. Rather they alternated as individuals in their support of the two major blocs, but when they did agree they were invariably on the predominant side in the party.[26]

---

[25] There were 100 votes designated as Administration support votes in the first session, 90 in the second. For a more detailed description of the criteria of selection and for a validation of the procedure, see the Appendix.

[26] This was characteristic of these men over the session as a whole. Their mean

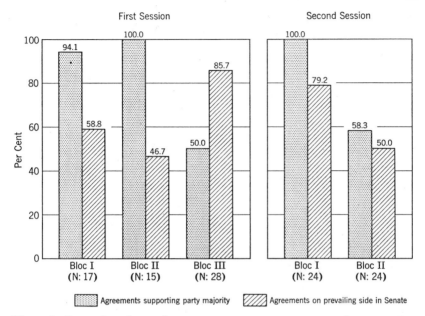

Figure 2. Proportion of agreed votes supporting party majority and on prevailing side in the Senate, principal Democratic blocs, low-cohesion roll calls, 81st Congress, 1st and 2nd sessions. (Agreements include all votes on which the bloc was unanimous plus those on which less than half the members were unrecorded and the remainder were unanimous.)

More striking are the data on the Southern bloc (Bloc III in the first session and Bloc II in the second). From these it is clear that this was the continuing Democratic component of the bipartisan coalition that often dominated the Senate in this Congress (Figure 2). In the first session six of every seven of its agreements (85.7 per cent) were on the prevailing side in the Senate while only half were on the side of the party majority. The excess of agreements on the prevailing side is an indication of successful coalition voting in association with one or more Republican factions and in opposition to a majority of Democrats. In the second-session set the issues were less conducive to a stable coalition arrangement, but the proportion of its agreements on the prevailing side was still high relative to the proportion on which it agreed with the party majority. (There were in this set a good many fewer votes dealing with labor, and on the long series of votes concerning the Displaced Persons Act a majority of the Republicans did not

party orthodoxy index for the whole session was 4.39, as compared with 4.36 for Bloc I and 3.78 for Bloc III. In the second session the mean party orthodoxy index of Bloc I was 4.18, that of Bloc II 3.79.

vote with this bloc.) The set of votes from the second session, more-over, illustrates the instability of the Southern bloc's dissenting posi-tion in the party, for, though the bloc as a whole was agreed more often on the side of the party majority than on the prevailing side in the Senate, the reverse was true of the four-man nucleus of the bloc.[27] This nucleus on various votes picked up enough support from other Democrats to form an effective coalition with the Republicans, but several of the other ten members of the bloc broke away from the dis-senters often enough so that the bloc as a whole was less often on the prevailing side than was the nucleus. These departures from the nu-cleus were most frequent on votes dealing with expenditures for wel-fare and foreign policy purposes, with immigration, with general eco-nomic policy, and with organized labor.

The contrasting positions of these blocs are further revealed by Figure 3. From this distribution of the Administration support votes on which the members of each bloc were agreed in the two sets it is apparent that Bloc I was conspicuously the bloc strongest in support

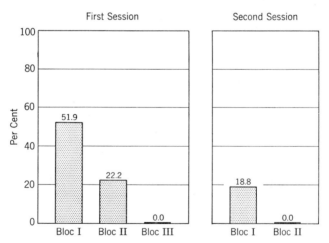

Figure 3. Proportion of Administration support votes in low-cohesion sets on which members of principal Democratic Senate blocs were agreed on the admin-istration side, 81st Congress, 1st and 2nd sessions. Administration support votes are those identified as involving an expressed presidential preference; there were 27 of these in the first-session set and 32 in the second-session set. Agreements include votes on which the bloc was unanimous plus those on which less than half the members were unrecorded and the remainder were unanimous.

---

[27] As shown in Figure 1, above: Senators McClellan, Holland, George, and Hoey.

of the Administration. The Southern bloc, on the other hand, agreed on the side of the Administration on none of these votes.[28]

To summarize in preliminary fashion, these two sets of low-cohesion votes reveal among the Senate Democrats a structure of two rather sharply opposed wings that was remarkably stable. The structure, though indicating that voting choices were not haphazard, was not so rigid, however, that the two wings were completely polarized. There was some overlapping between the blocs, enough in the first-session set to produce an intermediate bloc, and dissenting behavior by individuals was fairly common. Concerted, as distinguished from individual, dissent from the party majority, however, was sectionally based and covered a wide range of issues. The dominant bloc in the party, in terms of size and cohesion, was intersectional in its make-up. Its party dominance was often inadequate for control of the Senate, however, when the dissenting bloc agreed with a large majority of the opposition. In the structure as a whole the stability and cohesion of the principal blocs were sufficiently marked to permit one to infer not only that the voting was not fluid or haphazard, but also that these blocs were based on patterns of consultation and association and probably were not merely groupings produced by the mode of analysis.

THE DEMOCRATS IN HARMONY

At first glance the structure of the party as reflected in the high-cohesion votes seems to be completely altered, to present an appearance of consolidation and convergence in which the cleavages so obvious in the low-cohesion sets are undetectable. To a degree this is in fact the case, as increased party cohesion could have no other meaning. The structure of the party, as is evident from Tables 6 and 7, was of the uninuclear type. This means that on these roll calls there was a rough continuum of attitude within the party. A small nucleus of men, those ranking first in the blocs in Tables 6 and 7, were agreed on almost all of the votes. The other members of the party dissented in varying degrees from the positions taken by this nucleus, those dissenting most frequently ranking lowest in the bloc. These dissenters, however, were not sufficiently agreed among themselves to form an alternate nucleus or bloc.

---

[28] The records of these men over the sessions as a whole were consistent with the data in Figures 2 and 3. The mean Administration support indexes of the several blocs were, for the first session, Bloc I 4.67, Bloc II 4.52, Bloc III 3.61; for the second session, Bloc I 4.25, Bloc II 3.29.

Closer examination of these tables will indicate, however, that there was no real structural discontinuity between the low- and high-cohesion sets, that the cleavages whose stability was noted in analyzing votes on which the party was divided persisted in modified degree

Table 6

DEMOCRATIC UNITY: BLOC STRUCTURE OF SENATE DEMOCRATS ON 74 HIGH-COHESION ROLL CALLS, 81ST CONGRESS, 1ST SESSION

Bloc I

Members: 39
Mean Score: 55.5

RANK		FRINGE: 9
1	Green, R. I.	Miller, Ida.*
2	Kerr, Okla.	Gillette, Ia.
3	Anderson, N. M. (e)	O'Conor, Md.
4	Lucas, Ill. (e)	Robertson, Va.
5	Hayden, Ariz. (e)	Tydings, Md. (s)
6	Sparkman, Ala.	Frear, Del.
7	Hill, Ala.	George, Ga. (s)
8	Pepper, Fla.	Russell, Ga.
9	McKellar, Tenn. (e)	Graham, N. C.*
10	Myers, Pa. (e)	
11	Johnson, Tex.	
12	Connally, Tex. (s)	
13	O'Mahoney, Wyo. (s)	
14	Chapman, Ky.	
15	Kilgore, W. Va.	
16	Magnuson, Wash.	
17	Humphrey, Minn.	
18	Thomas, Utah (s)	
19	Kefauver, Tenn.	
20	Withers, Ky.*	
21	Stennis, Miss.	
22	Holland, Fla.	
23	Neely, W. Va. (s)	
24	Murray, Mont.	
25	Maybank, S. C. (s)	
26	Johnston, S. C. (s)	
27	Hoey, N. C.	
28	Fulbright, Ark.	
29	Ellender, La.	
30	Long, La.	
31	Thomas, Okla. (s)	
32	Taylor, Ida.	
33	McFarland, Ariz.	
34	McGrath, R. I. (s)*	
35	Downey, Cal.	
36	Chavez, N. M. (s)	
37	McMahon, Conn. (s)	
38	Hunt, Wyo.	
39	Douglas, Ill.	

* Senator not seated for whole session.

LEGEND: Each *bloc* member agreed with each other bloc member on 38 or more of the 74 votes in the set. *Mean score* of the bloc: the mean of the number of agreements between all pairs of bloc members. *Rank:* the rank of each bloc member according to the mean of his scores with all other bloc members, 1 designating the highest average number of agreements. *Fringe:* nonmember having scores of 38 or higher with at least half of the bloc members. (e): elective leader. (s): seniority leader.

Table 7

DEMOCRATIC UNITY: BLOC STRUCTURE OF SENATE DEMOCRATS ON 73
HIGH-COHESION ROLL CALLS, 81ST CONGRESS, 2ND SESSION

Bloc I		Bloc II		Bloc III	
Members: 30		Members: 22		Members: 28	
Mean Score: 49.2		Mean Score: 52.5		Mean Score: 49.8	
RANK		RANK		RANK	
30	Taylor, Ida.				
29	Murray, Mont.				
28	Humphrey, Minn.				
27	Graham, N. C.*				
26	McMahon, Conn. (s)				
25	Leahy, R. I.				
23	Kefauver, Tenn.				
20	Lehman, N. Y.				
24	Chavez, N. M. (s)	22	Chavez (s)	25	Chavez (s)
22	Hunt, Wyo.	21	Hunt	22	Hunt
16	Thomas, Utah (s)	19	Thomas (s)	20	Thomas (s)
11	Lucas, Ill. (e)	11	Lucas (e)	16	Lucas (e)
13	Kilgore, W. Va.	10	Kilgore	15	Kilgore
12	Myers, Pa. (e)	16	Myers (e)	19	Myers (e)
10	Green, R. I.	15	Green	18	Green
8	Magnuson, Wash.	9	Magnuson	9	Magnuson
5	Neely, W. Va. (s)	5	Neely (s)	6	Neely (s)
6	Anderson, N. M. (e)	6	Anderson (e)	7	Anderson (e)
7	O'Mahoney, Wyo. (s)	7	O'Mahoney (s)	8	O'Mahoney (s)
4	Hayden, Ariz. (e)	3	Hayden (e)	3	Hayden (e)
3	Sparkman, Ala.	4	Sparkman	4	Sparkman
2	McFarland, Ariz.	2	McFarland	2	McFarland
1	Hill, Ala.	1	Hill	1	Hill
9	Connally, Tex. (s)	8	Connally (s)	5	Connally (s)
14	Kerr, Okla.	13	Kerr	13	Kerr
15	Holland, Fla.	17	Holland	10	Holland
17	Johnson, Tex.	12	Johnson	12	Johnson
18	Chapman, Ky.	14	Chapman	11	Chapman
19	McKellar, Tenn. (e)	18	McKellar (e)	14	McKellar (e)
21	Maybank, S. C. (s)	20	Maybank (s)	17	Maybank (s)
				21	Hoey, N. C.
				23	Fulbright, Ark.
				24	Stennis, Miss.
				26	Ellender, La.
				27	George, Ga. (s)
				28	Johnston, S. C. (s)

FRINGE: 10

Closer to Bloc I	Closer to Bloc III
Benton, Conn.	Johnson, Colo. (s)
Tydings, Md. (s)	Gillette, Ia.
Pepper, Fla.	Russell, Ga.
Withers, Ky.*	Eastland, Miss.
Douglas, Ill.	Long, La.

* Senator not seated for whole session.

LEGEND: Each *bloc* member agreed with each other bloc member on 37 or more of the 73 votes in the set. *Mean score* of the bloc: the mean of the number of agreements between all pairs of bloc members. *Rank:* the rank of each bloc member according to the mean of his scores with all other bloc members, 1 designating the highest average number of agreements. *Fringe:* nonmember having score of 37 or higher with at least half of the bloc members. (e): elective leader. (s): seniority leader.

when the Senate Democrats were united. In other words, though the structure reflects the relatively high cohesion of these roll calls, the bases of dissent were essentially the same as in the low-cohesion votes. However, the instability of the dissenting Southern bloc, noted in the analysis of the low-cohesion votes, was so extended on the high-cohesion roll calls that the dissenters did not form a separate bloc.[29]

The list of isolates for the two high-cohesion sets further reinforces the evidence concerning structural continuity and the pattern of dissent (Table 8). Most of these isolates belonged to the dissenting minority blocs on the low-cohesion votes or were isolates voting with the opposition.[30] On the 1949 votes Johnson of Colorado, McClellan, Byrd, and Eastland, whose absences were moderate, stood apart from the consolidation of the minority bloc with the center of the party and continued to vote, individually but fairly regularly, with a Republican faction.[31] On the second-session set McClellan, Robertson, McCarran, Byrd, and Frear continued voting patterns which placed them indi-

---

[29] In the first place, though the blocs in the second-session set (Table 7) were based on a single nucleus, this central nucleus (Hill, McFarland, Sparkman, and Hayden) had adherents from two fairly distinct wings of the party, so that the resulting structure appears as two overlapping blocs or one central bloc (Bloc II) with two sets of affiliates, each of which was internally cohesive but at its extremes not significantly related to the other (Blocs I and III). The outer ranks of these two wings resembled the nuclei of the two distinct blocs of the low-cohesion set. Second, though the high-cohesion set of the first session revealed no such distinct wings (Table 6), most of the later adherents to the bloc, for example, those ranking 25 through 39, were in the opposed blocs of the low-cohesion set and in the separate wings of the party in the high-cohesion set of the second session.

[30] In the first-session set 54 Democrats are thus accounted for in Tables 6 and 8, though there were three additional individuals who served for such brief periods that only their predecessors or successors were included in the analysis (Barkley of Kentucky, Broughton of North Carolina, and Leahy of Rhode Island). In the second-session set 53 Democrats are accounted for in Tables 7 and 8. Senator Downey of California, who resigned in November of 1950 and was succeeded by Richard Nixon, was recorded on too few votes to be included in the analysis. Others serving too short a period to be included were Clements of Kentucky, Pastore of Rhode Island, and Smith of North Carolina; in each of these cases the predecessor is included in the analysis.

[31] On the 1949 votes Wagner clearly was unrecorded too many times to have a chance of appearing in the bloc system, and the same may have been true of McCarran, who was in Europe for several weeks investigating displaced persons. Byrd and Eastland, despite their high "absence" rate, are listed in the coalition category (but not McCarran) because of the limited number of their Democratic colleagues with whom Byrd and Eastland had scores of 38 or higher.

Table 8

DEMOCRATIC ISOLATES: SENATORS NOT INCLUDED IN IDENTIFIED BLOCS OR
FRINGES, HIGH-COHESION ROLL CALLS, 81ST CONGRESS

Senator	Number of "Absences"*	Number of Scores of at Least Minimum Magnitude†	Blocs in Which Scores Occur
First Session			
Johnson, Colo. (s)	3	1	I
McClellan, Ark. (s)	5	19	I
Byrd, Va.	22	0	– – –
Eastland, Miss.	24	3	I
McCarran, Nev. (s)	25	14	I
Wagner, N. Y.‡	35	9	I
Second Session			
McClellan, Ark. (s)	1	18	I, II, III
Robertson, Va.	5	12	I, II, III
Byrd, Va.	5	2	– – –
McCarran, Nev. (s)	6	5	I, II, III
O'Conor, Md.	12	7	I, II, III
Frear, Del.	14	1	I
Thomas, Okla. (s)	32	3	I, II, III

* "Absences" cover those roll calls in the set on which the senator did not vote and did not record his preference in any other way.

† In the first session, 38 or higher; in the second session, 37 or higher.

‡ Senator not seated for whole session.

(s) Seniority leader.

vidually and in varying degrees closer to a Republican grouping than to one of the Democratic blocs.[32]

The extent of intraparty consolidation to be expected on a set of high-cohesion votes and the compromise character of these roll calls are evident from various parts of the data, despite the indications of persistent cleavage. For example, in the first-session set the presence of Kerr in the nucleus of the bloc, with Green, Anderson, Lucas, and Hayden, is revealing (Table 6), since Kerr's position on the low-cohesion votes was that of the middleman tending fairly often to side with the Southern bloc. Similarly, the relatively high ranking of such Sena-

---

[32] In the votes of the second session Thomas of Oklahoma, "absent" on 32 roll calls, had no chance of bloc membership. O'Conor of Maryland again is difficult to account for, but the distribution of his seven scores suggests again the ambivalent position of many Border State legislators.

tors as McKellar, Connally, and Chapman in the first-session bloc and
the motley character of all three blocs in the second-session set (Table
7), judged on the basis of the low-cohesion votes, reflect the coales-
cence of the party.

Less obvious features of the data indicate more precisely the degree
of intraparty consolidation. In the first-session set, although the 39
members of the bloc were in complete agreement on only 5 of the 74
votes and there were thus divisions within the bloc on 69 roll

Table 9

DISSENT AND COHESION IN THE MAJOR BLOC AMONG SENATE DEMOCRATS,
74 HIGH-COHESION ROLL CALLS, 81ST CONGRESS, 1ST SESSION

	Within the bloc, among the first:				
	11 Members	16 Members	21 Members	28 Members	39 Members
Of all 74 votes there were agreements* on	58	48	40	18	5
And disagreements on	16	26	34	56	69
The proportion of these disagreements caused by the dissenting vote of more than one man was (per cent)	31.4	34.7	41.2	53.5	87.0

* Agreements include all votes on which the bloc was unanimous plus those
on which less than half the members were unrecorded and the remainder were
unanimous.

calls, in most cases the number of members dissenting from the majority of the bloc was low (Table 9).[33] The second-session set showed
a roughly comparable pattern.[34]

---

[33] On over four-fifths (56) of these disputed votes 4 or fewer of the 39 members
of the bloc dissented from the majority position. On only one of the 69 disputed roll
calls were there more than 7 dissenters among the bloc members. On this vote,
rejecting an amendment offered by Magnuson and aimed at extending rent control
for two years rather than for 15 months, there were 10 dissents in the bloc. These
10 supported the Magnuson motion, the only members of the Senate to do so, in
one of the fairly infrequent cases of "liberal" deviation from the party majority.
The average number of dissenters within the bloc on the 69 disputed votes was
just over 3.

[34] In the smaller central bloc (Bloc II, Table 7) there were 54 disagreed votes
out of 73, but over 90 per cent of these involved four or fewer dissenters, and

The disagreements within the bloc in the first-session set did not threaten its dominance in the party nor materially affect its position in the Senate. On none of the 69 disagreed votes was the majority of the bloc opposed by a majority of the party and on only four roll calls did the dissident position prevail in the Senate.[35]

Looking more closely at the substance of the disagreements within the bloc in this first-session set, the differences among the members ranking first through eleventh in Table 6 were neither numerous nor particularly important. Among the later adherents to the bloc and between these and the higher-ranking members the number of disagreements and the number of dissenters was larger (Table 9). Moreover, the substance of the disagreed votes was of more consequence. These later disagreements were more likely, for example, to involve Administration support votes, and the later adherents to the bloc less frequently voted with the party majority.[36]

Among the first 16 members of the bloc in Table 6 individual considerations, involving interest-group attachments and constituency pressures rather than major policy divergences, account for most of the dissents. For example, Senators Neely and Kilgore departed from the bloc in voting against the confirmation of James Boyd as director of the Bureau of Mines, an appointment strongly opposed by John L. Lewis and the United Mine Workers. The extraneous factors bearing upon the vote are suggested by the fact that among the other nine negative votes in the Senate, on the Democratic side the only other "nay"

---

the average was slightly over 2. There were 62 disagreed votes in each of the other two blocs. In Bloc III nearly three-fourths of these involved from 1 to 4 members, and the average was a little over 3. In Bloc I the average number of dissenters was identical with Bloc III, and 71 per cent of the disagreements were registered by 4 or fewer members.

[35] One of these was of some consequence, a Bridges amendment to the Independent Offices appropriation cutting funds for the Office of the Housing Expediter, a thrust at rent control, which was adopted by a vote of 45 to 42 with Hoey and 7 Democrats from outside the bloc on the prevailing side (Byrd, George, Johnson of Colorado, McClellan, O'Conor, Russell, and Tydings). The others concerned funds for building maintenance in the District of Columbia and an unsuccessful effort to exempt from the excise tax tickets to the Truman inauguration celebration.

[36] There were 33 Administration support votes in the high-cohesion set of the first session. The first 11 members of the bloc (Table 6) supported the Administration on 84.8 per cent of these; the last 11 members voted that way on only 9.1 per cent. The pattern for these men was, as usual, consistent over the session. The mean Administration support index for the whole first session was 4.66 for the first 11 members of the bloc; for the full 39 members it was 4.30. The comparable mean party orthodoxy index for the first 11 members was 4.48 and for the whole 39-member bloc was 4.28.

came from Johnson of Colorado. (On the Republican side the opposition to Boyd was composed of Johnson's colleague, Millikin, Capehart and Jenner of Indiana, Schoeppel of Kansas, Brewster of Maine, Wherry of Nebraska, Langer of North Dakota, and Bricker of Ohio.) Similarly, Senator Magnuson of Washington formed an unlikely combination with two other Democrats, Johnson of Colorado and Gillette of Iowa, to vote for the two amendments to the National Housing Act of 1949, vigorously sponsored by Senators Cain of Washington and Bricker of Ohio, that would have barred segregation or discrimination on account of race or creed in publicly supported housing. If adopted, they would have weakened Southern support for the bill as a whole, which presumably was the real intent of the sponsors. It seems likely that Magnuson, who was up for re-election in 1950, felt he could not oppose amendments nominally aimed at racial discrimination which were actively championed by his Republican colleague from Washington.

By way of contrast, the dissents registered by the last 18 adherents to the bloc much more often occurred in areas such as the foreign aid program, public power, public housing, rent control, and across-the-board appropriation cuts. The fact that the bulk of these dissents, excepting the last-named category, came from Southerners who belonged to the minority bloc in the low-cohesion sets again indicates the continuities of attitude underlying the low- and high-cohesion votes.

The data on the second session's high-cohesion votes suggest no markedly different inferences from those above, allowance being made for the lower average cohesion of this set. Again the disagreed votes in the central bloc (Bloc II, Table 7) included no instance in which the majority of the bloc was at odds with the majority of the party. On 8 of these 54 non-unanimous votes, however, the majority of the bloc (and of the party) was on the losing side in the Senate.[37] These were votes on which, though Democratic cohesion was high, Republican co-

---

[37] As would be expected, at least 6 of the disagreed votes on which the Democratic majority was not on the winning side were of considerable importance, and 5 were classified among the Administration support votes. Three concerned restrictive amendments to the Defense Production Act, sponsored by Bricker and by Johnson of Colorado, which the majority of the bloc opposed; they also voted against Knowland's amendment to the Social Security Act revision, which severely restricted the authority of the Secretary of Labor to withhold unemployment insurance funds from states not complying with his regulations, and they voted for Long's amendment to the same bill, aimed at granting public assistance to the needy disabled; finally, they supported Lucas's move toward modifying the registration provisions of the Internal Security Act.

hesion was still higher, so that the defection of a handful of Democrats could decide the issue. These defectors were not the same in all cases, but in each instance they included several of the "isolates" whom the discussion of Table 8 described as frequently voting with the Republicans, further indicating the nature of the party's dissenting wing.

The persisting cleavages within the party that were responsible for the two wings of the voting structure on this set (Table 7) were also apparent in the data. Some of the later adherents to the central bloc such as Chapman of Kentucky, who ranked higher in Bloc III than in Blocs I and II, tended to dissent more frequently on matters of substance, especially on Administration support votes. These were among the men who, along with some of those in the isolate category and some of the extremists in Bloc III, were responsible for the central bloc and the party majority being on the losing side in the Senate on eight of these votes.

Generally speaking the principal difference between Blocs I and III was the former's consistently stronger support of the Administration. Several members of Bloc III showed a corresponding tendency to break away from the party majority, particularly on domestic "welfare" policies and on economic issues.[38]

Bloc II in the second-session set looks like a stronger version of the intermediate bloc identified in the low-cohesion set of the first session (Bloc II, Table 3). Its high-ranking members include a number of the members of that bloc, but, more important, it occupied a similar, though more dominant, position in the structure of the party. Intermediate in its support of the Administration, its members most consistently voted with the party majority over the session as a whole.

Among the earlier adherents to this central group (Bloc II, Table 7), disagreements not only were relatively few but characteristically concerned matters of localized constituency importance or the claims of particular interest groups rather than broad policy issues. For example, the first 7 members of the bloc were not agreed on such matters as an amendment to the Revenue Act of 1950 providing that funds derived from the sale of breeding or dairy cattle should be treated as capital gains rather than as personal income. Here, as in many other votes of

---

[38] On the 28 Administration support votes in the high-cohesion set of the second session, Blocs I and II both supported the Administration on 17.9 per cent, Bloc III on 3.6 per cent. Their mean Administration support indexes over the whole session showed fairly marked differences: Bloc I 4.00, Bloc II 3.94, and Bloc III 3.82. The votes on which the members of these three blocs were agreed were in all cases on the side of the party majority. Over the session as a whole their mean party orthodoxy indexes were, Bloc I 4.24, Bloc II 4.29, and Bloc III 4.21.

the Senate Democrats, the general stability of the voting structure indicates that, while such specialized claims occasionally disrupt the "normal" pattern, typically they are either supplementary to the claims of the legislative party, in the sense of being supported by a majority of the party, or are subordinate to them.

Analysis of the high-cohesion votes thus supports the earlier inference that the structure of the Senate Democrats, while not rigid, was stable and was clearly not the product of haphazard or highly individualized behavior. The consolidation of the party produced no pattern that was essentially new. The lines of association and concerted action that were assumed to underlie the blocs on the low-cohesion votes were evident, though less conspicuous, on both sets of high-cohesion roll calls. Dissent from the majority of the party, though less concerted than on the low-cohesion votes, had essentially the same sectional base. The dissenters' effectiveness as part of a bipartisan coalition depended more on the size and cohesion of the Republican faction with which they agreed than upon their own unity and influence among the Democrats. They were, in fact, not a bloc, but a splinter of modest and variable proportions. The instability of this splinter, especially on these votes, underscores the point that a stable party structure existed among the Senate Democrats and indicates the influence of a central party tendency. Elaboration of this inference, however, must be delayed until the Republican patterns have been examined.

REPUBLICAN STRUCTURAL CLEAVAGES

The structure of the Republican party in the Senate on the two sets of low-cohesion votes was generally similar to that of the Democrats. The two parties differed in important respects, including the substance of the divisive issues, but the basic structural pattern was much the same in both cases: on both sets of votes the Republican party was split into sharply distinctive blocs composed of essentially the same members in both sessions. As with the Democrats, the cleavages among the Republicans did not occur in haphazard fashion, else these persistent structural differences would not have appeared.

A comparison of Tables 10 and 11 will show the extent of this structural stability. Treating the intermediate Bloc II of the first-session set as if it were a part of Bloc III, to which it is closer than to Bloc I, 30 of the 40 Republican senators who were included in the analyses of

Table 10

REPUBLICAN CLEAVAGE: BLOC STRUCTURE OF SENATE REPUBLICANS ON 74
LOW-COHESION ROLL CALLS, 81ST CONGRESS, 1ST SESSION

Bloc I	Bloc II	Bloc III
Members: 10 Mean Score: 50.0	Members: 5 Mean Score: 44.1	Members: 8 Mean Score: 47.5
RANK 1 Smith, Me. 2 Aiken, Vt. (s) 3 Saltonstall, Mass. (e) 4 Ives, N. Y. 5 Thye, Minn. 6 Flanders, Vt. 7 Lodge, Mass. 8 Smith, N. J. 9 Morse, Ore. 10 Knowland, Cal.	RANK	RANK
	X	
	1 Millikin, Colo. (e) 2 Cordon, Ore. 3 Gurney, S. D. 4 Hickenlooper, Ia. 5 Mundt, S. D.	
X		X X
		1 Wherry, Neb. (e) 2 Cain, Wash. (s) 3 Ecton, Mont. 4 Williams, Del. (s) 5 Bricker, Ohio 6 Butler, Neb. (e) 7 Kem, Mo. 8 Malone, Nev.
	X X X X	
FRINGE: 5 Tobey, N. H. (s) Hendrickson, N. J. Donnell, Mo. Vandenberg, Mich. (s) Baldwin, Conn.	FRINGE: 3	FRINGE: 7
	X X X	
	Cain, Wash. (s) Wherry, Neb. (e) Ecton, Mont.	
	X X X	Millikin, Colo. (e) Cordon, Ore. Watkins, Utah Schoeppel, Kan. Capehart, Ind. Martin, Pa. Jenner, Ind.

LEGEND: Each *bloc* member agreed with each other bloc member on 38 or more of the 74 votes in the set. *Mean score* of the bloc: the mean of the number of agreements between all pairs of bloc members. *Rank:* the rank of each bloc member according to the mean of his scores with all other bloc members, 1 designating the highest average number of agreements. *Fringe:* nonmembers having scores of 38 or higher with at least half the bloc members. X: member of a bloc or fringe who had scores of 38 or higher with some but less than half the members of another bloc. (e): elective leader. (s): seniority leader.

both sessions were in the same wing in both sets.[39] The structure was less stable than the Democrats', for there were two senators who shifted between wings. As in the equivalent Democratic sets, however, the bulk of the changes—nine in this situation—involved shifts into or out of the isolate category.[40]

In both sessions each of the blocs was essentially uninuclear in form, but the generally less cohesive roll calls of the second-session set produced a much greater degree of fragmentation than among the Democrats. In addition to the four blocs shown, there were no less than four others, omitted from Table 11 in the interests of simplicity, which were smaller and less cohesive wings of the principal blocs. These additional blocs are shown schematically in Figure 4 along with the blocs included in Table 11. As Figure 4 indicates, the omitted blocs differed slightly in their composition, much as I and II or III and IV differed

---

[39] Note that in Table 10 Millikin and Cordon from Bloc II are also in the fringe of Bloc III and that Cain, Wherry, and Ecton from the latter cluster are also in the fringe of Bloc II. There are no overlaps of this sort between Blocs I and II. In this connection it is worth noting that, according to press reports (*New York Times,* January 4, 1949), the bitter struggle within the Senate Republican Conference over the floor leadership for the Eighty-first Congress was settled by a vote of 28 for Senator Wherry, the incumbent, to 14 for Senator Knowland, the candidate of the insurgents. There is no record of how individual Republican senators voted on this question, but the close similarity between the reported totals and the sizes of the two wings indicated in Table 10 seems more than mere coincidence. The intraparty cleavage on organizational matters apparently persisted in the voting patterns. Carlson of Kansas and Nixon of California cast too few votes to be included in the analysis.

[40] In the second session Williams of Delaware was in both wings; in the first session he was only in Bloc III. He is therefore counted both among the shifters and among the stationary. Donnell of Missouri was in the Bloc I-II wing in the first session and appeared in the Bloc III-IV wing in the second. Two members of the intermediate Bloc II, Hickenlooper and Gurney, turned up among the isolates in the second-session set, like their structural equivalents among the Democrats, who shifted in the same way on the set whose mean index of cohesion was lower. Again, even with the Republicans, among whom sectional divisions follow a different pattern, note the peculiar behavior of men from the Border States such as Williams and Donnell. In the second session Williams voted with the Bloc II Republicans on a series of public works votes and a scatter of others, and with Bloc IV on votes dealing with displaced persons, foreign aid, and economic controls. Donnell's behavior included voting with Bloc I on a scattering of votes dealing with domestic matters and on a few votes dealing with foreign aid. He voted with Bloc IV on most of the votes concerning the liberalized Displaced Persons Act, in opposition to the repeal of taxes on oleomargarine, and on a number of other roll calls dealing with agriculture. It should be noted that he was a member of the Committee on the Judiciary, from whose chairman (McCarran) came most of the restrictive amendments to the Displaced Persons Act which he supported.

Table 11

REPUBLICAN CLEAVAGE: BLOC STRUCTURE OF SENATE REPUBLICANS ON 74 LOW-COHESION ROLL CALLS, 81ST CONGRESS, 2ND SESSION

Bloc I		Bloc II		Bloc III		Bloc IV	
Members: 10		Members: 9		Members: 9		Members: 8	
Mean Score: 47.6		Mean Score: 48.4		Mean Score: 46.8		Mean Score: 47.7	
RANK		RANK		RANK		RANK	
9	Morse, Ore.						
8	Thye, Minn.				X		X
7	Aiken, Vt. (s)						
6	Smith, Me.				X		X
10	Wiley, Wis. (s)	9	Wiley (s)				
5	Smith, N. J.	5	Smith				
4	Hendrickson, N. J.	4	Hendrickson				
3	Lodge, Mass.	1	Lodge				
2	Saltonstall, Mass. (e)	3	Saltonstall (e)				
1	Ives, N. Y.	2	Ives				
		6	Knowland, Cal.				
		7	Ferguson, Mich.				
		8	Taft, Ohio (e)				
				9	Kem, Mo.		
				6	Malone, Nev.		
	X			4	Ecton, Mont.	4	Ecton
				3	Dworshak, Ida.	2	Dworshak
				5	Mundt, S. D.	3	Mundt
				1	Wherry, Neb. (e)	1	Wherry (e)
	X			2	Butler, Neb. (e)	5	Butler (e)
				7	Donnell, Mo.	6	Donnell
				8	Watkins, Utah	7	Watkins
						8	Langer, N. D. (s)
FRINGE: 4		FRINGE: 7		FRINGE: 7		FRINGE: 10	
Knowland, Cal.							
Taft, Ohio (e)							
Ferguson, Mich.							
Flanders, Vt.		Flanders				X	
	X	Tobey, N. H. (s)					
		Thye, Minn.					
		Morse, Ore.					
		Aiken, Vt.					
		Smith, Me.					
	X	Williams, Del. (s)		X		Williams (s)	
				Darby, Kan.		Darby	
				Schoeppel, Kan.		Schoeppel	
				Cain, Wash. (s)		Cain (s)	
				Cordon, Ore.		Cordon	
				Langer, N. D. (s)			
				Jenner, Ind.		Jenner	
				Millikin, Colo. (e)		Millikin (e)	
						Bricker, Ohio	
						Kem, Mo.	
						Malone, Nev.	

LEGEND: Each *bloc* member agreed with each other bloc member on 38 or more of the 74 votes in the set. *Mean score* of the bloc: the mean of the number of agreements between all pairs of bloc members. *Rank:* the rank of each bloc member according to the mean of his scores with all other bloc members, 1 designating the highest average number of agreements. *Fringe:* nonmember having scores of 38 or higher with at least half the bloc members. X: member of a bloc or fringe who had scores of 38 or higher with some but less than half the members of another bloc. (e): elective leader. (s): seniority leader.

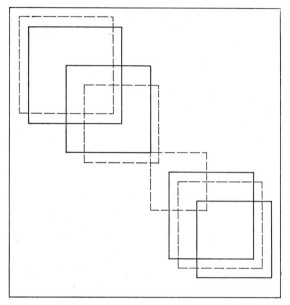

Figure 4. Structural fluidity: overlapping Republican blocs in Senate, 74 low-cohesion roll calls, 81st Congress, 2nd session. Area of blocs is proportionate to the number of members. Blocs bounded by solid lines are those identified in Table 11. Additional overlapping blocs are indicated by dash lines.

from one another. This structural "looseness" plus the fact that the principal wings in both sets were, unlike the Democrats', approximately equal in size, suggest the inference that lines of cleavage were considerably more varied within the minority party, that more reshuffling occurred from issue to issue, though not enough to eliminate the stabilities discussed in the preceding paragraph.

The isolates in these sets, of whom there were 10 in the first session and 9 in the second, present the same kinds of problems as did their counterparts among the Democrats (Table 12).[41] It seems likely that Ferguson and possibly Langer in the first session and Gurney in the second so split their support between the two systems that they became members of neither. The remaining isolates—Brewster, McCarthy, Taft, and Young in the first session and Hickenlooper in the second—almost certainly became disassociated from their colleagues

---

[41] A considerable number in each set had too many "absences" to have any chance of entering one of the systems. In the first session Bridges, Reed, and Wiley, each of whom had 22 or more "absences," fall into this group, as does Dulles, who held his seat for only four months. In the second session the 7 men with more than 15 "absences" must be so classified. (Vandenberg, of course, was ill during most of the second session.)

Table 12

REPUBLICAN ISOLATES: SENATORS NOT INCLUDED IN IDENTIFIED BLOCS OR
FRINGES, LOW-COHESION ROLL CALLS, 81ST CONGRESS

Senator	Number of "Absences"*	Number of Scores 38 or Higher	Blocs in Which Scores Occur
First Session			
Langer, N. D. (s)	1	6	I, III
Ferguson, Mich.	3	12	I, II, III
Dulles, N. Y. †	6	0	– – –
Taft, Ohio (e)	6	3	– – –
Young, N. D.	7	6	II, III
McCarthy, Wis. (s)	11	3	I
Brewster, Me. (e)	18	1	I
Wiley, Wis. (s)	22	3	I
Bridges, N. H. (s)	24	0	– – –
Reed, Kan.	39	0	– – –
Second Session			
Gurney, S. D.	8	5	II, IV
Hickenlooper, Ia	9	6	IV
Brewster, Me. (e)	16	3	II
McCarthy, Wis. (s)	16	2	IV
Bridges, N. H. (s)	17	1	II
Capehart, Ind.	17	2	IV
Martin, Pa.	20	2	IV
Young, N. D.	25	1	IV
Vandenberg, Mich. (s)	40	0	– – –

* "Absences" cover those roll calls in the set on which the senator did not
vote and did not record his preference in any other way.

† Senator not seated for whole session.

(e) Elective leader.

(s) Seniority leader.

because of the frequency with which they voted, as individuals, with
one or another wing of the Democrats.

The most striking general feature of the bloc structures shown in
Tables 10 and 11 is the sectional character of the division. It is less
sharply defined and somewhat less consistent than the geographic
cleavage within the Democrats, but it is still unmistakable. In the
first-session set all but 4 members of the Bloc I wing, including the
fringe, came from east of the Mississippi—Donnell, Knowland, Morse,
and Thye—while in Blocs II and III together only 4 came from states

east of the river—Bricker, Capehart, Jenner, and Williams. The division was even sharper in the second-session set, as there were only 6 "outlanders," Donnell having shifted to the "right" and Capehart having dropped into the isolate category although still showing a tendency toward membership in Bloc IV (Table 12).

Although for present purposes it is the structural fact of this division that is principally relevant, the possible reasons for it are a natural object of speculation, especially when the cleavage is along a line less familiar than that between the Democrats of North and South. The difficulty with such speculation, however, is that geographic cleavage in a legislative party is a symptom whose origins are multiple and complex and are not readily susceptible to isolation and rating except in general terms. Ignoring this fact leads to a crude and inadequate geographic determinism. Regional variations in culture are undoubtedly relevant, though in cases such as this their sources may be less geographic than demographic, reflecting rural-urban differences rather than, for example, market or commodity specializations. Such variations unquestionably are engaged by particular issues in a legislative session. As later discussion of voting in the House will show, however, there are intralegislative associations along the lines of state and region which seem to grow not only out of a common response to similarities in constituencies but also out of the facts of organization along state and regional lines within the legislative party.[42] Furthermore, the presence of "outlanders," such as those noted above or Hill, Sparkman, Kefauver, and Pepper among the Democrats, reflects either peculiarities of the particular constituency power structures on which such senators rely for support in elections or aspects of their personal attitudes, including their aspirations within the party, or more likely a combination of these.

The immediate source of this cleavage within the Republican party on these low-cohesion sets lay almost entirely in a single general area of policy, that of foreign affairs. Although the two wings took different positions on a scattering of votes, opposition between Bloc I and Bloc III was concentrated in the first-session set in a series of roll calls on the foreign aid program and in the second-session set in the votes concerning the amended Displaced Persons Act, which was a source of disunity for both parties.[43]

---

[42] See chap. 7.

[43] Nearly two-fifths of the agreements within Bloc I (9 out of 24) in the 1949 set dealt with foreign aid, and the proportion within Bloc III was roughly the same (11 out of 29). On 6 of the 16 foreign aid votes in the set the two groups were solidly opposed, Bloc I favoring the program. They were completely agreed

Bloc II in the first-session set, as we have already noted, was somewhat closer to Bloc III than to Bloc I. Its separate appearance in the structure is traceable to a variety of votes on both domestic and foreign matters, but its most distinctive feature is that its members as a group were agreed with Bloc III on none of the foreign aid votes and were lined up solidly with Bloc I on 3. Its agreements with Bloc III, of which there were several (8 of its 21 agreements), were almost entirely in connection with domestic issues of various sorts.[44]

The foreign affairs cleavage within the Republican party takes on added significance from the fact that in both these sets of roll calls there were other substantive policy areas in which a considerable number of votes was taken, yet none of these formed the basis for significant differences between blocs or wings. Thus in the first-session set there were almost as many votes concerning agriculture and housing (14) as there were on foreign aid (16), yet none of the principal blocs was agreed on more than two votes in these domestic categories, and in only one or two instances were the identified blocs solidly opposed to one another. In the second-session set there were 15 votes on public works questions, 13 dealing with economic controls, and 11 on agriculture, but these did not produce the agreement within blocs and the cleavage between blocs that was associated with the 17 votes on foreign policy (all but one of which dealt with displaced persons). To some extent this random pattern of voting in the domestic areas merely reflects the heterogeneous character of the categories used in the classification, but not entirely. The fact remains,

---

on the same side of none of these. There were 5 additional votes on which the two groups took opposite sides, roll calls concerning the reciprocal trade agreements extension, housing and rent control, and pay raises for officials in the executive branch. On all of these Bloc III took the "conservative" position. In the second-session set approximately half the agreements in each of the four blocs concerned the displaced persons bill (13 of 22 in Bloc I, 12 of 22 in Bloc II, 12 of 19 in Blocs III and IV). On 10 of these votes the two wings were solidly opposed.

[44] Between the blocs in each of the wings in the second-session set there were differences in the kinds of issues agreed upon, though there were of course no solid oppositions. In general, Bloc I was clearly somewhat to the "left" of Bloc II. Its members, for example, on several roll calls opposed the bill restricting the Federal Power Commission's authority to regulate the price of natural gas, favored the conference report on rent control, and supported the nomination of General Marshall as Secretary of Defense. Bloc II was agreed on none of these. Its largest cluster of agreements not shared with I involved 8 public works roll calls, including 3 on which it supported the California opposition to the Bridge Canyon (Arizona) reclamation project. Between Blocs III and IV the differences in the votes agreed upon showed no particular pattern.

moreover, that the foreign affairs issues in both sets marked out the main lines of structure within the party.

Given the substance of the crucial divisions among the Republicans, one would expect to find rather marked differences among the various blocs with respect to their identification with the party majority and with respect to the frequency with which they appeared on the prevailing side in the Senate. This is indeed the case, as the data in Figure 5 indicate. In both sessions Bloc I clearly was the spearhead element

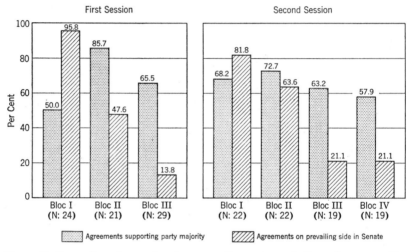

Figure 5. Proportion of agreed votes supporting party majority and on prevailing side in the Senate, principal Republican blocs, low-cohesion roll calls, 81st Congress, 1st and 2nd sessions. Agreements include all votes on which the bloc was unanimous plus those on which less than half the members were unrecorded and the remainder were unanimous.

within the Republicans who joined forces with the majority wing of the Democrats, frequently at the expense of deserting the bulk of their colleagues. That is, their agreements were more often on the prevailing side in the Senate than with the Republican majority.[45] The intermediate position of Bloc II in the first-session set is evident from

---

[45] Their party orthodoxy indexes were on the average consistently the lowest among the Republican clusters. These were, in the first session, Bloc I 3.56, Bloc II 4.16, Bloc III 4.03; in the second session, Bloc I 3.60, Bloc II 3.82, Bloc III 4.10, Block IV 3.99. The only Republican bloc disposed to give any significant degree of support to the Administration either on these sets of votes or in the sessions as a whole was Bloc I in each session. The mean Administration support indexes were, in the first session, Bloc I 3.71, Bloc II 2.90, Bloc III 1.72; in the second session, Bloc I 3.22, Bloc II 2.99, Bloc III 1.97, Bloc IV 2.08.

the high proportion of its agreements in the set on the side of the party majority. In the second-session set no bloc quite held this position. Bloc III in the first-session set and Bloc IV in the second have many of the earmarks of a cluster of die-hards. Though on the side of the party majority with moderate frequency, as in the first-session set, they were consistently low on the proportion of prevailing agreements. If they were combining with a Democratic faction, therefore, the resulting combination more often than not formed a minority of the Senate. This is illustrated by their agreements on the Displaced Persons Act votes in the second session. On 5 of the 12 a majority of Republicans opposed a majority of Democrats, and this cluster sided with the preponderance of their fellow partisans, but on the 6 votes on which majorities of both parties voted the same way this bloc was in the minority both in the Senate and among the Republicans. (On one vote the Republicans were evenly split.)

The tendency of the Senate Republican structure toward greater fragmentation, as the locus of the party majority shifted from one type of issue to another, has already been noted.[46] This tendency, evidence of which will appear also in the analysis of the Republicans in the House, is an important clue to some of the apparent differences between the two parties. A more striking contrast between the Republican and Democratic blocs on their low-cohesion roll calls, however, appears in the evidence from the Administration support votes concerning partisanship as such. Even the dissident Democratic blocs on the average supported the Administration more strongly than did any of the Republican blocs.[47] Only in the first session was there a Republican bloc (Bloc I, Table 10) with a higher mean Administration support index than one of the Democratic blocs. In the second session even the relatively anti-Administration Democratic Bloc II had a higher index than any of the Republican blocs. The importance of these differences is their indication that, despite internal divisions, there was evidently a strong tendency toward common partisanship among Democrats and among Republicans in the Senate, at least with respect to roll calls on which an Administration preference was at stake. One cannot effectively assert in the face of such evidence that within the legislature the party is a weak or meaningless factor, in content more ritualistic than substantial.

The Republican low-cohesion roll calls thus show some strong struc-

---

[46] See p. 74.

[47] Unlike the votes included in the sets for the bloc analyses, of course, the roll calls on which these indexes are based were the same for both parties. The indexes appear above in note 28, p. 63, and note 45, p. 80.

tural similarities and some interesting differences from the comparable Democratic votes. Republican voting was relatively stable and structured, rather than haphazard, and the resulting blocs were unified enough to indicate that they represented patterns of association and not merely accidents of agreement. The cleavages, chiefly reflecting differences of foreign policy, including immigration, were at least superficially sectional in character. As among the Democrats, clear evidences of coalition voting appeared in the behavior of some blocs. There was, however, less indication among the Republicans of dissent from a stable and continuing party majority. It was less clear that any one bloc was large enough consistently to represent a majority of the party, from which a minority dissented on a varying series of issues. The Republicans, moreover, showed more evidence of shifting associations from issue to issue, of a greater fluidity in the party structure, pointing to the possibility of a continuing difference between the parties in this respect. Despite shifting, however, and despite coalition voting, comparison of the two parties, on those votes in which the Administration had an expressed preference, showed a marked degree of stable interparty opposition which gave substantial meaning to the party labels.

THE REPUBLICANS UNITED

In the two high-cohesion sets the voting structure of the Senate Republicans, as Tables 13 and 14 suggest, resembled that of the Democrats in that it showed marked continuity with the patterns revealed in the low-cohesion roll calls, stability within the high-cohesion sets, and of course a consolidation of the party in the high- as compared with the low-cohesion sets. The patterns, however, showed the same kinds of differences between the two parties that were evident on the low-cohesion votes.

In the first place, though the Republican structure in both high-cohesion sets was essentially uninuclear, it was a good deal less tightly knit than the Democrats'. Thus the Republican structure on the high-cohesion votes of the first session (Table 13) shows a basic resemblance to the Democratic pattern on the comparable set in the second session (Table 7), on which the Democratic structure was composed of a central bloc and related wings, the outer ranks of which correspond to the nuclei of the opposed blocs in the low-cohesion sets. But the central bloc in the Republican structure (Bloc II), unlike its equiva-

Table 13

REPUBLICAN UNITY: BLOC STRUCTURE OF SENATE REPUBLICANS ON 74 HIGH-COHESION ROLL CALLS, 81ST CONGRESS, 1ST SESSION

Bloc I		Bloc II		Bloc III	
Members: 8		Members: 22		Members: 13	
Mean Score: 46.1		Mean Score: 50.0		Mean Score: 48.0	
RANK		RANK		RANK	
8	Flanders, Vt.				
7	Thye, Minn.				
6	Ives, N. Y.				
5	Smith, N. J.				
4	Smith, Me.				
1	Saltonstall, Mass. (e)	16	Saltonstall (e)		
2	Hendrickson, N. J.	14	Hendrickson		X
3	Ferguson, Mich.	6	Ferguson		X
	X	22	Brewster, Me. (e)		
		21	Bricker, Ohio		X
	X	19	Bridges, N. H. (s)		X
	X	18	McCarthy, Wis. (s)		X
	X	17	Donnell, Mo.		X
	X	13	Mundt, S. D.		X
	X	12	Cordon, Ore.		X
	X	11	Taft, Ohio (e)		X
	X	10	Martin, Pa.		X
	X	8	Gurney, S. D.		X
	X	5	Millikin, Colo. (e)		X
	X	1	Hickenlooper, Ia.	5	Hickenlooper
	X	2	Watkins, Utah	3	Watkins
	X	3	Schoeppel, Kan.	6	Schoeppel
	X	4	Cain, Wash. (s)	4	Cain (s)
	X	7	Williams, Del. (s)	1	Williams (s)
	X	9	Knowland, Cal.	7	Knowland
		15	Wherry, Neb. (e)	2	Wherry (e)
	X	20	Capehart, Ind.	9	Capehart
				8	Kem, Mo.
				10	Ecton, Mont.
				11	Jenner, Ind.
				12	Butler, Neb. (e)
				13	Malone, Nev.

FRINGE: 3	FRINGE: 3	FRINGE: 1
Wiley, Wis. (s)	Wiley (s)	
Vandenberg, Mich. (s)	Vandenberg (s)	
Lodge, Mass.		
	Young, N. D.	Young

LEGEND: Each *bloc* member agreed with each other bloc member on 38 or more of the 74 votes in the set. *Mean score* of the bloc: the mean of the number of agreements between all pairs of bloc members. *Rank:* the rank of each bloc member according to the mean of his scores with all other bloc members, 1 designating the highest average number of agreements. *Fringe:* nonmember having scores of 38 or higher with at least half of the bloc members. X: member of a bloc or fringe who had scores of 38 or higher with some but less than half the members of another block. (e): elective leader. (s): seniority leader.

lent in the Democratic structure (Table 7), included no member of all three blocs, whereas there were 22 such instances among the Democrats. Further, in the Republican second-session set (Table 14) not only was the intraparty consolidation less complete, but it seems

Table 14

REPUBLICAN UNITY: BLOC STRUCTURE OF SENATE REPUBLICANS ON 74 HIGH-COHESION ROLL CALLS, 81ST CONGRESS, 2ND SESSION

Bloc I			Bloc II
Members: 5			Members: 20
Mean Score: 46.7			Mean Score: 47.7
RANK			RANK
1 Ives, N. Y.			
2 Lodge, Mass.			
3 Hendrickson, N. J.		X	
4 Saltonstall, Mass. (e)		X	
5 Smith, Me.			
	X		1 Butler, Neb. (e)
	X		2 Wherry, Neb. (e)
	X		3 Dworshak, Ida.
	X		4 Ferguson, Mich.
			5 Ecton, Mont.
	X		6 Bricker, Ohio
	X		7 Kem, Mo.
	X		8 Malone, Nev.
	X		9 Capehart, Ind.
	X		10 Schoeppel, Kan.
	X		11 Martin, Pa.
	X		12 Mundt, S. D.
	X		13 Watkins, Utah
	X		14 Brewster, Me. (e)
	X		15 Donnell, Mo.
			16 Cordon, Ore.
	X		17 Hickenlooper, Ia.
			18 Knowland, Cal.
	X		19 Bridges, N. H. (s)
	X		20 Millikin, Colo. (e)
FRINGE: 5			FRINGE: 3
			Williams, Del. (s)
			Taft, Ohio (e)
			Jenner, Ind.
Knowland, Cal.			
Aiken, Vt. (s)			
Thye, Minn.			
Tobey, N. H. (s)			
Smith, N. J.			

LEGEND: Each *bloc* member agreed with each other bloc member on 38 or more of the 74 votes in the set. *Mean score* of the bloc: the mean of the number of agreements between all pairs of bloc members. *Rank:* the rank of each bloc member according to the mean of his scores with all other bloc members, 1 designating the highest average number of agreements. *Fringe:* nonmember having scores of 38 or higher with at least half of the bloc members. X: member of a bloc or fringe who had scores of 38 or higher with some but less than half the members of another bloc. (e): elective leader. (s): seniority leader.

clearly to have taken place without the dissident faction represented by the quite separate Bloc I.[48]

---

[48] Bloc I in Table 14 provides a useful illustration of the implications of the arbitrary choice of a stopping point in the construction of a matrix. The four-man nucleus of this bloc did not appear on the matrix until all scores of 43 or higher had

The looseness of the Republican structure was in part simply a reflection of their lower average cohesion on these roll calls as compared with the Democrats. But it also points to a more substantial factor, noted as well in connection with the low-cohesion sets, namely, a much greater degree of fragmentation than among the Democrats. This fragmentation was indicated at various stages of the analysis by the appearance on the matrix of a considerable number of wings of the principal blocs. These overlapping blocs, which were smaller and less cohesive than those shown in the tables, of course were not as numerous as those of the low-cohesion set shown earlier in Figure 4, but they carried the same implication. That is, the variation or fragmentation in the structure did not reflect opposition between these blocs but merely variation in the substance of issues agreed upon within them. This greater reshuffling of the structure from issue to issue, the minor shifting of the lines of cleavage within the party, indicates again that the Republican senators, more than the Democrats, conformed to the common stereotype of congressional voting as a sort of political kaleidoscope.

This fragmentation may have been merely a reflection of the problems and issues peculiar to the Republican senators in the Eighty-first Congress, but it is at least possible that fragmentation is a mark of the minority. The evidence to this effect appeared in both sessions and on both low- and high-cohesion roll calls, and, as a later chapter will show,[49] the same fractionation in a more extreme form also was evident in the minority party in the House of Representatives in this Congress. The issues in the two chambers, while of course roughly comparable, are by no means identical, and there are important procedural differences in connection with voting. This sort of difference makes comparison difficult, but the recurrent evidence of fragmentation at least suggests the hypothesis that the collective positions taken by the members of the minority party on substantive issues of legislation, perhaps especially when it is also out of power in the White House, tend to give it a loose and unprogrammed appearance, meaning

---

been entered, at which point Bloc II numbered 16 men. Had the work been stopped with scores of 44 and higher, the essential uninuclear structure of the party would have been accurately identified. Bloc I would not have been defined, but its dissident tendencies would have been evident from the fact that most of its members would have fallen into the isolate category despite their relatively low "absence" rate. The inference that they tended to vote fairly frequently *as individuals* with a Democratic faction would have been accurate, since the cohesion of the bloc is low and even at the level of 38 agreements only 2 of the 5 had scores with members of Bloc II.

[49] See chap. 5.

by "program" a tendency, from whatever cause, toward coherence along substantive policy lines in the votes.

The second contrast between the parties was that, on the high-cohesion votes as on those on which the parties were relatively disunited, there were substantial and consistent policy differences between the whole series of Republican blocs, on the one hand, and all the Democratic blocs, on the other. None of the Republican blocs, not even those most given to coalition voting, in either session had a mean Administration support index as high as that of the Democratic bloc whose record on this score was weakest.[50] In other words, although fluidity and fragmentation characterized the Republican structure and although the Democrats divided along the familiar sectional lines, recognizable partisan differences, as measured by these selected roll calls, existed despite the differences of internal structure. On votes that could be associated with an Administration preference, Democratic choices were perceptibly different from those of the Republicans.

The other features of the Republican structure on the high-cohesion votes are largely of descriptive interest. The seven isolates in the first-session set and the ten in the second further project the patterns of the bloc structure (Table 15). Among the first-session isolates Aiken, Morse, Langer, and Tobey were obviously voting with a wing of the Democrats even more frequently than were their colleagues in Bloc I, since their infrequent agreement with fellow Republicans cannot be explained by the number of their absences.[51] In the second-session set Wiley and Gurney seem to have divided their preferences between the two principal blocs and thus failed to belong to either. But McCarthy and Young apparently voted fairly frequently with one Democratic wing while Langer and Morse, most of whose scores were in Bloc I, sided with the other.[52]

---

[50] The mean Administration support indexes for the members of the Republican blocs on the high-cohesion sets were, for the first session, Bloc I 3.43, Bloc II 2.38, Bloc III 1.95; for the second session, Bloc I 3.27, Bloc II 2.16. The comparable indexes for the Democratic blocs are given above in note 36, p. 69, and note 38, p. 71. See also Figure 7. In the Republican high-cohesion set of the first session there were 35 Administration support votes. The members of Bloc I (Table 13) agreed in support of the Administration on 14 of these and the members of the other blocs on none. In the second-session set there were 32 Administration support votes. The members of Bloc I (Table 14) were agreed in support of the Administration on 11 of these, the members of Bloc II on none.

[51] Reed and Baldwin were absent too often and Dulles did not hold his place long enough to get into one of the blocs.

[52] Darby, who held his seat for only part of the session, and Cain, Flanders, and Vandenberg, who were "absent" 20 or more times, had no chance of bloc membership.

Table 15

REPUBLICAN ISOLATES: SENATORS NOT INCLUDED IN IDENTIFIED BLOCS
OR FRINGES, HIGH-COHESION ROLL CALLS, 81ST CONGRESS

Senator	Number of "Absences"*	Number of Scores 38 or Higher	Blocs in Which Scores Occur
First Session			
Langer, N. D. (s)	3	4	I
Morse, Ore.	7	5	I
Aiken, Vt. (s)	9	8	I
Dulles, N. Y.†	11	0	- - -
Tobey, N. H. (s)	17	4	I
Baldwin, Conn.	22	6	I, II, III
Reed, Kan.	31	3	II, III
Second Session			
Morse, Ore.	1	8	I, II
Wiley, Wis. (s)	7	11	I, II
Langer, N. D. (s)	8	2	I
Darby, Kan.†	12	8	II
Gurney, S. D.	14	6	I, II
McCarthy, Wis. (s)	16	9	II
Young, N. D.	16	5	II
Flanders, Vt.	20	1	I
Cain, Wash. (s)	23	7	II
Vandenberg, Mich. (s)	58	0	- - -

* "Absences" cover those roll calls in the set on which the senator did not vote and did not record his preference in any other way.

† Senator not seated for whole session.

(s) Seniority leader.

Despite the tendency toward fragmentation in the party as a whole, the degree of agreement within the two main blocs in these sets was roughly comparable to that among the Democrats. Votes on which some members dissented from the majority of the bloc were not very numerous, and the number of bloc members deviating from their colleagues on most of these was not significantly different from the number of dissenters in the equivalent Democratic blocs.[53] In both sessions

[53] In Bloc II of the first-session set there were dissents from the majority of the bloc on 68 of the 74 votes, but on roughly four-fifths (54) of these the number of dissenters was 4 or less, and the average number of dissenters on all 68 votes was slightly over 3. In Bloc II of the second-session set there were dissents on only 55 votes, reflecting both the smaller size of the bloc and the rather sharp

the central position of Bloc II in the party is evident in the fact that the majority of the bloc agreed with the majority of the party in the first session on all the votes on which there were dissenters within the bloc and in the second on all but one. As would be expected in a minority party, however, the dissenters were on the prevailing side in the Senate on a good many of the disputed roll calls.[54]

The general pattern of agreements and dissents within these blocs contains few surprises. Within Bloc II of the first-session set dissents were relatively few on the votes dealing with public power, on which a majority of the bloc took a negative view; on those concerning labor, indicating support for the anti-Administration version of the attempted Taft-Hartley Act alterations; and on those dealing with economic controls, most of the bloc voting against the extension of rent controls. The most conspicuous sources of disagreement, on the other hand, were the roll calls on the foreign aid program, those on reservations to the North Atlantic Treaty, and those on agriculture, a perennial focus for parochial loyalties.

In the second-session set the dissents and agreements within Bloc II both reflect and help to explain the separate position of Bloc I. Here the principal bloc was comparatively unified on the foreign aid votes, which, of course, tended to divide it from Bloc I. Even the later adherents to Bloc II were generally friendly to efforts at restricting foreign aid and reducing executive discretion in its administration. Bloc II also inclined toward agreement on most economic control votes. However, a good many of these separated the members of the two blocs, since the category here contained a number of votes on which Bloc I tended to support the Administration.[55] Moreover, this second-session set contained a relatively smaller number of votes on subjects like labor and public power, which in the first session tended to unite the members of Bloc I with their party colleagues in the larger bloc. Of course, a good many issues among these second-session votes divided Bloc I, as its relatively low cohesion indicates, including some dealing with foreign aid.[56] Agreement was sufficiently frequent, however, to maintain Bloc I as a separate cluster.

---

separateness of Bloc I, but a little less than two-thirds of these votes (35) involved dissents by 4 or fewer members, and the average number of dissenters on the 55 votes was slightly under 4.

[54] The dissenters were on the prevailing side in the Senate on 28 of 68 disputed votes in the first session and on 31 of 55 in the second.

[55] For example, the final votes on extending rent controls, those on presidential reorganization plans, and several of those concerning the Defense Production Act.

[56] The mean score of the five men in Bloc I was 46.7, that for the first 5 members of Bloc II was 57.5. Bloc I tended to support foreign aid on final votes and

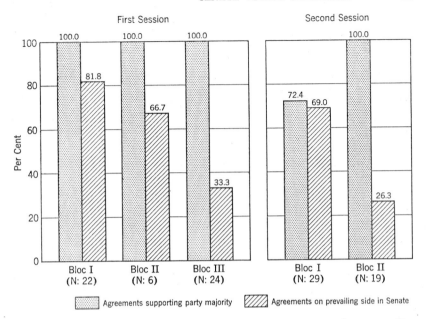

Figure 6. Proportion of agreed votes supporting party majority and on prevailing side in the Senate, principal Republican blocs, high-cohesion roll calls, 81st Congress, 1st and 2nd sessions. Agreements include all votes on which the bloc was unanimous plus those on which less than half the members were unrecorded and the remainder were unanimous.

In the first-session set both dissenting wings were less cohesive than Bloc II, indicating the limited range of their agreements outside of those in the main bloc. Bloc I, the smallest and least unified of the three, was agreed, generally on the side of the Administration, on a number of votes dealing with rent control, housing, and labor, as well as on a majority of those in the foreign affairs area. As would be expected on a collection of high-cohesion votes, the two wings were solidly opposed on none of the roll calls in the set, but the agreements within Bloc III were concentrated in the same subject-matter categories as those within Bloc I. In other words, some members of each group split off to vote with the other cluster on roll calls in all of these areas. But those on which the members of Bloc III were united did not involve agreement with the Administration position, while those within the looser Bloc I frequently did. Bloc I, moreover, clearly was

to resist drastic cuts in appropriations for the program, but they split on proposals for moderate reductions in funds and on efforts, spearheaded by Senator Wherry, to require withholding of aid from countries trading with the Soviet Union or in its orbit.

the wing of the party most likely to combine with the majority among the Democrats, both on this set and in the session as a whole. That is, not only was Bloc I the only one of the three in the first session to give united support to the Administration on any of the 35 votes in the set that involved a presidential preference, but over four-fifths of its agreements were on the prevailing side in the Senate (Figure 6). The equivalent bloc in the second-session set had the same tendency, but it was more isolated from the rest of the party when it indulged in coalition behavior. Its agreements accorded with the views of a majority of the party in less than three-fourths of the cases, whereas in the first session Bloc I's agreements were always shared by a majority of the party, even when they involved support of the Administration.[57]

SUMMARY

A number of general inferences concerning the legislative parties in the Senate emerge from this analysis of the voting structure in the 1949 and 1950 sessions. In the first place, it is clear that the voting was far from haphazard. Though particular issues produced eccentric patterns of agreement and disagreement within the party, in the sets of votes examined in this chapter a persistent structure was evident. The structure, moreover, appears to have been in general a stable one. Although the issues in the two sessions were by no means identical, the composition of the wings of the two parties remained virtually unchanged. There were, of course, differences in structure between the low- and high-cohesion votes, but between the two basic resemblances remained. Increased unity did not entirely obscure or completely eliminate persistent cleavages within either of the parties.

Second, because of the stable voting structure in the two parties, one does no violence to the data by inferring that the identified blocs, especially at their centers, reflected interaction and association. That is, the members of blocs such as these not only were in some measure aware of their common responses when the roll was called, but presumably also were in contact with one another prior to such votes and on a more or less continuing basis. The nature of such contact almost

---

[57] The relatively low party orthodoxy index and the comparatively high Administration support index of Bloc I show further that these Republican senators were disposed throughout both sessions to side with the Democrats on a number of issues. The Administration support indexes of the Republican blocs are given in note 50, p. 86. The mean party orthodoxy indexes are, for the first session, Bloc I 3.81, Bloc II 4.15, Bloc III 4.12; for the second session, Bloc I 3.66, Bloc II 4.07.

certainly is informal and relatively unorganized, though it may be far from simple, but its reality in the life of the legislative party seems unquestionable.

Superficially the basis of the intraparty cleavages, of these stable clusters, was geographic or sectional, and regional differences in economic activity, in attitude, and in political tradition undoubtedly were relevant in their make-up and in the pattern of preferences. It is important to bear in mind, however, that only one of the identified blocs, the minority wing of the Democrats, was regionally homogeneous. All the others were in varying degrees intersectional, though several of them drew their members disproportionately from one or another major region. Dissent within the Democratic party was peculiarly a Southern tendency, but not all Southern Democrats were dissidents. Cleavage within the Republican ranks tended to divide East from West, but there were some in each wing whose membership can not be explained in gross geographic terms. Thus it seems clear that these affiliations, especially the ones that deviated from the regional norm, reflected such factors as personal variations, peculiarities in the power structures within their constituencies, and associations within the legislative party.

Third, in addition to these evidences of division within the two parties in the Senate, the material drawn from these sets of votes points clearly to differences between the parties on a wide range of substantive policy matters. When the principal blocs of each set and session are ranked according to their mean Administration support indexes, as in Figure 7, it is evident that, with a single exception, the Democratic blocs were stronger in their support of the Administration than any of the Republican blocs. The exception was the Democratic Bloc III in the low-cohesion set of the first session (Figure 7). The mean index in the first session for the members of this extreme "right" Democratic bloc was slightly lower than that of the extreme "left" Republican Bloc I. In other words, the tendency was, despite the intraparty divisions, for the blocs in one party to resemble each other in this respect at least as much as any of the clusters on the opposite side of the aisle. This was only a tendency, of course, and one from which there were a number of individual deviations in both parties, but it was strong enough to warrant the inference that, at least on these votes, the Senate parties, as defined by their component blocs, showed a perceptible policy divergence.

Finally, less clearly but with comparable consistency, the Republican bloc structure had a much more fractionated appearance than the Democratic. This fractionation, shown particularly in a multiplicity

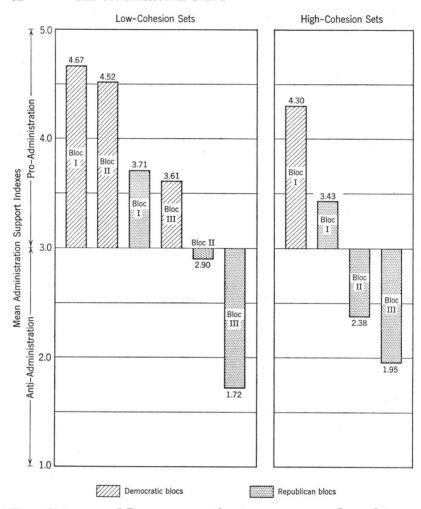

Figure 7. Interparty differences: mean Administration support indexes of Democratic and Republican blocs, Senate, 81st Congress, 1st session. A mean Administration support index of 5.00 would indicate that, on all the votes *in the session* that were classified as Administration support votes, all members of the bloc invariably voted on the Administration side, a mean index of 1.00 that none ever voted in that way.

of overlapping blocs, reflected a tendency within the minority party toward alignments that shifted rather readily from issue to issue within the major wings of the party.

These two differences between the Senate parties—in substantive policy orientation and in degree of structural fluidity—may have been peculiar to the Senate chamber and to the issues of this Congress. Their appearance in both sessions, however, and on both low- and high-cohesion votes raises at least the possibility that these contrasts in structure and substance were related to institutional characteristics of the two legislative parties. This possibility in turn suggests the hypothesis that the Democrats' policy tendencies and their more coherent structure were a consequence of their position as the majority party, both in the Senate and in the White House, and that the divergent policy views of the Republicans as well as their looser, somewhat kaleidoscopic voting structure are characteristics of a legislative party in the minority at both ends of Pennsylvania Avenue, a minority lacking the benefits of a coherent program.

Before attempting to explore and elaborate this hypothesis, however, it is appropriate to examine some features of the behavior of party leaders in the Senate and to compare both these and the voting patterns with comparable evidence on the House.

chapter four

Party leadership

ROLES IN THE SENATE

To raise the subject of party leaders and their roles in the congressional parties is to venture into a relatively uncharted area, one where, especially in the case of the Senate, regularities of behavior, if they can be identified at all, are difficult to isolate and to verify. Where a leader's influence is peculiarly personal, as is conspicuously the case with a position such as that of Floor Leader, the signs and sources of power tend to be obscured. Partly because they are so numerous and interstitial, they may be known only intuitively even by the occupant of the position; and because the influence is highly personal, the effectiveness of such leadership depends heavily upon the confidential, off-the-record character of the party official's activities.

A second handicap to dealing effectively with leaders of the legislative party is the lack of an adequate general theory about leadership. Everyone knows something of leaders and leadership of various sorts, but no one knows very much. Leadership, especially in the political realm, unavoidably or by design often is suffused by an atmosphere of the mystic and the magical, and these mysteries have been little penetrated by systematic observation. Progress has been made in recent years in less emotionally charged areas, in studies of small groups of school children, military units, friendship cliques, elements of industrial organization, and the like.[1] A characteristic common to most of these is that they have been problem-solving groups or situations, either in the sense that explicit problems or tasks are put to them in the natural or experimental setting or in the sense that the tranquility and even the survival of the members are closely dependent upon the effectiveness of the group's operations. The group's risks are their risks.

No imagination is required to recognize that the legislative party in the Senate is not closely analogous to the problem-solving type of group. It is clear from the evidence presented in the preceding chapter that the senatorial party has an identifiable existence as a group. The party labels do distinguish different patterns of attitude and value and different systems of interaction, in so far as these are reflected in the record votes. Moreover, these have a marked degree of stability and structure over at least the two-year period covered by the present investigation. Yet the degree of cleavage reflected in the low-cohesion votes in both parties indicates that the parties constitute a different and perhaps a special type of group. They have a vitality and persistence as organizations despite internal divisions which in most other groups would be the prelude to dissolution, secession, or ostracism. Their continuing existence cannot be dismissed as a stubborn adherence to tradition, for, even if this were the case, customary behavior in any realm is symptomatic of enduring function.

The roots of the legislative parties' persistence in some measure lie outside the groups themselves, perhaps chiefly in the rugged loyalty of broad sections of the electorate to the symbols of the party whose cause they, or their grandfathers, first espoused. Here is a clue to the peculiarity of the legislative party as a group. Apparently it is mediate and supplementary rather than immediate and inclusive in function. That is, from the viewpoint of the members it does some things of importance, and its failures may be of considerable consequence to them. On the other hand, retention of their status as senators is not so completely dependent on it—unlike the management of a corporation, the members of a labor union, or the components of a military organization—that its risks are entirely their risks or its failures necessarily theirs. Thus a senator's chances of re-election presumably are affected, perhaps even increasingly, by the accomplishments of the legislative

---

[1] In addition to the titles listed in note 1, chap. 3, see Harold H. Kelley and John W. Thibaut, "Experimental Studies of Group Problem Solving and Process," and Henry W. Riecken and George C. Homans, "Psychological Aspects of Social Structure," in Lindzey, editor, *Handbook of Social Psychology,* Cambridge, Mass.: Addison-Wesley, 1954, pp. 735–832, and literature cited therein.

party to which he belongs, but he may be able to best his challengers in the primary or the general election largely through his own efforts, through those of groups outside the legislative party, or even, one suspects, through forces beyond the control of any man or group. In some instances, of course, his chances may even be improved by the apparent failures of the legislative party. Thus support of a filibuster that successfully blocks a piece of legislation and in consequence prevents the enactment of a "solution" to a problem may help a senator in whose constituency the proposal is unpopular, and responsibility for provoking these obstructive tactics may raise the standing of a senator among whose constituents enthusiasm for the defeated project is high. Or again, membership in the legislative majority may be of great value to a senator in the greater opportunities it affords to advance or delay the consideration of bills in which his constituents are interested, but probably only infrequently is it crucial to his survival. His means of self-perpetuation are numerous, including the publicity mileage inherent in his being one of his state's two ambassadors in an assemblage conspicuously capable of generating headlines.

The mediate character of the legislative party is closely connected with the acknowledged independence of senators, which affects the atmosphere of the chamber and both delimits and defines the roles of the party leaders within it. As a breed senators are presumably no more self-reliant than other men, but a legislative day rarely passes without a reminder that the Great Compromise of 1787 still exists and that a senator is, or should be, an unregimented ambassador from his state, slave only to the interests of his constituents. Small wonder if the resources of leadership within the legislative party are personal and interstitial. Added to the self-conscious independence of its members is the mundane but fundamental fact, especially in comparison with the House, of the body's relatively small size. This permits not only the stylized informality of its proceedings, but, more important, the face-to-face contact of each, if he chooses, with all, which gives the Senate its clublike appearance. By comparison the House more nearly resembles a mass meeting. The importance of limited size, however, is that it helps to diffuse initiative. Since it is within reasonable physical limits for one man to establish some sort of personal contact with 48 or even 95 others, it is possible and fairly common for one senator, or a handful by concerted efforts with their colleagues, to affect materially the proceedings and the decisions of the upper chamber.[2] To

---

[2] Asked to compare service in the Senate and in the House a number of senators who had been members of both volunteered that the chief difference was that in the Senate it was easier for an individual to "get something done."

do this a senator need not have much seniority and need not hold an official position within the legislative party.

Here is the problem for the official party leaders in the Senate and for one who aspires to analyze "leadership" within the legislative party. If initiative is thus diffused, what is the substance of the leaders' roles? What are the tools of their trade which are not for all practical purposes shared with any member of the rank and file? Further, assuming that these questions can be adequately answered, at least in general terms, is it the case, and to what extent, that the "real" leaders of the Senate are the "official" ones? To what degree are the "informal" structure of influence in the Senate and the "formal" structure of leadership identical or even roughly congruent? [3]

Depending somewhat on the narrowness with which "initiative" or "leadership" is defined, one can recall numerous familiar cases in which the congruence seems to have been so slight that the formal leadership could be all but ignored.[4] Admittedly, for example, Senator Richard Russell of Georgia is a leader in the Senate and among the Democrats regardless of whether he holds a formal party leadership position, and the late Senator Robert A. Taft of Ohio played a similar role among the Republicans and in the Senate as a whole. On occasion even a nonmember, such as an experienced and skillful Secretary of the Senate, may informally be as important a leader in the majority party as any man in the formal party hierarchy.

It may be taken as a generally valid proposition that the larger an organization, the more probable—provided that the organization is not in the process of dissolution—is the convergence if not the complete congruence of the "formal" and "informal" structures of influence and leadership. The requirements of orderly communication, which are critically important in a large organization, are probably chiefly responsible for this tendency, which might be referred to as the "rule of numbers." This assumption may have little bearing on the legislative party in the Senate, which rarely has more than 60 members, though in the House its relevance would be high.[5]

---

[3] The reality of this question and the frequency with which, in conspicuous instances, the congruence is slight may help to account for the fact that even in comparison with the House there has been little or no solid historical research on the development and institutionalization of the modern legislative party.

[4] For examples see Stephen K. Bailey, *Congress Makes A Law*, New York: Columbia University Press, 1950, and William S. White, *Citadel*, New York: Harper, 1957, pp. 95–6, 114, 130, and *passim*.

[5] On this general point see "Quantitative Aspects of the Group," Part 2 of *The Sociology of Georg Simmel*, edited and translated by Kurt H. Wolff, Glencoe, Ill.: The Free Press, 1950. There are indications, which will be discussed spe-

There is warrant, however, for a concern with the formal leadership positions as such. If it is desirable to achieve a more accurate understanding of the legislative party, then it is important to know whether these positions have a distinctive, functional meaning. What in fact are these roles, especially those of the Majority Leader and Minority Leader? What are the relations among the various types of formal leaders? What evidence is there of corporate activity by the leaders? Are there indications of distinctive relationships between the Floor Leader and the chairmen of the standing committees? Is there evidence in the Majority Leader's behavior of relationships with the President that are characteristic of his position in the Senate? Does the White House appear to have a significant part to play in the functioning of the legislative party? Answers to such questions as these may also make possible some inferences concerning the congruence of "formal" and "informal" leadership, despite the fact that the "rule of numbers" is at best a limited working assumption in the case of the Senate parties.

Since the publication nearly seventy-five years ago of Woodrow Wilson's classic, *Congressional Government,* questions concerning the significance of legislative party leadership have usually been answered in the negative. General impressions and studies of the legislative

---

cifically in later sections, that the assumption of correspondence between formal and informal leadership is not entirely unwarranted in the case of the Senate parties; it is, of course, clearly more defensible in connection with the House. Some of these indications concerning formal leadership seem to be connected, moreover, with the matter of size, along with a range of other factors. Though no adequate historical investigation of the Majority Leader and associated positions has ever been made, even for the House, the indications are that much of the formal machinery of party leadership in both houses either emerged or was considerably strengthened during the period of rapid growth in the size of both chambers between 1870 and 1913. It is customary, in talking about these developments and about the institutionalizing of the standing committee system, to emphasize the increase in the business of the Congress. Certainly this is relevant, and one would expect to find also that the change in the character as well as the volume of the legislative business since the Wilson Administration had affected the number and nature of leadership roles. Especially from the standpoint of organization, however, it is perhaps worth bearing in mind that between 1870 and 1913 the Senate increased in size by nearly one-third, from 74 to 96, and the House grew by roughly four-fifths, from 243 to 435. This period saw the emergence of the strong Speakership in the House, the formalization of the floor leadership in both chambers, and the establishment of the whip system. These and other changes must certainly have facilitated the management of larger numbers even if they did not occur wholly in response to such increases. (See Arthur N. Holcombe, *Our More Perfect Union,* Cambridge: Harvard University Press, 1950, chap. 6; Floyd M. Riddick, *The United States Congress: Organization and Procedure,* Manassas, Va.: National Capitol Publishers, 1949, chap. 5.)

history of particular measures have provided reaffirmation of his assertions that ours is "government by the Standing Committees of Congress" whose chairmen "do not consult and concur in the adoption of homogeneous and mutually helpful measures" and that in the Senate and the House "No one may speak for his party as well as for himself; no one exercises the special trust of acknowledged leadership. . . ." [6]

As Wilson himself anticipated more than a decade before he became Chief Executive, the events of the twentieth century have resulted in a re-emergence of the prestige and initiative of the President.[7] However, given the difficulty of continuous and complete observation of a body such as a Senate party or of reconstructing the relationships within it except for very limited periods of time or for a single piece of legislation, the assumption has persisted, almost by default, that the legislative process has remained essentially as it was in the 1880's. To quarrel with the broad outlines of the Wilson position in the present day may be unreasonable, but it seems improbable, nevertheless, that the dramatic changes in the Presidency since 1900 have been accompanied by no alterations, at least in tendency, within the legislative party and among its leaders. An analysis of the formal record cannot explore these roles to their limits nor can it without extensive supplementation more than suggest the interstitial subtleties and informalities that seem to characterize them. But in pursuit of an answer to these problems the following pages will focus upon the roles of the formal party leaders, giving such attention as opportunity provides to indications concerning their correspondence to the "real" leadership.

THE POSITIONS

Within both legislative parties the formal leadership positions can appropriately be divided into two general classes: "elective leaders," those who are chosen by the members of the party caucus or conference or are designated by an official so chosen, with or without the confirmation of the entire party membership; "seniority leaders," the chairmen and ranking minority members of the standing committees of the Senate, positions acquired by virtue of having been continuously a member of the committee for longer than any other senator of the

---

[6] Woodrow Wilson, *Congressional Government: A Study in American Politics*, Meridian Edition, New York, 1956, with an introduction by Walter Lippmann, pp. 55–56, 59, and 147. (First edition, Boston: Houghton Mifflin, 1885.)

[7] In the Preface to the 1900 edition, Woodrow Wilson, *Congressional Government: A Study in American Politics*, Meridian Edition, New York, 1956, pp. 22–23.

same party.[8] The basis of the distinction is obvious; its relevance is that the sources of whatever authority the positions involve being different, it would be expected that the behavior of the incumbents, including their votes on the roll calls, would also differ.

[8] The "seniority leaders" in the Eighty-first Congress, chairmen and ranking members of the standing committees, were as follows:

COMMITTEE	DEMOCRATS	REPUBLICANS
Agriculture and Forestry	Thomas, Okla.	Aiken, Vt.
Appropriations	McKellar, Tenn.	Bridges, N. H.
Armed Services	Tydings, Md.	Bridges, N. H.
Banking and Currency	Maybank, S. C.	Tobey, N. H.
District of Columbia	McGrath, R. I.	Williams, Del.
	Neely, W. Va. (after 8/24/49)	
Expenditures in Executive Departments	McClellan, Ark.	McCarthy, Wis.
Finance	George, Ga.	Millikin, Colo.
Foreign Relations	Connally, Tex.	Vandenberg, Mich.
Interior and Insular Affairs	O'Mahoney, Wyo.	Butler, Neb.
Interstate and Foreign Commerce	Johnson, Colo.	Tobey, N. H.
Judiciary	McCarran, Nev.	Wiley, Wis.
Labor and Public Welfare	Thomas, Utah	Taft, Ohio
Post Office and Civil Service	Johnston, S. C.	Langer, N. D.
Public Works	Chavez, N. M.	Cain, Wash.
Rules and Administration	Hayden, Ariz.	Wherry, Neb.
Joint Committee on Atomic Energy	McMahon, Conn.	Vandenberg, Mich. Hickenlooper, Ia. (2nd Sess.)

Several comments are in order concerning this list. First, the last-named committee is the only joint committee included because it was the only one of the eight joint standing committees in this Congress that had legislative authority. Second, the number of individual men on the Republican list is the smaller, 14 as against 17, not only because of the succession of Neely to McGrath on the District of Columbia committee, but also because a senator may be ranking minority member of more than one committee—Bridges, Tobey, and Vandenberg—but he may be chairman of only one. Third, and most important, the overlaps between the list of individual elective leaders and the list of seniority leaders present some problems. On the Democratic side this involved Senators McKellar and Hayden; on the Republican side it affected more: Senators Butler, Millikin, Taft, and Wherry. In the following pages where comparisons are drawn between the elective and the seniority leaders collectively, these men were regarded as belonging to the former category. In comparisons between a single elective leader, such as the Floor Leader, and the individual seniority leaders, however, these men were classified among the seniority leaders.

The list of "elective" positions in the two Senate organizations is roughly identical, but the practices of the two parties in filling them are somewhat different. Thus among the Democrats the same man is simultaneously Floor Leader (Majority Leader in the Eighty-first Congress), Chairman of the Democratic Policy Committee, Chairman of the Democratic Conference (or Caucus), and Chairman of the Democratic Committee on Committees.[9] Senator Scott Lucas of Illinois occupied these positions in the Eighty-first Congress. Among the Republicans, however, the equivalent offices were parceled out among four men. In 1949–1950 the Minority (Floor) Leader was Senator Kenneth Wherry of Nebraska, the Chairman of the Republican Policy Committee was Senator Robert A. Taft of Ohio, the Chairman of the Republican Conference was Senator Eugene Millikin of Colorado, and the Chairman of the Republican Committee on Committees was Senator Hugh Butler of Nebraska.

This difference in form may make some difference in fact. Republican informants claim that their procedure permits a wider representation of all segments of the party, while Democrats, especially those who have been close to the Leader, argue that a man cannot be expected to assume the burdens of the floor leadership unless he can also hold the other three positions. Probably the amount of personal negotiation which an effective Floor Leader must engage in is about the same in either case, but it may well be that the Democratic Floor Leader can more easily bargain for support of his desires as a result of also wearing the other three hats.

The formal status of the two party Whips also differs somewhat. In both parties they may either be elected by the conference or be appointed by the Floor Leader upon authorization by the conference. The Democratic Whip, who in the Eighty-first Congress was Senator Francis Myers of Pennsylvania, is formally designated as Assistant Leader. The Republicans make no such designation; their procedure in

---

[9] The recent metamorphosis of the last-named of these bodies is symptomatic of the informality of life in the legislative party (as well as indicative of the rather more casual attitude of the Democrats toward the niceties of organization, as compared with the Republicans). Until 1947 it was the Steering Committee. When in that year the party policy committees in the Senate were created by law, such "steering" functions as it performed were absorbed by the new committee, whose membership was overlapping but not identical, and it continued to make up the Democratic slate for memberships on the standing committees of the Senate. It nevertheless continued for several years to be called the Steering Committee and only gradually and without solemnity came to be known by the more accurate title of Committee on Committees.

recent years seems to assume no high degree of intimacy between Leader and Whip. Certainly, given the circumstances of his selection, which were noted in Chapter 2, it is unlikely that Senator Leverett Saltonstall, the Republican Whip in the Eighty-first Congress, was privy to the most delicate calculations of the Minority Leader. Over the years in both parties, however, a Whip has often been chosen as Floor Leader when that position became vacant.

Included here among the elective leaders in both parties are the Chairmen of the Republican and Democratic Senatorial Campaign Committees, who are appointed by the Chairman of the Conference in each party. Admittedly these positions, occupied in 1949–1950 on the Democratic side by Senator Clinton Anderson of New Mexico and on the Republican by Senator Owen Brewster of Maine, are not key posts in the respective party hierarchies and are regarded as chores which it is often difficult to persuade a man to accept. They were included in this analysis for two reasons. First, in a fairly disciplined party system it would be unthinkable for the occupant of such a post to be sharply at odds with the principal leaders of the party; hence evidence of such disharmony may provide a rough indicator of the absence of discipline. Second, despite responsible judgments that these committees are not used for disciplinary purposes, according to recurrent rumors they are so used from time to time, less in the Senate than in the House and less among the Democrats than among the Republicans, whose financial resources are considerably greater and whose fund-raising structure is more centralized and more highly organized.[10]

On the Democratic side two other individual positions were included within the definition of "elective" leaders, the Chairman of the Senate Patronage Committee, Senator Carl Hayden of Arizona, and the President *pro tempore* of the Senate, Senator Kenneth McKellar of Tennessee. The former position, through which jobs on the Senate side of

---

[10] In one of the few reported studies of the campaign committees Hugh A. Bone concludes against the disciplinary use of these bodies: "This is one case where he who pays the fiddler cannot call the tune." (Hugh A. Bone, "Some Notes on the Congressional Campaign Committees," *The Western Political Quarterly*, Vol. IX, no. 1, March 1956, p. 134.) My own interviews with members of both parties in the Senate and the House lead to the conclusion that, though this is generally the case, there are some exceptions. It seems likely at least that ways are occasionally found disproportionately to reward the faithful even though a standard minimum of assistance is not denied the recalcitrant. And one regularly encounters reports indicating that it may be worth while for a deserving member to solicit the top leadership of the legislative party for supplementary financial and other assistance at the disposal of the campaign committee.

Capitol Hill are filled, appears to be important in the affairs of the majority party at least to the extent of avoiding disharmony over such matters. In major outline the reputation of this function is that it has been reduced, like so many other possible sources of friction within the legislative party, to a formula. How much flexibility in application exists is not clear, but the reasons for including the position in this category are essentially the same as those justifying the inclusion of the Chairman of the Campaign Committee, namely, that it might be used for disciplinary purposes and that in a reasonably unified party one would expect a certain harmony of view between its occupant and the principal elective leaders. The case for including the President *pro tempore* is more debatable. Though the position is largely honorific, including such perquisites as an official automobile, and though it usually in recent years has been filled from within the majority party mostly on seniority grounds, through the years there have been rather bitter controversies over filling it,[11] and it is usually the case that its occupant is close to the central councils of the legislative party. The power of the position, as distinguished from that of the occupant, is not great.[12]

Finally, for certain purposes the collective memberships of the Majority and Minority Policy Committees were regarded as part of the "elective" leadership.[13]

---

[11] For examples see George H. Haynes, *The Senate of the United States*, Boston: Houghton Mifflin Company, 1938, pp. 249–254.

[12] As these remarks suggest, delimiting the category of "elective" leaders is a somewhat arbitrary matter. This list certainly includes all the positions of major consequence; there are, however, others, such as the secretary of the party conference, which might have been included but were omitted in the interests of simplicity.

[13] The practices of the two parties again differ in the selection of these bodies. Among the Democrats the members are appointed by the Floor Leader and customarily hold their places as long as they remain in the Senate. The Republican committee is appointed by the Chairman of the Conference, subject to its approval, and all except the *ex-officio* members—Chairman of the Conference, Floor Leader, Whip, Secretary of the Conference, Chairman of the Policy Committee, and the President *pro tempore* of the Senate if a Republican—are limited to four consecutive years of service. In the Eighty-first Congress the members of the Democratic Policy Committee were: Senators Lucas, chairman, Tydings, O'Mahoney, Green, Russell, Hill, Myers, and McMahon. One vacancy remained unfilled throughout the Congress, reportedly because the place was desired by both senators from Arizona, and the Majority Leader wished to avoid offending either. The membership of the Republican Policy Committee was: Senators Taft, chairman, Millikin, Young, Wherry, Saltonstall, Smith of Maine, Cordon, Bridges, Ives, Hickenlooper, and Vandenberg.

THE FLOOR LEADERS

The most interesting and, in terms of its evolutionary potential, possibly the most significant position in the senatorial party is that of the Floor Leader, especially the Majority Leader. Though the development of this office has had no satisfactory historical treatment, it is clear that the Floor Leader, particularly on the majority side, has become highly "visible" to a national political audience. He has an assured place in the press coverage of Washington greater than that of most of his colleagues and of all but a few Representatives, and succession to the position is often the occasion for an intense rivalry.

A search for the substance and sources of power in the position, however, is frustrating, not because they do not exist but because they are tremendously varied and often inaccessible. One cannot draw up for this post a neat list of authorities and prerogatives that describes its power adequately if not exhaustively, as one can for a place in a tightly structured hierarchy. The sum total of influence in the role as played by any individual senator depends upon the skill with which he combines and employs the fragments of power that are available to him.[14] In this respect and possibly in the fact that the expectations imposed on him exceed the reach of his official powers, the Floor Leader's position bears some resemblance to the Presidency.

Each Floor Leader has a more than casual connection with the filling of committee vacancies, subject always to the willingness of his colleagues to "go along" with his advice. Each is able to grant or to facilitate the granting and withholding of favors ranging from the allocation of space in the Senate Office Building to the expeditious handling of a pet bill. Such favors and others, including, for example, personal assistance and useful advice in connection with a particularly difficult constituency problem or in an election campaign, create obligations which an adroit and determined Leader can attempt to "cash in" for a supporting vote or an abstention on a closely contested bill. He may gain something in leverage and as a source of political intelligence if, when the White House is occupied by a fellow-partisan, he is a major if not the exclusive means of contact with the President.[15]

---

[14] In this connection note White's instructive comment on Lucas, whom he assesses as ". . . not a great leader, because the weapons of accommodation did not neatly function in his hands." (White, *Citadel*, p. 106.)

[15] The late Senator Taft is reported to have said, upon assuming the Majority Leadership in 1953, "You can't have a lot of fellows running down to the White House and then coming back to the Senate to speak for the President. That voice has got to be one voice." (William S. White, *The Taft Story*, New York: Harper

He is almost certain to be privy to the development of any legislative plans of consequence among his party colleagues, not only because of his inclusion in the party hierarchy but also because of his responsibility for determining the program of the Senate.

The scheduling function is primarily in the hands of the Majority Leader, though formally the deliberations of the Majority Policy Committee are much concerned with it. The Minority Leader, however, is usually kept informed of the majority's plans concerning the order in which measures will be called up; he may be consulted about them and he even may be able to induce their alteration.

Control or predominant influence over the schedule provides a base for negotiation. Judging from the behavior of Majority Leaders and from the comments of informants, the Floor Leader on the majority side in both House and Senate regards with great jealousy his authority to set the schedule of debate in his chamber. Unlike his ability to influence committee assignments, it is a continuous authority and, while not a prerogative of shattering power, it is not trivial. A Majority Leader cannot indefinitely refuse to schedule a measure in which any considerable minority of the Senate is interested, but the time he chooses for calling it up may in no small measure affect its chances of enactment, and a reasonably aggressive Leader will fight to keep the function under his control.[16]

---

and Brothers, 1954, p. 216.) In the Eighty-fourth Congress the meetings of the Minority Policy Committee following the leaders' weekly consultations with President Eisenhower became for all practical purposes gatherings of the entire Republican membership of the Senate, so eager were the rank-and-file members for reports of the President's plans, presumably not merely those in the area of legislation.

[16] For example, there were three instances in the two sets of low-cohesion Democratic votes in which a record vote was taken on a move threatening this control. Majority Leader Lucas objected to all of these on the ground of their threat to the leadership; on two he was upheld. On August 24, 1949, while the Senate was considering H. Con. Res. 129, providing that the House adjourn for approximately a month in late August and September to allow the Senate to catch up on accumulated work, Senator Capehart offered an amendment to the effect that both House and Senate should adjourn *sine die* at the end of September. It was rejected 34 to 48 (22 Republicans and 12 Democrats to 13 Republicans and 35 Democrats). On April 10, 1950, Senator McCarran moved that the Senate proceed to take up the conference report on S. 1008, dealing with basing-point pricing; if accepted, this motion would have sidetracked consideration of the rivers-and-harbors bill then being debated; the McCarran motion was defeated 35 to 36 (24 Republicans and 11 Democrats to nine Republicans and 27 Democrats). On May 10, 1950, Senator Taft moved to take up S. Res. 248, disapproving the President's reorganization plan for the National Labor Relations Board; this would have set aside the F.E.P.C. bill, which was then being consid-

Of such fragments is the power of the Floor Leader composed. It is rarely or never peremptory. The character of the chamber and of the party make this indeterminateness inevitable. It is reinforced, moreover, by the fact that a Floor Leader does not drop his role as ambassador from his own state when he assumes the position. When promoting the claims of his constituency he can speak as more than a rank-and-file senator, but his actions as Floor Leader are often not free of the implication that he is also a senator from a particular state.

Given the depth and persistence of the cleavages in both parties indicated in the sets of low-cohesion votes, therefore, one would expect that a Leader who accepted any degree of responsibility for the substantive actions of the party would almost certainly be a middleman, not only in the sense of a negotiator but also in a literal structural sense. One would not expect that he could attract the support necessary for election unless his voting record placed him somewhere near the center in an evenly divided party, and one would not expect him to be effective in his role unless he continued to avoid identification with one of the extreme groups within his nominal following.

Examination of the tables in the preceding chapter showing the bloc structure of the two Senate parties (Tables 3, 4, 6, and 7 for the Democrats; Tables 10, 11, 13, and 14 for the Republicans) indicates that the voting behavior of Majority Leader Lucas conformed fairly closely to the middleman expectation. On the two low-cohesion sets he belonged to the "left" Bloc I system (Tables 3 and 4), but he was not one of the high-ranking members of the bloc. On the high-cohesion votes of the second session (Table 7) he was a member of all three blocs, but he ranked somewhat higher in the "left" Bloc I than in the "right" Bloc III. Only on the high-cohesion votes of the first session, which had the highest mean index of cohesion for the four sets and on which the structure of the party was of the clear uninuclear type (Table 6), was Lucas among the most prominent members of the bloc.[17]

The Minority Leader, Senator Wherry, did not display the expected

---

ered; Taft's motion was adopted, 50 to 22 (30 Republicans and 20 Democrats to four Republicans and 18 Democrats).

In the course of an interview a Representative who has served as Majority Leader in the House said that he would stage a fight in the party conference rather than permit removal of the scheduling function from the floor leadership, and he added that on a vote dealing with the schedule, such as a snap motion for adjournment, he would never forget and not soon forgive a member of his party who voted with the opposition.

[17] The close reader will note that these intrabloc rankings, since they cannot take account of variations in "absence" rates, are at best rough approximations. Allowance has been made for such variations in these comments.

pattern in his voting nearly as markedly as did Lucas. On the two low-cohesion sets he was a member of the "right" bloc system (Tables 10 and 11), but in addition he was consistently the most prominent member of the bloc. Although he was in the fringe of the center Bloc II on the low-cohesion set of the first session (Table 10) and on the high-cohesion set of that session was a member of the center Bloc II as well as of the "right" Bloc III (Table 13), his rank in the latter bloc was considerably higher than that in the central bloc. On the second session's high-cohesion votes Wherry was not only in the principal bloc, as would be expected, but also among its most prominent members, a long way removed from the dissident Bloc I (Table 14).

In short, Senator Wherry tended to occupy a rather extreme position in the party structure. His behavior is more significant in view of the fact that the two wings of the Republican party were for the most part equal in numbers. Had the bloc to which he belonged consistently composed a majority of the party, as was the case with Lucas's affiliation among the Democrats, Wherry's position would have been less remarkable, but to find the Floor Leader one of the most prominent members of a bloc tending toward a minority position in the party is a striking deviation from the expected pattern.[18]

In view of Lucas's rather moderate position in the blocs of which he was a member, one might suspect that on a number of votes important to the Southern members of the party's "right" wing he dissented from the position of his usual associates in order to support the preferences of those whom he normally opposed. A close analysis of his votes on the two low-cohesion sets, where this sort of behavior might be most likely to occur, indicates that he was no more inclined to shift his support in this way than were the two most prominent members of the "left" wing, Senators Neely and Humphrey. None of the three, moreover, voted with the Southerners against his own bloc on any issue of consequence. Among the Majority Leader's "absences," however, there were some that suggest a tendency toward accommodating the members of the minority bloc. For example, on March 29, 1950, Lucas's preferences were unrecorded on five votes dealing with the then current version of legislation designed to exempt the independent pro-

---

[18] These differences between Lucas and Wherry were confirmed by the more precise indicators of their voting behavior. Lucas voted more frequently on the side of the majority of his party than Wherry did on the majority side of his on every set but one. On the high-cohesion votes of the second session, largely owing to Lucas's relatively high "absence" rate, each cast about the same number of votes with the majority of his party. For the sessions as a whole Lucas's index of party orthodoxy was consistently higher, 4.47 and 4.42 as against Wherry's 4.09 and 4.27 for the first and second sessions, respectively.

ducers and gatherers of natural gas from regulation by the Federal Power Commission. These were the only record votes in the Senate on this measure, and the members of the Southern bloc were in complete agreement on them. As Majority Leader, Lucas certainly knew not only when these votes were likely to be taken but also what the issues were. (Three of the five were on modifying amendments, but there were also roll calls on a motion to recommit and on final passage.) It is reasonable to infer that if his preferences were unrecorded, even in his absence from the Senate, he intended that they should be. Since his Illinois colleague, Senator Douglas, was one of the chief opponents of the measure, Lucas could hardly afford, especially in an election year, to vote with the Southerners. His complete abstention would be almost equally welcomed by them, however.

There were no symptoms whatsoever in the Minority Leader's record of voting (or nonvoting) in deference to the views in an opposing wing of the party.

Given the several contrasts between the voting records of Lucas and Wherry, one would expect, if the earlier assumptions about the role of the Floor Leader are correct, that the Minority Leader was the less effective of the two, and there have been comments to this effect by responsible observers.[19] Arriving at an adequate measure of such a discrepancy, however, is difficult. A Leader may put his prestige to the test in a variety of subtle ways that are not identifiable, especially in the record votes. It is clear, however, that when a Floor Leader offers a motion, makes a point of order, or calls for the "yeas and nays" on a vote, he is staking his influence at least to the extent that repeated losses can be presumed to reflect adversely on his skill and standing in his party and in the Senate. Accordingly all such moves by Lucas or Wherry that resulted in a record vote were tallied for both sessions of the Eighty-first Congress, and the instances were noted on which these initiatives were supported by a majority of the Leader's party or by a majority of the Senate.[20]

The results, summarized in Table 16, tend to confirm the expecta-

---

[19] William S. White describes Wherry as ". . . a fair to good leader—but his outstanding characteristic in the post was a flatly uncompromising attitude and a brand of Midwestern small-town, Lions Club Republicanism so intolerant as sometimes to repel even the redoubtable Taft." (White, *Citadel*, p. 106.)

[20] For a roughly comparable technique see Robert A. Dahl, James G. March, and David Nasatir, "Influence Ranking in the United States Senate," a paper presented at the meetings of the American Political Science Association in Washington, D. C., September 6–8, 1956; see also Robert A. Dahl, "The Concept of Power," *Behavioral Science*, Vol. 2, no. 3 (July 1957), pp. 201–215 and the literature cited therein.

Table 16

PARTY INFLUENCE OF THE MAJORITY AND MINORITY LEADERS: RESPONSES
OF DEMOCRATIC AND REPUBLICAN SENATORS TO THE INIATIVES* OF THEIR
RESPECTIVE FLOOR LEADERS, 81ST CONGRESS, 1ST AND 2ND SESSIONS

	Majority Leader (Lucas, Ill.)	Minority Leader (Wherry, Neb.)
Number of initiatives	39	88
Number supported by a majority of the party	35	72
Per cent	89.7	81.8
Number supported by a majority of the Senate	26	23
Per cent	66.7	26.1

* Motions offered, points of order raised, record votes called for by Floor Leader, on which record votes were taken.

tions. It would be unreasonable to assume that the Minority Leader would do as well as the Majority Leader in the Senate as a whole, but, if they were performing equally effectively, their records within their respective parties should be equal. The deficiencies of Wherry, moreover, are underscored by the fact that while only about one-quarter (23) of his initiatives occurred on votes in the Republican low-cohesion sets, more than two-fifths (16) of Lucas's were taken on the equivalent Democratic votes. Yet the Majority Leader was supported by a majority of his party on a higher proportion (81 per cent) of these low-cohesion initiatives than was Wherry (61 per cent).

Judged by this measure both Leaders were fairly effective, but Wherry, though he took the initiative more often, was considerably less successful than Lucas. Further insight into the reasons for this appears in the substance of the votes on which the parties rejected their Leaders' initiatives. Three of the four votes on which Lucas was not followed by the party majority dealt with race issues, on which he was normally close to the party majority. Thirteen of the 16 votes on which a majority of the Republicans rejected Wherry's initiatives, however, dealt with foreign aid or foreign policy questions, matters on which he and his bloc tended to be in a minority position in the party, and his initiatives were more likely than Lucas's to attract only a minority of the party and of the Senate on lop-sided bipartisan decisions.

Senator Wherry's operating conception of the Minority Leader's role apparently did not preclude his behaving more as a senator from

Nebraska than as a spokesman for his legislative party. It is also possible that Wherry's was a reasonably correct conception of the role of Minority Leader, especially in the setting of this Congress. The demands upon the Senate Republicans and the opportunities available to them, as the minority both in the legislature and in the executive, may have been so slight as to make an extreme Floor Leader an inexpensive luxury. Especially may this have been the case if others in the party, possibly including Wherry, knew that if matters reached a really critical juncture, Taft or someone else nearer the center would step in. As later evidence will indicate, neither Taft nor anyone else seems to have functioned consistently as a substitute, but there is little doubt that Taft did so occasionally.

Although Senator Lucas was not in as extreme a position in his party as was the Minority Leader, he was nevertheless not at the very center of the Democratic structure but rather slightly to the "left." One explanation for this is that he displayed a strong tendency to vote in accordance with the preferences of the President on Administration support votes, a tendency whose further implications will be examined in detail later. Senator Lucas, of course, was not the only Democrat who strongly supported the President, but there are in his voting record indications of a distinctive pattern in this respect. Among the members of the bloc with which the Majority Leader was affiliated on each of the four sets of roll calls, he was one of two whose ranking on the Administration support votes in the sets was consistently higher than his rank in the bloc. On all the roll calls in the two sessions that were classified as Administration support votes Lucas opposed what was designated as the Administration position on fewer than any other member of the Senate. Among those who normally voted for the Administration position, moreover, he was least frequently "absent" (Table 17). In other words, Lucas's "left-of-center" position in the party structure, which was not extreme, seems to have been due less to a close identification with the other members of the bloc, as such, than to a strong propensity to vote in support of the Administration. Loyalty to the Administration apparently modified his ties to the center of the party.[21]

---

[21] Senator McMahon of Connecticut was the other whose rank on Administration support was higher than his rank in the bloc. The 12 instances in which Lucas failed to support the Administration can be summarized for the benefit of the curious. All but one of them, the last on the list, were included in the four sets of votes used in the bloc analyses. It may be worth noting that 10 of the 12 instances occurred in the second session, during most of which Lucas was a candidate for re-election. (The votes on which he was "absent" are designated "A"; on the others he voted against the inferred Administration position.) First session: against

Table 17

FREQUENCY WITH WHICH DEMOCRATIC SENATORS* WERE RECORDED AS NOT SUPPORTING THE ADMINISTRATION ON 190 SELECTED ROLL CALLS, 81ST CONGRESS, 1ST AND 2ND SESSIONS

Senator	Vote	Nonsupport Indicated by: Announcement or Pair	"Absence"	Total
Lucas, Ill.	8	0	4	12
McMahon, Conn.	9	1	8	18
Douglas, Ill.	16	1	1	18
Myers, Pa.	9	2	8	19
Green, R. I.	13	0	7	20
Humphrey, Minn.	15	1	6	22
Anderson, N. M.	11	2	10	23
Kilgore, W. Va.	20	2	2	24
Neely, W. Va.	11	9	6	26
Hill, Ala.	25	0	2	27
Magnuson, Wash.	20	6	3	29
O'Mahoney, Wyo.	17	2	12	31
Thomas, Utah	16	4	15	35
Hayden, Ariz.	14	11	10	35
Sparkman, Ala.	21	1	13	35
Murray, Mont.	17	0	21	38
Pepper, Fla.	11	1	32	44
Johnson, Tex.	33	0	11	44
Kefauver, Tenn.	11	0	35	46
Kerr, Okla.	31	3	13	47
McFarland, Ariz.	40	1	6	47
McKellar, Tenn.	41	0	7	48
Chapman, Ky.	46	4	5	55
Hunt, Wyo.	21	5	32	58
Fulbright, Ark.	49	0	9	58
Connally, Tex.	45	2	13	60
Chavez, N. M.	22	6	33	61
O'Conor, Md.	34	3	24	61
Holland, Fla.	57	3	2	62
Maybank, S. C.	37	8	19	64
Gillette, Iowa	41	4	19	64
Taylor, Ida.	25	7	33	65
Tydings, Md.	33	5	19	67
Hoey, N. C.	56	1	10	67
Ellender, La.	46	10	13	69
Stennis, Miss.	60	3	8	71
Robertson, Va.	52	7	13	72
Frear, Del.	38	10	25	73
Long, La.	41	8	27	76
Thomas, Okla.	31	4	43	78
Johnston, S. C.	50	10	20	80
George, Ga.	66	1	13	80
Russell, Ga.	68	10	16	94
Johnson, Colo.	83	0	12	95
McClellan, Ark.	96	3	6	105
Eastland, Miss.	41	15	53	109
McCarran, Nev.	50	16	46	112
Byrd, Va.	96	4	39	139

* 48 Democratic senators who were seated during the whole of both sessions.

If the proposition is valid, that a general qualification for the choice of a Floor Leader and for his effective performance is that he should be a "middle" man, it should predict the roster of possible aspirants from among whom the successors of the incumbent Leaders will be chosen. Five senators in the Eighty-first Congress have subsequently served as Floor Leader. Examination of their records in 1949 and 1950 should provide a test of the general proposition. On the Democratic side were Senator Ernest McFarland of Arizona, who became Majority Leader in the Eighty-second Congress following the defeat in the 1950 elections of Senator Lucas and Majority Whip Myers of Pennsylvania, and Senator Lyndon Johnson of Texas, who moved up in 1953 to the position of Minority Leader after serving as Whip in the Eighty-second Congress.[22] For the Republicans Senator Styles Bridges of New Hampshire was designated as Leader in January 1952, following the death of Senator Wherry, on the understanding that he would occupy the position for only one year.[23] He was succeeded by Senator

---

Magnuson amendment to rent control renewal extending authority for two full years; Gillette amendment to E.C.A. extension specifying that 15 per cent of corn shipments be in processed form ("A"). Second session: override veto of H. R. 87 granting to postal workers salary and promotion credit for time spent in the military service during World War II ("A"); against George-Millikin amendment to Revenue Act of 1950 directing committees to report early in 82nd Congress an excess profits tax retroactive to July 1 or October 1, 1950; against amendment to Highway Act of 1950 reducing funds for secondary roads; against amendment to Omnibus Appropriation Bill increasing funds for Voice of America and other State Department functions; against Aiken amendment to price support bill barring support for potatoes unless marketing agreements are in effect; override veto of War Contractors' Relief Act ("A"); override veto of Internal Security Act; for tabling motion to reconsider vote on amendment to Omnibus Appropriation Bill by which Spanish loan was agreed to; for passage of resolution disapproving plan for reorganization of Treasury Department; override veto of increased medical service for veterans of the Spanish-American War ("A").

[22] The selection of McFarland suggests a perhaps unnecessary reminder that structural position is only one of a number of factors bearing on the party's choice. He reportedly sought the position and found securing it the easier because competitors were few. The shock of the defeat of both Lucas and Myers in 1950 produced a widespread feeling in the Senate that the top leadership positions were not necessarily an asset in the constituency, an attitude that was strengthened when McFarland himself was defeated in 1952. He held no committee chairmanship, which augmented his availability even though there is no tradition in the Senate, as there is in the House, that a Floor Leader must relinquish his committee posts. The demands upon the time of a Floor Leader, especially if he is of the Senate majority, apparently make it difficult for him to be an active member of a committee, to say nothing of being a chairman. Since he was finishing his second term in the Senate, he was not a newcomer and was young enough (56) to carry the physical burdens of the job.

[23] *New York Times,* January 9, 1952.

Taft at the opening of the Eighty-third Congress, and he in turn by Senator William Knowland of California, who had been designated as acting Majority Leader by Taft when he was taken ill in June, 1953, and elected to the position in August following Taft's death.

Examination of the bloc structure of the Senate Democrats (Tables 3, 4, 6, and 7) indicates that both McFarland and Johnson satisfied the expected positional requirement. McFarland, whose lack of aggressiveness still makes his selection a source of wonderment to staff and press people on Capitol Hill, allegedly owed his position in large measure to the influence of key men in the "Southern" bloc, notably Senator Russell of Georgia.[24] There is no reason to doubt this report, especially as this bloc was more important in the Eighty-second Congress than in the Eighty-first—the five seats lost by the Democrats in 1950 were all in the North or the Border. The relevant point here is that the pattern of McFarland's voting on the four sets of roll calls for the Eighty-first Congress identified him with the center or even the "left" wing of the party, not with the "right." [25] Johnson, whose designation as Whip in 1952 and almost automatic succession to the leadership in 1953 were a result of the same kind of political factors responsible for McFarland's elevation, was also clearly a "middle" man, although he may have leaned somewhat more to the "right." Evidence the fact that in his position among the "isolates" on the low-cohesion set of the second session two of his three top scores were with members of Bloc II (Table 5) and that on the high-cohesion votes of the same session he ranked somewhat higher in Bloc III than in Bloc I (Table 7).[26]

Inferences from the Republican structure (Tables 10, 11, 13, and 14) are less clear, notably because Senator Bridges was "absent" so frequently that it is difficult to locate him with complete assurance (Table 12).[27] With variations, nevertheless, Bridges, Taft, and Knowland all fit the expected pattern. Bridges on the high-cohesion roll calls

[24] *New York Times*, July 22, 1951.

[25] On the four sets McFarland most frequently agreed with Hayden, his colleague from Arizona, Sparkman of Alabama, Anderson of New Mexico, and Kerr of Oklahoma.

[26] On the four sets of votes Johnson agreed most frequently with his Texas colleague, Senator Connally, Kerr of Oklahoma, Hayden of Arizona, Sparkman of Alabama, Chapman of Kentucky, and Fulbright of Arkansas.

[27] Bridges's high "absence" rate, which is characteristic of his behavior in Congresses before and since the Eighty-first, provides one clue to his unwillingness to retain the Floor Leader position on more than a temporary basis. One of the arduous features of the job is that the Leader must be on the floor most of the time when the Senate is in session, which means, incidentally, that he is recorded on most roll calls. Probably more important in his calculations, however, was his position as ranking Republican on the Appropriations Committee.

clearly stood near the center of the party. His votes on the low-cohesion sets showed a somewhat greater tendency toward the "right" wing but not a complete identification in that direction.[28] Taft, who obviously could have had the Floor Leader position long before the Eighty-third Congress if he had wanted it, displayed in his voting both his well-known individuality and his central position in the party. Although he was among the "isolates" in the low-cohesion set of the first session, his high scores were with Ferguson of Michigan, himself a man of the center, Watkins of Utah, who was in the fringe of the "right" bloc, and Donnell of Missouri, who was similarly located with respect to the "left" bloc (Table 10). On the low-cohesion votes of the second session Taft was a member of the "left" bloc system, though not one of its extreme affiliates (Table 11). On the two high-cohesion sets, however, he was clearly part of the central element in the party (Tables 13 and 14).[29]

The voting pattern of Senator Knowland not only conforms to that expected of a future Floor Leader but also goes a long way to explain why Senator Taft should have chosen him as his heir in the Eighty-third Congress. In both low-cohesion sets he was one of the less conspicuous affiliates of the "left" blocs (Tables 10 and 11). On the high-cohesion votes of the first session Knowland was a member of both the center Bloc II and the "right" Bloc III, ranking somewhat higher in the latter than in the former (Table 13). Yet on the comparable votes of the second session he was not only one of the more moderate members of the principal bloc (II) but also in the "fringe" of the "left" Bloc I (Table 14). To a marked degree, therefore, Knowland's voting fit the pattern of a moderate with effective attachments to the dissident "left" of the party and, somewhat less strongly, to the "right" as well.[30]

Taft and Knowland were not particularly close in their voting, if the pattern of these sets is representative, even though they both stood toward the center of the party.[31] Since identity of view on the sub-

---

[28] Bridges agreed most often on the four sets with Taft of Ohio and Ferguson of Michigan, but he also voted with considerable frequency with Bricker of Ohio, Schoeppel of Kansas, Kem of Missouri, and Millikin of Colorado.

[29] On all four sets Taft voted most frequently with Senators Ferguson of Michigan and Watkins of Utah.

[30] Over the four sets Knowland agreed most frequently with Senators Ferguson of Michigan and Saltonstall of Massachusetts, illustrating his center-left orientation. Ferguson, who was close to all three of the men under discussion, was himself suggested after the 1952 elections as an alternative to Knowland as Majority Leader, should Taft not want the position. (*New York Times*, November 9, 1952.)

[31] Their scores on the four sets were as follows: Low-cohesion, first session, less than 38, second session, 45; high-cohesion, first session, 50, second session, 44.

stance of legislation does not seem to explain Taft's choice of Knowland, it appears more than likely that the structural factor was influential. Knowland, who in the first months of 1953 was serving as Chairman of the Majority Policy Committee, must have appeared eligible to Taft at least in part because he occupied a central position in the party which involved effective contacts with both extremes but not strong identification with either.[32]

This characteristic of the Senate Floor Leader's role—holding a position in the structural middle of the party—is a logical correlate of the mediate function of the legislative party. The party as a mediate group both reflects and fosters the self-conscious independence of the individual senator, records and in a degree perpetuates the deep cleavages that persist within it. And the mediate group imposes upon even a most talented Leader the necessity to build his influence upon a combination of such fragments of power, and hence such groupings of men, as are available to him. He must, in other words, be a middleman in the sense of a broker. To operate this way, however, he must in turn be a middleman in the structural sense, if only because of the difficult communication problem with which he is faced.

In a group of this sort, despite its institutional persistence, a stable and functioning leadership inevitably is engaged in repeated, even continuous, efforts at restructuring, reconstituting the group. That is, the Leader's lines of communication within the party—and, of course, within the Senate as a whole—must be open and efficiently operating, "efficiency" here implying speed and accuracy in a changing tactical setting in which the demands of the message-sender must, almost by definition, compete for attention and response with those from other

---

These are equal to or a little below the mean scores in the blocs of which they were both members.

[32] On less formal grounds William S. White seems to be making essentially the same point when he comments concerning Taft's choice: "He took Knowland upon faith and upon observation and without the remotest sense of personal favoritism; while friendly these two were not mutually and deeply sympathetic men in the personal sense." (White, *Citadel*, pp. 261–2.) White also says (pp. 259–260) that Knowland was chosen to prevent the selection of a "Dewey" man such as Saltonstall or one from the extreme right. Probably also pertinent to the choice of Knowland was, among other considerations, the fact that he had no committee chairmanship within sight. It is relevant to point out that structural considerations seem to have been influential with the dissidents who opposed the re-election of Senator Wherry as Minority Leader at the opening of the Eighty-first Congress. In supporting Knowland against Wherry they picked a moderate with some affinity for them or, to put it the other way, one of their less extreme affiliates who might attract support in the conference from the party's center. See chap. 2, and chap. 3, note 39.

sources. In this type of group the continuing burden of restructuring tends to fall upon a few or one, such as the Floor Leader. For him, or them, a middle position in the structure is a prerequisite to efficient communication.

The Leader must be able easily and largely without intermediaries to deal with the full range of the party membership, an unlikely possibility if he is identified with one of its extremes. In a "problem-solving" group the leadership is expected to display extreme attachment to the goals of the group and can directly or, if the organization is large enough, through an established hierarchy identify and define from an extreme position authoritatively relevant intermediate goals. Or in a mediate group where size or other factors not conspicuous in the Senate party give the leadership more formidable sanctions, cues may effectively be transmitted from an extreme position with or without an established hierarchy of intermediate communicators.[33] In a group such as the Senate party, however, location far from the center of the structure apparently is almost a disqualifying handicap to an incumbent or aspiring leader.[34]

Even granting that Wherry's conception of his role was not crippling, especially with a Taft in the background, the observed discrepancies between him and Lucas are still troubling. How does it happen that there can be two such divergent interpretations of roles that appear to be so similar? Political accidents and exigencies may, of course, greatly narrow the range of choice open to a party, especially one which, like the Republicans between 1933 and 1947, has long been in a minority. From all accounts, however, the Wherry case is not unique, which suggests that it may be traceable partly to the characteristics of the legislative party in the Senate.

In a group organized around and sharply focused upon shared goals in which all members have a considerable stake, one would expect that the optional component of a leader's role, as distinguished from the required and forbidden elements, would be relatively nar-

---

[33] As, for example, in the House under Speaker Cannon, whose downfall in 1910 suggests the dangers of ignoring the limits to such sanctions if the essential mediate character of the group remains unaltered.

[34] These general speculations are not meant to imply that an effective Senate Floor Leader has no use for intermediaries. Senator Lyndon Johnson, who in the Eighty-fourth and Eighty-fifth Congresses played the Majority Leader's role with extraordinary technical elegance, apparently made use of them. Some observers of the Senate, for example, report that Senator Humphrey of Minnesota was more often Johnson's representative in the "left" wing of the party than its emissary to him. But presumably even this sort of relationship depends upon the principal being not too far removed in the structure from the agent.

row. In a group of the mediate type, however, where the members' stakes in the group are not high, one would expect the discretionary segment of the leader's role to be relatively broad. That is, where the character of the group limits the authority of the leader, successive incumbents likely will interpret very differently the requirements and opportunities of the position. Hence the tendency in comments on the Floor Leader in the Senate to emphasize the importance of the skills and personality of the individual in determining what the position is.[35] As White has put it, "There is in fact not even any fixed and general concept of just what a leader is and just what he *ought* to do, except that when the Senate is in characteristic mood and tone there is general agreement on what he is *not* and what he ought *not* to do." [36]

Party members may grumble at the extremes of a Wherry or at the inactivity of a McFarland, and the dropped ball may be picked up by a Taft or a Russell, but even this substitution may not occur. The function of the group does not require standardized performance of the role as a condition of tenure, and ineffective performance may produce no compensating behavior elsewhere in the party.

THE WHIPS

If the role of the Floor Leader in the Senate is not sharply defined, that of the Whip is even less so. The formal elements of the position, which bears only the most remote family resemblance to its nominal equivalent in the British parliamentary party, are essentially two. The Whip is expected to keep informed of the attitudes and voting intentions of the members of the party and he is supposed to be responsible for their attendance in the chamber, which also entails his supervision of the process of arranging pairs. For the most part, however, these duties can be and are performed by a competent member of the party staff, usually the Floor Secretary, and they are in any case rarely a source of independent power. The significance of the Whip therefore depends upon his position in the party structure and upon his relations with the other elective leaders, particularly the Floor Leader.

In their relations with the Floor Leaders the differences between Senators Myers and Saltonstall, respectively the Democratic and Republican Whip, went far beyond the difference in their formal status. Although the Republican Whip, unlike his Democratic counterpart,

---

[35] See, for example, White, *Citadel*, pp. 95 ff.; Haynes, *The Senate of the United States*, pp. 480 ff.; Riddick, *The United States Congress*, pp. 93 ff.

[36] White, *Citadel*, pp. 95–96.

is not designated as Assistant Floor Leader, the rules of the conference do specify that the Whip "shall perform such other duties as the
Chairman or Floor Leader may require." Yet it is fairly evident from
what has gone before that cooperation between Senator Wherry and
Senator Saltonstall in the Eighty-first Congress must have been minimal at best. Senator Lucas and Senator Myers were close enough, by
the indications of the record votes, so that the Whip could function as
a supplement to or a substitute for the Majority Leader, but the two
Republicans appeared as leading members of opposing wings of the
party.

Table 18

FLOOR LEADERS AND WHIPS: CONTRASTING BEHAVIOR OF DEMOCRATIC AND
REPUBLICAN ELECTIVE LEADERS, 81ST CONGRESS, SENATE

| | Democratic | | Republican | |
| | Floor | | Floor | |
	Leader	Whip	Leader	Whip
Party orthodoxy index				
First Session	4.47	4.51	4.09	3.78
Second Session	4.42	4.10	4.27	3.74
Administration support index				
First Session	4.72	4.79	1.40	3.55
Second Session	4.58	4.33	1.76	3.33

For each of the indexes a score of 5 would indicate perfect support of the
Administration or party majority, a score of 1 would indicate complete non-
support.

Table 18 summarizes the contrasting behavior of Whip and Floor
Leader on the majority and minority sides. Lucas and Myers were
both fairly close to the center of the party, as their high party orthodoxy indexes show, with Myers somewhat closer in the first session.
(That is, Myers's party orthodoxy index was higher—4.51—than Lucas's
—4.47.) Although, as Table 17 has revealed, Lucas over the votes of
the whole Congress was particularly strong in his support of the Administration, Myers was not far behind, and in the first session his
Administration support index was slightly higher.[37] Senator Wherry on

---

[37] At various points the Democratic Whip's record shows signs of the same sort
of avoidance of open opposition to the President that was noted earlier in connection with the Majority Leader. For example, Myers was "absent" on the Senate
vote in the first session confirming the appointment of James Boyd as Director of
the Bureau of Mines. Boyd was vigorously opposed by John L. Lewis and the

the average was not close to the center of his party, but he was nevertheless much closer than was the Republican Whip. The degree and in general terms the source of their differences are shown in the Administration support indexes. Wherry voted against the President almost without exception, while Saltonstall's index shows moderately strong support by a member of the opposition. His indexes would rank him among the last dozen Democrats listed in Table 17; Wherry's were lower than those of any other member of the Senate, Democrat or Republican.

Senators Lucas and Myers recorded opposing preferences on approximately 5 per cent of the votes in the four Democratic sets. Since their constituencies were not the same, at least this rate of disagreement might have been expected. Indeed several of their oppositions can easily be explained on the grounds of differing responses to interest group and constituency claims.[38] Some of their disagreements, including

United Mine Workers, who had successfully delayed Senate action for more than a year. They were, of course, an important element within Myers's constituency. Since he was recorded as voting on several other roll calls taken on March 22, 1949, his "absence" on this vote can be interpreted as a deliberate abstention.

[38] Lucas and Myers were recorded in opposition as follows: first session, 3 votes on the low-cohesion set and 2 on the high-cohesion; second session, 8 votes on the low-cohesion set and 4 on the high. In the two low-cohesion sets they differed on 3 votes concerning the bill designed to amend the antitrust laws so as to legalize basing point pricing. The demand for such legislation was vocal in Pennsylvania and Senator Myers not only supported it but also was the author of one version of the bill. In the second session Myers supported and Lucas opposed the resolution disapproving the President's plan for reorganizing the Interstate Commerce Commission, the Whip's position presumably again reflecting demands or anticipating consequences in his constituency. Also in the second session Lucas supported and Myers opposed one of Senator Douglas's losing efforts to cut the ship construction funds of the Maritime Commission. Douglas, Lucas's Illinois colleague, was engaged in a much-publicized effort to cut the "pork" from the Omnibus Appropriation Bill, and Lucas's refusal to support him in most of these futile attempts was known to be embarrassing the Majority Leader's efforts at maintaining a good press for his re-election campaign.

This situation is a revealing one, if reasonably authenticated reports are correct. During the Senate debate in July 1950, Douglas offered a long list of amendments, all rejected, to cut funds for highways, reclamation, rivers and harbors, and ship construction subsidies. These were in a sense a sequel to his efforts in April to cut the authorizations in the Rivers and Harbors and Flood Control Act. Lucas and his associates were concerned with heading off economy attacks on the foreign-aid portion of the bill, which would have been encouraged if the leadership appeared to be aiding Douglas. In April Lucas had been similarly worried about cuts in the Foreign Economic Assistance Act authorizations, which were taken up after the rivers and harbors bill. The Majority Leader's mail, however, stimulated by the publicity his colleague was getting, was heavy with condemnation of his

those traceable to constituency differences, were on matters of some consequence, but about half dealt with comparatively trifling issues.[39]

In contrast Senators Wherry and Saltonstall opposed one another on more than three-fifths of the Republican votes, among which were a very large number in the general area of foreign policy, including foreign aid. However, some of their agreed votes, practically all of them in the high-cohesion sets, suggest a measure of coordinated activity by the Republican leaders. They hint at the elements of what might be called a program, that is, a coherent line of substantive policy, especially as on most of them the votes of the Minority Leader and Whip coincided with those of the other four Republican elective leaders.[40] These votes may have been merely instances in which Senator Saltonstall attempted to "go along" with the consensus among the elective leaders. Since most of them were roll calls on which Saltonstall voted against the members of the bloc to which he normally belonged, this interpretation is a reasonable one. Whatever the motive assigned, however, some of the agreed votes suggest a degree of concerted effort by the minority leadership.[41] Nevertheless most of the agreements

---

failure to join in these economy efforts. Lucas reportedly asked Douglas to drop the campaign when it became obvious that it was getting nowhere. The amendment on which Lucas voted with Douglas was the last one which the latter called up. The incident might give pause to some uncritical enthusiasts for omnibus appropriation bills, and it clearly indicates the delicate, broker position in which a Majority Leader is likely to find himself. (For a somewhat different account of the April incidents, see Stephen K. Bailey and Howard D. Samuel, *Congress at Work,* New York: Henry Holt, 1952, pp. 188–192.)

[39] The important differences between Lucas and Myers, in addition to the five easily traceable to constituency factors, were four: Low-cohesion, second session: Amendment to Omnibus Appropriation Bill increasing funds for the Voice of America and related activities, Lucas for; high-cohesion, first session: Myers for amendment to rent control bill, extending program for full two years; Myers for amendment to first deficiency appropriation eliminating funds for new T. V. A. steam generating plant; second session: Lucas for amendment to Highway Act reducing funds for secondary roads.

[40] Wherry and Saltonstall were recorded in opposition on 56 votes in each of the low-cohesion sets; on the high-cohesion votes they were opposed on 30 votes in the first session and on 40 in the second. Among their agreements showing some traces of deliberate coordination were the following: in the first session (high-cohesion set) the Whip and the Floor Leader agreed on a series of 6 votes aimed at across-the-board appropriation cuts, on 3 votes hostile to public power development, on 5 votes on the projected amendment of the Taft-Hartley Act, and on 2 votes concerning the Wherry substitute for the Senate cloture rule. In the second-session set they were agreed in support of 7 restrictive amendments to the Defense Production Act. On all of these, excepting 2 of the second-session votes, the other 4 elective leaders were in agreement with the Whip and Floor Leader.

[41] There were other minor signs of deliberate convergence between Wherry and

between Wherry and Saltonstall have a much more accidental appearance. Many of them were on minor matters or a few major ones on which their agreement seems likely to have represented no more than an unplanned convergence, especially on domestic economic matters, on which Saltonstall's conservative attitudes happened to coincide with Wherry's less immoderate ones.[42]

The discussion of Republican structure in Chapter 3 called attention to the greater tendency of the Republicans toward fragmentation and shifting of the lines of cleavage from issue to issue and suggested this as possibly characteristic of the unprogrammed and looser situation of a minority party.[43] The indicated relationships between Wherry and Saltonstall point in the same direction. Unlike the Majority Leader, Senator Wherry could hardly have placed substantial reliance on the Whip for assistance in effectuating a program, assuming his desire to develop one. One suspects that there is little inclination in that direction within a minority party, especially if the White House also flies the majority's pennant, and that Wherry and Saltonstall went about as far in the direction of accommodation as their minority situation required, which, as these comments indicate, was not very far.

A Minority Leader with stronger aspirations toward the development of a coherent program and record for his party, yet faced with the virtual impossibility of close collaboration with the Whip, as was the case here, might look elsewhere for reliable and congenial lieutenants. He might, for instance, use each seniority leader as an assistant or colleague on all legislation coming from his committee. Just as the device of reliance on the seniority leaders has apparently been a characteristic practice of relatively unaggressive Floor Leaders, both

---

Saltonstall. Thus, although a number of the votes on which they agreed were ones on which the prevailing side was made up of majorities of both parties, the incidence of such nonparty votes among their agreements was slightly lower in 3 cases out of 4 than in the sets as a whole. The exception was the high-cohesion set of the first session, that on which the Republicans were most cohesive (Table 1). In other words, they were somewhat more likely, on 3 of the 4 sets, to agree, if at all, when a majority of their colleagues opposed a majority of the Democrats.

[42] Note the occurrence of votes such as the following among the Wherry-Saltonstall agreements: support of an amendment to the 1950 Revenue Act reducing the holding period for capital gains taxation from six to three months, a number of public works votes, opposition to two foreign aid amendments aimed at encouraging European integration, support of a number of "economy" amendments on several domestic and a few foreign issues, and support of several amendments restricting cooperative, middle-income housing. This interpretation is also consistent with the tendency, noted in chap. 3, for Wherry's bloc to cast "die-hard" votes, especially in the low-cohesion sets.

[43] Above, chap. 3, pp. 82–86.

minority and majority, so its use by Wherry, faced with an uncongenial Whip, would seem rather to promote segmentation than to encourage program coherence. Alternatively a Minority Leader in this kind of predicament might find compensation for his estrangement from the Whip in his relations with the other elective leaders. Or, as seems possible in Wherry's case, one or more of the latter might informally supplant either or both Leader and Whip. Their ability to do so, however, would depend on the roles of these other leaders. What of the behavior of the other elective leaders on the Republican side in the Eighty-first Congress? How did it compare with the voting of their opposite numbers among the Democrats?

OTHER ELECTIVE LEADERS

As a group the elective leaders among the Senate Republicans were much less cohesive than were the Democrats. Comparisons here are to be drawn with caution, not only because of differences in the distribution of the principal offices within the two parties but also because of the generally lower cohesion of the Republican party in the Eighty-first Congress (Table 1). Allowing for the latter qualification, however, the disunity among the Republican leaders is still evident. The mean scores and number of complete agreements listed in Table 19 indicate that the elective leaders on the majority side were about as unified on the low-cohesion votes as the minority leaders were on the high-cohesion votes. If Senator Saltonstall, the most deviant of the Republicans, is omitted from the calculations, the number of agreements among the remaining five minority leaders is increased considerably, but the means of the scores between the pairs of Republicans are altered very little. If, on the other hand, the most deviant of the Democrats, Senator McKellar, is omitted, the contrast between the majority and minority is enhanced.

The number of votes each Republican elective leader cast in opposition to a majority of the party on each of the four sets of votes may be taken as a rough measure of how central his position was in the party structure. These figures, assembled in Table 20, indicate that of the four principal Republican leaders Millikin was consistently, though by fairly narrow margins, nearer the center of the party than either Wherry or Saltonstall. Taft's record on this score was less strong, in large measure because he, more than any of the other Republican leaders was likely to agree fairly frequently with Saltonstall, especially on

Table 19

RELATIVE COHESION OF REPUBLICAN AND DEMOCRATIC ELECTIVE LEADERS,
81ST CONGRESS, SENATE

	Republicans		Democrats	
	Six Leaders	Five* Leaders	Five Leaders	Four† Leaders
Low-cohesion votes				
First Session				
Mean score	30.1	34.4	42.7	47.6
Number of complete agreements	5	11	24	42
Second Session				
Mean score	31.6	34.3	40.9	49.2
Number of complete agreements	5	18	21	42
High-cohesion votes				
First Session				
Mean score	44.3	44.7	68.1	68.8
Number of complete agreements	33	46	68	69
Second Session				
Mean score	43.3	45.8	52.5	54.3
Number of complete agreements	23	38	56‡	55‡

* Excluding the most deviant member, Senator Saltonstall.

† Excluding the most deviant member, Senator McKellar.

‡ There were 73 roll calls in the Democratic high-cohesion set of the second session. In all other sets there were 74. The reason for there being one more "complete agreement" among the five elective leaders than in the smaller group of four is that in both groups the same two men were "absent" on one roll call. Since "complete agreement" was defined to include agreement among all in a group who were recorded, provided at least half were recorded, this roll call was counted as an "agreement" in the larger group but not in the smaller.

MEAN SCORE: the mean of the number of agreements between all pairs in the group.

COMPLETE AGREEMENTS: includes all roll calls in the set on which the group was unanimous plus all those on which less than half the group were unrecorded and the remainder were unanimous.

the low-cohesion votes.[44] By way of cautious comparison, Lucas, who was not the most central figure in the Democratic party, voted against a majority of the Democrats on the low-cohesion votes only 18 times in

---

[44] Senators Brewster and Butler can be ignored in this comparison not only because their posts were less important but also because both, especially Brewster, had very high "absence" rates. Over the four sets, 296 roll calls, Butler was "absent" on 11.5 per cent and Brewster on 22.3 per cent.

Table 20

LEADERSHIP OF THE REPUBLICAN CENTER: NUMBER OF VOTES AGAINST
MAJORITY OF THE PARTY CAST BY SIX ELECTIVE LEADERS, 81ST CONGRESS,
SENATE

	Wherry	Millikin	Taft	Saltonstall	Butler	Brewster
Low-cohesion votes						
First Session	33	29	27	37	20	18
Second Session	30	24	30	35	26	12
High-cohesion votes						
First Session	14	5	10	16	12	2
Second Session	12	11	15	22	8	3

the first session and only 20 times in the second. On the high-cohesion votes of the first session he never opposed the party majority and he did so only 5 times on the comparable roll calls of the second session. As a group, moreover, the 6 Republican elective leaders were less strong in their support of the party than were their Democratic counterparts. The mean party orthodoxy index for the Republican leaders was 4.05 in the first session and 4.08 in the second; the equivalent means for the Democratic group were 4.52 and 4.34.

The lower mean values of the party orthodoxy index for the Republican leaders and the indications that as a group they were less cohesive than the Democratic leaders reflects not only the generally lower cohesion of the Senate Republicans in this Congress but also the fragmentation of the minority party that has been noted elsewhere. This fragmentation, as the data in Table 19 suggest particularly, was projected into the group of elective leaders and seems not to have been effectively resisted by them. This tendency is particularly marked in the behavior of the Minority Leader. Again the Minority Leader appears as a diehard.[45] Twelve of the 14 votes on which he was against a majority of the Republicans in this set were nonparty votes.

The deficiencies of the Floor Leader apparently were not entirely offset by the efforts of any of his colleagues among the elective leaders.

---

[45] Note especially (Table 20) that Senator Wherry cast more votes against the majority of his party and was in this respect farther from the position of Senator Millikin on the high-cohesion votes of the first session than he was on the equivalent votes of the second session. Yet the earlier set had a higher mean index of cohesion for the party as a whole than any of the remaining three. This set also had the highest proportion of votes on which the prevailing side in the Senate was made up of a majority of both parties.

Millikin and, to a lesser degree, Taft were somewhat less eccentric than Wherry. Either or both provided more support for Wherry than did the Whip. Both of them, but judging from these data especially Millikin, may have supplied the Republicans in the Senate with a more effective and a more acceptable leadership than that of either Wherry or Saltonstall. But, if the evidence of the record votes can be relied upon, they did not do so to an extent sufficient to give them a position in the party as central as that occupied by the principal elective leaders among the Democrats. The party orthodoxy indexes of Taft and Millikin in both sessions were lower than those of any of the five Democratic elective leaders.[46]

If the mean scores of the elective leaders in both parties are compared with those in the principal blocs identified in the preceding chapter (Tables 3, 4, 6, 7, 10, 11, 13, and 14), it becomes evident that collectively these leaders agreed with one another less frequently than did senators in the major blocs. Apparently, therefore, at least on substantive policy matters, neither group of elective leaders functioned collectively as a unified and disciplined spearhead of the party. This conclusion, moreover, applies with particular relevance to the Chairman of the Campaign Committee and the Chairman of the (Majority) Patronage Committee. If these roles were used as a means of discipline, the evidence for this is not given by the roll calls. The elective leaders were split, especially the Republicans, by the same issues and to much the same degree as was the party as a whole. On the low-cohesion votes they did not, for example, present the appearance of an integrated cadre holding an agreed line against the threat of cleavage within the party. The leaders of the majority, with the exception of Senator McKellar, at least belonged to the same bloc within the party. The minority leaders, however, were distributed over the whole range of the party structure. Among the minority the scores of only one pair of leaders, Wherry and Butler, approached those of the Majority Leader and his Whip, and their rate of agreement seems likely to have reflected the marked tendency, evident in both parties, toward identi-

---

[46] It is perhaps unnecessary to add the precaution that these inferences apply to the record of the Congress as a whole, not to particular measures. On individual bills or votes it is more than likely that both Taft and Millikin were highly influential within their party and in the Senate generally, but as much might also be said of a senator who occupied no post in the party hierarchy. The concern here is with the general pattern of party leadership and behavior, and on this score it does not appear that Millikin or Taft entirely compensated for Wherry's shortcomings.

cal voting by senators from the same state rather than a concerted discharge of leadership obligations.[47]

The implications of this admittedly tenuous evidence are principally two. First, the comparatively low level of agreement among the elective leaders of both parties suggests again the singular role of the Floor Leader, one which, if not adequately performed by the incumbent, is not likely to be fully absorbed on a continuing basis by others in the formal leadership hierarchy, and which need not be shared by the other elective leaders to the extent of identical voting on most roll calls. Second, although the considerably lower level of agreement among the Republican elective leaders may in part reflect both their different formal organization and the generally lower cohesion of the party in this Congress, it also raises again the possibility that fragmentation and fluidity of voting patterns may be a tendency peculiarly characteristic of a minority party.

THE POLICY COMMITTEES

If the voting of the individual elective leaders shows slight tendency toward solidarity, even less can be said of the Majority and Minority Policy Committees. These party organs in the Senate were established by law in 1947 for "the formulation of over-all legislative policy of the respective parties." [48]

If the Senate parties conformed to the misleading stereotype of a legislative party as a completely disciplined group, one would expect that the party Policy Committees would display a high degree of cohesion. One might even entertain this expectation as a contingent possibility in the face of the evident fact that the legislative parties in the Congress, though they display real differences in central tendency and enjoy a corporate existence that is not simply formal, are rather deeply divided internally.

---

[47] Lucas and Myers voted the same way on 79.5 per cent of the 295 roll calls in the four Democratic sets. Wherry and Butler agreed on 78 per cent of the 296 Republican votes, Taft and Saltonstall on 57.5 per cent, Wherry and Millikin on 57 per cent, Millikin and Taft on 51.6 per cent, Wherry and Taft on 50.6 per cent, and Wherry and Saltonstall on 36.5 per cent.

[48] As it passed the Senate, the Legislative Reorganization Act of 1946 carried a provision for such committees in both House and Senate. The provision was deleted in the House, but in 1947 the Senate committees were established by an item in the appropriation for the legislative branch in the First Supplemental Appropriation Act passed in the second session of the Seventy-ninth Congress (60 *U. S. Stat. at L.* [1947], 911).

As the evidence presented below will demonstrate, the Policy Committee of neither party in the Eighty-first Congress fitted this expectation. It would be tempting and easy, therefore, to dismiss them as meaningless formalities. This interpretation seems somewhat too hasty. Places on the Policy Committee are coveted by many senators. Since the establishment of the Committees in 1947 several attempts have been made in both parties to enlarge or otherwise to alter their composition. In 1953, for example, Senator Capehart of Indiana led an abortive movement to require that the Republican Policy Committee include the chairmen of all standing committees, only three of whom were then members.[49] If the Policy Committees were without meaning or function in the party and in the Senate, it is unlikely that incidents such as these would occur. What, then, can be said of these bodies? Judging from the voting patterns in the Eighty-first Congress, how are their functions to be interpreted?

The low frequency of agreement within the Committees is indicated clearly in Table 21. Comparison of the majority and minority is hazardous, both because of the difference in the size of the two groups and because of variations in the "absence" rate. Bearing these factors in mind, however, it appears that the Minority Policy Committee, like the Republican elective leaders, were a good deal less cohesive than their Democratic counterparts. The difference probably was of slight consequence, for neither displayed much unity. If Table 21 is compared with Table 19, it will be evident that, however poor the record of the elective leaders on this score, that of the Policy Committees was even less impressive.

The handful of votes on which the Minority Policy Committee was agreed are of no significance. All five were roll calls carried by rather lopsided bipartisan majorities. The agreements within the Majority Policy Committee are somewhat more interesting, and some of them suggest the bare possibility of consensus on substantive policy.[50] There

---

[49] *New York Times,* September 15, 1953.

[50] For example, in the first session: They supported a Kerr amendment to the Interior Appropriation Bill aimed at a compromise between public and private power advocates over funds for the Southwestern Power Administration; they supported a move to refer to the Foreign Relations Committee, and thus kill, Wherry's resolution calling on the President to halt the dismantling of German war plants; they opposed Morse's proposal in connection with the cloture issue to limit debate by simple majority vote. In the second session: They supported Lucas's vain effort to substitute detention for registration provisions in the Internal Security Act; they opposed a move by McCarran to refer to his Judiciary Committee the bill setting up a uniform code of military justice, reported by the Armed Services Committee; they supported a compromise provision in the Omnibus Ap-

Table 21

RELATIVE COHESION OF MAJORITY AND MINORITY POLICY COMMITTEES,
81ST CONGRESS, SENATE

	Majority (Democrats)*	Minority (Republicans)†
Low-cohesion votes		
First Session		
Mean score	37.4	32.3
Number of complete agreements	5	0
Second Session		
Mean score	39.7	27.0‡
Number of complete agreements	2	1
High-cohesion votes		
First Session		
Mean score	51.9	43.3
Number of complete agreements	28	3
Second Session		
Mean score	46.9	29.8‡
Number of complete agreements	20	1

* The 8 members of the Majority Policy Committee were: Lucas of Illinois, chairman, Green of Rhode Island, Hill of Alabama, McMahon of Connecticut, Myers of Pennsylvania, O'Mahoney of Wyoming, Russell of Georgia, and Tydings of Maryland.

† The 11 members of the Minority Policy Committee were: Taft of Ohio, chairman, Bridges of New Hampshire, Cordon of Oregon, Hickenlooper of Iowa, Ives of New York, Millikin of Colorado, Saltonstall of Massachusetts, Smith of Maine, Vandenberg of Michigan, Wherry of Nebraska, and Young of North Dakota.

‡ Senator Vandenberg was "absent" on 98 of the 148 votes included in the second-session sets. If he were excluded from the calculations for that session, the mean scores of the remaining 10 members would be: low-cohesion, 29.2; high-cohesion, 34.5.

MEAN SCORE: The mean of the number of agreements between all pairs in the group.

COMPLETE AGREEMENTS: Includes all roll calls in the set on which the group was unanimous plus those on which less than half the group were unrecorded and the remainder were unanimous.

were, however, many more votes equally significant in policy terms, some in the very same policy areas, on which they were not agreed.

propriation Bill authorizing a loan rather than an outright grant of E. C. A. funds to Spain; and they supported a Long amendment to the social security bill designed to provide coverage for the disabled.

Many of their agreements were on patently trivial matters, and virtually all of those bearing the earmarks of policy consensus fell in the high- rather than the low-cohesion sets.

If the Committee were functioning as a unified source of cues on substantive policy, one would expect that a significant proportion of its agreements would occur when the party itself was not very unified. There were instances of this sort, but on the average the indexes of cohesion for the party on the votes on which the Policy Committee were agreed were about the same as for the set as a whole, indicating the likelihood that agreement within the Committee reflected at least as often as it influenced the cohesion of the party.[51] *In a relatively undisciplined party* one would expect the means of the party cohesion indexes to be consistently lower on those votes on which a Policy Committee agreed than on a sample such as one of these sets, if the Committee were with some frequency setting substantive policy. If they were markedly lower, the Committee obviously would be out of step with the party; if they were very much higher, it would be performing no policy function at all, being less unified than the party itself. (This seems to have been the situation with the Minority Policy Committee in this Congress, given the almost complete absence of agreements, even on the high-cohesion sets.) When, as here, the means are practically identical, the only firm inference is that, though the Committee *may* be providing voting cues, this is a minimal function and typically it is mirroring tendencies within the party.

The record of the Majority Policy Committee was even rather spotty on those votes on which the scheduling function was at stake. On two of the three such roll calls listed earlier in this chapter the Committee was divided five to three, and there was one dissenter on the third.[52] There were two more such votes, in the high-cohesion set of the first session, on both of which the Policy Committee voted as a unit, "absentees" excluded. One was a motion by Ellender of Louisiana that the Senate recess during the debate on public power funds in the Interior Department Appropriation Bill, a move aimed at deferring action until more opponents of public power were present. This the Committee solidly and successfully opposed. The second was on

---

[51] On the high-cohesion votes: first session, the mean index of cohesion for the party on the whole set was 73.09, on the 28 votes on which the Committee were agreed, 74.96; second session, the equivalent means were, on the whole set, 62.6, and on the 20 votes on which the Committee agreed, 62.3.

[52] See note 16, above. The lone dissent occurred on the Capehart motion that the House and Senate adjourn *sine die* at the end of September, 1949. Tydings was the only member of the Committee to support the motion. The splits on the other two votes were not identical.

a motion by Lucas, after the Senate had overridden the Vice President's ruling that cloture could be applied to a motion to take up a bill, that the Senate adjourn until the next day. The Committee—and all but four members of the party—voted with Lucas to carry the motion, one which normally would not have been brought to a record vote.

One is thus forced to the conclusion that neither the Majority nor the Minority Policy Committee was characterized by consensus on substantive legislative matters. Even the Majority Committee did not function with marked frequency as a unified source of cues to guide the voting of the remainder of the party. Despite some contrasts between the two Committees, both seem to have constituted not the sources of substantive policy guidance, but means of representing the geographic and bloc structure of their parties. And here, one suspects, lies the explanation for the seeming paradox that while the Policy Committee does not seem to establish a consensus on the substance of policy, at the same time, judging by the apparent attractiveness of belonging to it, it is an important element in the life of the party and of the Senate.

An explanation for the significance of the Policy Committees leads again into the nature of the legislative party as a group and in turn into the peculiarities of the governmental process, especially at the national level. Finally, it points once more to the pivotal position of the Floor Leader, if he chooses and is able to exploit the potentialities of his role. If the proposition is correct that, from the standpoint of its members, the legislative party is a mediate group of which the individual member is comparatively independent, the likelihood is strong that any reasonably conscientious and alert senator will place a premium upon knowing what is going on within the group and upon gaining access to those places in the group where such communication occurs and where decisions may be taken affecting matters in which he is interested or upon which he must take a position. Between the standing committees, in whose intimate concerns he usually cannot share unless he is a member, and the floor of the Senate, where designs usually transpire too late for the individual senator not already "in the know" to do more than arrive at his own view of them, there is no institutionalized spot except the Policy Committee where such information is regularly available.[53] The Committee does not monopolize the

---

[53] Despite impressions to the contrary, the uniform testimony of informants in and around the Senate is that, while bills may be "written on the floor" in the sense that the fortunes of measures and amendments are settled there, rarely is a design incorporated into a bill unless it has been developed well in advance, with or without the cooperation of the leaders.

intelligence function. Important sources of information are available in the cloakrooms, in the office of the Secretary of the Senate, in the suites of prominent senators, and elsewhere. But these are unregularized and usually segmental, whereas the Policy Committee, through its regular meetings, through the investigations of its staff, and through its discussions of the Senate agenda, is an institutionalized communications center.

When the President is of the same party, the Policy Committee is also strategically placed as a source of White House preferences and intentions, given the regular practice of weekly conferences between the President and one or more key members of the Committee. In a governmental system in which the executive branch bulks large and in which the influence structures that determine public policy are varied and shifting,[54] information on the plans of the President and his staff is a major asset. Hence membership on the Committee has value over and above any policy decisions that it may make.[55]

The decisions of the Policy Committees, especially the Majority Committee, again point to the importance of the Floor Leader and perhaps his immediate associates. Decisions in the Committees typically are not registered by formal vote but are reached, after discussion, by consensus which may or may not be formally stated by the chairman. In the case of the Democrats, if they have a reasonably aggressive Floor Leader, the choices on schedule matters are characteristically his, guided to the extent he chooses by the advice of the representative elements on the Committee. Thus informants close to the Majority Committee in the Eighty-first Congress indicate that the Southerners on the Committee "went along" with Lucas's feeling that he had to call up F.E.P.C. and the revision of the cloture rule even though they were going to oppose passage of the measures. Among the Republicans an aggressive Majority Leader or one working closely

---

[54] David B. Truman, *The Governmental Process: Political Interests and Public Opinion*, New York: Alfred A. Knopf, 1951, chap. 11 and *passim*.

[55] When a party is in the minority in the Senate, the communications function presumably becomes the chief if not the only importance of the Committee, especially if the minority "party" controls the White House, as with the Republicans in the Eighty-fourth and Eighty-fifth Congresses. The Committee's influence over the Senate schedule becomes minimal, but as an information source its position is relatively enhanced. Presumably this was the major reason for the decision of the Republicans at the opening of the Eighty-fourth Congress to increase the size of the Policy Committee from 11 to 24, to include on it all members of the party up for re-election in 1956, and informally to permit any Senate Republican to attend those meetings at which the leaders reported on their weekly conferences with President Eisenhower. (See note 15; also see *New York Times*, January 12, 1955.)

with the chairman of the Committee can operate with the Committee in much the same way.[56]

Membership on the Policy Committee thus may be presumed to have value because it provides access both to an important communication center and to the decisions of the Floor Leader, especially the Majority Leader. Any senator in the legislative party presumably must enjoy access to the Floor Leader in some degree, but as a member of the Policy Committee he has it on a generalized basis and as a sort of institutional right, which may be a very different thing.

As earlier comments have indicated, moreover, the Floor Leader's influence over the Senate's agenda need not be a purely routine matter. And it need not stop at scheduling. He can go back to the standing committees to learn the direction and rate of their deliberations on a bill. Through the chairman or even directly to the whole committee he can, and in some instances does, influence not only the timing but even the substance of their actions, using the admittedly limited sanctions involved in the scheduling function and more characteristically his key position in the communications network. By these activities, in turn, his own importance as a source of information is enhanced, and by skillful use of staff, his own and that of the Policy Committee, it may be further extended.[57]

Despite superficial anomalies, therefore, it may not be unreasonable to say that the Policy Committee is properly named, though its actions, including the votes of its members, may not fit a layman's blueprint but rather reflect the peculiar group character of the legislative party. Its importance rests principally upon its value as a center of communication and upon its connections with the Floor Leader's part in setting

---

[56] In this connection the following comments by William S. White are relevant. Concerning the Eightieth Congress he says, "The policy committee became famous, where it had been rather pedestrian before. After each of its meetings, in which rarely was anything so binding as an actual vote on policy taken, Taft [Chairman of the Committee] was careful to announce that it was his 'impression' that this or that had been 'the general view' of the session. This unexpected regard for the sensibilities of other Senators (which did not come naturally, ever, to Taft) fooled nobody. It became, and pretty correctly so, the custom to consider Taft *as* the policy committee." And, concerning the Eighty-third Congress, in which Taft assumed the majority leadership, he comments, ". . . though Taft continued to sit in the Policy Committee he was careful never to attempt to run it out of hand and always to leave its functioning to Chairman Knowland. Taft . . . really kept on making policy but now he made it elsewhere." (White, *The Taft Story*, pp. 60–61 and 256.)

[57] There is a widespread view about the Senate that much of Lyndon Johnson's effectiveness as a Floor Leader lies in his use of staff in this way. By some it is even referred to as a spy system.

the Senate schedule, but in a group of this sort this may be far from trivial.[58]

THE SENIORITY LEADERS

Wilson's classic description of government at the national level in the 1880's made the bipartisan standing committees and their imperious chairmen, if not the villains, at least the chief actors in a spectacle of political depravity. The seniority leaders, removable only by their heavenly Maker or their collective earthly ones, by his account acted in magnificent disregard of one another, often in jealous hostility, and, none among them or among their colleagues standing acknowledged as leader, the legislative party could never speak with a single voice. The opening pages of this chapter suggested that the functioning of the congressional party may have changed more in the seven decades since Wilson wrote than most contemporary estimates indicate. Subsequent sections have described the Floor Leader and particularly the Majority Leader as the pivotal element in the legislative party and as in some measure the voice that was silent in the days of Wilson's initial study.[59] This he seems to be in the potentialities of his role if not always in the actuality of his performance.

The seniority leader, however, whether committee chairman or his heir-apparent on the minority side, remains a figure of obvious power, especially in his ability, when chairman, to delay or prevent action. His place in the party structure, therefore, must be established. Is Wilson's charge of independence and nonconcurrence still valid? What of the relations between the seniority leader and the Floor Leader? What evidence is there of collaboration between them? Or conflict? For, even if there are to be grounds for modifying the Wilsonian view, one would still expect the leaders of an imperfectly disciplined party to differ on occasion. Who prevails when they fall out? What answers to these questions are suggested by the record votes of the Eighty-first Congress?

---

[58] The best published comment on the Senate Policy Committees is to be found in Hugh A. Bone, "An Introduction to the Senate Policy Committees," *American Political Science Review*, Vol. 50, no. 2 (June 1956), pp. 339–359. Bone's conclusions differ somewhat from those outlined here.

[59] For a thoughtful, provocative, and informed analysis of the contemporary Congress, which slightly modifies the early Wilsonian interpretation in a way different from but not inconsistent with that proposed here, see Dean Acheson, *A Citizen Looks at Congress*, New York: Harper and Brothers, 1956.

Table 22

RELATIVE COHESION OF THE DEMOCRATIC AND REPUBLICAN SENIORITY
LEADERS, 81ST CONGRESS, SENATE

	Democrats	Republicans
Low-cohesion votes		
First Session		
Mean score	27.8	28.9
Number of complete agreements	0	0
Second Session		
Mean score	33.4	27.4*
Number of complete agreements	0	0
High-cohesion votes		
First Session		
Mean score	43.1	36.2
Number of complete agreements	1	4
Second Session		
Mean score	41.0	29.5*
Number of complete agreements	5	3

* Senator Vandenberg was "absent" on 98 of the 148 votes included in the second-session sets. If he were excluded from the calculations for that session, the mean scores of the remaining Republicans would be: low-cohesion, 29.5; high-cohesion, 33.4.

MEAN SCORE: The mean of the number of agreements between all pairs in the group.

COMPLETE AGREEMENTS: Includes all roll calls in the set on which the group was unanimous plus all those on which less than half the group were unrecorded and the remainder were unanimous.

Judging from the voting structure of the two parties in the Senate, no reason exists for revising Wilson's conclusion that the seniority leaders do not function as a collegial body. If they consult, they do not concur. In both parties, in both sessions, and on both low- and high-cohesion votes, they were distributed throughout the bloc structure.[60] Even more than the elective leaders, especially among the Democrats, they appear as individuals, acting in response to variations in personal ideology, region, or constituency rather than to the demands of a collective leadership role. Even on the high-cohesion votes, on which the elective leaders tended to be relatively cohesive, a considerable number of the seniority leaders were still to be found in one of the extreme wings of the party.

[60] See Tables 3, 4, 6, 7, 10, 11, 13, 14.

The same conclusion emerges from an examination of those roll calls on which the seniority leaders were in agreement, as Table 22 indicates. The mean scores of the seniority leaders were generally lower than those of either the elective leaders or the Policy Committees, and on almost no votes were the ranking committee personnel within each party agreed among themselves.[61] Allowing for the differences between the two parties in the general level of cohesion, the seniority leaders on the majority side were generally somewhat more cohesive than the ranking Republican committee members, with the marked exception of the low-cohesion votes of the first session. The prominence of several Democratic seniority leaders in the opposing blocs in this set made the mean scores of the whole group unusually low.

The substance of the agreements among the Republican seniority leaders is of some interest. Six of the 7 were roll calls on which a majority of one party was opposed to a majority of the other, whereas only 4 of the 6 Democratic agreements were on such party votes. The Republican agreements, moreover, have some coherence. Four of the 7 were votes to cut appropriations, 2 were in support of Senator Wherry's efforts to bar foreign aid funds to countries trading behind the Iron Curtain, and one opposed a ban on time studies of workers in naval establishments and those working on Navy contracts. In contrast, the Democratic agreements covered 3 attempts by Senator Douglas to cut ship construction subsidies, one hotly contested but minor flood control authorization, and the votes on passage and adoption of the conference report on the Internal Security Act, both of which were lopsided bipartisan votes. The Republican votes thus suggest some minimal tendency toward the programmatic, but the number of agreements is too low to justify altering the inference of general nonconcurrence.

Since collegial action by the seniority leaders in the Senate was for all practical purposes nonexistent in the Eighty-first Congress, it is clear that any significance in the relations between the Majority or Minority Floor Leader, on the one hand, and the ranking committee members, on the other, must be sought in the connections between the former and the latter taken as individuals rather than as a group. That is, a Floor Leader who, for whatever reason, interpreted his role as permitting or requiring him to be the "voice" of his party in the Senate, to be in some sense the trustee of the party's record, and, therefore, to pro-

---

[61] Compare Tables 19 and 21, above. As noted earlier, for purposes of tabulations such as those in Table 22 Senators Hayden and McKellar were included among the Democratic seniority leaders and Senators Butler, Millikin, Taft, and Wherry among the Republican seniority leaders.

mote a substantive legislative program, would be likely to work with the individual seniority leader on the measures being handled by his committee. In a relatively undisciplined party an aggressive Floor Leader would attempt to achieve agreement with the appropriate seniority leader on the form of reported bills and on floor strategy, would try to further the agreed matter in the Senate, and would support it with his own vote. If this were the case, it would then follow, given members' independence in a mediate group such as a Senate party, that the individual seniority leaders would agree with the Leader more frequently on votes dealing with measures reported by their committees than on other record votes. This would apply particularly to seniority leaders belonging to a wing of the party other than that with which the Leader was identified.

Looking first at the Democrats, it is clear from Table 23 that the

Table 23

AGREEMENTS BETWEEN SENATE MAJORITY LEADER AND COMMITTEE CHAIRMEN ON VOTES CONCERNING MEASURES REPORTED BY THEIR COMMITTEES AND ON ALL OTHER VOTES, 81ST CONGRESS, 1ST AND 2ND SESSIONS

	Agreements on Committee Measures* (per cent)	Agreements on Other Votes† (per cent)
Low-cohesion votes	43.6	36.7
High-cohesion votes	80.7	66.2

* In the low-cohesion sets, based on 140 roll calls; 6 votes on measures from the District of Columbia Committee were omitted because of a change of chairmen midway in the first session, and two adjournment votes were not assigned to a committee. In the high-cohesion sets, based on 145 roll calls; two votes on measures referred to both the Foreign Relations Committee and the Armed Services Committee were included, in the votes of both chairmen; two recess motions and two votes on a resolution not referred to committee were omitted.

† In the low-cohesion sets, based on 1784 votes, those of each of the 13 committee chairmen on all 148 roll calls, minus those on measures reported by his committee. In the high-cohesion sets, based on 1913 votes, handled in the same way for the 147 votes in the sets, for each of 14 chairmen of committees votes on whose measures fell into these sets.

proposition holds in general, somewhat more strongly on the high- than on the low-cohesion votes, as might be expected. However, the details underlying the table show that the pattern was not consistent from one seniority leader to another, especially on the low-cohesion votes. In these sets the differences were insignificant or the individual proportions were actually lower on committee measures than on other votes in the cases of seven of the thirteen chairmen. In the cases of George (Finance) and Johnston of South Carolina (Post Office and Civil Service) the differences were slight. Johnson of Colorado (Interstate and Foreign Commerce), McCarran (Judiciary), and McClellan (Expenditures in the Executive Departments) clearly were inconsistent with the hypothesis; the level of agreements between them and the Majority Leader was uniformly low, but lower on measures coming from their committees than on other roll calls. The other two exceptions, Chavez (Public Works) and Hayden (Rules) are rather surprising, since one would not expect two chairmen in the Leader's bloc to disagree with him so frequently on votes dealing with the affairs of their committees.[62] The voting of three chairmen from the "right" wing of the party, Connally (Foreign Relations), Maybank (Banking and Currency), and McKellar (Appropriations), was entirely consistent with the hypothesis. Each of these members of the "right" wing agreed with Lucas more often on committee measures than on other votes, and it is also significant that Thomas of Utah (Labor and Public Welfare) and Tydings of Maryland (Armed Services), both of whom were in or relatively close to the "left" wing of the party, voted more often with Lucas (or he with them) on measures from their committees than on the other roll calls.

The evidence in Table 23 on the high-cohesion sets more strongly supports the hypothesis. The data underlying the summary figures indicate that 12 of the 14 individual patterns were in the expected direction. Thomas of Oklahoma, whose voting on the low-cohesion sets was somewhat ambiguous, again turned up in the deviant column, and Chavez again displayed a fairly anomalous record on the public works votes.[63]

Given the evidence in Chapter 3 indicating a structural looseness and an unprogrammed character in the voting of the minority party and given also the data in the present chapter suggesting that the Minority

---

[62] The nonagreements between Lucas and Hayden all involved votes on changes in the cloture rule in the first session. The explanation for Chavez's behavior, which was highly consistent, may lie in a tendency for public works legislation to be a law unto itself, unrelated to any general program, and comparatively impervious to the initiatives of outside leadership. (See below, Table 27, and accompanying text.)

[63] Thomas's record on these votes does not seriously challenge the proposition, since the four differences between him and Lucas (who was also a member of the Committee on Agriculture and Forestry) were non-agreements rather than disagreements, one or the other of them having been "absent" on all four.

Leader interpreted his role in rather narrow terms and was somewhat less effective than his Democratic opposite-number, one would expect that the record of accommodation between Senator Wherry and the Republican seniority leaders would be a good deal less marked than that on the Democratic side.[64] Table 24 indicates that this was indeed

Table 24

AGREEMENTS BETWEEN SENATE MINORITY LEADER AND REPUBLICAN SEN-
IORITY LEADERS ON VOTES CONCERNING MEASURES REPORTED BY THEIR
COMMITTEES AND ON ALL OTHER VOTES, 81ST CONGRESS, 1ST AND 2ND
SESSIONS

	Agreements on Committee Measures* (per cent)	Agreements on Other Votes† (per cent)
Low-cohesion votes	32.4	44.2
High-cohesion votes	51.4	49.6

* In the low-cohesion sets, based on 142 roll calls; one vote from the Joint Committee on Atomic Energy was excluded because of a change in seniority leaders, 2 votes from the Rules Committee were omitted since Wherry himself was ranking minority member, and 3 votes were on resolutions not referred to committee. In the high-cohesion sets, based on 144 roll calls; 4 concerning the Committee on Rules were excluded, since this was Wherry's committee.

† In the low-cohesion sets, based on 1634 votes, those of each of the 12 seniority leaders on all 148 roll calls, minus those on measures reported by his committee. In the high-cohesion sets, based on 1484 votes; these were handled in the same way for the 148 votes in the sets, for each of the 11 seniority leaders of committees, votes on whose measures fell into these sets.

the case, especially in the low-cohesion votes. At the same time, the data underlying the table show some signs of a pattern of accommodation in individual cases.

On both low- and high-cohesion sets some evidence suggests that Wherry achieved some sort of *modus operandi* with Aiken (Agricul-

---

[64] There is difficulty in applying the general proposition concerning relations between the Floor Leader and the individual seniority leaders to the minority party, even speculatively, principally because the ranking minority member of a committee normally has less leverage on his colleagues than does the chairman. He does not control the committee agenda, for example, and for this and other similar reasons there may be a good deal less incentive for the Floor Leader to seek him out. If the structural looseness of the minority party in this Congress were found to be a normal thing, the different position of the minority seniority leaders might well be one reason—but only one—for this pattern and for a tendency toward lack of program.

ture and Forestry), Bridges (Appropriations, Armed Services), and even Tobey (Banking and Currency, Interstate and Foreign Commerce), all of whom were in varying degrees identified with the wing of the party that normally opposed Wherry. This was conspicuously not the case, however, with Vandenberg (Foreign Relations) and Wiley (Judiciary). Even allowing for "absences," the low level of agreement with the ranking minority members of the Foreign Relations and Judiciary Committees was marked. Wherry, moreover, unlike the Majority Leader, seems not to have worked out a strong pattern of agreement with many of the seniority leaders who were in or near his wing of the party, notably Millikin (Finance) and Taft (Labor and Public Welfare), at least on the low-cohesion votes.

The record votes, therefore, provide some support for the proposition that collaboration occurs between the Floor Leader and the individual seniority leaders, especially on the majority side. These data do not, of course, indicate anything about relationships not directly reflected in the roll calls: They say nothing about attempts to modify the provisions of bills reported, to arrange the timing of reports, or to prevent or facilitate placing a measure on the Senate calendar. Nevertheless, the data do indicate the existence of specialized relations between the Floor Leaders and the individual seniority leaders.

A crucial question remains, however. Granting the specialized relations between the Floor Leader and the individual seniority leaders, who in these pairs was the dominant partner? Agreements between Floor Leader and individual seniority leaders are merely indications of association. They can as easily mean that the Leader was "going along" with the committee chairman as that he was guiding the latter along the lines of a more or less coherent program or deliberately working out an accommodation of their differing views. And if the Floor Leader was not exercising a coordinating initiative, he was not speaking as the voice of his party in the Senate but successively with a dozen or more voices. Some measure of the relative strength and influence of the principal elective leader in comparison with the individual seniority leaders is necessary, therefore, before the former's position as party spokesman can be established, even for the Eighty-first Congress.

One indicator of the relative strength of the Floor Leader is provided by those roll calls on which he and the chairman of the committee reporting a measure disagreed. A Leader who was effectively acting as the voice of his party would more often than not carry a majority of his party with him. He might even be expected to have on his side a majority of his party's membership on the committee, and, if he were Majority Leader, his would be more often than not the prevail-

Table 25

FREQUENCY WITH WHICH MAJORITY LEADER WAS ON PREVAILING SIDE IN
THE PARTY, IN THE SENATE, AND AMONG DEMOCRATIC COMMITTEE MEM-
BERS WHEN HE AND COMMITTEE CHAIRMEN DISAGREED ON VOTES CON-
CERNING MEASURES REPORTED BY THEIR COMMITTEES, 81ST CONGRESS, 1ST
AND 2ND SESSIONS

	Number of Dis- agreed Votes	Majority of Party with Leader on:	Majority of Senate with Leader on:	Majority of Committee Democrats		
				with Leader on:	with Chair- man on:	"Absent"* or Evenly Divided on:
140 Low-cohesion roll calls†	66	46	35	32	30	4
145 High-cohesion roll calls‡	18	13	10	12	6	0

* "Absent" means those votes on which half or more of the Democrats on the committee were not recorded.

† Six votes on measures dealt with by the Committee on the District of Columbia were omitted because of a shift in the chairmanship during the first session. Two adjournment votes did not go to committee. The 66 disagreements were distributed among 10 committee chairmen.

‡ Two votes on recess motions and two on a resolution not referred to a committee were excluded. Two votes on measures referred to both the Foreign Relations Committee and the Armed Services Committee were counted for each. The 18 disagreements were distributed among 5 committee chairmen.

ing view in the Senate. Table 25 indicates that the Majority Leader's behavior conformed fairly closely to this expectation. Especially on the low-cohesion votes, on which he voted more often against the views of the seniority leaders than with them (compare Table 23), a majority of the Democrats supported Lucas in approximately five out of every seven instances, and his vote was on the prevailing side in the Senate in more than half the cases. Finally, on those votes on which the majority of Democrats on a committee were recorded, one can conclude that a preponderant element was somewhat more likely to support Lucas than to vote with the chairman, though the inference must be drawn with caution.[65] There were, of course, fewer disagreements between

[65] More than two-thirds of the cases on which committee members voted with Lucas rather than with the chairman involved a single chairman, McCarran of Judiciary. This does not destroy the argument for Leader predominance, but it does suggest that among the members of a committee it occurs primarily in cases where the seniority leader takes an extreme position. The comparable

the chairmen and the Majority Leader on the high-cohesion votes, but on those where there were divergences the same general pattern appeared.

Although, as in the comparable earlier analyses, the number of disagreements with any individual chairman is too small in most cases to permit very confident inferences, a few of the cases that deviate from the general pattern are worth mentioning. Senator George, chairman of the Committee on Finance, is the most interesting of these. Although Lucas did fairly well with the party majority when he disagreed with George, he rarely carried the Senate with him and never the majority of the committee.[66] One suspects that this is an illustration of the outer limits on the Leader's role: George for the most part was his own leader, and Lucas was merely a promising younger member of the committee.[67] Somewhat the same situation may have obtained with McKellar (Appropriations), with Johnson of Colorado (Interstate and Foreign Commerce), and with Hayden (Rules), and it was clearly relevant in the case of Chavez (Public Works), who again was a conspicuous exception to the norm. Public works measures, though they might be an instrument of party discipline, apparently are built on a system of interdependent adjustments that is beyond the reach of the Majority Leader's influence.

The Minority Leader's record on votes on which he disagreed with the ranking Republicans on the standing committees was less impressive, as would be expected, but even Wherry was supported by a majority of his party in at least half the cases. (Table 26.) The Minority Leader was also somewhat less influential with the rank-and-file members of the committees, and of course he was on the prevailing side in the Senate much less often than Lucas. Wherry's relations with

---

record of McCarran on the high-cohesion votes argues for a similar caution in interpreting the evidence there.

[66] Lucas was a member of Finance, but a majority of the Democrats on the committee were from the "right" wing. The other Democratic members were Byrd, Connally, Hoey, Johnson of Colorado, and Kerr.

[67] This presumably is the kind of situation William S. White had in mind when he commented: "There are far-separated times when a chairman loses his moral primacy over his issue or reaches with a majority of his committee a conclusion so starkly and hopelessly at variance with the wishes of the Senate generally that he is overruled. But even then to repudiate his leadership and workmanship is a delicate and queasy task and one not relished by any general Senate majority, however great. If, reluctantly, it is undertaken, the victim is nearly always a lesser committee in the tradition of the Senate, say that on Labor." (White, *Citadel*, pp. 180–181.) These figures would suggest that the event occurs somewhat more frequently than White claims, but they are consistent with his proposition that some chairmen are virtually beyond challenge.

Table 26

FREQUENCY WITH WHICH MINORITY LEADER WAS ON PREVAILING SIDE IN
THE PARTY, IN THE SENATE, AND AMONG REPUBLICAN COMMITTEE MEM-
BERS WHEN HE AND SENIORITY LEADERS DISAGREED ON VOTES CONCERNING
MEASURES REPORTED BY THEIR COMMITTEES, 81ST CONGRESS, 1ST AND 2ND
SESSIONS

	Number of Dis-agreed Votes	Majority of Party with Leader on:	Majority of Senate with Leader on:	Majority of Committee Republicans		
				with Leader on:	"Absent"* with Seniority Leader on:	or Evenly Divided on:
142 Low-cohesion roll calls†	78	39‡	19	33	26	19
144 High-cohesion roll calls§	53	31	9	18	28	7

* "Absent" means those votes on which half or more of the Republicans on the committee were not recorded.

† One vote on a measure reported by the Joint Committee on Atomic Energy omitted
because of a shift in the ranking minority membership during the Congress; 2 votes from
the Rules Committee omitted, since Wherry himself was ranking minority member;
3 votes were on resolutions not referred to a committee. The 78 disagreements were
distributed among 11 seniority leaders.

‡ The party was evenly divided on three additional roll calls.

§ Four votes dealing with reports of the Rules Committee omitted since Wherry was
its ranking Republican member. The 53 disagreements were distributed among nine
seniority leaders.

Taft (Labor and Public Welfare), and to a lesser degree with Millikin
(Finance), are suggestive of the same sort of limitation on the Floor
Leader that was noted earlier in connection with Lucas and George.
Taft, as one might have expected, apparently was his own leader, at
least with respect to the affairs of the committee of which he was the
ranking Republican member.[68]

The independence of Taft suggests the desirability of checking his
relations with the other seniority leaders to see whether the earlier
tentative conclusion is sustained, that Wherry's limitations in his role

---

[68] The solidarity of the Republican members of the Committee on Labor and
Public Welfare behind Taft and against Wherry is not astonishing. The Republicans on it, in addition to Taft, were Aiken, Smith of New Jersey, Morse, and
Donnell. They agreed with Taft on all 11 disagreed votes included in this table;
a majority of the Republicans in the Senate supported Taft on all but one of these.

as Leader were not fully compensated for by the behavior of the Senate's most prominent Republican. Table 27 indicates that, although Taft somewhat more often had the majority of the party with him and was much more frequently on the prevailing side in the Senate when he disagreed with the Republican seniority leaders, his record with the rank-and-file committee members was not materially different from

Table 27

FREQUENCY WITH WHICH SENATOR TAFT, CHAIRMAN OF MINORITY POLICY COMMITTEE, WAS ON PREVAILING SIDE IN THE SENATE, IN THE PARTY, AND AMONG REPUBLICAN COMMITTEE MEMBERS WHEN HE AND SENIORITY LEADERS DISAGREED ON VOTES CONCERNING MEASURES REPORTED BY THEIR COMMITTEES, 81ST CONGRESS, 1ST AND 2ND SESSIONS

	Number of Dis-agreed Votes	Majority of Party with Taft on:	Majority of Senate with Taft on:	Majority of Committee Republicans		
				with Taft on:	with Seniority Leader on:	"Absent"* or Evenly Divided on:
136 Low-cohesion roll calls†	43	25‡	14	21	14	8
138 High-cohesion roll calls§	43	26	16	13	23	7

* "Absent" means those votes on which half or more of the Republicans on the committee were not recorded.

† Excluding one vote from the Joint Committee on Atomic Energy because of a shift in the seniority leadership, 8 votes from the Committee on Labor and Public Welfare, of which Taft was ranking Republican member, and 3 votes on resolutions not referred to a committee. The 43 disagreements were distributed among nine seniority leaders.

‡ On one additional roll call the party was evenly divided.

§ Excluding 10 votes on measures reported by the Committee on Labor and Public Welfare, of which Taft was ranking Republican member. The 43 disagreements were distributed among nine seniority leaders.

Wherry's. These votes, therefore, as far as they go, reaffirm the earlier impression that when the Minority Leader dropped the ball or was unable to carry it, his colleague at the head of the Policy Committee did not fully take over for him. Given the rather slight differences between Wherry and Taft, they also suggest that the contrasts between the Majority and Minority Leaders may not have been entirely a matter of Wherry's peculiarities as an individual. They may also have had something to do with the role of the Minority Leader as such. This inference and the fact that both Taft and Wherry disagreed with the Republican seniority leaders rather more frequently than Lucas with his committee chairmen, even considering the generally lower cohesion of the Republicans, again call attention to the looseness and the un-programmed character of the minority party's voting.

In summary, it is clear that in neither party in the Senate were the seniority leaders functioning as a collegial body. Nonconcurrence was still characteristic of their behavior. Their individual power was evident at various points in these record votes. In consequence, the leadership pattern, especially within the majority party, was a matter of the relations between the Floor Leader and the individual seniority leaders. In these relations the Floor Leader, particularly on the majority side, seems to have spoken as the voice of the party when he and the seniority leaders differed. The Majority Leader, and less frequently his colleague on the minority side, more often than not prevailed within the party, in the Senate, and among the seniority leader's own committee colleagues when there were differences between the leaders on the record votes. The Majority Leader in particular seems to have worked toward accommodation with the individual committee chairmen, and apparently this accommodation was not merely a matter of acting as mouthpiece for the chairmen.

The data on the seniority leaders and, in fact, the inferences from all the analyses in this chapter point to the pivotal character of the Floor Leader's role in the functioning of the legislative party in the Senate. The Majority Leader especially seems to represent, sometimes in cooperation with one or two other elective leaders, a continuous leadership such as is displayed in connection with no other role in the Senate. His behavior seems to emphasize and to reflect the common ties of party, a kind of trusteeship for the party record and for the survival of this somewhat anomalous group. He is supplanted and his efforts are defeated with some frequency by the leadership of other Senators, especially by one or another of the more influential seniority leaders, but this does not occur consistently. The coincidence between the formal and the "real" leadership of the party in the Senate is not perfect, but the evidence of the Eighty-first Congress indicates that more often than not, at least on the majority side, the two are convergent. Even in the minority party much the same pattern exists, though in a muted and less stable form. An attempt to explain further why the Floor Leader's role should have these characteristics, and particularly to indicate why such marked differences should exist between the Majority and Minority Leaders must be deferred until the comparable voting patterns in the House have been explored.

chapter five

DIVISION AND COHESION:

The Structure of Party Voting
in the House of Representatives

The same questions are in order in approaching the problem of the structure of party voting in the House of Representatives as were raised in the analysis of the Senate parties. Did the parties have a reality that was more than simply formal? What were the structural patterns, the constituent cliques and blocs? How were they composed? What was their relative cohesion? How stable were the patterns, both in their personal composition and in the substance of their views? Were there perceptible differences, both of structure and of attitude, between the two parties? Did any of these differences relate to the positions of the majority and the minority as such?

In putting these questions, however, one must constantly keep in mind the commonplace but important fact that in the House they are being raised in a very different context. Institutional life in the two chambers differs in a great many respects and for many reasons, but perhaps the most fundamental of these is also the most obvious: the House has four and one-half times as many members as the Senate. From this schoolboy fact comes the tendency for the formal leadership in the House to correspond closely to the actual; from it also follow the strict controls on debate under the rules and practices of the House, the relative impotence of the rank-and-file representative, and his heavy dependence upon mechanisms such as those provided by the party. These in turn account in large part for the smaller number of record votes in the House, in consequence of which the roll call has a more standardized meaning and a more limited range of uses in the House as compared with the Senate. These are obvious effects of the chamber's size. But there are also many more subtle and less immediate ones, as in the relations of the elective and seniority leaders, some of which will be noted later. They are alluded to here as a general warning against the dangers of ignoring the pervasive consequences of the size difference in comparing the two bodies. The observer who moves from the Senate to the House wing of the Capitol finds himself in a position resembling that of the Westerner on his first visit to the Orient. Prepared for differences from the setting with which he is familiar, he will be continually baffled by behaviors which he sees until he discovers or recalls some simple cultural fact that makes them understandable. The size of the House and its legislative parties is a fact of this simple and basic order.

In analyzing the House, its greater size and its larger parties also dictated some modifications in the procedure that was applied to the Senate. Since the House took only 121 record votes in the first session and 154 in the second, it was impossible to have for each party four sets of 74 votes each, especially as a number of the votes were automatically ruled out of consideration because the party were unanimous on them, because they were explicitly overruled by subsequent votes, or because they dealt with private bills. Accordingly, from the first-session votes of each party a single set of 74 roll calls was drawn, those with the lowest indexes of cohesion. These will be referred to as the intermediate-cohesion set (Table 28). From the second-session roll calls in each party a low-cohesion set of 74 was drawn and a smaller high-cohesion set covering 62 Democratic votes and 66 Republican roll calls. These differences must be kept in mind in making comparisons between the parties and between the House and Senate blocs.

Again, because of the numbers involved, in developing the House matrixes it was deemed wise not to enter agreement scores of as low frequency as those included in the Senate bloc analyses. As noted in an earlier chapter, the use of these higher cut-off points permits a less complete account of the party structure, since a smaller proportion of the members was placed in blocs at these levels.[1] Nevertheless in each case the basic structure of the party was clear by the time these scores had been entered on the matrix. Entering scores lower than these seemed, therefore, to involve an uneconomical expenditure of time, especially as the matrixes, even when thus abbreviated, required accommodations whose proportions began to resemble a sail-maker's loft.[2] These modifications in procedure render impossible precise comparisons of the cohesiveness of House and Senate blocs; they also make it unprofitable to distinguish sharply the "fringe" and "isolate" members among those not included in the identified House blocs. As later sections will indicate, certain of the handicaps imposed by this simplified procedure were reduced by contriving alternative analytical devices.

SOURCES OF CLEAVAGE

The Democrats in the House, unlike their fellow partisans in the Senate, were generally less cohesive than the Republicans, as Table 28 indicates. (Both parties in the House appear more cohesive than those in the Senate, judging from the means of the indexes in the low-cohesion sets shown in Tables 1 and 28. This apparent difference, however, is in part merely a reflection of the House practice of taking fewer record votes at the amending stage of the legislative process.) With the exception of the low-cohesion sets, however, the means of the comparable sets of the two parties in the House are closer than was the case in the Senate.

Within the House there were interesting differences between the parties on the distribution of "party votes"—those on which a majority of Republicans opposed a majority of Democrats. In the Senate they tended in both parties to be slightly more frequent in the high-cohesion sets.[3] In the House, however, party votes were most frequent in the Democratic high-cohesion set and among the Republican low-cohesion votes. It was also the case that the Democratic high-cohesion

---

[1] Above, note 13, chap. 3. In the low- and intermediate-cohesion sets only scores of 46 or higher were entered on the matrix; in the high-cohesion sets scores of 52 or higher were entered for the Democrats and 56 or higher for the Republicans (that is, the top 11 score levels in each case).

[2] For example, the matrix for the Democratic intermediate-cohesion set (first session) included 9508 scores of 46 or higher. The number of scores of 38 or more was 17,375.

[3] See above, note 11, chap. 3.

Table 28

DISTRIBUTION OF PARTY COHESION INDEXES ON SIX SELECTED SETS OF ROLL CALLS, HOUSE OF REPRESENTATIVES, 81ST CONGRESS

	Republican	Democratic
FIRST SESSION		
Intermediate-cohesion set		
Number of roll calls	74	74
Range of indexes	2.2–87.6	0.4–88.4
Mean of indexes	51.01	47.6
Median of indexes	57.05	47.45
SECOND SESSION		
High-cohesion set		
Number of roll calls	66	62
Range of indexes	73.0–98.7	68.6–99.2
Mean of indexes	88.5	86.5
Median of indexes	87.95	89.3
Low-cohesion set		
Number of roll calls	74	74
Range of indexes	2.3–72.9	0.0–67.4
Mean of indexes	43.08	33.3
Median of indexes	45.05	34.6

votes contained a slightly higher proportion of final votes—on passage, adoption of conference reports, and the like—while this type of vote among the House Republicans was somewhat more common among the low-cohesion votes. The Democrats, in other words, tended to be cohesive on these final, ratifying votes, which were likely to be passed over the opposition of a small majority of Republicans, while the Republicans drew together on the preliminary skirmishes over votes on amendments, which were often carried by bipartisan majorities in which slightly over half of the Democrats voted with the Republicans. It would be tempting to infer from this that the Democrats were unified on the "final" votes because they were the responsible majority party and that the Republicans, because they were the minority, were cohesive on the preliminary, modifying proposals but, when the impending result was clear, split between those willing to support the emerging decision and those still opposed to it. However, it would be equally logical to infer that these differences were principally a reflection of the setting and the peculiar issues of the Eighty-first Congress. Analysis of the Eighty-third Congress (1953–1954), in which the Republicans were in the majority, does not show this majority-minority difference, which suggests that the pattern probably had more to do

Table 29

THE SUBSTANCE OF PARTY UNITY AND DISUNITY IN THE HOUSE OF REPRE-
SENTATIVES: DISTRIBUTION OF ROLL CALLS, CLASSIFIED BY SUBJECT, AMONG
HIGH- AND LOW-COHESION SETS AS COMPARED WITH INCIDENCE IN SESSIONS
AS A WHOLE, 81ST CONGRESS

	Subject	
Voting Pattern	Republicans	Democrats
1. High unity (subjects over-repre-sented* in high-cohesion set and under-represented† in low- and intermediate-cohesion sets)	1. Civil rights and internal security 2. Labor 3. Housing 4. Taxation and general appro-priation cuts	1. Foreign policy 2. Agriculture 3. Miscellaneous
2. Unity (subjects slightly over-rep-resented in high-cohesion set and under-represented in low- and in-termediate-cohesion sets)	1. Miscellaneous 2. Foreign policy	1. Foreign aid 2. Public works 3. Taxation and general appro-priation cuts
3. Disunity (subjects slightly under-represented in high-cohesion set and over-represented in low- and intermediate-cohesion sets)		1. Labor 2. Housing
4. High disunity (subjects under-represented in high-cohesion set and over-represented in low- and intermediate-cohesion sets)	1. Foreign aid 2. Agriculture 3. Public works 4. Veterans 5. Economic controls	1. Civil rights and internal security 2. Economic controls 3. District of Columbia
5. Ambiguous (subjects showing no consistent pattern of incidence)	1. Social security 2. District of Columbia 3. General govern-ment organiza-tion	1. Social security 2. Veterans 3. General govern-ment organiza-tion

* OVER-REPRESENTED: proportionately more votes on the subject in the set specified than in the session as a whole.

† UNDER-REPRESENTED: proportionately fewer votes on the subject in the set specified than in the session as a whole.

with the circumstances of 1949–1950 than with the characteristic behavior of majority and minority parties in the House.[4]

Classifying the roll calls into subject-matter categories and comparing the incidence of these categories in the various sets with their incidence in the roll calls of the whole session one can see roughly the
substantive sources of unity and disunity in the two parties (Table 29).
Comparing this table with the equivalent one for the Senate (Table
2), it is evident that in both houses the parties were divided by much
the same kind of issue. The tables are not identical, but again the
Democrats were badly split on issues concerning civil rights and internal security and those dealing with labor, and they were relatively
united on votes dealing with foreign policy, foreign aid, and public
works. Among the Republicans, as in the Senate, the position of these
categories was generally the reverse. In contrast with the Senate, agriculture questions tended to divide the Republicans and unite the
Democrats in the House, issues involving economic controls tended
to split both groups, and housing votes tended to unify the Republicans but not the Democrats.

THE STRUCTURE OF DEMOCRATIC CLEAVAGE

The Democrats in the House of Representatives, like their fellow
partisans in the Senate, were divided on the low-cohesion roll calls
into two highly distinctive blocs or wings whose composition was
almost the same in the two sets.[5] The cleavage, of course, was again
essentially sectional, one wing in each set being composed entirely of
men from the South and Border (Tables 30B and 31B) and the other
including Northern and Border representatives, plus a few from the
South in the intermediate-cohesion set (Tables 30A and 31A). This
cleavage was a deep one; the names of only two men, Albert of Oklahoma and Priest of Tennessee, appear on the rosters of both the North-

---

[4] Key reports that an analysis of the 1953–1954 House roll calls showed *both*
parties to be more cohesive on the preliminary votes than on the final ones (V. O.
Key, Jr., *Politics, Parties, and Pressure Groups*, 4th edition, New York: Thomas Y.
Crowell and Co., 1958, pp. 730–731). The question deserves precise analysis over
a series of Congresses, for which it might be possible to control for such variable
factors as the vigor of the White House leadership.

[5] In this section the intermediate-cohesion set will be discussed along with the
low-cohesion one, since the mean of the cohesion indexes for the former is fairly
close to that of the latter. Where differences resulted from the higher cohesion of
the first-session set, these will be noted.

Table 30A

DEMOCRATIC CLEAVAGE: BLOC STRUCTURE OF HOUSE DEMOCRATS, NORTH-
ERN WING, ON 74 LOW-COHESION ROLL CALLS, 81ST CONGRESS, 2ND
SESSION

Bloc N-I

Members: 66
Mean Score: 55.8

RANK	Name and District				
1	Karsten, Mo. 13		33	Mack, Ill. 21
3	Price, Ill. 25	Nucleus N-I*a*	34	Blatnik, Minn. 8
4	Sullivan, Mo. 11	Mean score: 67.3	35	Staggers, W. Va. 2
8	Jackson, Wash. 2		35	Tauriello, N. Y. 43
16	Multer, N. Y. 14		37	Karst, Mo. 12
16	Rodino, N. J. 10	Nucleus N-I*b*	38	O'Brien, Ill. 6
14	Addonizio, N. J. 11	Mean score: 64.7	39	McSweeney, Ohio 16
6	Rooney, N. Y. 12		40	Biemiller, Wis. 5
2	Forand, R. I. 1		41	Rabaut, Mich. 14
15	McGuire, Conn. 3	Nucleus N-I*c*	42	Marsalis, Colo. 3
12	Gorski, N. Y. 44	Mean score: 61.8	43	Holifield, Cal. 19
28	Buckley, Ill. 4		44	O'Toole, N. Y. 13
53	Chesney, Ill. 11		45	Carnahan, Mo. 8
5	O'Sullivan, Neb. 2		46	Kelly, N. Y. 10
7	Havenner, Cal. 4		47	O'Hara, Ill. 2
9	Shelley, Cal. 5		48	Aspinall, Colo. 4
10	Madden, Ind. 1		49	Perkins, Ky. 7
11	Klein, N. Y. 19		50	Burnside, W. Va. 4
13	Feighan, Ohio 20		51	Delaney, N. Y. 6
18	Garmatz, Md. 3		52	Doyle, Cal. 18
19	Lane, Mass. 7		54	Flood, Pa. 11
20	Linehan, Ill. 3		55	Yates, Ill. 9
21	King, Cal. 17		56	Wagner, Ohio 2
22	Lind, Pa. 21		56	Howell, N. J. 4
23	Zablocki, Wis. 4		58	Crosser, Ohio 21 (s)
24	Gordon, Ill. 8		59	Heller, N. Y. 7
25	O'Neill, Pa. 10		60	Kirwan, Ohio 19 (e)
26	McKinnon, Cal. 23		61	Welch, Mo. 3
27	Rhodes, Pa. 13		62	Denton, Ind. 8
29	Bolling, Mo. 5		63	Granahan, Pa. 2
30	Dollinger, N. Y. 24		64	McCarthy, Minn. 4
31	Miller, Cal. 6		65	Chudoff, Pa. 4
32	Buchanan, Pa. 33		66	Crook, Ind. 3

LEGEND: Number of representatives in Northern wing blocs: 66. Each *bloc*
member agreed with each other bloc member on 46 or more of the 74 votes
in the set. *Mean score* of the bloc: the mean of the number of agreements
between all pairs of bloc members. *Rank:* the rank of each bloc member according to the mean of his scores with all other bloc members, 1 designating the
highest average number of agreements. *Nucleus:* a highly cohesive cluster or
small bloc, around which a more inclusive bloc develops. (e): elective leader.
(s): seniority leader.

Table

DEMOCRATIC CLEAVAGE: BLOC STRUCTURE OF HOUSE
ROLL CALLS, 81ST

	Bloc S-I		Bloc S-II
	Members: 10		Members: 16
	Mean Score: 54.8		Mean Score: 52.5
RANK	Name and District	RANK	Name and District
1	Albert, Okla. 3	2	Albert
2	Beckworth, Tex. 3	4	Beckworth
5	Thornberry, Tex. 10	6	Thornberry
6	Underwood, Ky. 6	8	Underwood
7	Lanham, Ga. 7	5	Lanham
8	Chelf, Ky. 4	11	Chelf
9	Hays, Ark. 5	14	Hays
10	Priest, Tenn. 6 (e)	12	Priest (e)
		10	Evins, Tenn. 5
		13	Rains, Ala. 5
		15	Sims, S. C. 2
		16	Bates, Ky. 8
3	Trimble, Ark. 3	2	Trimble
4	Jones, Ala. 8	1	Jones
		9	Cooper, Tenn. 9
		7	Mills, Ark. 2

Nucleus S-IIa
Mean score: 58.2

LEGEND: Number of representatives in Southern wing blocs: 42. Each *bloc* member agreed with each other bloc member on 46 or more of the 74 votes in the set. *Mean score* of the bloc: the mean of the number of agreements between all pairs of bloc members. *Rank:* the rank of each bloc member according to the mean of his scores with all other bloc members, 1 designating the highest average number of agreements. *Nucleus:* a highly cohesive cluster or small bloc, around which a more inclusive bloc develops. (e): elective leader. (s): seniority leader.

30B

DEMOCRATS, SOUTHERN WING, ON 74 LOW-COHESION
CONGRESS, 2ND SESSION

Bloc S-III		Bloc S-IV	
Members: 18		Members: 21	
Mean Score: 52.7		Mean Score: 53.8	
RANK	Name and District	RANK	Name and District
17	Mills		
17	Whittington, Miss. 3 (s)		
13	Hardy, Va. 2		
9	Burton, Va. 6		
7	Bonner, N. C. 1		
8	Gary, Va. 3		
2	Burleson, Tex. 17	8	Burleson
1	Harrison, Va. 7	7	Harrison
3	Fisher, Tex. 21	4	Fisher
		6	Teague, Tex. 6
4	Wilson, Tex. 5	4	Wilson
4	Whitten, Miss. 2	1	Whitten
6	Lucas, Tex. 12	8	Lucas
		3	Davis, Ga. 5
		1	Abernethy, Miss. 4
12	Camp, Ga. 4	18	Camp
15	Abbitt, Va. 4	21	Abbitt
11	Herlong, Fla. 5	13	Herlong
14	Gathings, Ark. 1	12	Gathings
9	Andrews, Ala. 3	11	Andrews
16	Poage, Tex. 11	17	Poage
		10	Smith, Va. 8
		14	Gossett, Tex. 13
		15	Rankin, Miss. 1 (s)
		15	Murray, Tenn. 8 (s)
		19	Wheeler, Ga. 8
		21	Preston, Ga. 1

Nucleus S-IIIa Mean score: 56.3

Nucleus S-IVb Mean score: 60.3

Nucleus S-IVa Mean score: 61.5

Table 31A

DEMOCRATIC CLEAVAGE: BLOC STRUCTURE OF HOUSE DEMOCRATS, NORTH-
ERN WING, ON 74 INTERMEDIATE-COHESION ROLL CALLS, 81ST CONGRESS,
FIRST SESSION

	Bloc N-I			Bloc N-II
	Members: 77			Members: 42
	Mean Score: 56.7			Mean Score: 57.9
RANK	Name and District		RANK	Name and District
77	Baring, Nev. A L			
76	McKinnon, Cal. 23			
75	Davenport, Pa. 29			
74	Christopher, Mo. 6			
73	Fogarty, R. I. 2			
71	Sims, S. C. 2			
70	Hays, Ohio 18			
69	Lynch, N. Y. 23			
66	Lesinski, Mich. 16 (s)			
62	Mansfield, Mont. 1			
61	O'Hara, Ill. 2			
60	Burke, Ohio 9			
59	Flood, Pa. 11			
58	Delaney, N. Y. 6			
57	Granger, Utah 1			
56	McCarthy, Minn. 4			
55	King, Cal. 17			
51	Dollinger, N. Y. 24			
48	Chesney, Ill. 11			
47	Dawson, Ill. 1 (s)			
46	Rhodes, Pa. 13			
45	Miller, Cal. 6			
44	McGuire, Conn. 3			
43	Multer, N. Y. 14			
41	Kirwan, Ohio 19 (e)			
40	Biemiller, Wis. 5			
39	O'Sullivan, Neb. 2			
38	Jacobs, Ind. 11			
34	Lane, Mass. 7			
33	Morgan, Pa. 24			
31	Douglas, Cal. 14			
30	Gorski, N. Y. 44			
26	Rooney, N. Y. 12			
25	Zablocki, Wis. 4			
20	Havenner, Cal. 4			
19	Mitchell, Wash. 1			
13	Yates, Ill. 9 ⎤			
16	Madden, Ind. 1		21	Madden
15	Rodino, N. J. 10		16	Rodino
14	Wagner, Ohio 2		18	Wagner
12	Price, Ill. 25		12	Price
10	Howell, N. J. 4		14	Howell
9	Rabaut, Mich. 14	Nucleus N-Ia	9	Rabaut
8	Jackson, Wash. 2	Mean score: 65.9	13	Jackson
7	Crook, Ind. 3		7	Crook
6	Karst, Mo. 12		6	Karst
5	Bolling, Mo. 5		4	Bolling
4	Sullivan, Mo. 11		5	Sullivan
3	Forand, R. I. 1		2	Forand
2	Carroll, Colo. 1		3	Carroll
1	Karsten, Mo. 13 ⎦		1	Karsten

Table 31A (continued)

Bloc N-I		Bloc N-II		
Members: 77		Members: 42		
Mean Score: 56.7		Mean Score: 57.9		
RANK	Name and District	RANK	Name and District	
49	Buckley, Ill. 4			
36	Linehan, Ill. 3			
32	O'Brien, Ill. 6			
37	Gordon, Ill. 8	27	Gordon	
18	Gorski, Ill. 5	15	Gorski	
11	Spence, Ky. 5 (s)	8	Spence (s)	
24	Marsalis, Colo. 3	10	Marsalis	Nucleus N-IIa
50	Aspinall, Colo. 4	23	Aspinall	Mean score: 63.8
67*	Priest, Tenn. 6 (e)	28*	Priest (e)	
68	McCormack, Mass. 12 (e)	33	McCormack (e)	
17	Doyle, Cal. 18	11	Doyle	
26	Perkins, Ky. 7	17	Perkins	
21	Eberharter, Pa. 32	19	Eberharter	
23	Denton, Ind. 8	20	Denton	
22	Addonizio, N. J. 11	22	Addonizio	
29	Buchanan, Pa. 33	24	Buchanan	
28	Holifield, Cal. 19	25	Holifield	
35	Cannon, Mo. 9 (s)	26	Cannon (s)	
53	Carnahan, Mo. 8	29	Carnahan	
42	O'Neill, Pa. 10	30	O'Neill	
54	Polk, Ohio 6	31	Polk	
52	Welch, Mo. 3	32	Welch	
64	Lind, Pa. 21	34	Lind	
63	Moulder, Mo. 2	35	Moulder	
65	Garmatz, Md. 3	36	Garmatz	
72	Noland, Ind. 7	37	Noland	
		38	Thomas, Tex. 8	
		39	Monroney, Okla. 5	
		40*	Albert, Okla. 3	
		41	Bates, Ky. 8	
		42	Stigler, Okla. 2	

* Also member of a bloc in Southern wing, see Table 31B.

LEGEND: Number of representatives in Northern wing blocs: 82. Each *bloc* member agreed with each other bloc member on 46 or more of the 74 votes in the set. *Mean score* of the bloc: the mean of the number of agreements between all pairs of bloc members. *Rank:* the rank of each bloc member according to the mean of his scores with all other bloc members, 1 designating the highest average number of agreements. *Nucleus:* a highly cohesive cluster or small bloc, around which a more inclusive bloc develops. (e): elective leader. (s): seniority leader.

Table 31B

DEMOCRATIC CLEAVAGE: BLOC STRUCTURE OF HOUSE DEMOCRATS, SOUTH-
ERN WING, ON 74 INTERMEDIATE-COHESION ROLL CALLS, 81ST CONGRESS,
FIRST SESSION

	Bloc S-I				Bloc S-II
	Members: 23				Members: 28
	Mean Score: 54.2				Mean Score: 54.2
RANK	Name and District			RANK	Name and District
23	deGraffenried, Ala. 6				
22	Rains, Ala. 5				
20	Boggs, La. 2				
20*	Priest, Tenn. 6 (e)				
19*	Albert, Okla. 3				
17	Thompson, Tex. 9				
16	Patman, Tex. 1				
15	Evins, Tenn. 5				
13	Lyle, Tex. 14				
12	Fugate, Va. 9				
10	Hardy, Va. 2				
10	Frazier, Tenn. 3				
9	Beckworth, Tex. 3				
7	Trimble, Ark. 3				
7	Thornberry, Tex. 10				
5	Mills, Ark. 2				
4	Cooper, Tenn. 9	⎱			
3	Jones, Ala. 8	⎰ Nucleus S-Ia			
1	Elliott, Ala. 7	Mean score: 63.0			
2	Brown, Ga. 10	⎰			
6	Harris, Ark. 7			14	Brown
14	Preston, Ga. 1			7	Harris
18	Battle, Ala. 9			21	Preston
				27	Battle
				28	Tackett, Ark. 4
				26	Winstead, Miss. 5
				25	Gathings, Ark. 1
				24	Rogers, Fla. 6
				23	Whitten, Miss. 2
				21	Passman, La. 5
				20	Cox, Ga. 2
				19	Fisher, Tex. 21
				18	Andrews, Ala. 3
				16	Gossett, Tex. 13
				16	Kilday, Tex. 20
				15	Doughton, N. C. 9 (s)
				13	Burleson, Tex. 17
				12	Bryson, S. C. 4
				11	Pickett, Tex. 7
				10	Wilson, Tex. 5
				9	Lucas, Tex. 12
				6	Wheeler, Ga. 8
				4	Whittington, Miss. 3 (s)
				8	Colmer, Miss. 6 ⎱
				4	Davis, Ga. 5 ⎱ Nucleus S-IIa
				3	Abernethy, Miss. 4 ⎰ Mean score: 62.5
				2	Murray, Tenn. 8 (s)
				1	Hare, S. C. 3 ⎰

* Also member of bloc in Northern wing, see Table 31A.

LEGEND: Number of representatives in Southern wing blocs: 47. Each *bloc* member agreed with each other
bloc member on 46 or more of the 74 votes in the set. *Mean score* of the bloc: The mean of the number of
agreements between all pairs of bloc members. *Rank:* The rank of each bloc member according to the mean
of his scores with all other bloc members, 1 designating the highest average number of agreements. *Nucleus:*
A highly cohesive cluster or small bloc, around which a more inclusive bloc develops. (e): elective leader.
(s): seniority leader.

ern and the Southern wings of the party, and these only on the inter-mediate-cohesion set (Tables 31 A and B).

A more exact indication of the depth and character of the cleavage can be had by noting the number and substance of the roll calls on which two or more of the nuclear clusters shown in these tables were agreed despite their general opposition.[6] This analysis suggests that on questions of foreign policy and on domestic issues not sharply sec-tional in character even some of the more widely separated nuclei could agree, but these occasions were too infrequent to obscure the basic divisions within the party.[7]

A close examination of the tables will reveal, as in the Senate, a remarkable stablity in the structure of the party from one session to the other. The point can be summarized as follows: Of the 233 Demo-crats who were members of one of the systems in the intermediate set (that is, had some scores on the matrix but may not have been part of a bloc), only 6 occupied significantly different positions in the low-cohesion set of the second session. These were the only changes in the two systems except for men who belonged to a bloc in one session but not in the comparable set of the other session.[8]

---

[6] As in the Senate analysis, the blocs in these tables are identified by Roman numerals. As a rough guide the blocs may be thought of as being arranged on a continuum from "left" to "right," with the lower numbers to the "left." This guide should be used with caution, however, especially in connection with the Republican tables, since the blocs are not obviously divided along these ideologi-cal lines. In addition, the blocs in the two major sectional wings of the Demo-cratic party are designated by capital letter, "N" for the Northern wing and "S" for the Southern. Where it seemed useful to identify the nuclear clusters around which the blocs were constructed, they are designated by lower-case letters fol-lowing the number of the bloc of which they are the nuclei. A bloc, of course, may have more than one nucleus. (See chap. 3, note 20.)

[7] Among the nuclei shown in Tables 30A and B there were 22 votes on which N-Ia, N-Ib, S-IVa and b, and S-IIIa were agreed in various combinations, the bulk of them, 15, being among N-Ia, N-Ib, and S-IIIa. Fourteen of the 22 dealt with foreign aid, economic controls, and railway labor. In the intermediate-cohe-sion set, shown on Tables 31 A and B, there were 38 common agreements among nuclei N-IIa, S-Ia, and S-IIa. Most of these, 23, were between N-IIa and S-Ia and were concentrated on foreign aid, foreign policy, rent control, and public housing.

[8] The "shifters" changed as follows: Two men, Bates of Kentucky and Sims of South Carolina, "shifted" from the Northern wing in the first-session set to the Southern wing (Bloc S-II) in the low-cohesion set of the second session (Tables 31A and 30B); two others, Priest of Tennessee and Albert of Oklahoma, were in both wings in the intermediate set but only in the Southern wing in the low-cohe-sion set (Tables 31A, 31B, and 30B); finally, two men, Hardy of Virginia and Preston of Georgia, were in the "left" bloc of the Southern wing in the intermedi-ate set but in one of the "right" blocs in the low-cohesion set (Tables 31B and

As the tables of bloc structure indicate, both wings of the party and even some of the individual blocs were multinuclear in form. In fact, in the interests of simplicity, only a few of the more cohesive nuclei that appeared on the matrixes are shown on the tables. The Southern wing in particular had several additional ones.[9] The omission of these is of no consequence, but the multinuclear form suggests that within the general stability of the party structure there was a good deal of fluidity in detail. It also raises a question: How significant were the differences between these nuclei in a given wing of the party?

In the Northern wing the differences among the principal nuclei were not marked, although on both sets the N-Ia nucleus tended to stand somewhat more to the "left" than the others. In the low-cohesion set of the second session, for example, these four men (Table 30A) were among the 48 members of the House who voted against overriding the President's veto of the Internal Security Act of 1950. But by and large the differences within the Northern wing were comparatively minor.

At first glance it may be astonishing to find two overlapping blocs in the Northern wing on the intermediate-cohesion votes while there is only one bloc on the low-cohesion set (Tables 30A and 31A). This reflects the intersectional character of the "Northern" wing on the first-session votes rather than a division among the usual Northern members of the party. The factor chiefly responsible for this intersectional, North-South accommodation was the difference in the number and character of the votes dealing with civil rights. Not only were there

---

30B). There were 74 "drop-outs," 44 who belonged to a bloc in the first-session and not in the second-session set and 30 who were in the reverse situation. Most of these reflect fluctuations in the "absence" rate, but not all of them do. The larger number who "dropped out" of blocs in the low-cohesion set suggests that on these controversial votes some members of the party divided their allegiances between the opposing wings in such fashion that they appeared as members of blocs in neither. Possible examples would include Stigler of Oklahoma, Spence of Kentucky, Cannon of Missouri, and McCormack of Massachusetts, the Majority Leader.

[9] For example, in the Southern wing on the intermediate-cohesion set (Table 31B) 5 Texans and one Mississippian—Fisher, Lucas, Burleson, Picket, Wilson, and Whittington—composed a separate nucleus with a mean score of 57.4. The pattern of its agreements located it midway between the other two nuclei, S-Ia and S-IIa, shown in the table. Also, in the Northern wing, intermediate-cohesion set (Table 31A), 5 men from Illinois—Buckley, Linehan, O'Brien, Gordon, and Gorski—formed a distinct nucleus with a mean score of 63.6. Its divergences from the other nuclei were not great, mostly involving issues of local consequence. For comment on such state groupings, see below, chap. 7.

fewer votes in this category in the first-session set, but the bulk of these dealt with the anti-poll tax bill, whereas most of the votes in this category in the second-session set dealt with the more controversial F.E.P.C. bill. The lower boiling point of the poll-tax issue not only allowed some of the more moderate Southerners to go along with the majority of the party but also reduced the number of roll calls on the bill and permitted greater prominence for other kinds of issues that tended to divide the Southern wing internally rather than to split it off from the North. Neither Bloc N-I nor N-II (Table 31A) was agreed on all the poll-tax votes, but they both supported two moves to prevent dilatory action on the bill, and N-II took a similar position on four other attempts of this sort. Aside from this issue N-II was somewhat the stronger in support of foreign aid, and N-I was agreed on more of the votes dealing with such domestic questions as public housing and rent control. N-I also solidly supported adoption of the 21-day rule,[10] weakening the power of the Rules Committee, while N-II did not.

As these remarks suggest, the Northern wing of the party was a good deal more cohesive on both sets than was the Southern. Various details support this inference. In the first place, it is apparent from a glance at Tables 31A, 30B, and 31B that there is a lower degree of fusion between the blocs in the Southern wing. In the second place, within the Northern wing the overlapping segment includes most of the members of the nuclear clusters, while in the Southern wing it does not. Thus the cleavages between these Southern nuclei, and presumably also between the blocs, apparently were marked and deep.[11] Third, the number of overlapping blocs in the Southern wing, a portion of which are not indicated on the tables, was greater than in the Northern, which is always a sign of shifting and unstable alignments. Finally, in each set the largest bloc in the Northern wing of the party included in its membership a considerably larger proportion of those

---

[10] See above, chap. 2.

[11] Eight of the members of nucleus N-I*a* in Table 31A also ranked at the top of Bloc N-II, though they were not members of its nucleus. This indicates that the mean scores of these men were high in both blocs but the range of their scores in Bloc N-II was narrower. The wide range of scores by the N-II*a* nucleus within its bloc, indicated by the relatively low ranking of its members in the bloc, reflects a cleavage between the two nuclei but one not deep enough to prevent both from being in the overlapping sector of the two blocs. In contrast, none of the members of the S-II*a* nucleus in Table 31B is in Bloc S-I, and only one member of the S-I*a* nucleus, Brown of Georgia, appears in the S-II roster. Table 30B indicates a similar pattern.

in the system, that is, men with at least one score on the matrix, than did the largest bloc in the Southern wing.[12]

Given the evidence of division within the Southern wing of the party, one is impelled to ask whether these oppositions between nuclei and between blocs were indeed substantial. If they were, how can they be explained? These groupings were generally agreed, in opposition to the other wing of the party, on votes of peculiar relevance to the region, notably, of course, those concerning matters of race. On questions of foreign policy, however, and on domestic economic and social issues related to problems of foreign relations or growing out of the strains of an urban, industrial society, they were by no means united and in a number of cases were directly opposed.

On the low-cohesion votes of the second session all of the nuclear groupings in the Southern wing (Table 30B) were agreed in opposition to the prevailing view in the House on the 3 crucial votes dealing with F.E.P.C., that is, one weakening amendment, recommital, and passage. However, only the S-IVa nucleus was consistently solid in support of the 14 dilatory moves on this bill. Moreover, as one goes from "right" to "left" in Table 30B one encounters among the nuclei increasing support for the Administration and the majority of the party on foreign aid, labor, social security, public housing, rent control, and similar issues.[13] The differences between these nuclear groups do not, of course, appear as sharply when the whole blocs are compared, but the same tendencies are evident. Half the members of Bloc S-II, for example, opposed Representative Cox's move to repeal the 21-day rule, but only one member of Bloc S-IV did so.

On the intermediate-cohesion votes of the first session (Table 31B) the two principal nuclei were again agreed on some regionally important issues: 12 of the 13 votes dealing with civil rights and internal security, roll calls on such matters as exempting independent produc-

---

[12] Bloc N-I in Table 30A included just under 48 per cent of the members of the system, Bloc N-I in Table 31A a little over 46 per cent. On the other hand, Bloc S-IV in Table 30B covers only a little over 22 per cent of the men in that system and Bloc S-II in Table 31B just under 29 per cent.

[13] No useful purpose would be served by presenting all the detail in support of this observation; a few comparisons between the S-IVa and S-IIa nuclei will illustrate it. The former was in opposition to the party majority on three votes concerning economic assistance in the Far East, on the passage of and conference report on the bills extending rent controls, and on three votes on the bill to amend the Railway Labor Act to permit the union shop and related practices. It supported an amendment to the Defense Production Act, aiming at restricting to new construction credit controls on real estate transactions. On all nine of these the S-IIa nucleus was solidly agreed on the other side.

ers of natural gas from regulation by the Federal Power Commission, and those on repealing the tax on oleomargarine. They were solidly opposed to each other, however, on votes dealing with housing and rent control, on adoption of the 21-day rule, and the like. Further, when one examines the votes, dealing with both foreign and domestic issues, on which one of these nuclei was unified and the other was not, it is evident that the "left" bloc (S-I) tended to unite and to join with the majority of the party as the Democrats became relatively cohesive.[14] On the other hand, the "right" bloc (S-II) was most likely to draw together on votes that sharply split the party.[15] In other words, votes of clear regional import aside, the behavior of these nuclei indicates that while *individual* members of the "left" bloc deserted the majority when the party became divided, the bloc as a whole did not. In contrast, the "right" bloc *as a group* was likely to desert when Democratic cohesion declined, though *individual* members on the "right" might vote with the party majority on roll calls that were less divisive for the party. As these comments suggest, the S-II*a* nucleus was the spearhead of a bipartisan coalition on this series of votes, an inference that follows from two items of evidence: first, on none of these votes was this nucleus in agreement with a majority of the Democrats; and, second, on nearly three-quarters of them it was on the prevailing side in the House.

Both the similarities within the Northern wing and the contrasts within the Southern wing are evident from Figure 8. In particular, the penchant of the "right" Southern bloc for voting in coalition with the Republicans is clear from the fact that in both sets the proportion of its agreements on the prevailing side of the House exceeded that on the side of the party majority. The general substance of these differences, moreover, is suggested in Figure 9, which shows for each of the principal blocs the proportion of the Administration support votes in the set on which its members unanimously backed the presidential preference. The differences in the party orthodoxy and Administration support indexes indicate, moreover, that the contrasts between

---

[14] Nucleus S-I*a* was agreed and nucleus S-II*a* was divided on a series of votes, most of them dealing with foreign policy, labor, and social security, on which the mean cohesion indexes of the party were relatively high. There were 16 of these votes. On them the mean cohesion index of the party was 67.0, which was 19 points higher than the mean of the party on the set as a whole.

[15] The S-II*a* nucleus was agreed on a series of votes, most of them on foreign policy and domestic economic issues, that split the S-I*a* group. The mean cohesion index of the party for this series was relatively low. On those votes, of which there were 14, the mean cohesion index of the party was 30.7, which was 17 points below the mean of the party for the whole set.

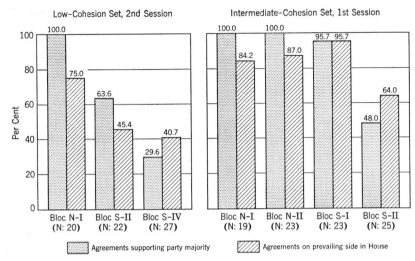

Figure 8. Proportion of agreements supporting party majority and on prevailing side in the House, principal Democratic blocs, low- and intermediate-cohesion roll calls, 81st Congress, 1st and 2nd sessions. Agreements include all votes on which the bloc was unanimous plus those on which less than half the members were unrecorded and the remainder were unanimous.

these blocs were characteristic of their members over the sessions as a whole.[16]

It is thus evident that within the Southern wing of the Democratic party in the House, more clearly even than in the Senate, issues that were not peculiarly regional in their reference but rather reflected the common strains of society in the midtwentieth century split the representatives into opposing groupings. One fairly sizable segment strongly resisted change in both realms and effectively utilized the device of the bipartisan coalition to further its views. A generally smaller but significant number were, so to speak, in the middle between the views of their die-hard colleagues and the demands strongly reflected in the votes of the Northern wing. This middle position is peculiarly that of what may be called the "bridge" man, one from the

---

[16] The mean party orthodoxy indexes of the principal blocs were, first session, Bloc N-I 4.56, Bloc N-II 4.60, Bloc S-I 4.11, and Bloc S-II 3.53; second session, Bloc N-I 4.45, Bloc S-II 4.17, and Bloc S-IV 3.30. The corresponding Administration support indexes were: First session, Bloc N-I 4.73, Bloc N-II 4.77, Bloc S-I 4.11, and Bloc S-II 3.32; second session, Bloc N-I 4.52, Bloc S-II 4.06, and Bloc S-IV 2.87. In the first session 56 votes were designated as Administration support votes. In the second session 73 were so classified. For the purpose of some comparisons, as in the mean indexes given above, the latter number was reduced to 59 by eliminating 14 tactical votes dealing with the F.E.P.C. bill.

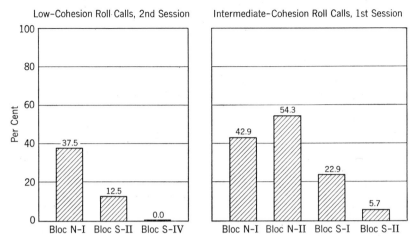

Figure 9. Proportion of Administrative support votes among low- and inter-mediate-cohesion roll calls on which principal Democratic blocs in House were agreed, 81st Congress, 1st and 2nd sessions. Votes identified as involving an expressed presidential preference; there were 40 Administration support votes in the low-cohesion set and 35 in the intermediate-cohesion set. Agreements include votes on which the bloc was unanimous plus those on which less than half the members were unrecorded and the remainder were unanimous.

South or Border who agreed with members of both the Southern and the Northern wings of the party on enough votes to put him on the matrix. Six of these "bridge" men formed the nucleus of Bloc S-I of the low-cohesion set (Table 30B), which was really a wing of Bloc S-II and distinguishable from it by a somewhat more latidudinarian position on the F.E.P.C. controversy.[17] A larger contingent in the intermediate-cohesion set, the bridge men included 22 of the 23 members of Bloc S-I (Table 31B), all but Rains of Alabama.

A middle position approaching the embarrassment of a dilemma was also the lot of many Democrats from the six Border states, Delaware, Maryland, West Virginia, Kentucky, Missouri, and Oklahoma. Many of these were "bridge" men, and a considerable number were in blocs in one or the other wing of the party, but in proportion to their numbers they were less likely to fall into any bloc than were Democrats from the North or South. On the low-cohesion votes of the second session, as Table 32 indicates, the rate of bloc membership among the Border men was six percentage points lower than that for the party as

---

[17] The "bridge" men in Bloc S-I on Table 30B were Albert of Oklahoma, Beckworth of Texas, Priest of Tennessee, Trimble of Arkansas, and Chelf and Underwood of Kentucky.

Table 32

THE BORDER DILEMMA: PROPORTION OF HOUSE DEMOCRATS FROM THE
NORTH, THE SOUTH, AND THE BORDER STATES BELONGING TO BLOCS, 74 LOW-
COHESION ROLL CALLS, 81ST CONGRESS, 2ND SESSION

	South	North	Border	Total
Number of Democratic representatives	100*	121	37	258
Number in Northern-wing blocs	0	56	10	66
Number in Southern-wing blocs	43	0	4	47
Total in blocs	43	56	14	113
Per cent	43.0	46.3	37.8	43.8

* Excluding Speaker Rayburn.

a whole; the pattern was essentially the same on the intermediate-cohesion votes. Although these differences are small and unreliable, they are consistent with other indications that the men from these states were more likely than those from other regions so to divide their votes between the two wings of the party that they agreed with neither consistently enough to appear in a bloc.

The breaking away of the Border State members of the party thus accounts in small measure for the division and lack of cohesion in the Southern wing, but not all the "bridge" men were Border men. Were there other facts, aspects of the constituencies, which would explain why some in the Southern wing exhibited die-hard opposition to their Northern colleagues and others broke away at least often enough to form an alternative Southern bloc? Was one segment in some way representative of the "Old South" and the other some sort of "New South"?

A cursory examination of the constituency characteristics of the opposing nuclei in the blocs of the two sets of votes showed no promising answers to these questions. To pursue the matter an attempt was made to compare a selection of the extreme cases from each Southern bloc in the intermediate set (Table 31B). From each bloc were selected those members who had no more than one score in the other bloc. Seven men were thus selected from Bloc S-I and nine from Bloc S-II.[18]

While in some respects there were slight differences between these two groupings, no single attribute of those tested consistently and

[18] From Bloc S-I: Albert of Oklahoma, Boggs of Louisiana, Evins and Priest of Tennessee, Rains of Alabama, and Patman and Thornberry of Texas. From Bloc S-II: Abernethy, Colmer, Whitten, and Winstead of Mississippi, Cox and Davis of Georgia, and Fisher, Gossett, and Pickett of Texas.

markedly discriminated between the two sets of Southerners. Thus the S-II group represented districts that tended to be somewhat more rural than the constituencies of the S-I group; the mean per cent of the male population employed on farms in 1950 in the former was 38.5 and in the latter 26.5. But Davis of Georgia was elected from one of the most urban constituencies in the South; his district included two of the three counties in the Atlanta metropolitan area. And Gossett's district, the Texas 13th, had a lower proportion of farmers than all but two of the seven S-I constituencies.[19] There were no differences of consequence in the size of urban places contained within the two sets of districts, in their rate of growth between 1940 and 1950, or in a general tendency toward loss or gain of population in that decade. All of these were essentially one-party districts. Those in one group were no more likely than those in the other to have had serious primary opposition in 1948, though the primary contests of Davis of Georgia and Pickett of Texas, in the S-II group, were close in that year, both winning by narrower margins than any others in the two groups.[20]

All members of the two groups, with the exception of Priest of Tennessee, took the same positions on the votes dealing with the anti-poll tax bill. However, given the established proposition that one-party politics in areas in the South with a substantial Negro population tends to suppress issues of national importance and to perpetuate the preferences of an established order,[21] one might expect to find between these two groups of districts a substantial difference in the size of the non-white population. There is a tendency in this direction, but again it is not consistent. The mean per cent non-white in the S-II districts was approximately 29 and that in the S-I districts was approximately 19, but both Boggs and Priest in the latter group represented districts with sizable non-white populations (almost one-third and approximately one-fifth, respectively), and Fisher and Gossett in the S-II group came from districts that were more than 95 per cent white.[22]

---

[19] I am indebted to Duncan MacRae, Jr., for the data on the occupational characteristics of the districts. These have been published in the Appendix to his *Dimensions of Congressional Voting*, Berkeley and Los Angeles: University of California Press, 1958.

[20] The data on primaries were collected by the late Julius Turner and have been made available to me through the courtesy of Duncan MacRae, Jr.

[21] Key, *Southern Politics*, pp. 665 ff. and *passim*.

[22] The lower non-white population in the S-I districts may be of somewhat more consequence than these exceptions imply, since the districts of Boggs and Priest were in or contained metropolitan-urban areas (New Orleans and Nashville, respectively). In the highly urban setting a sizable Negro population does not produce quite the same characteristics in the one-party system that are evident in rural and small-town areas.

In some districts in both groups the States Rights presidential ticket got a higher proportion of the 1948 vote than in the state as a whole; and in some the proportion was about the same or lower. The incidence of the Eisenhower vote in 1952 was similarly inconsistent.

Some significance may be attached to the fact that, on the average, the S-I group were younger than the men in S-II.[23] It may also be relevant to note that the S-I group were on the average somewhat less senior in the House than their colleagues from the opposing bloc.[24] There were relatively young and junior and relatively older and senior men in both groups, but it may be that the younger representatives among these Southerners tended to be less intransigent and less hostile to the designs of the party majority than those of more advanced years.

The point of these inconclusive factors is not that a combination of them could not be used to explain the behavior of one or another of the men in the two groups. It is rather that none of them accounts for the groupings as such. One could legitimately conclude that the more die-hard Southern Democrat in the House tended to be a somewhat older man representing a more rural constituency with a fairly numerous non-white population. But one would not be saying very much, because he would not be accounting for the many deviations from the asserted pattern. The sharp and persistent cleavages within the Southern wing indicate that there were signs of what might be called an old and a new South in the Democratic party. An explanation for these divergent tendencies is apparently not to be found, however, in aggregate demographic or political data.[25] Unquestionably it lies rather in a combination of three rather different factors: (1) differences in the factional and general power structure within the constituencies, of which data of the sort analyzed above are weak indicators; (2) differences in the personal values and attitudes of the individual representatives; and (3) differences in the impact of influences within the House itself. It would be impossible with any confidence to rank these except on the basis of a separate and detailed investigation, but of the three the last is almost certainly of more than casual consequence, as later evidence will indicate. Intralegislative groupings may

---

[23] The mean age in 1949 of the 7 men selected from Bloc S-I was 43. That of the 9 men from Bloc S-II was 49. The differences between the medians were of the same order. The S-II group contained three men over 50 in 1949, while the S-I group included only one over that age.

[24] Among the men from S-I the mean terms served in the House, including the Eighty-first Congress, were 4, while among those from S-II they were 6.

[25] Thus, for example, Gossett of Texas could be classified as "old" South in a political sense but hardly in an economic one. He was, to be sure, born in western Louisiana, but the chief concerns of his district were with oil and cattle-raising.

be fully as important in determining voting behavior in the House as any influences coming from outside the chamber.

In summary, the cleavages within the Democratic party in the House showed marked parallels to those in the Senate. The familiar North-South division was again the dominant characteristic, and it is evident, even more than in the Senate, that deviation from the party majority and coalition with the Republican opposition were peculiarly characteristic of Southern representatives but by no means of all Democrats from the South. Voting choices were clearly not haphazard, and consequently the voting structure of the party was highly stable from one to the other of the two sets of roll calls examined. There was, however, a clear tendency, as regionally significant issues decreased in frequency and in intensity, for sizable numbers of Southern Democrats and even larger proportions of men from the Border states to vote with their fellow partisans in the Northern wing. Despite a fluidity in the Southern wing that was much more striking than that among the Northerners, however, the evidence is clear that there was a solid and sharply identifiable die-hard element among the Southern Democrats, whose opposition extended well beyond the issues of intense regional loyalty to almost the whole range of questions growing out of the strains and stresses to which the American society is subjected in the midtwentieth century. The source of these divisions within the South is not easily identified, but it seems clear that it is not in some aggregate demographic characteristic of the constituencies or an equally inclusive feature of their political complexion. The power structure, including the factional cleavages, within the congressional districts is unquestionably relevant, though it has not been investigated in the present analysis, but it seems equally likely that factors of an individual character cannot be ignored in attempting to account for these voting patterns. These individual factors would include influences within the legislature, as distinct from those emanating from the constituency, influences pointing to the range of discretion open to the representative.

THE DEMOCRATS IN HARMONY

As would be expected on a set of roll calls on which the cohesion of the party ranged upward from an index of 68.6 (Table 28)—indicating dissent from the majority of the party by 15 per cent or less of those voting—the voting structure of the Democrats on the high-cohesion set of the second session was clearly uninuclear. This structure, indicated in Table 33, was so strongly apparent that, as noted at the opening of the chapter, in developing the matrix nothing was to be gained by entering scores indicating less than 52 agreements out of the 62 possible in the set. At this point there were 38 men in the bloc, and 112 of the 258 Democrats—excluding Speaker Rayburn—were in the extended system, that is, had at least one score of 52 or higher with members of the bloc. The voting patterns of the 74 men in the system who were not in the bloc indicated agreement most frequently with the members of the Ia-1 nucleus and a scattering of scores—more numerous, of course, in some cases than in others—with the remaining members of the bloc. Inspection of Table 33 indicates that the bloc contained 11 men from the South, some of them ranking very high. Most of these were in the "left" wing of the Southerners on the low-cohesion votes of the second session, but not all of them. Specifically, Representative Hardy of Virginia and Representative Bonner of the adjacent district in North Carolina, who ranked 7th and 38th, respectively, in Bloc I, were both members of the "right" S-IIIa nucleus in low-cohesion set of the second session (Table 30B). Among the other men who were in the system but not in the bloc there were several whose positions on the low-cohesion set were of the same sort.[26]

It is thus evident that on these votes the essential structure of the party in the House reflected a rough continuum of attitude shading from no dissents on any of the 62 votes among the members of the principal nucleus (Ia-1, Table 33) to complete agreement on 40 of the votes among all members of Bloc I. These dissents were so haphazardly distributed, moreover, that they resulted in no separate bloc at the time the matrix was completed and seemed most unlikely to do so except possibly in a bloc of small size and very low cohesion.

The uninuclear character of the voting structure in this set is further suggested by the fact that, as was not the case on the low-cohesion sets, whether a man was in the system or a member of the bloc was largely, though not entirely, a function of the frequency with which he was "absent." An illustrative example of general importance in the study is Representative McCormack of Massachusetts, the Majority Leader. He was not a member of Bloc I. He entered the system, however, with a score of 54 (with the men who ranked first and second in Bloc I); he was "absent" on eight roll calls; together these account for

---

[26] For example, the following men listed in the extreme "right" Bloc S-IV in Table 30B were in this system, and their scores were distributed in a manner consistent with the expected uninuclear pattern: Camp and Preston of Georgia, Andrews of Alabama, Gathings of Arkansas, and Herlong of Florida.

Table 33

DEMOCRATIC UNITY: BLOC STRUCTURE OF DEMOCRATIC REPRESENTATIVES
ON 62 HIGH-COHESION ROLL CALLS, 81ST CONGRESS, 2ND SESSION

	Nucleus Ia-1		Nucleus Ia-2		Bloc I
	Members: 3		Members: 12		Members: 38
	Mean Score: 61.3		Mean Score: 59.5		Mean Score: 55.7
RANK	Name and District	RANK	Name and District	RANK	Name and District
1	Brown, Ga. 10	1	Brown	1	Brown
1	Sullivan, Mo. 11	4	Sullivan	2	Sullivan
3	Forand, R. I. 1	4	Forand	4	Forand
		2	Price, Ill. 25	3	Price
		3	Hardy, Va. 2	7	Hardy
		4	Karst, Mo. 12	7	Karst
		4	Jones, Ala. 8	4	Jones
		4	Trimble, Ark. 3	6	Trimble
		9	Karsten, Mo. 13	10	Karsten
		10	Beckworth, Tex. 3	9	Beckworth
		11	McGuire, Conn. 3	13	McGuire
		12	Elliott, Ala. 7	15	Elliott
				11	Buchanan, Pa. 33
				12	Murdock, Ariz. 1 (e)
				14	Mills, Ark. 2
				16	Rooney, N. Y. 12
				17	Addonizio, N. J. 11
				18	Rodino, N. J. 10
				19	Lind, Pa. 21
				19	Hart, N. J. 14 (s)
				21	Bolling, Mo. 5
				22	Mansfield, Mont. 1
				23	Garmatz, Md. 3
				23	Crook, Ind. 3
				23	McSweeney, Ohio 16
				26	Peterson, Fla. 1 (s)
				27	Spence, Ky. 5 (s)
				28	Grant, Ala. 2
				29	Walter, Pa. 20 (e)
				30	Aspinall, Colo. 4
				30	Albert, Okla. 3
				32	Lanham, Ga. 7
				33	O'Brien, Ill. 6
				34	King, Cal. 17
				35	Jones, Mo. 10
				36	Marsalis, Colo. 3
				37	O'Sullivan, Neb. 2
				38	Bonner, N. C. 1

LEGEND: Number of Representatives in the bloc: 38. Each *bloc* member agreed with each other bloc member on 52 or more of the 62 votes in the set. *Mean score* of the bloc: the mean of the number of agreements between all pairs of bloc members. *Rank:* the rank of each bloc member according to the mean of his scores with all other bloc members, 1 designating the highest average number of agreements. *Nucleus:* a highly cohesive cluster or small bloc, around which a more inclusive bloc develops. (e): elective leader. (s): seniority leader.

all 62 in the set, though explaining the pattern of his voting is another matter, to be taken up in the following chapter.

Though the dissenting votes in the structure indicated in Table 33 were not numerous by comparison with the low-cohesion sets, they are of some interest. Among the members of Bloc I and the two nuclei they were of little substantive importance. On the 22 nonunanimous votes in Bloc I there was only one dissenter on 10, and 3 or fewer on 20. Among all of these disputed votes little pattern was evident, since most involved only one or two men and no member of the bloc dissented from his colleagues with any frequency. The most characteristic thread among these dissents was local or regional economic interest,[27] but even this accounts for no more than half the votes on which disagreements were registered among members of the bloc.

Dissent elsewhere in the party, however, indicated the persistence at lower frequency of the divisions that produced opposing blocs on the low-cohesion roll calls. None of the 38 members of Bloc I (Table 33) was "absent" on more than 4 of the roll calls in the set. In the whole party there were 25 men who were not members of the bloc and who had 4 or fewer "absences." Their nonmembership thus was not due to their preferences being unrecorded and must be explained on other grounds. Seventeen of these were in the system—that is, had one or more scores with members of the bloc—and their dissents from the majority position differed only in degree from those that occurred within the bloc itself. The remaining 8 men, however, were not even in the system; their disagreements with the majority presumably were of a different order. Who were these men? What patterns appear in their disagreements with the majority of the party?

Six of these 8 extremists were Southerners, and all but one of them were in the extreme "right" bloc of the Southern wing on the low-cohesion votes of the second session (Bloc S-IV, Table 30B).[28] The substance of the 29 votes on which one or more of these 5 dissented from the party majority had nothing to do with racial questions. These votes rather dealt almost entirely with foreign policy and with domestic economic questions of general character.[29] These votes illustrate

---

[27] For example, votes concerning repeal of the oleomargarine tax, suspending the tariff on copper imports, authorizing particular local construction projects, and creating additional judicial positions in some of the states.

[28] These five were Abernethy and Rankin of Mississippi, Burleson and Wilson of Texas, and Davis of Georgia. The sixth, Bennett of Florida, belonged to none of the principal blocs in any of the sets.

[29] They included all of the votes in the set that were concerned with foreign aid, most of those dealing with other matters of foreign policy (guarantees of private investment in economic development enterprises abroad and appropriations for

the consistency of the party structure on all three sets of votes. More important, they underscore again the point that among the Democrats opposition to the party majority on the key questions of midcentury national policy had its base primarily in Southern constituencies even though it is true that such views were not characteristic of the Southern representation as a whole. This Southern contingent were both the Democratic spearhead of the bipartisan coalition in the House (indicated by the fact that nearly 80 per cent of their dissents were on roll calls on which most Republicans also opposed the Democratic majority) and a die-hard element within the House as a whole (since the remaining 20 per cent of their dissents were on lop-sided bipartisan votes on which the minority in the House numbered no more than two dozen men).

The other two men who, in view of the low number of their "absences," might have been expected to belong in the system—Secrest and Huber of Ohio—illustrate, respectively, the case of the representative whose constituency has political characteristics that almost compel him to deviate from the norm of his party and that of the representative whose voting seems to reflect a particularly close attachment to the claims of a single interest group.

Secrest's fifteenth district in southeastern Ohio was rural—containing only one place whose population was 25,000 or more in 1950—to a degree usually associated in the Middle West with Republican control, and it gave a majority of its votes to the Republican presidential candidate in 1940, 1944, and 1948. Secrest, however, was a local boy, raised, educated, and employed in the district. During World War II he resigned the position in the House to which he had first been elected in 1932, at the age of 28. For three successive Congresses thereafter the district was Republican by a margin larger than that usually accumulated by Secrest, but in 1948 he was able to recapture the seat. His tendency to vote with the Republicans, indicated not only by the number of his dissents but also by the fact that more than four-fifths of these deviations were on votes on which majorities of the two parties were opposed, presumably reflected an accommodation to the political characteristics of his district.

Huber represented the 14th district—four counties west, south, and southeast of Cleveland, three of which were fairly Republican and one, containing the city of Akron, strongly Democratic. Though the district as a whole was normally a fairly close one, the pattern of Huber's dis-

---

support of organizations affiliated with the U.N., among others), and several concerned with domestic economic policy (principally rent control and provisions in the Defense Production Act).

sents would not show it, as he voted rather like a Rankin of the "left." Conspicuously, for example, on a series of votes dealing with the Internal Security Act of 1950, passed over the President's veto, he was one of a handful in the House as a whole who voted against the prevailing view. In fact, three-fifths of his dissents from the party, an unusually high proportion, were on such one-sided bipartisan roll calls. Whether, as his opponent successfully implied in the 1950 campaign, he was taking his lead from the labor groups concentrated in Akron,[30] it is impossible to say, but his voting record suggests a closer identification with the views of a single interest group than would be expected in the representative of a heterogeneous and evenly balanced district.

The two Ohio deviants may be regarded as "sports" of a type occasionally found in both parties.[31] The six Southerners, however, and a number of their less deviant colleagues illustrate in attenuated form the persistence of the party's characteristic voting structure into the high-cohesion roll calls. This persistence demonstrates that the voting structure of the Democrats in the House, as in the Senate, was not random and did not lack pattern. Its consistencies are evident even on those votes on which the party as a whole was comparatively unified.

REPUBLICAN STRUCTURAL CLEAVAGES

The most striking feature of the voting structure of the House Republicans on the intermediate- and low-cohesion sets is fractionation and fluidity. The bloc structures shown in Tables 34 and 35, despite their complexity, do not include all of the numerous small, overlapping clusters that appeared on the matrix. These clusters cannot be shown in all their variety, as was possible with the less dramatic evidence in the Senate (Figure 4), because they overlap at so many individual points. Figure 10, however, presents a simplified comparison of the bloc structures of the Republicans and the Democrats on their respective low-cohesion votes. Several more precise indications of the relatively greater fragmentation of the minority party will be discussed

---

[30] For an illuminating account of the 1950 contest in this district see Stephen K. Bailey and Howard D. Samuel, *Congress at Work*, New York: Henry Holt, 1952, pp. 30–48.

[31] For a Republican equivalent of Secrest, compare the record of Jacob K. Javits, who represented the 21st New York district from the Eightieth through the Eighty-third Congresses. This district was normally Democratic except when Javits ran for the House, and it returned to the Democratic side when Javits in 1954 ran for state office. Javits's voting deviated toward the Democrats as Secrest's did toward the Republicans.

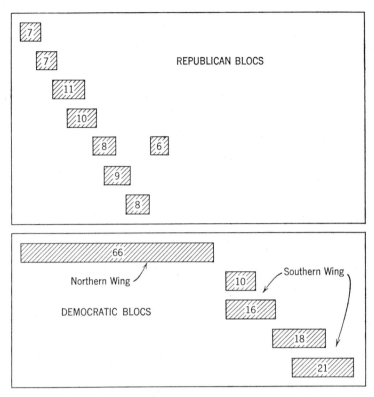

Figure 10. Relative fragmentation: schematic comparison of Republican and Democratic bloc structures in the House, low-cohesion roll calls, 81st Congress, 2nd session. LEGEND: Each *bloc* member agreed with each other bloc member on 46 or more of the 74 votes in the set. These diagrams are simplified representations of the blocs shown in Tables 30 A and B, 31 A and B, 34, and 35. The horizontal dimension of the blocs is proportionate to the number of their members. The numbers within each figure indicate the size of the bloc. The proportion of a bloc lying under another indicates the number of members common to both.

later. For the present, the meaning of Figure 10 is clear. There was among the Republicans no single and sharp line of cleavage such as that which divided the Northern from the Southern wing of the House Democrats, but rather a series of noncongruent lines which, though they permitted the identification of contrasting tendencies within the party, reflected shifting and fluid bases of agreement and, presumably, of association. The tendency is all the more striking in view of the generally higher means of the Republican cohesion indexes as compared with the Democratic on these sets (Table 28). The Republican

Table

REPUBLICAN CLEAVAGE: BLOC STRUCTURE OF HOUSE REPUBLICANS

	Bloc I		Bloc II		Bloc III		Bloc IV
	Members: 7 Mean Score: 51.5		Members: 7 Mean Score: 50.6		Members: 11 Mean Score: 52.0		Members: 10 Mean Score: 53.6
RANK	Name and District	RANK	Name and District	RANK	Name and District	RANK	Name and District
6	Corbett, Pa. 30						
5	Fulton, Pa. 31						
4	Wolverton, N. J. 1 (s)						
3	Canfield, N. J. 8						
2	Case, N. J. 6						
1	Heselton, Mass. 1	2	Heselton				
7	Rogers, Mass. 5 (s)	3	Rogers (s)				
		4	Herter, Mass. 10				
		5	Riehlman, N. Y. 36				
		6	Bolton, Ohio 22				
		1	Wigglesworth, Mass. 13	9	Wigglesworth		
		6	Elston, Ohio 1	1	Elston	2	Elston
				11	Gamble, N. Y. 28		
				10	Keating, N. Y. 40		
				8	St. George, N. Y. 29		
				7	Martin, Mass. 14 (e)		
				6	Dague, Pa. 9	5	Dague
				5	LeFevre, N. Y. 30	8	LeFevre
				4	Fenton, Pa. 12	3	Fenton
				2	Goodwin, Mass. 8	4	Goodwin
				3	Graham, Pa. 25	1	Graham
						6	Gavin, Pa. 19
						9	James, Pa. 7
						10	McCulloch, Ohio 4
						7	Weichel, Ohio 13 (s)

34

ON 74 LOW-COHESION ROLL CALLS, 81ST CONGRESS, 2ND SESSION

	Bloc V		Bloc VI		Bloc VII		Bloc VIII
	Members: 8		Members: 9		Members: 8		Members: 6
	Mean Score: 52.2		Mean Score: 51.0		Mean Score: 49.5		Mean Score: 51.7
RANK	Name and District	RANK	Name and District	RANK	Name and District	RANK	Name and District
6	Graham	5	Graham				
7	McCulloch						
				6	Weichel (s)		
5	Miller, Neb. 4						
4	Davis, Wis. 2						
2	Byrnes, Wis. 8						
3	Rees, Kan. 4 (s)	8	Rees (s)				
1	Scrivner, Kan. 2	1	Scrivner				
8	Smith, Wis. 1	6	Smith				
		2	Clevenger, Ohio 4				
		3	Hoffman, Mich. 4 (s)				
		4	Taber, N. Y. 38 (s)				
		7	Curtis, Neb. 1	3	Curtis		
		9	Reed, N. Y. 45 (s)				
				8	Dondero, Mich. 17 (s)		
				7	Reed, Ill. 14		
				5	Arends, Ill. 17 (e)		
				4	Jensen, Iowa 7		
				2	Brown, Ohio 7		
				1	Simpson, Ill. 20 (s)		
						1	LeCompte, Iowa 4 (s)
						2	Cunningham, Iowa 5
						3	Hoeven, Iowa 8
						4	Talle, Iowa 2
						5	Stefan, Neb. 3
						5	Gross, Iowa 3

LEGEND: Number of representatives in blocs: 48. Each *bloc* member agreed with each other bloc member on 46 or more of the 74 votes in the set. *Mean score* of the bloc: the mean of the number of agreements between all pairs of bloc members. *Rank:* the rank of each bloc member according to the mean of his scores with all other bloc members, 1 designating the highest average number of agreements. (e): elective leader. (s): seniority leader.

Table

REPUBLICAN CLEAVAGE: BLOC STRUCTURE OF HOUSE REPUBLICANS

	Bloc I		Bloc II		Bloc III
	Members: 8		Members: 29		Members: 32
	Mean Score: 53.1		Mean Score: 53.4		Mean Score: 53.8
RANK	Name and District	RANK	Name and District	RANK	Name and District
8	Judd, Minn. 5				
7	McDonough, Cal. 15				
5	Holmes, Wash. 4				
4	Heselton, Mass. 1				
1	Wigglesworth, Mass. 13	4	Wigglesworth	15	Wigglesworth
2	Herter, Mass. 10	17	Herter	28	Herter
3	Auchincloss, N. J. 32	29	Auchincloss		
6	Nixon, Cal. 12	28	Nixon		
		22	Ford, Mich. 5		
		20	McConnell, Pa. 16 (s)		
		27	Anderson, Cal. 8	31	Anderson
		25	Cotton, N. H. 2	32	Cotton
		26	Goodwin, Mass. 8	25	Goodwin
		18	Vorys, Ohio 12	23	Vorys
		23	Miller, Md. 1	26	Miller
		24	McMillen, Ill. 22	26	McMillen
		21	LeFevre, N. Y. 30	24	LeFevre
		11	Scudder, Cal. 1	14	Scudder
		9	Hope, Kan. 5 (s)	16	Hope (s)
		3	Michener, Mich. 2 (s)	3	Michener (s)
		15	Hoeven, Iowa 8	17	Hoeven
		12	Allen, Cal. 7	13	Allen
		6	LeCompte, Iowa 4 (s)	9	LeCompte (s)
		5	Talle, Iowa 2	10	Talle
		19	Arends, Ill. 17 (e)	20	Arends (e)
		1	Graham, Pa. 25	1	Graham
		7	Brown, Ohio 7	4	Brown
		2	Cole, Kan. 1	2	Cole
		16	Jenkins, Ohio 10	18	Jenkins
		8	Simpson, Ill. 20 (s)	7	Simpson (s)
		14	McCulloch, Ohio 4	11	McCulloch
		10	Meyer, Kan. 3	7	Meyer
		13	Rees, Kan. 4 (s)	6	Rees (s)
				21	Bramblett Cal. 11
				29	Halleck, Ind. 2
				11	Barrett, Wyo. AL
				5	Scrivner, Kan. 2
				19	Chiperfield, Ill. 19
				22	Dague, Pa. 9
				30	Wolcott, Mich. 7 (s)

LEGEND: Number of representatives in blocs: 55. Each *bloc* member agreed with each other bloc member on 46 or more of the 74 votes in the set. *Mean score* of the bloc: the mean of the number of agreements between all pairs of bloc members. *Rank:* the rank of each bloc member according to the mean of his scores with all other bloc members, 1 designating the highest average number of agreements. (e): elective leader. (s): seniority leader.

35

ON 74 INTERMEDIATE-COHESION ROLL CALLS, 81ST CONGRESS, 1ST SESSION

Bloc IV		Bloc V		Bloc VI	
Members: 32		Members: 23		Members: 6	
Mean Score: 53.9		Mean Score: 54.3		Mean Score: 51.6	
RANK	Name and District	RANK	Name and District	RANK	Name and District
18	Wigglesworth				
27	McConnell (s)				
31	Anderson				
32	Cotton				
26	Goodwin				
24	Vorys				
30	Miller				
25	McMillen				
28	LeFevre				
14	Scudder				
8	Michener (s)	17	Michener (s)		
17	Hoeven				
12	Allen				
9	LeCompte (s)				
10	Talle	11	Talle		
19	Arends (e)	14	Arends (e)		
1	Graham	1	Graham		
4	Brown	5	Brown		
2	Cole	7	Cole		
16	Jenkins	12	Jenkins		
7	Simpson (s)	4	Simpson (s)		
11	McCulloch	8	McCulloch		
6	Meyer	6	Meyer		
5	Rees (s)	3	Rees (s)		
23	Bramblett				
29	Halleck				
12	Barrett				
3	Scrivner	2	Scrivner		
15	Chiperfield	13	Chiperfield		
22	Dague	16	Dague		
20	Church, Ill. 13	9	Church		
21	Dondero, Mich. 17 (s)	9	Dondero (s)		
		15	Gillette, Pa. 14		
		21	Smith, Kan. 6		
		20	Nicholson, Mass. 9		
		19	Jensen, Iowa 7		
		18	Werdel, Cal. 10		
		22	Byrnes, Wis. 8		
		23	Reed, Ill. 14		
				6	Davis, Wis. 2
				5	Murray, Wis. 7
				4	Gross, Iowa 3
				3	Anderson, Minn. 7
				2	Lemke, N. D. AL
				1	Hagen, Minn. 9

lower-cohesion votes, that is, showed on the average somewhat less deep fissures within the party, but the basis of their slightly greater unity was a shifting one. This tendency, as would be expected, was less conspicuous on the intermediate-cohesion votes of the first session than on the low-cohesion votes of the second.

A symptom of the fractionation, especially on the low-cohesion set of the second session (Table 34), is the concentration of representatives from a particular state in several of the blocs.[32] This clustering of state delegations, less obvious in the Democratic sets, will be examined in more detail in Chapter 7. In the present context its significance is as an indicator of the looseness or fluidity of the party, which was apparently greater than in the Senate Republican structure.[33]

---

[32] In Table 34 note, for example, the New Jersey cluster in Bloc I, the Massachusetts cluster in Bloc II, the Wisconsin cluster in Bloc V, and the Iowa cluster in Bloc VIII, among others.

[33] It may be in order here to make as explicit as possible the difference between two aspects of voting structure: fluidity and noncohesion. They are not identical. Noncohesion means that within a party the majority element on a series of votes is comparatively small. If this majority is usually composed of the same men, the structure is stable; if, however, its composition tends to change perceptibly from one issue to another, the structure is fluid or loose. Thus the House Democratic structure was less cohesive but also less fluid than the Republican. In the Senate, on the other hand, the Republican structure was both less cohesive and more fluid than the Democratic. These comparisons within the House or Senate are reasonably reliable. Comparisons between the two chambers on a point such as this, however, can be justified only on the basis of impression. As noted earlier in this chapter, the mean cohesion indexes of both parties in the House are likely to be higher than in the Senate as they were in the Eighty-first Congress:

	DEMOCRATS	REPUBLICANS
First Session		
Senate (215 roll calls)	64.1	51.7
House (118 roll calls)	65.9	68.2
Second Session		
Senate (229 roll calls)	61.0	51.0
House (151 roll calls)	61.8	67.1

A reason for this appearance of greater cohesion in the House is that, given the severe restrictions on House debate and the normal practice of disposing of most amendments in the Committee of the Whole, without record votes, the House roll calls generally include fewer votes on amendments, preliminary matters on which cohesion is often low. Thus, were the House roll calls more exactly comparable to those in the Senate—in number and in kind of motion—the parties of the lower house might appear no more cohesive.

For essentially the same reason the structure of the Senate parties is almost certain to appear less fluid. Since the Senate roll calls usually include more votes on preliminary matters, they provide a larger "sample" of recorded preferences on any one issue or series of closely related issues on which the voting structure of

The fluidity of the Republican structure is reflected in a lack of close resemblance between the blocs in Tables 34 and 35. Stability of position was not completely lacking, however. No name appearing in one of the blocs on the extreme right or left side of Table 34 is in the reverse position in Table 35. Despite some shifting, moreover, there were several men whose positions were essentially the same on the two sets. For example, Herter, Heselton, and Wigglesworth of Massachusetts, who were members of Blocs I or II on the "left" of the party in the second-session set (Table 34), were also in the equivalent position (Bloc I) on the intermediate-cohesion votes (Table 35). At the other extreme, while most of the members of Bloc VIII, the cluster on the "right" side of Table 34, occupied a more central position on the votes of the intermediate-cohesion set (Table 35), Gross of Iowa remained in essentially the same "right" location (Bloc VI, Table 35).

The superficial attributes of such stability as appears in the structure of these two sets are not perfectly clear. In the low-cohesion set (Table 34) there was an evident connection between geographic region and position in the structure. With a few exceptions the men who belonged to the blocs on the left side of the table were from the East and those in the blocs on the right were from the Middle West. The cleavage on these votes thus resembled that among the Senate Republicans. Traces of the same sort of division were evident on the intermediate-cohesion votes. Only 4 of the 29 men in Blocs V and VI in Table 35 were from east of the Appalachians, while the proportion in Blocs I and II was more than twice as great, 10 out of 33. But the correlation between region and position in the voting structure is not consistent nor nearly as close as in the case of the Democrats.

The substantive differences among the blocs in a multinuclear system as fluid and fractionated as this should appear as slight gradations between adjacent blocs with marked oppositions only between the extremes. This is in fact generally the case. As one moves from the left to the right sides of Tables 34 and 35 he encounters increasing opposition to the foreign aid program, increasing hostility to the Administration on other foreign policy matters, a larger number of negative votes on such domestic programs as rent control and social security

---

the parties is essentially the same. In the House, where the "sample" is smaller, the number of issues (or closely related series) per hundred record votes is normally larger. Hence the number of structural shifts is likely to be larger, with a resulting appearance of great fluidity. (The best analogy, perhaps, is to the difference between a slow-motion and a fast-motion picture of the same action. If there are on a film more frames per minute, movement will appear to be slight; if there are few pictures per minute, they will give an impression of great activity.)

extension, and a reduced enthusiasm for such civil rights measures as
F.E.P.C. and the bill outlawing poll taxes.

This characterization is accurate in only the most general terms,
however, for it exaggerates the consistency of a "left-to-right" distribution within the party. Bloc I in both Tables 34 and 35 supported the
Administration on both foreign and domestic issues more regularly than
any other bloc. Its "left" tendencies are clear, at least in relative terms.
Among the blocs to the right in the tables, however, there is less consistency. Which is regarded as more to the "right" in its voting depends on the issues. For example, most of the oppositions between
Blocs I and VIII (Table 34) in the low-cohesion set dealt with agricultural matters, the latter bloc having been almost alone among the
Republicans in supporting upward revision of cotton and peanut acreage allotments. It voted in opposition to Bloc I on some foreign policy
matters, but not all, supported the F.E.P.C. bill, and generally opposed rent control. On the other hand, between Blocs I and VI in the
same set the principal disagreements were in the realm of foreign policy, although in addition the latter bloc was opposed to rent control,
to the F.E.P.C. bill, and to the retention of the 21-day rule. Largely
because of its votes on farm policy, Bloc VIII was more isolated from
the rest of the party than Bloc VI, but which was more to the "right"
in its views? Similarly, in the intermediate-cohesion set of the first
session (Table 35) Bloc VI was conspicuous in its support of several
farm measures (although it was not unexpectedly opposed to the repeal of the oleomargarine tax), in its opposition to the bill restricting
F.P.C. jurisdiction over natural gas producers, and in its strong hostility to foreign aid, but it consistently favored efforts to outlaw poll
taxes. Bloc V, on the other hand, though divided on most of the farm
votes, consistently supported the gas bill and, especially among its
nuclear members,[34] was opposed to the anti-poll-tax legislation.

As in the case of the Southern wing of the House Democrats, no
obvious demographic or political factor was identified that consistently
distinguished the components of the Republican "right" from one another. Bloc VIII in Table 34 and Bloc VI in Table 35 clearly had a
regional base, but Blocs VI and VII in Table 34 and particularly Bloc
V in Table 35, even its nucleus, were intersectional in composition.
Between these blocs, moreover, there was no reliable difference in the
proportion of the population classified as urban. Again the general
pattern of voting points to the influence of such factors as the personal

---

[34] The nuclear members of Bloc V were Gillette of Pennsylvania, Jensen of Iowa,
Nicholson of Massachusetts, and Smith of Kansas.

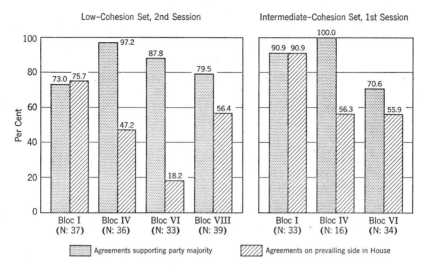

Figure 11. Proportion of agreements supporting party majority and on prevailing side in the House, principal Republican blocs, low-, and intermediate-cohesion roll calls, 81st Congress, 1st and 2nd sessions. Agreements include all votes on which the bloc was unanimous plus those on which less than half the members were unrecorded and the remainder were unanimous.

preferences of the representative and his associations in the constituency and in the House, all operating within the general context of the differences between the parties in the House.[35] This may be peculiarly the case in a structure that is marked by both fractionation and fluidity.

In view of the difficulty involved in labeling one wing of the House Republicans as "left" and the other as "right" on these roll calls, it is not surprising to find that blocs on either extreme of the structure showed a tendency toward voting in coalition with one or another segment of the Democrats and in opposition to the majority of their own party. Figure 11, which represents data on a selection of the blocs shown in Tables 34 and 35, illustrates this point by comparing the proportion of intrabloc agreements on the side of the party majority

[35] A factor of interest that seems to be related to some but not all die-hard voting by representatives in both parties is that the constituencies of several of these men were small in population and included a number of counties whose population had declined between 1940 and 1950 and in which income levels were relatively low as compared with the rest of the state. It may be that the effect of "rotten borough" representation upon a legislative body derives less from its usual rural character than from the attitudes that may be characteristic of a population that has been literally left behind.

with the proportion on the prevailing side in the House. In the low-co-hesion set of the second session the members of Bloc I were actually agreed more often on the prevailing side than on that of the party majority, a clear sign of coalition voting. The equivalent Bloc I in the intermediate-cohesion set was less extreme, but its members were never-theless agreed as often on the prevailing side as on the side of the majority of the party. The blocs on the "right" wing (Bloc VIII in the low-cohesion set and Bloc VI in the intermediate) were less disposed than these to coalition behavior but were more likely to vote with a Democratic faction than were any of the clusters in the middle. The ratios of their prevailing agreements to their party-majority agreements were higher than in any other blocs except those on the far "left." [36] The mean party orthodoxy indexes of these blocs over the sessions as a whole were generally consistent with this pattern. The mean Admin-istration support indexes, which tended to be high at the "left" and "right" extremes, testify to the loose meaning of these terms when ap-plied to the Republican blocs and they also point to the maverick tendencies of these clusters at the two extremes of the structure.[37]

It thus seems clear that the fractionation of the Republican party in the House involved, if it did not cause, a tendency for generally op-posed wings of the party to break away and side with one or another bloc among the Democrats. Coalition voting was not a peculiarity of

---

[36] By way of precaution the point should be made that this device of identify-ing coalition voting by the difference between the proportion of prevailing and party-majority agreements does not exhaust the possibilities of such behavior. In fact, it points to such coalitions only when the bipartisan group constitutes a majority in the House. Those cases in which a coalition is in the minority in the House as a whole, especially if it is part of a majority in the party being examined, are not detected. Signs of such minority coalitions may be seen elsewhere in the data, however. Thus in Table 35 Bloc V, though none of its agreements was against the party majority, had the third lowest mean party orthodoxy index over the session as a whole and also the lowest Administration support index. Given the evidence on the substance of its agreements, notably its hostility to the anti-poll-tax bill, it seems likely that these indexes reflect a proclivity for voting with a minority group on the right wing of the Democratic party.

[37] The mean party orthodoxy indexes of the several Republican blocs were as follows: low-cohesion set, second session: Bloc I 4.04, Bloc II 4.30, Bloc III 4.52, Bloc IV 4.52, Bloc V 4.34, Bloc VI 4.21, Bloc VII 4.28, Bloc VIII 4.21; intermedi-ate-cohesion set, first session: Bloc I 4.26, Bloc II 4.53, Bloc III 4.55, Bloc IV 4.55, Bloc V 4.49, Bloc VI 4.04. The corresponding mean Administration support in-dexes were: low-cohesion set: Bloc I 3.57, Bloc II 3.03, Bloc III 2.59, Bloc IV 2.39, Bloc V 2.21, Bloc VI 2.02, Bloc VII 2.15, Bloc VIII 2.57; intermediate-cohesion set: Bloc I 3.55, Bloc II 2.92, Bloc III 2.82, Bloc IV 2.78, Bloc V 2.46, Bloc VI 2.98. (The Administration support indexes for the second session do not include 14 tactical votes on the F.E.P.C. bill and consequently are based on 59 votes.)

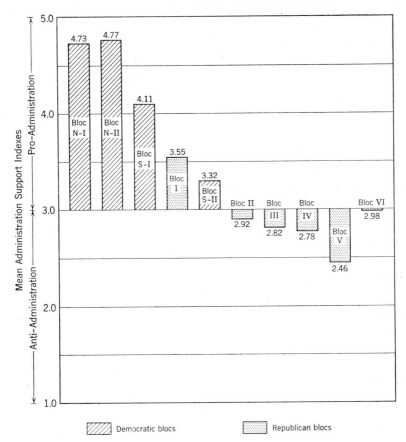

Figure 12. Interparty differences: mean Administration support indexes of Democratic and Republican blocs, House, 81st Congress, 1st Session, intermediate-cohesion votes. A mean Administration support index of 5.00 would indicate that, on all of the votes *in the session* that were classified as Administration support votes, all members of the bloc invariably voted on the Administration side, a mean index of 1.00 that none ever voted in that way.

only one wing of the party but occurred among blocs at both extremes and on quite different kinds of issues.[38]

Lest these references to coalition voting be misleading, attention should be called to the evidence in these data that in the House, as in

---

[38] On this score it may be noted that the blocs at the extremes of Tables 34 and 35 had few agreements in common, about one-third of the total of the first-session set and less than one-quarter in the low-cohesion set of the second session. In each case, moreover, approximately half of these common agreements dealt with civil rights, the poll tax issue in the first session and F.E.P.C. in the second.

the Senate, the structural cleavages within the parties were on the whole less marked than the divisions between the parties. This is clear from a comparison of the mean Administration support indexes of the various Democratic blocs with those of the Republican blocs. In the first session (Figure 12) only one Republican bloc, the "left" Bloc I, had a higher mean index of Administration support than the Democratic bloc that was most deviant on this count, Bloc S-II. In the second session the pattern was slightly less contrasting, since both "left" Republican blocs had higher mean Administration support indexes than did the extreme "right" Democratic bloc, but the essential tendencies were the same as those shown in Figure 12. The interparty differences are less marked than they were in the Senate, suggesting a wider range of tendency in the larger body.[39] But even in these circumstances the Republican "left" was nearer the Democratic "right" than the Democratic "left." Even on these low-cohesion votes the relevance of party as such to voting patterns in the House is unmistakable.

The most striking characteristic of the House Republican party on these low- and intermediate-cohesion roll calls, fractionation and structural fluidity, has been noted at several points in the preceding paragraphs. Despite the fact that the means of the cohesion indexes for the Republican sets were higher than for the Democratic ones, the composition of the Republicans' majority apparently was more changeable than the Democrats', with the result that the Republican structure, especially in the second-session set, was a complicated series of relatively small, overlapping blocs. This peculiarity of the Republican structure can be summarized in the following fashion: In the second-session sets the largest Republican bloc, 11 men, included approximately 6 per cent of the total party membership, while the largest

---

[39] This point should not be exaggerated, since, as noted at the opening of the chapter, differences in analytical procedures as well as peculiarities in the two chambers make Senate-House comparisons risky. For example, as additional scores are entered on a matrix, the mean Administration support index of extreme blocs tends to be moderated, downward in the case of "left" blocs and upward in the case of those on the "right." Had it been profitable on other counts to carry the House matrixes below 46 agreements to 38, as was done in the case of the Senate, it is likely that the distribution of the mean Administration support indexes in the House would have resembled more closely that in the Senate. In addition, there is the complication introduced by differences in the size of the parties in the two chambers. A nine-man bloc among the 171 House Republicans represents approximately 5 per cent of the party. A bloc representing this proportion of the 42 Senate Republicans would include two men. Had the Senate analysis dealt with clusters of this size, other things being equal, it is likely that some of the apparent differences between the chambers would have disappeared.

Democratic bloc, 66 men, included slightly over a quarter of that party's members; in the first-session sets just under 19 per cent of the Republicans, 32 men, were in that party's largest bloc, while slightly more than 29 per cent of the Democrats, 77 men, were in the largest bloc on the other side of the aisle.

When the same sort of tendency was identified among the Senate Republicans, a suggestion was offered that the minority legislative party might, especially if the White House were of the opposite party persuasion, show a rather loose, kaleidoscopic voting structure because it lacked or was unable to develop a coherent, programmed approach to the legislative agenda. In addition to the data already presented, there are two other indicators that seem to point in the same direction, both of which involve the tricky but perhaps revealing factor of "absences." In the first place, on both sets of votes the Republicans on the average were more often "absent," that is, not present and no preference recorded, than the Democrats. On the intermediate-cohesion votes of the first session the mean of the Republican "absences" was 10.8, of the Democrats, 8.5; on the low-cohesion set of the second session the Republican mean was 11.6, the Democratic, 9.2. These differences, though consistent, are not large, but they suggest a lack of involvement within the minority party, greater indifference to the outcome. There are no obvious indications that the votes in the Republican sets included a higher proportion on trivial matters. To be sure, as pointed out earlier, more of the Republican votes in these sets dealt with final actions, votes taken at a stage when the probable result was clear. If this were the explanation of the higher Republican "absence" rate, however, it would still be consistent with the proposition that voting patterns, including "absences," reflected distinctive aspects of the minority party's role.

In the second place, on both sets of votes a smaller proportion of Republicans than of Democrats who might have been expected to belong to one of the identified blocs actually did so. This estimate was made on essentially the same basis as that used to analyze the "isolate" category in the Senate. Taking the mean "absences" recorded by the entire membership of the party, one may assume that any member of the party whose "absences" were equal to or lower than the average for the party and who was not in a bloc was voting in an unstructured fashion, first with one and then with another segment of the party, or was siding as an individual or as part of a tiny cluster with the opposition. The proportion of such men in the party is thus a rough measure of fractionation, and the comparative size of these proportions in the two parties is an indicator of relative fluidity. In the low-cohesion sets of the second session there were 48, or slightly over 28 per cent, of the Republicans and 51, or less than 20 per cent, of the Democrats in this position. In the intermediate-cohesion sets of the first session the comparable numbers were 50 Republicans and 44 Democrats, representing slightly more than 29 per cent and just under 17 per cent of the party memberships, respectively. There were 81 Republicans and 77 Democrats in this ambiguous position on one or both of the sets.

It thus seems evident that, on the intermediate- and low-cohesion sets, the House Republicans, even perhaps somewhat more than their Senate colleagues, displayed a relatively fluid, kaleidoscopic pattern of voting. This inference, of course, does not warrant an assertion that this kind of voting pattern is an inevitable tendency of the minority legislative party, but as a hypothesis it is at least tenable. Though it is consistent with the data of the Eighty-first Congress, it cannot be regarded as established on the basis of these data alone. Moreover, if there is a disposition toward fluidity inherent in the position of a minority situated as were the Republicans in 1949 and 1950, variations in the associated conditions, including the skill with which the majority's President exploited the issues, would materially affect the extent to which the disposition became a dominant characteristic. Some of these variations will be discussed more fully in a later chapter.[40] For the moment it is sufficient, on the basis of evidence from both House and Senate, again to record the possibility that a minority party also out of power in the White House inherently tends to face special handicaps to coherent and structured voting.

THE REPUBLICANS UNITED

The voting structure of the Republican party on the high-cohesion set of the second session superficially bears almost no resemblance to the two sets just discussed. As is clear from Table 36, the structure was uninuclear. Virtually all those who had at least one score of 56 or higher on the 66 votes in the set—that is, who were in the system whose bloc structure is shown in the table—had their highest scores with one or more of the four men in Nucleus Ia-1. There was none of the isolated clustering and fluidity characteristic of the two sets with lower mean indexes of cohesion.

The consolidation of the Republican structure on this set is high-

---

[40] See chap. 8, pp. 289–316. For confirmatory evidence on the fluidity of the Republicans in this Congress, derived by quite different methods, see MacRae, *Dimensions of Congressional Voting*, p. 231.

Table 36

REPUBLICAN UNITY: BLOC STRUCTURE OF HOUSE REPUBLICANS ON 66 HIGH-COHESION ROLL CALLS, 81ST CONGRESS, 2ND SESSION

	Nucleus Ia-1		Nucleus Ia-2		Bloc I
	Members: 4		Members: 12		Members: 31
	Mean Score: 65.2		Mean Score: 63.0		Mean Score: 60.4
RANK	Name and District	RANK	Name and District	RANK	Name and District
1	Ford, Mich. 5	1	Ford	1	Ford
1	Fenton, Pa. 12	1	Fenton	1	Fenton
3	Elston, Ohio 1	3	Elston	3	Elston
3	Wigglesworth, Mass. 13	4	Wigglesworth	4	Wigglesworth
		5	McGregor, Ohio 17	5	McGregor
		5	Gamble, N. Y. 28	6	Gamble
		7	Hope, Kan. 5 (s)	7	Hope (s)
		8	Cole, Kan. 1	8	Cole
		8	Phillips, Cal. 22	9	Phillips
		10	Beall, Md. 6	10	Beall
		11	Auchincloss, N. J. 3	14	Auchincloss
		12	Rogers, Mass. 5 (s)	15	Rogers (s)
				11	Bramblett, Cal. 11
				12	Heselton, Mass. 1
				12	Keating, N. Y. 40
				15	Graham, Pa. 25
				17	Herter, Mass. 10
				18	Cotton, N. H. 2
				19	Scrivner, Kan. 2
				20	McConnell, Pa. 16 (s)
				21	Gavin, Pa. 19
				21	Holmes, Wash. 4
				23	Anderson, Minn. 7
				24	Rees, Kan. 4
				24	Davis, Wis. 2
				26	Cunningham, Iowa 5
				26	Michener, Mich. 2 (s)
				28	Scott, Hardie, Pa. 3
				29	Corbett, Pa. 30
				30	Jensen, Iowa 7
				31	Horan, Wash. 5

LEGEND: Number of representatives in bloc: 31. Each *bloc* member agreed with each other bloc member on 56 or more of the 66 votes in the set. *Mean score* of the bloc: the mean of the number of agreements between all pairs of bloc members. *Rank:* the rank of each bloc member according to the mean of his scores with all other bloc members, 1 designating the highest average number of agreements. *Nucleus:* a highly cohesive cluster or small bloc, around which a more inclusive bloc develops. (s): seniority leader.

lighted by the appearance of a number of men among the 31 members of Bloc I who on the other two sets were in the more isolated blocs or were in no bloc at all despite a relatively low "absence" rate. Some of these, moreover, ranked fairly high in this bloc. For example, Fenton of Pennsylvania, who belonged to no bloc on the other sets though his "absence" rate was low, ranked first in this bloc. Heselton of Massachusetts, who was consistently on the "left" of the other structures, ranked in the upper half of this bloc. Cunningham of Iowa, who was on the "right" wing on the low-cohesion votes of the second session, became a member of this bloc, though not a very prominent one, as did Jensen of Iowa, who appeared on the "right" in both of the sets previously discussed.

With some exceptions, which will be discussed later, membership in Bloc I and its nuclei tended to be a function of the individual's "absence" rate, as was the case on the equivalent Democratic set. For example, though Martin of Massachusetts, the Minority Leader, was not in the bloc, he was in the system. His highest scores were with Fenton and Ford, the top-ranking members of the bloc. He agreed with both of these men on 59 of the 66 roll calls, the difference being attributable to his seven "absences."

On this set of votes, in contrast with the other two, Republican "absences" were relatively low. The Republican mean of 9.5 was, in fact, lower than that of the Democrats, who were "absent" on an average of 10.7 of their high-cohesion votes. In terms of this indicator of structural looseness, therefore, the Republicans were in an obviously stronger position than on the other sets, somewhat more so than the Democrats. Other factors confirm this inference. Thus the 82 men in the system, that is, with at least one score of 56 or higher, and the 31 men in Bloc I represented slightly larger proportions of the Republican party, 48 and 18 per cent, respectively, than did the equivalent formations among the Democrats, in which the comparable percentages were 44 and 15. The rate of dissent from Bloc I was about the same as in the Democratic bloc. Twenty-four of the 66 votes in the set were not unanimous among the members of Bloc I. Thirteen of these, however, involved only one dissenter from the rest of the bloc and on 22 of the 24 there were 3 or fewer dissenters.

This was a highly consolidated structure, but among the 24 votes on which the bloc was not unanimous there was a trace of pattern, more than in the equivalent Democratic bloc. The pattern was continuous with the lines of cleavage most conspicuous in the votes on which the party was less cohesive. That is, there were two identifiable types of dissenters. First, a number of disagreeing votes were cast by men who were in one of the "right" blocs on the low-cohesion set of the second session (Table 34), such as Jensen and Cunningham of Iowa and Rees of Kansas. One or more of this group, for example, voted with the Southern Democratic bloc on several of the tactical maneuvers concerning F.E.P.C. Second, a somewhat larger number of dissenting votes was cast by men who on the low-cohesion roll calls were in one of the "left" blocs, for instance, Heselton of Massachusetts and Corbett of Pennsylvania. Among the disagreements registered by one or more of these men were votes opposing restrictive amendments to the Defense Production Act, opposing the basing-point pricing bill, and favoring the legislation authorizing the Export-Import Bank to guarantee American private investments in underdeveloped countries. Not all of the 24 dissents fit this pattern, but enough did to reveal in attenuated form the persistence of the cleavages evident on the low-cohesion votes.[41]

To the "right" and to the "left" of these dissenters there were, as among the Democrats, a number of "extremists," men whose "absence" rate was low but who nevertheless were not members of the bloc. There were 19 men not in Bloc I who had 4 or fewer absences, 4 being the highest number of absences for any bloc member. Twelve of these men were in the system, however, indicating relatively slight degrees of dissent from the majority. The remaining 7, the real "extremists," divided into a "right" group of 4 and a "left" group of 3. Those in each of these groups had voting *tendencies* in common, but it is important to note that they did not agree on enough *specific votes* to form separate nuclei or blocs. The 4 on the "right" were Hoffman of Michigan, Taber and Kilburn of New York, and Nicholson of Massachusetts. Those among these 4 who were in blocs on the low-cohesion votes were on the "right" wing, and their common tendencies on this set included opposition to the F.E.P.C. legislation and a general conservatism on such domestic issues as were involved in the Defense Production Act, the legislation authorizing the union shop for railway labor, and the cooperative middle-income housing bill. On the "left" were Hull of Wisconsin and Case and Canfield of New Jersey. Their location on the low-cohesion votes was either among the low-"absence" dissenters, as here, or in one of the "left" blocs. Their tendency was to vote with the Democratic majority on such measures as the middle-income housing bill, the Defense Production Act, and the few foreign policy questions in the set. The contrast between these two groups can be seen in the fact that most of the "left" dissents were on party votes. That is, they sided with the Democratic majority on a number of votes that were fairly controversial between the parties. The "right" grouping, however, dissented primarily on non-party votes. In other words, like a handful of the Southern Democrats, they were die-hards, voting against sometimes lop-sided bipartisan majorities on issues that were

---

[41] There were even some indications of a persistence of the East-West division, with men from the former region somewhat overrepresented in Bloc I. There were in the party 64 men from the 6 New England states plus New York, New Jersey, and Pennsylvania, slightly over 37 per cent of the party. Of the 31 men in Bloc I, however, 14 or slightly over 45 per cent were from these states.

almost completely lacking in controversy within the House as a whole.

Despite these evidences of a persistence of structural tendency between the low- and high-cohesion votes, some comment may be in order on the contrasts in the Republican structure at these two stages. Why is there no evidence on this set of the fluidity characteristic of the others? In a sense the question is pointless, since it seems to ask why high-cohesion votes are not low-cohesion. There is a point, however, for, while low cohesion implies a degree of fractionation, it does not, as the contrast with the House Democrats suggests, necessarily imply fluidity. Why were there no signs of fluidity when the Republicans were comparatively unified, for example in the mean "absence" rate, in the proportion of the party who were members of the bloc or in the system? Indicators such as these, of course, could not be as strong in a high-cohesion set, but why were they so inconspicuous? They were evident on the Republican high-cohesion sets in the Senate. Why not in the House? The explanation is quite simple. Although the House votes in the second session contained a number dealing with subjects that tended to split the Republicans, a somewhat higher proportion dealt with topics, conspicuously civil rights, on which they were usually relatively unified. The reverse was true of the Senate Republicans and of the House Democrats. In other words, the high-cohesion set for the House Republicans was "higher" than the high-cohesion votes of the Senate Republicans. The peculiarities of the House Republicans on this set, therefore, do not contradict the general finding that when the minority party split in the Eighty-first Congress, the lines of cleavage varied with the issue, whereas in the majority party they tended to follow the same lines almost regardless of the substance of the vote.

SUMMARY

Drawing together the principal implications of this analysis, it is evident that the parties in the House, as in the Senate, showed a structural stability throughout the Eighty-first Congress. It was, however, less perceptible in the House, especially among the Republicans. Despite their generally higher cohesion on the votes of both sessions, the Republicans divided not on either side of a single line of cleavage but along a series of lines that shifted almost from issue to issue. In these circumstances the inference that the voting blocs within the party reflect patterns of association and not merely coincidental agreements is less tenable. The voting behavior of the Republicans when they were divided resembled the kaleidoscopic stereotype, a moving pattern of shifting individuals or small clusters based on state delegations or even less inclusive aggregations.

The main lines of division, even among the Democrats, were not merely sectional. Among the Republicans there was a tendency toward an East-West split, but it was not perfectly consistent. Among the Democrats, the majority wing, even on the votes with the lowest mean index of cohesion, was clearly intersectional. As in the Senate, deviation from the Democratic majority was peculiarly a characteristic of representatives from the South, but this was not true of all Southerners, nor was it consistently the case with very many. The few consistent recalcitrants, moreover, the die-hards, opposed the majority of the party not merely on issues involving race, a position they shared with almost all representatives from the South, but even more conspicuously on a wide range of issues of both foreign and domestic policy reflecting the strains and demands of midcentury society.

In neither party did the die-hards have in common any aggregate demographic or political characteristic of their constituencies that consistently accounted for their voting behavior, with the possible exception that most of them represented districts in which one party was overwhelmingly dominant. This feature and the absence of any others suggest that explanation of their behavior lies in peculiarities of the power structure in their constituencies, in special features of the attitudes and values of the individual representatives, and in the characteristics of their associations within the legislature. The last two of these three point to discretionary features of the voting choice. The factors of individual attitude and intralegislative relations, moreover, may be subject to influence from within the legislative party, perhaps especially from the party leadership, which will be examined in the following chapter.

Despite intraparty cleavages, the evidence is clear, as it was in the Senate, that there were real differences in the policy tendencies and in the structural characteristics of the two legislative parties as reflected in the record votes. The policy difference was indicated particularly in the contrasting behavior of the parties on those roll calls in both sessions that were classified as Administration support votes. Although some Republicans supported the Administration more strongly than some Democrats, the central tendencies of the blocs within the parties were in opposite directions. The fluidity of the Republican structure when the party was divided also marked a difference from the Democrats. Among the latter, fluidity, the tendency for lines of cleavage to change with the issues, was confined to the Southern wing; among the Republicans it was so clearly evident, especially in the low-cohesion votes of the second session, that it was virtually impossible to identify a stable majority segment of the party.

It is probably not the case that fluidity and fractionation are always characteristic of a minority legislative party, one that faces a President of the opposite label, but it seems likely that a party in this situation, as the Republicans in the Eighty-first Congress, may suffer special handicaps to the development of a coherent and viable legislative position or program.

chapter six

PARTY LEADERSHIP ROLES
IN THE
HOUSE OF REPRESENTATIVES

The difference in the size and the composition of the House of Representatives is sharply reflected in the machinery of its leadership. Yet in the House, as in the Senate, the power of the party leaders is in considerable measure informal and interstitial in character—less so than in the Senate, to be sure, but still far from completely described by the formal rules.

The characteristics of the leadership roles in the House derive necessarily, as in the Senate, from the attributes of the legislative party as a group as well as from the distinctive formal features of the House itself. As the material in the preceding chapter has indicated, to think of the legislative party as a group does not violate the evidence of the record votes. Each is reasonably viewed as a system of interactions, and each labels an identifiable tendency of attitude as well as of behavior. Yet the cleavages within the parties in the House were at least as conspicuous as those in the Senate; they suggest again an apparent contradiction between stability and persistence, on the one hand, and fluidity and disunity, on the other, which cannot be resolved by analogy to simpler groups where such oppositions are neither character-

193

istic nor persistent. The explanation must rather be found in an underlying difference of function, in what the legislative party does for its members and within the political system as a whole that distinguishes it from groups lacking this contradictory appearance. In short, it seems appropriate to think of the legislative party in the House as a mediate group. Like its counterpart in the Senate, it does some things of real importance for its members, but their continuing status does not depend entirely upon how or whether these activities are carried on.

But there are significant differences between the legislative party in the House and that in the Senate, differences in degree if not in kind which may make the larger group functionally more inclusive, more critical for the survival of its members. Fundamentally these differences are traceable to the greater size of the House. In a body four and one-half times as large as the Senate, whose parties are larger than those in the upper chamber by approximately the same proportions, the individual member is scarcely visible to the electorate. Even in a state that chooses one or more representatives at large it seems likely that the House provides too large and diffuse a setting for the individual member to stand out as conspicuously and independently as does a senator. Political visibility is a function less of geographic than of psychological distance, and probably increasingly in the United States proximity in the latter sense reflects the opportunity to be conspicuously associated with major matters of obvious national importance. Even in the Washington arena, where the chance of such association is generally greater than in the geographically nearer seats of government in the states and the localities, a representative, in contrast to a senator, is more likely to be perceived as one member of a party than as a name and a person in his own right.[1]

A member of the House, in short, is almost certainly more dependent than a senator. His dependencies may be many, but one of them is the party, and especially the legislative party. If he is not visible as an individual, re-election, constantly impending in the House, will rest at bottom upon how the electorate perceives and responds to the label he carries. Far more than in the Senate, the fortunes of the party are,

---

[1] Many members of the House are aware of this difference in visibility. For example, an able younger representative, publicly chiding the press for its partiality toward the senators, illustrated his point that the deserved prominence of senators sometimes is carried too far by citing a case in 1955 in which a policy statement issued by 20 House members was almost ignored in the press yet received front-page treatment a week later when its ideas were propounded by a senator. (See Stewart L. Udall, "A Congressman Defends the House," *New York Times Magazine,* January 12, 1958.)

except in the safest districts, his fortunes. Whether these perceptions of the party relate to national or regional or even local issues, moreover, he is dependent on the machinery of the House and of the legislative party for favors, for support, and for the design of a favorable current image of the party.

The machinery of the House and of its parties is normally available to the ordinary member only, so to speak, on its own terms, because the source of its strength is also the source of his own disabilities, namely, numbers. In a House of 435 or in a body roughly half that size, as one of the parties, there is a tendency, as suggested in an earlier chapter, for the real and the formal leadership closely to coincide. A formal, standardized system of communication and control is indispensable to the conduct of affairs in a body of that size. In a smaller group, such as the Senate, it is feasible to improvise and to restructure a communication pattern because the number of individuals to be reached is fairly limited. In the House this is rarely feasible.[2] This standardization of the communication structure implies that initiative tends to be centralized or at least that there are central controls on the flow of business. These the rank-and-file member cannot command or, as sometimes happens in the Senate, supplant. Hence, excepting some aspects of his own voting decisions, the independence of the ordinary member is restricted.

The machinery of the House and of its parties thus takes on a special importance. Access to it and advancement within the hierarchy of communication and control accordingly become of more significance to the individual representative than are the comparable features to the rank-and-file senator. The cooptative powers in the hands of the party leadership, though far from unlimited, can affect materially both access and advancement and thus the prospects of a fuller and more secure political future for the rank-and-file member. His dependence upon the party, in this more restricted sense of the influential hierarchs, is correspondingly great.

These peculiarities of the House differentiate its parties from those

---

[2] For example, this is probably one reason—but only one—for the infrequency with which petitions for the discharge of a committee from further consideration of a bill receive the number of signatures (a majority of the total membership) necessary to calling up the discharge motion. (See Floyd M. Riddick, *The U. S. Congress,* Manassas, Va.: National Capitol Publishers, 1949, pp. 236–57.) On the general matter of numbers see P. D. Hasbrouck, *Party Government in the House of Representatives,* New York: Macmillan and Company, 1927, pp. 102, 225–226, and Lindsay Rogers, *The American Senate,* New York: Alfred A. Knopf, 1926, pp. 202 and *passim.*

of the Senate, but in terms of degree. They modify but do not eliminate the mediate character of the group. For the low-visibility representative has a set of additional, even alternative, dependencies in his
constituency and in the region or state in which it is located. These
include politically significant interest groups, whether organized or
not, and the local machinery of the electoral party—the constituency
power structure—on which he must rely for support in primary and
election campaigns. The expectations from these sources, often highly
ambiguous, must be recognized as fully as possible in the functioning
of the legislative party. If they are not, or cannot be, the representative may feel obliged to oppose the legislative party's majority in defense of them. He may, by such behavior and with the inevitable
"nursing" of his constituents, be able to create a distinction between a
negative image of the party in Washington and himself as the local
party representative that will permit him to withstand an electoral
swing against the party in general.[3] Without such effort, however, he
may be doomed to defeat. Thus, though the rank-and-file representative is, in comparison with the senator, peculiarly dependent on the
legislative party, this dependence is far from complete. These different sorts of dependencies are responsible for the apparent contradiction between stability and disunity in the legislative party and for the
informal character of much of the influence exercised by the leadership.

In order to explore more adequately these differences in degree between the parties in the Senate and the House, it is appropriate to raise in
connection with the latter the same kinds of questions asked about the
Senate party leadership. What in fact are the leader roles in the parties
of the lower chamber? What are the relations among them? To what
extent must Wilson's early generalizations about the parties and their
leaders still be accepted? In the record votes what evidence is there
of corporate or collegial activity among those in the leadership positions? Is it "exactly accurate" that "the House has as many leaders as
there are subjects of legislation"?[4] Is there no one who may "speak for
his party as well as for himself"?

---

[3] As, for example, in the case of Representative Secrest of Ohio, discussed above,
chap. 5, pp. 171–2.

[4] Woodrow Wilson, *Congressional Government*, New York: Meridian Edition,
1956, p. 58. For the sake of accuracy it should be noted that in 1900 Wilson himself specifically recognized that his analysis of nearly two decades earlier was "not
as accurate" as at the time when it was written and particularly called attention to
"the gradual integration of the organization of the House of Representatives."
(*Ibid.*, pp. 19, 21.)

THE POSITIONS

At the outset an admission must be made that, in attempting an analysis of party leadership roles in the House through an examination of the record votes, one finds himself in a position which inevitably brings to mind the hackneyed analogy to *Hamlet* without the Prince of Denmark. That is, he is obliged to talk about the House, its parties, and its leaders, without adequate data on the key figure, the Speaker. Since he is not obliged to vote, except to break or make a tie, and rarely does, the Speaker's name is not even listed on the roll that is used for record votes. This index of his behavior is not in the formal record, although his influence in the House and in the party is, to say the least, pervasive.

This handicap is the more serious in a study of the Eighty-first Congress because Speaker Rayburn brought the position to an unusually high level of importance in the House and in the government generally. Faced by the deep cleavage within the Democratic party, he used his formal powers, and even more the behind-the-scenes personal influence which he apparently preferred, to minimize the division. Although he did not, as one informant expressed it, "own" his Rules Committee, he frequently was the only man in the party who could negotiate a compromise with dissident members of the committee. The 21-day rule was approved in the Democratic caucus in January 1949, and was adopted in the House with his endorsement.[5] A year later he went so far as to take the floor to speak against the unsuccessful attempt to repeal the rule. The rule, of course, was repealed eventually, at the opening of the Eighty-second Congress in 1951, but it was taken from the books at that time partly because the Speaker had arrived at more congenial means for dealing with the Rules body.[6] To the very considerable formal powers of his office as party leader and Speaker he added an enormous personal influence built up over nearly half a century as a member of the House and perhaps particularly in the years after 1940, when he first became Speaker. Through wise use of his powers, generosity as adviser, and shrewd sponsorship and promotion of many able younger men—that informally defined

---

[5] *New York Times,* January 2, 1949; *Congressional Record,* 81st Congress, 1st Session, 95:1 (January 3, 1949), 10–11.

[6] *Congressional Record,* 81st Congress, 2nd Session, 96:1 (January 20, 1950), 719–720; Lewis J. Lapham, "Party Leadership and the House Committee on Rules," unpublished doctoral dissertation, Harvard University, 1953, p. 280.

company known on Capitol Hill as "the Speaker's boys"—he, in John Marshall's phrase about Jefferson, "embodied himself in the House of Representatives." He seldom called upon the full resources of his role openly or in wholesale fashion, but their importance in the House and in the party were unmistakable.

It follows, therefore, that the Majority Floor Leader, whose votes are available for analysis, was inevitably the second-ranking elective leader of the majority. It is no derogation of John McCormack, who was Floor Leader in the Eighty-first Congress, to say that his position was in a sense that of deputy to the Speaker or at most his collaborator, as this would almost inevitably be the case with any Majority Leader serving with an able Speaker. He would not entirely lack independence nor functions peculiar to his role, but it would be almost inherent in the relationship that neither the Speaker nor the Majority Leader, but especially the latter, could hope to accomplish much without the effective collaboration of the other. Rivalry in these positions is not unknown, but this sort of thing could not for long eliminate a collaborative relationship between the two without precipitating a major crisis in the party.

The assumed general harmony of view between the Speaker and the Majority Leader means that the latter's votes take on a particular importance as an index, not only of his own role, but also of the point of view of the two top leaders of the majority party. Speaker Rayburn presumably would not have voted as McCormack did on all roll calls, but the tendencies in his voting would not have been greatly different unless the assumption about the interdependence of the two roles is completely untenable.[7]

As in the Senate, the list of elective party leadership positions in the House is essentially the same in both parties, though the practices of the two parties differ slightly in formal detail. Both floor leaders are, of course, elected by their respective party caucuses. In Republican practice since 1919 the Floor Leader, in the Eighty-first Congress Representative Martin of Massachusetts, does not hold membership on

---

[7] This assumption is not peculiar to the present study. Lapham, for example, observes: "In determining the position of the leadership on the measures and issues that have been discussed . . . , it was found that the most reliable indicator was the majority leader . . . , John McCormack." ("Party Leadership and the House Committee on Rules," p. 341.) In the Eighty-third Congress, 1953–1954, which recorded an unusually low number of roll calls, Rayburn, who was Minority Leader, and McCormack, who had stepped down to Minority Whip, disagreed on only 14 of the 147 votes taken in the two sessions, or less than 10 per cent. Some of the disagreements occurred on matters of more than minor importance, but their total was not large.

any standing committee of the House, but he serves on the party's Committee on Committees and on the policy committee, of both of which he is normally chairman. McCormack, under the less strict Democratic practice, retained his membership on the House Committee on Expenditures in the Executive Departments. He was not formally a member of the party's Committee on Committees, since this is composed entirely of the Democratic members of the Committee on Ways and Means, and, though he was an *ex officio* member of the steering (policy) committee, as was the Speaker, he was not its chairman.

The majority and minority Whips (in this Congress, Priest of Tennessee and Arends of Illinois, respectively) are formally chosen by the caucuses but in fact on nomination by the Leader. Neither is formally designated as Assistant Leader, although both tend to function in that fashion, the Republican less regularly than the Democrat in recent years since, in the Eightieth and Eighty-third Congresses, when the Republicans were in the majority and Martin moved to the Speaker's chair, the Floor Leader's position was occupied by Halleck of Indiana rather than by Arends. When the party was in the minority, therefore, Halleck sometimes functioned as an unofficial assistant leader.

In both parties the Chairman of the Caucus or Conference is separately elected by that body. In the Eighty-first Congress Walter of Pennsylvania served in this capacity for the Democrats and Woodruff of Michigan for the Republicans.

The chairmen of the respective Congressional Campaign Committees were included among the elective leaders in this analysis for the same reason as in the Senate. These were, on the Democratic side, Kirwan of Ohio, and on the Republican, Leonard Hall of New York.

For the Democrats a fifth elective leader was analyzed along with those previously listed, since their practice is to make the Chairman of the steering (policy) committee a separate post rather than to assign it to the Floor Leader. The occupant of this position was Murdock of Arizona.

As in the Senate, for certain purposes the collective memberships of some committees were also treated as part of the elective leadership. The policy committees (by the Democrats still designated the steering committee) are set up somewhat differently in the two parties. Among the Republicans the committee is composed of five elective leaders, *ex officio*—the four listed here plus the conference secretary—the Republican members of the Rules Committee, and additional members nominated by the Committee on Committees. Among the Democrats the *ex officio* members are the Speaker, Floor Leader, Whip, Chairman of the Caucus, and the ranking Democrats on the Appropriations, Ways and Means, and Rules Committees. The remainder of the committee, 15 to 18, are elected from geographic zones by the state delegations in those zones.[8] For reasons that will be developed later, the differences in composition of these two are not of much consequence, but it is worth noting that in all probability the Republican method of designation, more centralized than the Democratic, would, if the committees were to function in a significant fashion, produce a more cohesive and, presumably, more effective body.

Given the importance of the standing committees in the House, it seemed appropriate for some parts of the analysis to include the collective memberships of the two Committees on Committees among the leadership elements. As noted above, the two parties follow different methods in designating these bodies. The membership of the Republican Committee, outside of the chairman, is elected by the state delegations, one member being chosen by each state with Republican representation. Among the Democrats since 1911 it has been customary for the Democratic members of the House Committee on Ways and Means to serve as the Committee on Committees, a reflection of the older practice of designating the chairman of Ways and Means as the Majority Floor Leader. Under both arrangements the principal elective leaders have a good deal to say about the choices for committee positions, and there is no evidence that the more decentralized Republican system is less amenable than the Democratic to the suggestions of the leaders, perhaps owing to the presence of the Republican leader as chairman.[9]

---

[8] In the Eighty-first Congress the members of these committees were: Democrats: Murdock, chairman, Rayburn, McCormack, Priest, Walter, Doughton, Cannon, and Sabath, *ex officio;* Woodhouse of Connecticut, Byrne of New York, Hart of New Jersey, Kerr of North Carolina, Peterson of Florida, Brown of Georgia, Colmer of Mississippi, Hobbs of Alabama, Cooper of Tennessee, Crosser of Ohio, Dingel of Michigan, O'Brien of Illinois, Blatnik of Minnesota, Morris of Oklahoma, Patman of Texas, and Jackson of Washington. Republicans: Martin, chairman, Woodruff, Arends, L. W. Hall, Allen of Illinois, Brown of Ohio, Wadsworth of New York, and Herter of Massachusetts, *ex officio;* Case of South Dakota, Wigglesworth of Massachusetts, Simpson of Pennsylvania, Towe of New Jersey, Cole of New York, Jennings of Tennessee, Andresen of Minnesota, LeCompte of Iowa, Halleck of Indiana, Bolton of Ohio, Jenkins of Ohio, Stefan of Nebraska, Hill of Colorado, Anderson of California, Ellsworth of Oregon, Keefe of Wisconsin, Michener of Michigan, and Phillips of California.

[9] The members of the Committees on Committees who served for the entire Congress were: Democrats: Doughton of North Carolina, chairman, Cooper of Tennessee, Dingell of Michigan, Mills of Arkansas, Gregory of Kentucky, Camp of Georgia, Lynch of New York, Forand of Rhode Island, Eberharter of Pennsyl-

Finally, the key importance of the Committee on Rules in the House made it desirable to include the eight Democrats and four Republicans on that body among the collective leadership elements, even though technically they are not elective leaders.[10] The chairman and ranking minority member of this committee, like the chairman of Ways and Means, were also included among the seniority leaders.

Unlike their Senate counterparts, the House seniority leaders did not overlap the list of individual elective leaders.[11]

vania, King of California, O'Brien of Illinois, Combs of Texas, Boggs of Louisiana, Carroll of Colorado, and Young of Ohio. Republicans: Martin of Massachusetts, chairman *ex officio,* Phillips of California, Hill of Colorado, Sanborn of Idaho, Allen of Illinois, LeCompte of Iowa, Morton of Kentucky, Fellows of Maine, Miller of Maryland, Woodruff of Michigan, Anderson of Minnesota, Short of Missouri, D'Ewart of Montana, Curtis of Nebraska, Cotton of New Hampshire, Kean of New Jersey, Wadsworth of New York, Lemke of North Dakota, Jenkins of Ohio, Stockman of Oregon, Simpson of Pennsylvania, Lovre of South Dakota, Plumley of Vermont, Horan of Washington, and Barrett of Wyoming.

[10] Rules Committee members: Democrats: Sabath of Illinois, chairman, Cox of Georgia, Smith of Virginia, Colmer of Mississippi, Madden of Indiana, Lyle of Texas, McSweeney of Ohio, and Delaney of New York. Republicans: Allen of Illinois, Brown of Ohio, Wadsworth of New York, and Herter of Massachusetts.

[11] The chairmen and ranking minority members of the standing committees of the House (seniority leaders) were:

COMMITTEE	DEMOCRATS	REPUBLICANS
Agriculture	Cooley, N. C.	Hope, Kans.
Appropriations	Cannon, Mo.	Taber, N. Y.
Armed Services	Vinson, Ga.	Short, Mo.
Banking and Currency	Spence, Ky.	Wolcott, Mich.
District of Columbia	McMillan, S. C.	Bates, G. J., Mass.
		Simpson, Ill.
		(after 11/2/49)
Education and Labor	Lesinski, Mich.	McConnell, Pa.
	Barden, N. C.	
	(after 5/28/50)	
Expenditures in Executive		
Departments	Dawson, Ill.	Hoffman, Mich.
Foreign Affairs	Bloom, N. Y.	Eaton, N. J.
	Kee, W. Va.	
	(after 3/8/49)	
House Administration	Norton, N. J.	LeCompte, Ia.
Interstate and Foreign		
Commerce	Crosser, Ohio	Wolverton, N. J.
Judiciary	Celler, N. Y.	Michener, Mich.
Merchant Marine and Fisheries	Bland, Va.	Weichel, Ohio
	Hart, N. J.	
	(after 2/17/50)	
Post Office and Civil Service	Murray, Tenn.	Rees, Kans.

THE FLOOR LEADERS

Although it is somewhat overshadowed by the Speakership, the position of Floor Leader in the House is only slightly less significant than the comparable post in the Senate. Its functions in the House are very old. In fact, until Henry Clay assumed the Speakership in 1811, the unofficial position of floor leader in the House, especially in Jefferson's Administration, far outranked the Speakership in importance.[12]

In its more recent development, both before and since the revolt of 1910, the Floor Leader has been in a sense an arm of the Speaker on the majority side and the post of the "shadow" Speaker on the minority side. Nevertheless, its contemporary characteristics mark it in both cases as a position of more than secondary importance. In particular, the practice established by the Republicans in 1919, under which a man relinquishes his positions on the standing committees of the House upon assuming the Floor Leader's post, indicates both that its burdens are heavy and that its importance is not simply derivative. The precedent is less strong among the Democrats, but it is still normal for their Floor Leader either to hold no other post in the House or to serve only on one of the less important standing committees. Before 1919 the Majority Leader characteristically was chairman either of Ways and Means or of Appropriations, as the ranking member of one of these was likely to be *de facto* Leader in any case because the bulk of the important House business was divided between them, especially in the four or five decades before the Wilson Administration.[13]

COMMITTEE	DEMOCRATS	REPUBLICANS
Public Lands	Somers, N. Y.	Welch, Cal.
	Peterson, Fla.	Crawford, Mich.
	(after 4/7/49)	(after 9/11/49)
Public Works	Whittington, Miss.	Dondero, Mich.
Rules	Sabath, Ill.	Allen, Ill.
Un-American Activities	Wood, Ga.	Thomas, N. J.
		Nixon, Cal.
		(after 1/2/50)
		Case, S. D.
		(after 12/30/50)
Veterans' Affairs	Rankin, Miss.	Rogers, Mass.
Ways and Means	Doughton, N. C.	Reed, N. Y.
Atomic Energy (Joint)	Durham, N. C.	Cole, N. Y.

[12] Ralph V. Harlow, *The History of Legislative Methods in the Period Before 1825*, New Haven: Yale University Press, 1917, pp. 176–177.

[13] DeAlva S. Alexander, *History and Procedure of the House of Representatives*, Boston: Houghton Mifflin, 1916, pp. 107, 234–235.

The emergence of the Floor Leader on both sides of the aisle as in effect a full-time official is an index, not only of the increased volume of the Congress's business and of the shifting substance of its concerns, but also of the development of a distinctive role important in the machinery of House and party.

At the heart of the Floor Leader's position on the majority side of the House, as in the Senate, is the scheduling function. The power to control or significantly to influence the time-table of any deliberative body is a key one, but in the House, where, if the leaders are working in harmony with the Rules Committee, it is possible to control not only the timing but also the form and substance of the debate, even a share in this power becomes formidable. It is a continuous authority, as in the Senate, but in the House it reaches a peak of importance in the closing days of a session when most business is conducted by unanimous consent or under suspension of the rules. Therefore, though it is shared, especially with the Speaker, it supplies leverage for negotiation with the rank and file, with the seniority leaders, and with the Minority Leader. The consultative relation of the Minority Leader, usually scrupulously observed, in turn supports his influence in his own ranks.

Again in cooperation with the Speaker,[14] the Majority Leader derives influence from an assortment of formal and informal functions, ranging from "assistance" in securing a coveted committee assignment —it being an acknowledged fact in the House that the respective Committees on Committees usually act favorably on the "suggestions" of the leadership—to help with a favorite legislative project. Though in absolute terms somewhat diminished on the minority side, these sources of power are relatively even more important for the Minority Leader, since his is the principal post in the party.

To these more formal sources of influence the Floor Leaders (and, of course, the Speaker) bring a range of personal, more intimate claims to loyalty. For, despite the imposing machinery of the House and the characteristic centralization of initiative as compared with the Senate, much of the power of the party leadership is uncodified and personal, reflecting the skills of the individuals playing these roles.

Testimony to this effect is easily found on Capitol Hill. For example, Martin, Rayburn, and McCormack, among other elective leaders, know or have a reputation for knowing a great deal about the House con-

---

[14] The point may be a minor one, but it is worth reporting that Representative McCormack, in an interview concerning his role, regularly used the plural pronoun in the first person, indicating agreement, perhaps negotiated or perhaps spontaneous, between himself and the Speaker.

stituencies, especially the more closely contested ones, and about the personal and political backgrounds of their representatives. Advice from the leaders, often unsolicited, is referred to gratefully by many members, and there are indications that in some instances this extends to advice not to vote with the party on an issue likely to create trouble in a constituency.

Many freshman representatives are carefully cultivated by one or another of the party's principal elective leaders, and this extends in various ways to help in campaigns. There are stories of the Speaker or Floor Leader appearing in a constituency during a hard campaign, holding a press conference along with a young representative, in the course of which complimentary remarks are made about his record and photographs are taken. There are similar stories of unsolicited financial assistance coming to a hard-pressed candidate from the leaders.[15] The Speaker in particular has a number of little ways in which he can provide a representative with useful publicity. For example, Speakers in recent years have frequently chosen a promising junior representative to perform the annual ceremonial reading of Washington's Farewell Address, a small matter but one that is good for some notice in the local press. It is also a mark of recognition that is noticed in the House. There are a number of other devices in the latter class— in addition, of course, to an assignment to a key committee—such as designation as Chairman of the Committee of the Whole, which is among the Speaker's prerogatives. On a minor bill a junior man is often named Chairman, both as a means of trying him out and as a form of modest recognition.

By such marks the "Speaker's boys" can be identified. These actions tend to create or cement loyalties. They may also contribute to the existence of a kind of network of influence within the party, for to be regarded as close to a seat of power is to acquire power. Just as a Floor Leader's influence may be augmented by the assumption that he will one day be Speaker, and correspondingly diminished if the feeling gets around that he is not first in the line of succession, so it seems likely that the "Speaker's boys," especially the older ones, may have their informal followings which help to knit the party together.

The convertibility of these ties of loyalty may be highly conditional, and the means of calling upon them will vary according to the skill and personality of the leader. He will rarely issue a peremptory demand, but apparently more commonly will make an implicit assump-

---

[15] One young representative, in recounting such an experience, said of the two principal leaders in his party, "They somehow always seem to have a few thousand dollars at their disposal in a campaign."

tion that the "follower" will "go along" if he feels that he possibly can. Informal and in gross probably unmeasurable, these ties are part of the stuff of party leadership in the House as they are in the Senate.

The Floor Leaders in the Eighty-first Congress had need of the full range of their formal and informal powers if they had any desire to achieve coherence in their parties. The deep divisions in both are illustrated by the wide range of the Administration support indexes in both groups. Among the Democrats over the two sessions these ranged from support of the Administration on every roll call to fairly consistent opposition. The Republican range was equally broad, from almost perfect support to almost invariable opposition, although the center of the distribution was, of course, lower.[16]

Given the cleavages within both parties and the admissibility of the assumption that the legislative parties in the House, like those in the Senate, are mediate groups, one would expect to find the Floor Leaders located toward the center of their respective parties. The three sets of data on the voting structures in each of the parties are consistent with expectation, although neither McCormack nor Martin was a member of an identified bloc except in a single set.[17] McCormack, on the intermediate-cohesion set (Table 31A) was in both blocs in the Northern wing. He ranked very low in the one that stood more to the "left" (Bloc N-I), and, despite his membership in the nucleus of the other (Bloc N-II), his ranking in that group was not very high. These rankings indicate that his scores with at least some of the more extreme elements in these blocs were fairly low. Bloc N-II was obviously a moderate aggregation, since included in its membership were two men who belonged to the bloc structure of both the Northern and Southern wings. On the low-cohesion set McCormack was not in a bloc but was most closely identified, as might be expected, with the principal bloc in the Northern Wing (Table 30A). Finally, on the high-cohesion set he was not in the bloc chiefly because of his "absence" rate, as has previously been explained, but he was strongly identified with its nuclear members. Martin on the low-cohesion set was a member of one of the central blocs (Bloc III, Table 34), which

---

[16] In the two sessions 3 Democrats had perfect scores (5.00) on the Administration support index, Spence of Kentucky, Karsten of Missouri, and Marsalis of Colorado. The lowest score was 2.05, by Rankin of Mississippi. Among the Republicans in the two sessions Javits of New York had the highest Administration support index (4.46), and Taber of New York had the lowest (1.51).

[17] Duncan MacRae, Jr., *Dimensions of Congressional Voting*, Berkeley and Los Angeles: University of California Press, 1958, p. 295, arrived at similar findings on the middle position of the Floor Leaders in the party structure in this Congress.

was by a small margin the largest of the many Republican blocs on that set. On the intermediate-cohesion set he was in no bloc, largely because he was unrecorded too frequently, but he was most closely identified with a group that was close to the party's center (Bloc II, Table 35). His position on the high-cohesion set was essentially comparable to McCormack's on the corresponding Democratic votes.

Both McCormack and Martin, as Table 37 indicates, characteristically voted with the majorities of their parties on those roll calls on

Table 37

INCIDENCE OF HOUSE FLOOR LEADERS' AGREEMENTS WITH PARTY MAJORITIES ON VOTES WHERE THEIR PREFERENCES WERE RECORDED, 81ST CONGRESS, 1ST AND 2ND SESSIONS

	Majority Leader (McCormack, Mass.)			Minority Leader (Martin, Mass.)		
	Number of Votes	Number with Party	Per Cent	Number of Votes	Number with Party	Per Cent
Second Session 74 Low-cohesion votes	65	50	76.9	66	57	86.4
First Session 74 Intermediate-cohesion votes	70	62	88.6	61	55	90.2
Second Session 62 Democratic and 66 Republican high-cohesion votes	54	54	100.0	59	59	100.0

which they were recorded, Martin slightly more often than McCormack, though the differences were not great except on the low-cohesion sets. The Republican Leader's party orthodoxy index was slightly lower in the first session (4.44 to McCormack's 4.53) and slightly higher in the second (4.55 to McCormack's 4.41). The indexes for both men were among the highest in their respective parties.

Both men appeared to satisfy the middleman requirements of the Leader role; neither was especially prominent in the bloc structure of his party; both occasionally voted against the majority of the party; and both were "absent" with some frequency. In view of these characteristics of their voting, are there also indications that either McCormack or Martin was casting his vote or absenting himself in such fashion as to accommodate one of the dissenting wings of his party? In the Senate there was little evidence that either of the principal leaders was behaving in this way. What of the House? A few not very startling indications of this sort of tendency appeared in Mc-Cormack's record on the low- and intermediate-cohesion sets. In the former set, for example, he agreed with the extreme "right" bloc in the Southern wing in support of a bill restricting "apprentice" positions in the civil service to veterans. Because of a retroactive provision written into the bill by the committee, it was charged that this was "lily-white" legislation. In the same set he voted for the Lodge-Gossett proposal to change the electoral college, along with a good many Southerners and relatively few Democrats from the North. In the intermediate-cohesion set there were 10 votes on which the Northern blocs were divided and McCormack supported one of the Southern blocs.[18]

Martin's record on this score is a good deal less clear. Some votes might be interpreted as accommodating the extremes of the party, such as votes first with one wing and then with another on rent control in both sessions, but on closer examination they look like no more than opposition to the measure on the preliminary votes and support of it only on final roll calls—recommittal, passage, conference report—when it was slated for approval, a common pattern on the Republican side. More instructive are certain of his "absences," notably those dealing with the repeal of the oleomargarine tax, which badly divided the party. He was unrecorded on 3 crucial votes on this measure, 2 in the first session and one in the second. Most of his remaining "absences," however, shown no particular pattern.

Aside from these scattered examples, there were no indications that the middleman Leaders in the House were any more likely than their Senate counterparts to vote in such fashion as conspicuously to accommodate dissenting segments of their parties.

No one among the Democrats in the Eighty-first Congress had moved at the time of the analysis into the Floor Leader position, so it is impossible to check the voting behavior of such aspirants against the assumed characteristics of the role. Among the Republicans, however, there was one such case, Halleck of Indiana, who had been Majority Leader in the Eightieth Congress, when Martin assumed the Speakership, and who reassumed the position when the Republicans next won a majority, in the Eighty-third Congress. In terms of position

---

[18] Only three of these were of much consequence, an amendment to the Housing Act of 1949 requiring a special loyalty oath of employees and two votes concerning the restriction of F. P. C. powers over the price of natural gas. These last two could be regarded as accessions to the wishes of the Speaker, since Rayburn had appealed for support of the bill in one of his rare speeches from the floor.

in the structure, Halleck satisfied the chief requirement of the role. That is, his votes tended to place him toward the center of the party. On the one set where his "absence" rate permitted his membership in a bloc, the intermediate-cohesion set of the first session, he belonged to the two largest blocs at the center of the structure (Table 35). In the second session, he agreed most frequently with the nuclear members of the bloc on the high-cohesion set (Table 36), and he was most closely identified with the two larger central blocs on the low-cohesion set (Blocs III and IV, Table 34), although his high score on this set was with Arends, the Minority Whip, who was located more to the right of the structure (Bloc VII). These comments suggest that Halleck's position generally may have been somewhat less moderate than Martin's, and the party orthodoxy indexes, which for both sessions were slightly lower in Halleck's case than in Martin's, tend to confirm this indication. Despite these differences and others to be noted later, however, Halleck's voting pattern was consistent with the middleman characteristics that the Floor Leader's role seems to require in both chambers.

Given the similarity of the structural positions of the two Floor Leaders in the House, one would anticipate that, though there were differences between them in various respects, indicators of relative effectiveness would not reveal striking contrasts. One such indicator in the Senate—the frequency with which the party and the chamber supported the Leader when he assumed the initiative by offering a motion, calling for a record vote, and the like—is of comparatively little value in the House. Proceedings in the House are more standardized than in the Senate, and the Leaders less frequently take the formal initiative on the floor. This is largely because of the extensive use of the Committee of the Whole, in which roll calls are not in order, and the limited range of circumstances in which the special orders reported by the Rules Committee permit a record vote to be taken in the House proper. In the three sets of votes there were only 6 such moves by McCormack and only 4 by Martin. The response in these few cases, however, was what one would have expected. A majority of the party supported the Leader on all of them; in addition, McCormack was supported by a majority of the House on 5 of his 6 moves, Martin on 2 of his 4.

In the analysis of the Senate the point was made that the Majority Leader, whose position was somewhat "left" of the center of the party, appeared in this location partly because of a strong tendency to support the Administration. What of the House? Did McCormack's clearly central position mean that he was less strong on this score than Lucas? Comparison in precise terms is impossible because neither the number nor the substance of the votes included in the Administration support index in the two chambers was identical. Nevertheless, the tendency is at least as clear in McCormack's case. On none of the 129 roll calls classed as Administration support votes in the two sessions was he recorded, by vote, by pair, or by announcement, against the Administration. On 7 of the votes, all in the second session, he was "absent." The evidence on several of these, especially on 4 which involved presidential vetoes that were overridden by wide margins, indicated that the "absences" were deliberate in order to avoid both open opposition to an Administration position and the awkwardness of being in a minority in House and party. For example, on June 26, 1950, the House took up the President's veto of a bill to grant promotion credit to employees of the Post Office for time spent in the military in World War II. A preliminary motion to return the bill to committee and thus to dispose of it lost by nearly a two-to-one margin, McCormack present and voting for the motion. The veto was then overridden by a vote of 213 to 72, on which McCormack was unrecorded.[19] In consequence of his "regularity" on votes of this sort, McCormack, on the one set of votes on which he was in a bloc, ranked considerably higher on the Administration support index than he did in the bloc.[20] The indications are thus strong that in the House as in the Senate the Majority Leader's role included a marked tendency to support the Administration or at least to avoid openly opposing it.

In this analysis of the House the bloc structures reveal less about the Floor Leaders than did the comparable materials on the Senate, partly because the House matrixes were not developed as fully. Moreover, as has already been noted, the formal practices of the House are such that the other means used to analyze the record votes in the Senate do not as readily indicate the characteristics of leader behavior

---

[19] Senator Lucas was also "absent" when this veto was taken up in the Senate. In both cases the preferences of the influential postal unions may have had something to do with a disinclination to vote with the Administration. The other three cases in which McCormack was unrecorded on votes dealing with vetoes were: H. J. Res. 238, on naturalization of Asians, overridden 307–14; H.R. 6217, providing free medical service for certain veterans, overridden 321–12; and H.R. 9490, Internal Security Act of 1950, overridden 286–48.

[20] Table 31A indicates that he ranked 33 out of 42 in Bloc N-II and 68 out of 77 in Bloc N-I, but on the Administration support index for the session he ranked, among the members of these blocs, fifth in the former and sixth in the latter. In the second session, although he was in a bloc in neither set, his Administration support index of 4.73 was exceeded by only five members of the party. (His index for the first session was 4.92.)

in the larger body. It is possible, however, to convert the size of the parties in the House from a handicap to an advantage by using a slightly different form of analysis. This involves a close examination of the top scores of each of the Floor Leaders, that is, the lists of men who voted most often with McCormack or Martin.[21] From this examination one can discern a number of new features of the behavior both of the Floor Leaders and of the respective parties. Specifically, it becomes apparent, first, that those who scored high with the leaders had certain characteristics that distinguished them from their party colleagues; second, that there were significant contrasts between these "followings" of the two leaders; and, third, that the majority and minority parties seem to have performed somewhat different functions in relation to representatives whose political situations were generally contrasting.

What were the peculiarities that distinguished those Democrats who tended to score fairly high with the Majority Leader?[22] At the outset one can discount the possibility that high agreement with McCormack was merely a function of constituency similarity, especially in areas outside the South. If there were nothing distinctive about McCormack in these lists of scores, one might expect to find that they included a disproportionately large number of men the socio-economic features of whose constituencies were superficially like his, that is, urban with a sizable proportion of wage workers. Some evidence points in this direction, but it is neither consistent nor conclusive.[23] It thus seems

[21] "Top scores" or "high agreement" on the low- and intermediate-cohesion sets means scores of 46 or more with the respective Floor Leaders; on the high-cohesion sets it means scores of 40 or more with McCormack and scores of 42 or more with Martin, since there were 62 roll calls in the Democratic high-cohesion set and 66 in the Republican.

[22] This is a difficult question to handle, since it is apparent that, once party and the basic regional division have been taken into account, there could have been and almost certainly was a great variety of factors that would result in frequent agreement with McCormack, as with any other member of the party, and to identify these and rank them in order of importance is a risky undertaking. The risk derives chiefly from the problem of dealing with the matter of "absence." Obviously the less frequently a representative's preferences were recorded, the less likely he would be to agree frequently with the Floor Leader, other things being equal. Since the "absence" rates varied widely, from none to 20 or more, these alone could produce a distribution of scores. But it might tell next to nothing about the Leader and his associations. The concern here, therefore, must be with identifying the "other things" that are not or may not be equal.

[23] McCormack's district, the twelfth Massachusetts—South Boston—in 1950 contained a population 52.2 per cent of whose employed males were workers (laborers, craftsmen, operatives, and foremen). Excluding McCormack's own, in 55.7 per cent of the Democratic districts in the non-Southern states in 1950 half

reasonably clear that frequent agreement with McCormack, certainly among the non-Southerners, was not simply a matter of similarity of constituency. Except on the low-cohesion votes, where, almost by definition, there was a weakening of leadership influence as such, factors other than constituency similarity apparently were operative.

The Southern districts tell a slightly different story. Including them in these comparisons is difficult, first, because there were no Southerners among those scoring high with McCormack on one of the sets, the low-cohesion votes of the second session, and, second, because the heavily urban, working-class districts in the South are few and they present contrasts with the remaining constituencies in the region that are sharper and more varied than those found elsewhere in the country. In any case they differed somewhat from the non-Southern constituencies in their distribution among McCormack's top scores.[24] The Southern Democrats whose districts most resembled McCormack's in occupational composition were somewhat more likely to vote as he did than were their regional colleagues. Neither this evidence nor that on the non-Southern Democrats, however, eliminates the general inference that high agreement with McCormack was not simply a function of similarity of constituency.

Support for this conclusion emerges from a further examination of the 65 top scores in the low-cohesion set. Far from being confined to representatives from strongly urban districts, some of these scores were with men from decidedly rural constituencies. Seven, for example, represented districts in which 20 per cent or more of the employed males in 1950 were farmers. More interesting than the occupational make-up of these districts, however, is the fact that 5 of these 7 men were "freshmen" in the Eighty-first Congress. Four of the 5, moreover,

---

or more of the employed males were workers. What was the incidence of such districts among the non-Southern constituencies represented among McCormack's top scores on the three sets of votes? Among the 65 top scores of the low-cohesion set they were more frequent (63.1 per cent) than among all non-Southern Democrats, by slightly over 7 percentage points. On the other two sets, however, they were less frequent. Among the 104 top scores of the intermediate-cohesion set, they accounted for 54.4 per cent, and among the 122 top non-Southern scores of the high-cohesion set they represented 53.3 per cent. It does not seem likely that the lower incidence of men from the "working-class" districts on the intermediate- and high-cohesion sets was due to variations in "absence" rates.

[24] Using the same occupational criterion, 17 per cent of the Southern Democratic constituencies in 1950 were working class. However, 18.5 per cent of the 27 Southerners who were among McCormack's top scores on the intermediate-cohesion set came from such districts, and on the high-cohesion votes the proportion was even higher. On these roll calls 24 per cent of the 50 Southerners among the Majority Leader's top scores represented working-class constituencies.

were from districts that were close in 1948, that is, were carried by less than 55 per cent of the two-party vote for representative.

Was there a general tendency for the more junior members of the party and for those from districts that were close in 1948 to agree more frequently with the Majority Leader? The answer to the first of these questions appears in Table 38. In its first four columns this table compares, by categories of seniority, the distribution of the party's whole membership with the distribution of those who most frequently agreed with McCormack. The second four columns make the same comparison for the non-Southern members (those from the "North" and Border states). The assumption here is that if there was indeed a tendency for the newer members of the party to vote more regularly with the Leader, proportionately more of them than of the more senior members of the party should appear among McCormack's top scores.

The distributions in Table 38 are not completely smooth, which was to be expected, not only because the numbers in some cases are fairly small, but, more important, because the table isolates only a single factor (other than region), and it is obvious that many influences in addition to seniority must have affected the rate of agreement with the Floor Leader. Nevertheless, the data here support the inference that both in the party as a whole and in its non-Southern wing the more junior members were consistently overrepresented among Mc-Cormack's "following." In both categories the first-term representatives were overrepresented among the Leader's top scores on all three sets. The less stable pattern among the non-Southern Democrats indicates that the relationship within the party as a whole was partly a function of region. Nevertheless, omitting the Southerners from the analysis does not entirely eliminate the tendency toward an inverse relation between seniority and support of the Leader.[25]

---

[25] The probability of a distribution like that within the whole party on the low-cohesion set occurring by chance is less than 5 in 100 ($x^2 = 8.426$; $d.f. = 3$). Though the statistical significance of the other distributions is lower, the consistency of the pattern permits confidence in the inference. The Southern members of the party were omitted from Table 38 not only because none of them appeared among McCormack's top scores in the low-cohesion set, but also because the pattern in the other two sets was confused. On the intermediate-cohesion votes the first-term Southerners were the only group in that wing to be overrepresented among the top scores, suggesting that when the party began to close ranks the younger Southerners led the way for their more senior colleagues. On the high-cohesion votes, however, no pattern at all was evident; those with 8 to 22 terms and those with 2 to 4 terms were overrepresented, while the other two groupings showed a lower incidence.

Table 38

RELATION BETWEEN SENIORITY IN PARTY AND HIGH AGREEMENT[*] WITH
HOUSE MAJORITY LEADER, 81ST CONGRESS

Terms of Service	All Democrats				Non-Southern Democrats			
	Distribution in Party		Distribution in Leader's Top Scores		Distribution in Party		Distribution in Leader's Top Scores	
	Number (1)	Per Cent (2)	Number (3)	Per Cent (4)	Number (5)	Per Cent (6)	Number (7)	Per Cent (8)
A. LOW-COHESION SET, 2ND SESSION								
8–22	32	12.4	3	4.6	14	8.8	3	4.6
5–7	56	21.8	13	20.0	30	19.0	13	20.0
2–4	86	33.3	20	30.8	45	28.5	20	30.8
1	84	32.5	29	44.6	69	43.7	29	44.6
Total	258	100.0	65	100.0	158	100.0	65	100.0
B. INTERMEDIATE-COHESION SET, 1ST SESSION								
8–22	34	13.1	11	7.8	14	8.8	6	5.3
5–7	58	22.3	28	19.9	31	19.6	22	19.3
2–4	87	33.4	45	31.9	46	29.2	35	30.7
1	81	31.2	57	40.4	67	42.4	51	44.7
Total	260	100.0	141	100.0	158	100.0	114	100.0
C. HIGH-COHESION SET, 2ND SESSION								
8–22	32	12.4	18	10.4	14	8.8	8	6.6
5–7	56	21.8	35	20.4	30	19.0	23	18.9
2–4	86	33.3	55	32.0	45	28.5	33	27.0
1	84	32.5	64	37.2	69	43.7	58	47.5
Total	258	100.0	172	100.0	158	100.0	122	100.0

[*] "High agreement" on the low- and intermediate-cohesion sets means voting as McCormack did on 46 or more of the 74 roll calls in the set; on the high-cohesion set it means agreement with the Majority Leader on 40 or more of the 62 roll calls in the set.

What about the close districts? There were 51 Democratic seats, all outside of the South, that were carried in 1948 by less than 55 per cent of the two-party vote for representative. In all three sets the representatives from these close districts were overrepresented among Mc-

Cormack's top scores, though by fairly small margins. For example, slightly more than four-fifths of this "marginal" group were among those who scored high with the Leader on the high-cohesion votes as compared with a little over three-fourths of the Northern members of the party as a whole.

The evidence suggests that marginality rather than some common demographic factor in these constituencies was primarily responsible for the tendency to agree with McCormack. The districts by any reasonable measure were highly varied. They ranged from Representative Wayne Hays's eighteenth in Ohio, nearly two-thirds of whose employed males in 1950 were workers, to Representative Franck Havenner's fourth in California, covering a portion of San Francisco in which more than one-quarter of the employed males were professionals and managers, to Representative Fred Marshall's sixth in Minnesota, in which nearly half the employed males were farmers. The principal characteristic these men seem to have had in common, outside of being Northern Democrats, thus was that they came from districts that were carried by narrow margins in 1948.

Although both lack of seniority and election in 1948 by a narrow margin apparently tended to produce frequent agreement with the Majority Leader on record votes, it is all but impossible to rank these two factors, principally because roughly four-fifths of the representatives from close districts were also first-termers. This would of course almost inevitably be the case in a fairly competitive political situation. Comparisons among the first-term men from close districts, first-termers from safe districts, and men with two or more terms from close and safe districts show no reliable indications that men of low seniority tended to vote with the Leader regardless of their electoral margins or that men from close districts agreed with him whatever their seniority.

Some rather slight, indirect signs, however, suggest that the marginality of the district may have been the more influential of the two factors, signs involving the troublesome matter of "absences," which must be dealt with in any attempt at inferences from these data on McCormack's "following." [26] Turning first to the matter of seniority

---

[26] The troublesome features about "absences" are, briefly, two: a clerical difficulty in arriving at their exact number and a much more serious problem of interpretation. On the first matter, it was comparatively easy in preparing the materials for the matrixes to arrive at the number of times a man's preference was unrecorded, and this figure has been used in various ways throughout the analysis. In analyzing the agreements between a single man, such as McCormack, and all other members of his party, however, one cannot satisfactorily work with the total of their "absences." One needs rather a net figure that would take into account the number of roll calls on which both men were unrecorded if one is to arrive at the

and support of the Majority Leader, grounds exist for at least the suspicion that differences in "absence" rates may have had something to do with the differences shown in Table 38. Among the House Democrats there was a definite tendency, clear but by no means perfectly consistent, for the more junior members of the party to be recorded more regularly than their senior colleagues. It seems to follow, therefore, that a part of the high agreement rates of the first-term members of the party with McCormack was due to their being somewhat more frequently on the record. The question is, were these differences, as shown in Table 38, entirely a function of "absences"?

Judging from the data in Table 39, this question can be answered in the negative. The table shows the mean "absences" of the Democratic representatives by seniority levels and, in percentage points, the degree of over- or underrepresentation of each seniority grouping among McCormack's top scores, as compared with their representation in the party as a whole.[27] The general tendency toward higher "absence" rates at the more senior levels is evident, but the suspected inverse relation between these rates and representation among the Leader's top scores is neither close nor consistent. The men serving in their eighth to twenty-second term had the highest mean absences on all three sets, and they were also most underrepresented, but those serving in their second to fourth terms, who had the lowest mean absences in all three sets, were not overrepresented in any set.[28] And

---

maximum possible number of agreements between them. In a large group this would be laborious, but it could be done. One would still confront the second problem, that of determining the meaning of such "absences," for a failure to be recorded on a roll call may mean literal absence from the chamber, with or without a "general" pair on which the preferences of the participants normally are not announced, it may indicate deliberate avoidance of an issue, as in several of the cases noted in earlier pages, or it may indicate hostility to a proposal but a disinclination to vote or even to pair against the preferences of supporters in the constituency, colleagues in the party, or leaders in the chamber. In fact, an "absence" may mean opposition to the leadership or a kind of indirect support, as when a member is induced, if he cannot go along with the leaders, at least to abstain from voting, with merely an announcement of his preference or without, in which case he would appear in these data as "absent." An advantage for the legislator but a disadvantage for the analyst is that it is next to impossible to tell what meaning a series of "absences" has. Given this fact, to deal with the clerical problem without solving that of interpretation would be to achieve precision at the expense of accuracy. In consequence the approximations discussed in the text were resorted to as alternatives.

[27] These percentage-point differences were derived from Table 38 by subtracting the percentage in the fourth column from that in the second.

[28] The coefficients of deviation for these absence rates were practically identical in all cases.

Table 39

RELATION BETWEEN MEAN ABSENCES AT VARIOUS LEVELS OF SENIORITY
AND FREQUENCY OF AGREEMENT WITH HOUSE MAJORITY LEADER, 81ST
CONGRESS*

Terms of Service	Low-Cohesion Set, 81:2		Intermediate-Cohesion Set, 81:1		High-Cohesion Set, 81:2	
	Mean Absences	Over- (+) or Under- (−) represen- tation in Leader's Top Scores	Mean Absences	Over- (+) or Under- (−) represen- tation in Leader's Top Scores	Mean Absences	Over- (+) or Under- (−) represen- tation in Leader's Top Scores
8–22	11.8	−7.8	14.3	−5.3	13.3	−2.2
5–7	9.2	−1.8	8.6	−2.4	11.6	−0.1
2–4	8.1	−2.5	7.9	−1.5	9.6	−1.5
1	9.4	+12.1	8.0	+9.2	10.4	+3.8

* Over- (+) or underrepresentation (−) among the Leader's top scores is expressed in
percentage points. The index was derived from Table 38 by subtracting the incidence of
the seniority grouping in the Leader's top scores (column 4) from its incidence in the party
as a whole (column 2).

the first-termers, who were most overrepresented on all three sets,
ranked second or third from the top in mean absences. It seems reasonable to conclude, therefore, that only part of the relation between
seniority and agreement with the Majority Leader must be attributed
to differences in absence rates.

The 51 representatives from the close districts present a slightly
different picture. On two of the three sets of votes, all but the high-
cohesion set, the mean and the median absences of these "marginal"
men were not lower, but slightly higher, than the means and medians
for the party as whole. It is therefore possible to say that absence rates
had little to do with their apparent tendency to be overrepresented
among McCormack's top scores. Since it was necessary to regard absences as having relation to the comparable tendency among the more
junior members of the party, one may cautiously infer that narrowness
of the election margin was probably slightly more important than low
seniority in the party in producing frequent agreements with the
Leader.

What summary inferences can be drawn from these data concerning
the role of the Majority Leader in the House and the way in which
McCormack played it? The effects of the obvious North-South cleav-

age aside, it seems clear that similarity in the socio-economic composition of the constituencies as a factor accounting for McCormack's
"following" was not controlling. That is, the evidence suggests that
strictly political factors, such as inexperience in the House and narrowness of the electoral margin in the district, reveal more about those
members of the party who tended to agree frequently with the Majority Leader than does a socio- economic index such as the occupational
composition of the district. In turn these factors indicate something
of the functions and sources of influence of a party leader such as the
Floor Leader.

It thus appears that among the Democrats in the House the mediate
functions of the legislative party and of its formal leadership were
different in degree for the new and marginal members from what they
were for the older and more secure. The situation of those from close
districts presumably was such that they needed the support of a party
whose public image suggested a record of orderliness and effectiveness.
Its fortunes were with a peculiar intimacy their fortunes. In addition,
they had more than ordinary need of the party and its leadership if
they were to achieve results in a single legislative term that might
give assurance of a wider electoral margin at the succeeding election.
Presumably many of the newcomers to the party had similar needs,
but they also would seem to have had special need of cues in their
voting. Because of their inexperience in the House, lack of personal
contacts, and unfamiliarity with the complexities of its operation, the
value to them of a salient source of clues, such as the Majority Leader,
would be far greater than to their more established colleagues. Many
of the newcomers, moreover, who had not yet developed the substantive legislative specialties common among older representatives,
especially those who have or are approaching the status of seniority
leaders, would be particularly receptive to such cues. Following them,
moreover, might be expected to pay off in terms of advancement within
the House.[29]

---

[29] A rough indication of this "pay-off" can be found by comparing the committee
posts of Democratic representatives who were "freshmen" in the Eighty-first
Congress with the assignments of those who were still in the House six years later,
in the Eighty-fourth Congress. One would expect that first-termers who went
along with the leadership would have more chance to switch committees, and
that more of those who voted with the Leader would turn up on such major committees as Rules, Ways and Means, and Appropriations. The data are not inconsistent with these expectations, as the following summary indicates: of the
29 first-termers in 1949 who were on McCormack's list of top scores on the low-
cohesion set, in 1955 14 were no longer in the House, 6 were on the same standing
committees, and 9 had switched committees, 4 of them to one of the three major

It is possible to argue, of course, that the high agreement between the new and the marginal members of the party, on the one hand, and the Majority Leader, on the other, was simply a matter of coincidence between the latter's marked disposition to support the President's preferences and the likelihood that the interests and attitudes of men elected for the first time or by narrow margins in 1948 would also resemble those of the President. In other words, this level of agreement may have had nothing to do with any active effort on McCormack's part. Circumstantial evidence consistent with this view appears in the fact that the Administration support indexes of the party newcomers, even those from the South, were generally higher than the average in the party. Taking these scores in context, however, it seems more likely that there was an interdependence here, that the position of the new or marginal party member made him peculiarly sensitive to current and topical demands, as reflected in the President's preferences, but that the Majority Leader had some active part, along with the rest of the party hierarchy, in communicating those preferences and in defining the alternatives implied for these precariously situated members of the party.

If these speculations are warranted, they necessarily imply that the majority legislative party and its Floor Leader had less important functions to perform for many of the more senior members and for those from relatively safe districts.[30] They also carry the implication that agreement between these men and McCormack was more a reflection of similarity of constituency than was the case among the newer and

---

committees. Of the 30 first-termers who were on the list for the intermediate-cohesion set but not for the low-cohesion set, in 1955 21 were no longer in the House, 2 were on the same standing committee, and 7 had switched committees, 1 of them to one of the three major committees. Of the 14 first-termers who were only on the list for the high-cohesion set, in 1955 10 were no longer in the House, 1 was on the same standing committee, and 3 had switched committees, 2 of them to one of the three major committees. Of the 11 first-termers who were not on any of these lists, in 1955 5 were no longer in the House, 4 were on the same standing committee, and 2 had switched committees, but no one of these had been assigned to the Committees on Rules, Ways and Means, or Appropriations, and none of the 6 remaining in the House had at any time been a member of one of these three major committees.

[30] This proposition is consistent with observations of informants close to the Democratic leadership in the House, to the effect that members who have been in the House for several terms can be less easily counted upon to "go along" with the leaders than can the more junior men. It also has some bearing on the comments of several representatives, both "freshmen" and "old hands," that they were astonished and puzzled to find when they were first elected to the House that the legislative party made relatively few formal demands upon its members in connection with voting.

marginal men.[31] Some evidence supports this implication. For example, in the low-cohesion votes 14 men of the 65 who had scores of 46 or more with the Majority Leader represented districts in which less than 45 per cent of the employed males in 1950 were workers, districts, in other words, that by this criterion tended not to resemble McCormack's. Of these 14, 9 were first-termers, 2 were serving in their second terms, and one had served for more than 2 terms but had been re-elected by a narrow margin in 1948. Only 2 represented safe districts and had served more than 2 terms. Those who agreed frequently with the Majority Leader despite differences in the composition of their districts were not the more senior men with few election worries.

The pattern of Martin's top scores shows interesting and revealing contrasts with the McCormack roster. The chief differences were, first, that on two of the three sets the frequency of these scores was appreciably lower on the Republican side than it was on the Democratic; second, that except on the high-cohesion set of the second session there was no tendency for the more junior members of the party to be overrepresented among Martin's top scores; third, that on the other two sets, those where the party was least cohesive, the relation between time of election and agreement with Martin showed a curious but significant pattern; and, finally, that the base of Martin's following within his party was much less stable than was McCormack's.

The proportion of Republicans who had top scores with Martin was smaller than the proportion of Democrats who had such scores with McCormack on both the low- and intermediate-cohesion sets. These differences can be accounted for only in part by differences in "absence" rates, either for the Leaders or for the party as a whole.[32] In view of

---

[31] "More" rather than "primarily" because, as earlier data have indicated, party membership itself was apparently a basic and pervasive source of agreement. On the general matter of party loyalty and similarity of constituencies, compare Duncan MacRae, Jr., "The Relation Between Roll Call Votes and Constituencies in the Massachusetts House of Representatives," *American Political Science Review,* Vol. 46, no. 4 (December 1952), pp. 1046–1055.

[32] On the low-cohesion sets only 26 of the 171 Republicans, 15.2 per cent, agreed with Martin on at least 46 roll calls, while 65 of the 258 Democrats, 25.2 per cent, voted at least that frequently with McCormack. On the intermediate-cohesion sets of the first session the Republican proportion was 39 out of 171, or 22.8 per cent, and the Democratic was 141 out of 260, or 54.2 per cent. Martin was unrecorded more frequently than McCormack on the intermediate-cohesion votes, but the reverse was true on the low-cohesion roll calls. Given the difficulty of dealing with "absences," especially for aggregations as large as the parties in the House (see note 26), the second part of this conclusion is less reliable. Obviously the fact that on the average the Republicans were on both sets recorded

this and considering that the means of the Republican cohesion indexes were higher than the Democrats', these differences point to one or both of two possible inferences. At the least they suggest again the relative fluidity of the Republican voting patterns, and they may also indicate that the Minority Leader, out of choice or necessity, was less effective in his relations with the other Republicans in the House than McCormack was among the Democrats. Further comment on both of these points will be offered in subsequent paragraphs.

Of the 17 first-term members of the Republican party none agreed with Martin on as many as 46 of the roll calls in the low-cohesion set, and, as Table 40 indicates, if there was a relation between rank and support of the Minority Leader on the low- and intermediate-cohesion sets, the tendency was for the more senior members to agree with him more frequently.[33] It is also evident from Table 40 that differences in the mean absences of the several groupings do not account for the variations in their over- or underrepresentation among Martin's top scores. For example, those Republicans who were serving in their fifth, sixth, or seventh terms had a mean absence rate on both the low- and the intermediate-cohesion sets equal to or greater than any of the other groupings, yet they were consistently overrepresented among Martin's top scores.

The meaning of the pattern on the high-cohesion set is not clear, but, whatever the explanation, it is evident that the more junior members of the party were somewhat more likely than those with greater seniority to agree with Martin on the high-cohesion votes. Given the lower absence rate for the party as a whole on this set and given the fact, noted in Chapter 5, that the high-cohesion votes on the Republican side included a relatively high proportion of votes on matters of a preliminary sort, such as amendments, the inference is possible that many of the votes in this set were ones on which the leadership exerted a maximum of effort. Were this the case, it might indicate that among the Republicans, as with the Democrats, the less senior members of the party were more receptive to Leader initiatives but that the Republican hierarchy attempted such guidance over a fairly narrow

---

on approximately two fewer votes than were the Democrats made some difference in the incidence of agreements with Martin. Confidence in the conclusion rests on the following fairly crude correction: If the Republicans who were one or two agreements short of inclusion on Martin's lists of top scores are added to the lists, the Republican proportions still are lower than those of the Democrats.

[33] The probability that a distribution like that on the low-cohesion set in Table 40 could occur by chance was high, more than .9 ($x^2 = 0.360$; $d.f. = 3$). Confidence in the table thus must rest entirely on the consistency of the pattern in the two sets.

Table 40

RELATION BETWEEN SENIORITY IN PARTY AND HIGH AGREEMENT* WITH
HOUSE MINORITY LEADER, 81ST CONGRESS

Terms of Service	Distribution in Party		Distribution in Leader's Top Scores		Difference (Col. 4 − Col. 2)	Mean Absences
	Number (1)	Per Cent (2)	Number (3)	Per Cent (4)	(5)	(6)
A. LOW-COHESION SET, 2ND SESSION						
8–16	29	17.0	4	15.4	−1.6	11.5
5–7	46	26.9	8	30.7	+3.8	12.1
3–4	46	26.9	8	30.7	+3.8	10.7
1–2	50	29.2	6	23.2	−6.0	12.1
Total	171	100.0	26	100.0	− − −	− − −
B. INTERMEDIATE-COHESION SET, 1ST SESSION						
8–16	30	17.6	7	17.9	+0.3	10.6
5–7	49	28.6	13	33.3	+4.7	11.9
3–4	46	26.9	10	25.7	−1.2	9.5
1–2	46	26.9	9	23.1	−3.8	10.7
Total	171	100.0	39	100.0	− − −	− − −
C. HIGH-COHESION SET, 2ND SESSION						
8–16	29	17.0	21	15.5	−1.5	9.3
5–7	46	26.9	33	24.5	−2.4	10.2
3–4	46	26.9	41	30.4	+3.5	8.5
1–2	50	29.2	40	29.6	+0.4	10.2
Total	171	100.0	135	100.0	− − −	− − −

* "High agreement" on the low- and intermediate-cohesion sets means voting as Martin did on 46 or more of the 74 roll calls in the set; on the high-cohesion set it means agreement with the Minority Leader on 42 or more of the 66 roll calls in the set.

range of issues. In more restricted terms, the data may mean no more than that the junior Republicans did not lag behind when the party tended to draw together.

The most striking feature, however, of the Minority Leader's top scores on the low- and intermediate-cohesion sets was not their distribution from one level of seniority to another, nor even the proportion of the party on the lists, but a tendency, particularly among those who had been elected for six terms or less, for the Republican representatives who were serving their second, fourth, or sixth terms to be overrepresented among Martin's top scores in proportion to their incidence in the party and for those who were serving their first, third, or fifth terms to be underrepresented. In other words, there was something about those who had won election to the House for the first time in the years 1948, 1944, and 1940, when Democratic Presidents were returned to the White House, that made them vote with Martin less regularly than those who first entered the House following the midterm elections of 1946, 1942, and 1938, when the Republicans made gains in the number of their House seats.

In the low-cohesion set of the second session this pattern was perfectly consistent through those who were serving their seventh terms, that is, were elected first in 1936. In the same set not only were those elected in 1932 underrepresented, but also those who were returned for the first time in the midterm election of 1934, when the Democrats set a record by increasing the majority they had held in the House for two years.[34]

In the intermediate-cohesion set of the first session the pattern was less consistent. The first-termers were very slightly overrepresented, and those in their second terms were under the expected percentage. For those in their third, fourth, fifth, and sixth terms, however, the alternation was like that of the low-cohesion set. These data are summarized in Table 41, which also includes the same material on the high-cohesion set.[35]

What does this curious pattern of alternation on the votes of lower cohesion signify? In the first place, it is important to point out that it was apparently not a function of differences in absence rates. As Table 41 indicates, a slight but not consistent relation existed between these rates and the frequency of agreement with Martin, and the detailed data not shown in the table are consistent with the summary figures.

---

[34] Of the 6 Republicans who had been elected first in 1932 and were thus serving their ninth terms, none had scores as high as 46 with Martin on the low-cohesion set. There were 9 Republicans in the House who had been elected first in 1934.

[35] As was suggested in discussing the distribution by seniority levels, Table 40, the pattern on the high-cohesion set seems to indicate a rather uniform convergence within the party. In fact, the probability is not much less than .5 that a distribution like that on the high-cohesion set could have occurred by chance. On the low- and intermediate-cohesion sets, however, the probabilities that the distributions could have occurred by chance were less than .02 and slightly more than .10, respectively. (x^2 for the low-cohesion distribution $= 8.062$; $d.f. = 2$. x^2 for the intermediate-cohesion distribution $= 4.242$; $d.f. = 2$.)

Table 41

RELATION BETWEEN ELECTION AT MIDTERM OR IN PRESIDENTIAL YEARS AND
HIGH AGREEMENT* WITH HOUSE MINORITY LEADER, 81ST CONGRESS

Terms of Service and Year of First Election	Distribution in Party		Distribution in Leader's Top Scores		Mean Absences
	Number	Per Cent	Number	Per Cent	
A. LOW-COHESION SET, 2ND SESSION					
1, 3, or 5 ('48, '44, '40)	42	24.6	1	3.9	11.8
2, 4, or 6 ('46, '42, '38)	93	54.4	20	76.9	10.5
7–16 ('36 or earlier)	36	21.0	5	19.2	12.0
Total	171	100.0	26	100.0	- - -
B. INTERMEDIATE-COHESION SET, 1ST SESSION					
1, 3, or 5 ('48, '44, '40)	38	22.2	4	10.3	10.8
2, 4, or 6 ('46, '42, '38)	93	54.4	24	61.5	9.4
7–16 ('36 or earlier)	40	23.4	11	28.2	11.8
Total	171	100.0	39	100.0	- - -
C. HIGH-COHESION SET, 2ND SESSION					
1, 3, or 5 ('48, '44, '40)	42	24.6	36	26.7	10.1
2, 4, or 6 ('46, '42, '38)	93	54.4	73	54.1	9.7
7–16 ('36 or earlier)	36	21.0	26	19.2	8.2
Total	171	100.0	135	100.0	- - -

* "High agreement" on the low- and intermediate-cohesion sets means voting as Martin did on 46 or more of the 74 roll calls in the set; on the high-cohesion set it means agreement with the Minority Leader on 42 or more of the 66 roll calls in the set.

For example, in the low-cohesion set the first termers were absent less often on the average than the second, the third less often than the second, fourth, and sixth, and the fifth less often than any of these.

Since differences in absence rates thus do not explain this distribution, its meaning must lie in more substantial factors. Apparently something about the Republicans first elected in years when the Democrats recaptured the White House and increased their majorities in the House worked against their support of the Minority Leader on the votes that divided the party. Alternatively or in addition, something about Martin's leadership may have meant that in his voting he could not or did not accommodate the attitudes of these men. In any case they evidently tended to look elsewhere for their voting cues.

The crucial question to ask about these nonfollowers is whether they were in fact a homogeneous group. Had they any important characteristic in common outside of the dates of their first election to the House?[36] Looking at the 17 first-termers—none of whom was on Martin's list of top scores in the low-cohesion set—and at the 11 fifth-termers—all of whom were missing from the lists for both the low- and intermediate-cohesion votes—one finds no single characteristic in either group that alone would explain their rates of agreement with Martin. They came from all parts of the country, outside the South. Some of their districts were quite rural, some urban, some mixed; the occupational patterns in the constituencies were equally varied; some of the districts were close in 1948, and some were safe. Apparently these men did not constitute a homogeneous group, at least in terms of these presumably relevant criteria.

When, however, the voting patterns of these men are examined, it is at once evident that they split into two quite different groupings. One of these groupings identified with blocs on the "left" of the party structure, and the other was associated with the formations on the "right." The same inference emerges from their Administration support indexes, the mean in one grouping being considerably higher and that in the other being considerably lower than Martin's own index.[37]

Apparently those Republicans who succeeded in gaining entrance to the House in the face of a general endorsement of Democratic presidential and congressional candidates were at the policy extremes of

---

[36] A few of these men were first chosen at special elections to fill vacancies. For example, in the second session 4 of the 17 "first-termers" fell in this category, so the general description of them as running at the same time as a Democratic President is only roughly accurate.

[37] This kind of cleavage is also evident on the high-cohesion votes, despite the general consolidation of the party on those roll calls. On this set there were 9 men whose absence rates were low enough so that they might have been expected to have scores of at least 42 with Martin, yet none of them did. Five of these mavericks frequently voted with the Democratic "right," and 4 tended to support the "left" wing of the opposition.

the party. Through choice or necessity, those at one extreme resembled the Northern Democrats in their voting, and those at the other shared with some of the Southerners an unreconstructed hostility toward the position of the dominant segment in the majority party. This pattern again points to the degrees of independence that may be expected from the members of a mediate party group. Republicans elected under these generally unfavorable circumstances, like the senior Democrats from safe districts, did not strongly need or could not completely depend upon the apparatus of the legislative party.

It is clear that these men were not following Martin's lead, particularly on the votes on which the party was relatively disunited. The alternative sources of their voting cues are not so apparent. They were evidently quite diverse. Judging by the top scores of the 17 first-termers, however, a good many of them, from one-third to one-half, were strongly disposed, particularly on the low-cohesion votes, to go along with members of their own state delegations in the party or with men from adjacent states. This pattern of disintegrated voting will be analyzed in some detail in the following chapter.

The characteristics of these Republican mavericks having been examined, can one also infer that some peculiarity of Martin's behavior as Leader contributed to their deviation? Was the Minority Leader simply unable to accommodate to the extremes in his party? Or was he ineffective or deficient in his efforts at such accommodation? There is no reliable way of determining which of these explanations is relevant, but bits of evidence point toward deficiency on the Minority Leader's part.

In the first place, unlike the Democrats, the 58 Republicans who represented districts that were close in 1948 were consistently underrepresented among Martin's top scores on the low- and intermediate-cohesion sets. Neither inexperience in the House nor electoral marginality seems to have produced reliance on the Minority Leader in connection with these votes.

Secondly, a lack of correspondence between Martin's top scores on the low- and intermediate-cohesion sets indicates that his "following" within the party was a shifting and unstable one. Of the 26 men who scored high with Martin on the low-cohesion set, 12, or 46 per cent, were not on the list for the intermediate-cohesion set. In contrast, only 6 men, less than 10 per cent of those on McCormack's list for the low-cohesion set, were not on both lists. Variations in absence rates account for some of the noncorrespondence in the cases of both Martin and McCormack, but the chief explanation for the Republican behavior seems to be that the differing issues in the two sessions, which were reflected in fluidity within the voting structure of the Republican party as a whole, also produced a shift in the composition of the Minority Leader's following.

The evidence on these several contrasts between the followings of Martin and McCormack is not strong enough to support a firm conclusion that the former was less capable as a Leader, but it does indicate that, as in the Senate, the discretionary segment of the Leader's role is very broad. McCormack and Martin appear not to have operated in the same way, whatever may be said of their relative effectiveness. Both were fairly close to the center of their respective parties, but in Martin's case that "center," especially on the votes of lower cohesion, had a shifting composition, despite the generally higher unity of the Republican party in the House. It would be difficult to argue, therefore, that his voting agreements reflected a stable pattern of association within his party, one as stable as that behind the Majority Leader. Martin's "following," like the structure of the party as a whole, had a kaleidoscopic, unprogrammed character. Whether it could have or not, his leadership did not meet the expectations and attitudes at the extremes of the party and it rested on a comparatively fluid base at the center.

This fluidity and the peculiarities of the Minority Leader's performance, both of which had their rough parallels on the Republican side of the Senate, may have been characteristic only of this minority party rather than of the minority side in the Congress generally, but they lead one again toward the suspicion that the contrasts with the majority side were more than slightly a reflection of the centripetal effect of the Executive programming role upon his legislative party. This may be, as has been suggested earlier, one reason why McCormack's "support" among the newcomers tended to bridge the basic split within the party. The young Democrats were asked, in effect, to choose whether they would support a known President and a fairly definite program. Their Republican counterparts were, so to speak, divided between the unspecified programs of two prospective candidates for President whose identities were not yet known.

Assuming, for the purposes of discussion, that the peculiarities of Martin's following did reflect, at least in part, deficiencies in his own performance,[38] it is important to an understanding of the role to note that no one else in the hierarchy of the party seems to have picked up

---

[38] The assumption is not utterly groundless, for one hears from Republican representatives, especially the younger ones, fairly frequent criticism of Martin, whether as Minority Leader or as Speaker, for alleged indifference to matters of a general program character.

the ball that he dropped. Halleck, who would have been a likely candidate, in this Congress displayed essentially the same peculiarities in his voting pattern as did Martin. His top scores showed much the same pattern of alternation between those elected at midterm and those first entering the House after a presidential election, and he was apparently no more influential than was Martin among the more junior members of the party.[39] His scores showed, in fact, a definite leaning toward the more senior members of the party; all those serving in their first through fifth terms, for example, were underrepresented among his top scores on the low-cohesion votes. Halleck as Leader in a Martin Speakership may have been more influential with the rank and file, but this would merely underscore the point that, as in the Senate, when the principal elective leader defines his role narrowly and, out of choice or necessity, underexploits its potentialities, no other individual is likely to take over the functions. In this case Halleck did not and, as will be indicated shortly, the Whip's voting pattern indicated that he did not. The role is apparently an integral one, and those segments not performed by the occupant, especially if he is the Minority Leader, are likely not to be performed by anyone.

THE WHIPS

In its formal features the position of Whip is not materially different in the House from what it is in the Senate parties. In neither chamber does the post constitute a source of power independent of the other leadership positions. In fact, apparently even more than in the Senate, the Whips in the House are influential in consequence chiefly of their relations with the other elective leaders and secondarily of their individual positions in the voting structure of the party. Operating through an organization of assistants whose task is to get in touch with fellow-representatives in the region assigned to them, they discharge the function of sounding opinion and intentions within the party in at least as routine a way as in the Senate. Although the House Whips, like their Senate counterparts, are expected to assist the Floor Leaders, this seems to be a less important component of their role, for in debate even the Floor Leader plays a less active part in the House than in the Senate, as the data on leader initiatives suggest.

---

[39] The evidence indicates also that Halleck was less influential than Martin in the party as a whole. The two men disagreed on 22 of the 214 roll calls in the three sets. On 14 of these 22 Martin was on the side of the party majority and on 16 his was the prevailing view in the House.

In the House the differences between the Republican and Democratic Whips in their relations with their respective Floor Leaders were not as great as they were in the Senate, but some contrasts still were evident. In both chambers the structural peculiarities of the minority party seem to have been reflected in the relations of Leader and Whip. In neither party were the Leader and Whip consistently as close to one another in the voting structure as were the Democratic Leader and Whip in the Senate, but also neither were they as separated as the Republican Leader and Whip in the upper chamber.

The Democratic Whip, Representative Priest of Tennessee, was closer to the Floor Leader, McCormack of Massachusetts, than the Republican Whip, Representative Arends of Illinois, was to his Floor Leader, Martin of Massachusetts. This pattern parallels that in the Senate. In the one set on which both Priest and McCormack were in blocs, the intermediate-cohesion set, they occupied adjacent ranks in the blocs of the Northern wing (Table 31A), though Priest was also in one bloc of the Southern wing (Table 31B). In the low-cohesion set McCormack, though not in a bloc, was most closely identified with the Northern wing (Table 30A) and Priest was a member of a Southern bloc (Table 30B), but the Whip was on the "left" of the Southern wing in the bloc nearest to the Northern wing of the structure.

Martin and Arends, who were both in blocs on only one set—the low-cohesion set of the second session—were pretty well separated in the structure. Martin belonged to Bloc III toward the "left" of the center and Arends affiliated with Bloc VII nearer the dissenting "right" (Table 34). On the intermediate-cohesion set Arends was a member of all four blocs in the center of the party (Table 35), but he was somewhat more prominent in the "right" Bloc V than in the others. Martin on this set, though not in a bloc, was not at all identified with Bloc V but rather with the "left"-of-center Bloc II.

Despite these differences in the structural positions of the two sets of leaders, on the roll calls of all three sets Martin and Arends voted on opposite sides of an issue only a little more frequently than McCormack and Priest.[40] The substance of the disagreements is a good deal more informative than their number, however. Nineteen of the 21 McCor-

---

[40] The Republican leaders disagreed on 27 of the 214 votes in the three sets, approximately 13 per cent, and the Democrats were opposed on 21 out of 210, 10 per cent. In both parties the Floor Leader was normally in the dominant position on disagreements with the Whip. On the 27 Martin-Arends disagreements the former was on the side of the party majority on 17 and with the prevailing view in the House on 24. On the 21 McCormack-Priest oppositions the Leader voted with the party majority on 15 and on the prevailing side on an equal number.

mack-Priest disagreements occurred on the low-cohesion set, and 15 of these were votes dealing with the F.E.P.C. bill. The remaining 6— 4 on the low-cohesion set, 2 on the intermediate, and none on the high-cohesion votes—were comparatively minor. Priest, not surprisingly, voted like a Southerner on most of the F.E.P.C. roll calls, but interestingly enough he voted with McCormack on two tactical moves concerning this legislation, both of them involving a challenge to the Leader's control of the schedule.[41] Priest also voted with McCormack on all 9 of the roll calls in the intermediate-cohesion set dealing with the anti-poll tax bill, a position which must have entailed some risk for a representative from central Tennessee, even though there were in the area influential elements opposed to the poll tax, including *The Nashville Tennessean,* on whose editorial staff Priest served for 14 years prior to his election to the House.

The 27 disagreements between Martin and Arends covered a wider range of issues, but their most important feature was that their content implied the existence of real differences between the two men on policy and tactics, differences indicating either genuine opposition or failure to concert on matters of policy. Thus Arends voted with the opposition on 9 of the 17 F.E.P.C. votes, 5 in the low-cohesion set and 4 in the high, and on 3 of the 7 poll tax votes in the intermediate set. These were not votes dictated by his constituency or they would not have been confined to the preliminary moves on these bills. They rather were tactical moves on legislation of more than casual consequence to the Republican party. Of Arends's 15 other disagreements with Martin, all in the low- and intermediate-cohesion sets, 4 in the low set and one in the intermediate set dealt with agriculture, including 3 favorable votes by the Republican Whip on the proposal to increase cotton and peanut acreage allotments. His votes on these measures and on civil rights questions may have been based on an agreement between some Middle Western Republicans and the "right" wing of the Southern Democrats for solidarity on farm policy in return for support against measures involving racial issues, but if they were, the agreement operated without the blessing or at least without the voting support of the Minority Leader. The remaining 10 disagreements dealt with foreign policy (7) and rent control (3), Arends voting against the Administration and Martin even on passage of the Mutual Defense Assistance Act.

---

[41] Both of these were on motions to dispense with further proceedings under quorum calls, motions of a sort normally accepted by the House without a roll call. The quorum calls and insistence on roll calls to order their interruption were part of the delaying tactics of the F.E.P.C. opponents.

The substance of these oppositions and the indications that Arends, unlike Priest, ran no political risks by any of his votes in agreement with Martin suggest that the unprogrammed character of the minority party noted in the discussion of party structure and in the analysis of the Minority Leader carried over into the relations of the Leader and Whip. This was not an especially wide gulf, since Arends was on Martin's list of top scores on all three sets. But the character of the disagreements seems to signify the peculiar tendencies of the minority. Is this feature of the Republican leadership also evident among the other elective leaders? Do contrasts with the majority persist here also?

OTHER ELECTIVE LEADERS

The cohesion of the Republican elective leaders as a group in the House was closer to that of the Democrats than was the case in the Senate, but it nevertheless reflected the looseness noted elsewhere in the minority party. As Table 42 indicates, the mean scores of the four Republican elective leaders were lower than those of the five Democrats on all three sets, and they were agreed on a smaller number of the roll calls on all but the low-cohesion set. The Republican leaders had a mean absence rate slightly higher than that of the Democrats, but the pattern holds even if this is taken into account. It is the more striking because the mean cohesion indexes of the Republican party as a whole were higher than those of the Democrats on all three sets (Table 28). The mean party orthodoxy indexes of the two groups of leaders tell much the same story; the Democratic leaders more regularly voted with the majority of the party than did the Republicans in both sessions.

Despite these differences between the Democratic and Republican elective leaders, it is clear that neither group functioned as a unified and disciplined source of cues to the rank and file of their respective parties. The mean scores shown in Table 42 are consistently lower than those of the principal blocs identified in the preceding chapter (Tables 30A and B, 31A and B, and 33 through 36). This contrast is particularly striking in view of the larger size of the blocs, which normally would result in lower mean scores. Thus the nuclear clusters of these blocs, comparable in size to the leader groups, had mean scores even more in contrast with the leaders than did the complete blocs. In the House as in the Senate, the elective leaders as groups were not, judging from the evidence of the roll calls, acting in concert to define the policy of the legislative parties.

Table 42

RELATIVE COHESION AND PARTY ORTHODOXY OF DEMOCRATIC AND REPUBLI-
CAN ELECTIVE LEADERS,* 81ST CONGRESS, HOUSE OF REPRESENTATIVES

	Five Democratic Leaders	Four Republican Leaders
Low-cohesion votes		
Second Session		
Mean score	42.3	37.8
Number of complete agreements	33	36
Intermediate-cohesion votes		
First Session		
Mean score	48.4	42.0
Number of complete agreements	54	40
High-cohesion votes		
Second Session†		
Mean score	48.6	45.7
Number of complete agreements	57	50
Mean party orthodoxy index		
First Session	4.45	4.32
Second Session	4.36	4.27

* Democrats: McCormack, Majority Leader; Priest, Whip; Walter, Chairman of the Caucus; Murdock, Chairman of the Policy Committee; and Kirwan, Chairman of the Campaign Committee. Republicans: Martin, Minority
Leader; Arends, Whip; Woodruff, Chairman of the Conference; and L. W. Hall,
Chairman of the Campaign Committee.

† In the high-cohesion sets there were 66 Republican and 62 Democratic
votes; in all other sets there were 74 roll calls.

LEGEND: *Mean score:* the mean of the number of agreements between each
member of the group and each other member. *Complete agreements:* number
of votes on which all members of the group were unanimous or on which less
than half the members were unrecorded and the remainder were unanimous.
A *mean party orthodoxy index* of 5.00 would mean support of the party majority
on all votes in the session, an index of 1.00 would mean equally consistent opposition.

THE COMMITTEES ON POLICY, ON RULES, AND ON COMMITTEES

When the Joint Committee on the Organization of Congress proposed in 1946 that the legislature authorize the establishment of policy committees for each party in each house, the members of the House

of Representatives rejected the idea. The obvious explanation for this action is that for decades, at least for the majority party, party policy had effectively been set by the party's membership on the Rules Committee, working smoothly or in uneasy harmony with the Speaker and the Majority Floor Leader. Both parties in the House for several years had had Steering Committees, the Republicans since the period of World War I and the Democrats since 1933. In 1949 the Republicans formally designated a policy committee, and the Democrats, with the casualness common in these matters, have gradually come to refer to their steering committee by the same term. But, with the possible exception of a brief period in the early 1920's, neither of these has amounted to much. A major reason for this, as for the rejection of the Joint Committee's proposal, is that the principal elective leaders on both sides of the aisle have had no desire to complicate their tasks by assuming an obligation to consult with or to delegate power—if in fact that could be done—to a body with a sizable elective membership which they might control even less effectively than the Rules Committee. Speakers and prospective Speakers, like Presidents, have been little inclined to support reductions in the importance of the office with which they are concerned.[42]

The Republican policy committee in the House apparently has met a good deal more frequently than the Democratic, especially since 1955, when the Republicans became the minority congressional party. The Republican policy committee's continued frequent meetings since 1955 reflect in part the function of this committee, as of its Senate counterpart, as a communication center, especially in connection with the plans and preferences of the President. The contrasting inactivity of the Democratic body, however, probably has its roots partly in the same factor that makes meetings of the Democratic caucus rare, namely, that any assembly of Democrats gathered to discuss policy

---

[42] However it may appear, resistance of this sort is not an indication of personal perversity or self-aggrandizement. The Speakership, altered in authority but little reduced in power since the days of Cannon, is a response to the size and the internal organization of the House. Its influence probably could not be transferred intact to any representative body. (Cf. Mary Parker Follett, *The Speaker of the House of Representatives*, New York: Longmans, Green, 1896, chap. 11 and *passim.*) The inactivity of the Democratic Steering (or Policy) Committee also may be traceable in part to the circumstances of its origins in 1933 as a consolation prize for the leader of a House Democratic faction that had lost out in a three-way struggle over the Speakership rather than as a serious effort to create improved party machinery.

would almost surely break apart over the explosive racial issue.[43] This fragility of the Democratic organization helps to account not only for the inactivity of its policy committee but also for the somewhat greater concentration of power in the hands of its principal elective leaders.

In the Eighty-first Congress neither of the policy committees constituted a body agreed upon an appreciable fraction of the wide range of issues reflected in the roll calls. This is evident from Table 43, which gives comparative data on these groups, on the Committees on Committees, and on the respective parties' memberships on the Rules Committee. Among the Democrats the policy committee agreed on fewer votes than either of the other two groups, partly owing to its larger size. It was somewhat more closely identified with the party majority than was the contingent on Rules, however, and its general cohesion, as indicated by the mean scores in Table 43, was higher. The Republican policy committee was not much different, though it was somewhat more unified and more regular than the Committee on Committees. In both parties, moreover, the roll calls on which the members of the policy committees were agreed not only were confined almost entirely to the high-cohesion sets, but also even within these sets included a disproportionate number of votes on which the party's index of cohesion was high. In other words, voting unity in the policy committees did not precede or produce agreement within the parties but merely reflected such unity as had developed on other grounds.

The contrast between the two parties' delegations on the Rules Committee is marked and illustrates well the reasons for Speaker Rayburn's willingness to experiment with the 21-day rule in this Congress. The number of agreements among the Democrats was smaller than in any group except the policy committee, and the group's mean party orthodoxy indexes in both sessions were lower than those of any bloc in the party except the extreme "right" of the Southern wing. The Democratic membership on Rules was anything but a unified instrument.

During the debate in the second session precipitated by the unsuccessful attempt to repeal the 21-day rule, McCormack, taunted by Halleck with undermining the power of the House and the Committee by his opposition to the repeal resolution, stated: ". . . the Rules Committee functions as a traffic light for the leadership. But it is not

---

[43] In an interview, a former Democratic representative somewhat ruefully recalled having once forced a caucus on a civil rights issue only to have it end in failure as he watched the party almost literally dissolve before his eyes when the touchy question was raised.

Table 43

UNITY AND PARTY ORTHODOXY OF DEMOCRATIC AND REPUBLICAN COMMITTEES ON POLICY AND ON COMMITTEES AND OF PARTY DELEGATIONS ON COMMITTEE ON RULES, 81ST CONGRESS, HOUSE OF REPRESENTATIVES

	A. DEMOCRATS			B. REPUBLICANS		
	Policy Committee	Committee on Committees	Rules Committee	Policy Committee	Committee on Committees	Rules Committee
Low-cohesion votes						
Second Session						
Mean score	33.7	33.5	25.6	33.6	32.9	32.5
Number of complete agreements	0	3	1	2	1	27
Intermediate-cohesion votes						
First Session						
Mean score	38.6	42.6	32.2	40.6	38.0	44.1
Number of complete agreements	3	16	9	8	2	42
High-cohesion votes						
Second Session*						
Mean score	40.6	41.8	31.5	44.1	41.6	43.5
Number of complete agreements	31	40	32	43	30	47
Mean party orthodoxy index						
First Session	4.16	4.30	3.89	4.27	4.18	4.35
Second Session	4.07	4.18	3.70	4.12	4.10	4.15

* In the high-cohesion sets there were 66 Republican and 62 Democratic votes; in all other sets there were 74 roll calls.

LEGEND: *Mean score:* The mean of the number of agreements between each member of the group and each other member. *Complete agreements:* Number of votes on which all members of the group were unanimous or on which less than half the members were unrecorded and the remainder were unanimous. *A mean party orthodoxy index* of 5.00 would mean support of the party majority on all votes in the session, an index of 1.00 would mean equally consistent opposition.

now a traffic light for the leadership. When the gentleman's party was in power [in the Eightieth Congress] I agree that it was." [44] Although the Republican membership was of course only half what it was in the Eightieth Congress, 4 as against 8, the superior signaling capacity of the four senior Republicans is evident. They were agreed about as often as were the Republican elective leaders. As the minority on the Committee, they were not formally responsible for the program of the House and they could not have their way on the Committee except through divisions among the Democrats, which were deep and violent enough so that they even erupted on the floor of the House. Nevertheless, on the 18 record votes dealing with resolutions from Rules that occurred in the three Republican sets, these 4 men were agreed on all but 6; by way of contrast, the 8 Democrats were split on all but 4 of the 13 that fell into their three sets. The Rules Republicans were rarely agreed in opposition to the Minority Leader, but Representative Allen of Illinois, the ranking Republican member, opposed him fairly frequently. These disagreements included 3 votes on resolutions reported by the Rules Committee, but one suspects that these reflected not an inability on Martin's part to control his Rules delegation but rather the Leader's unconcern with such matters of policy while his party was in the minority. It apparently did not mean that the Rules Republicans were more ready to follow an alternative leadership, since as a group they opposed Halleck's voting position far more frequently than they did Martin's. [45]

The two Committees on Committees are interesting in several ways.

---

[44] *Congressional Record*, 81st Cong., 2nd Sess., 96:1 (January 20, 1950), 734.

[45] The contrasting position of the two Rules delegations was nicely illustrated in a vote on a key move in connection with the proposed repeal of the 21-day rule. Martin and the other Republican leaders wanted repeal, because without the rule their ability to embarrass the Majority was increased and presumably because they were not anxious to have such a provision on the books when they one day took over the majority position in the House. The repeal motion was to be decided on Friday, January 20, 1950, but the House was also scheduled—provided that the 21-day rule, permitting the bypassing of the Rules Committee, was still on the books—to take up the F.E.P.C. bill on Monday, January 23. With conference backing, therefore, Martin moved adjournment at the opening of the session on Friday; since the Democratic leaders favored retention of the rule, McCormack was opposed to the Martin strategy. The Minority Leader's motion failed by a vote of 161 to 255, 5 Republicans voting on McCormack's side and 4 Democrats voting with Martin. However, all the Republican elective leaders, every member of the Republican policy committee, and all their members on the Rules Committee voted with the Floor Leader. On the Democratic side the policy committee was solidly with McCormack, as were the elective leaders, but the Rules Committee was divided, Smith of Virginia voting with Martin.

On the Democratic side the cohesion of this group, the Democratic members of the Committee on Ways and Means, roughly resembled that of the elective leaders (Tables 42 and 43). This is impressive chiefly for the contrast with the Rules group. Because of their party functions, the Democratic composition of the Ways and Means Committee is a matter of about as much concern to the principal elective leaders as is that of the Rules body. The contrast between their voting records is symptomatic of the leaders' difficulties with Rules. The Republican Committee on Committees was even less united than the policy committee. Given the looseness of the Republican structure in this Congress, this is not astonishing, and it probably does not indicate that the group was unresponsive to the Leader's initiatives concerning committee assignments. Its disunity on the roll calls does suggest, however, the limitations in the policy realm of a body whose members do not owe their positions directly to the leadership but rather to their state delegations. The relative unity of the Democrats' Committee on Committees may derive in part from the fact that they share common membership on a standing committee of the House, but their mode of selection seems a more likely explanation.

It is thus apparent that in neither party in the House were the policy committees, the Rules Committee memberships, or the Committees on Committees functioning strongly as unified elements in the definition of policy. By the evidence of the roll calls, all of them were generally even less impressive in this respect than were the elective leaders as a group. The generally low cohesion of the Democratic bodies and especially of the Rules group indicates the extent to which the power of the leaders, Rayburn and McCormack, must be interstitial and must rest on a basis of personal negotiation. The operation of the collective machinery of the majority party was faulty, so that the legislative party's effectiveness depended peculiarly upon the personal skills of the principal leaders, notably the Speaker.[46]

---

[46] Even in the second session of the Eighty-fourth Congress, when the difficulties with the Democrats on the Rules Committee were not nearly as great, its membership having changed somewhat by 1956, it was frequently said that, when Speaker Rayburn was obliged to be away from Washington for several weeks, the refusal of the Rules Committee—chiefly in the person of Chairman Smith of Virginia—to clear certain controversial measures for floor debate had to stand unchallenged until the Speaker returned and was able to attempt a negotiated settlement.

THE SENIORITY LEADERS

As in the Senate, a crucial feature of the roles of the principal elective leaders and of the legislative party in the House is the part played by the seniority leaders. The questions raised by Woodrow Wilson's observations in the 1880's, summarized in Chapter 4, are as relevant to the House as to the Senate.[47] Are the seniority leaders independent autocrats? Are there in the House ". . . as many leaders as there are subjects of legislation"?[48] Do the seniority leaders, and especially the committee chairmen, operate without the restraints of collegial obligation or common policy? What are their relations with the principal elective leaders? To what degree are these characterized by collaboration? When disagreement occurs between seniority and elective leaders, as it must, whom does the party follow?

In the analysis of the Senate in Chapter 4 the evidence pointed to the influence and the pivotal position of the Floor Leader. How close a parallel is to be expected in the House? Is the relative power of the principal elective leaders and the seniority leaders essentially the same in the two chambers? Or are there factors such as the greater size of the House that produce a different pattern? In the Eighty-first Congress were there differences between the two parties in these respects? If so, how are they to be accounted for? As a consequence of the setting in this Congress? Of continuing differences between Republicans and Democrats? Of features inherent in the positions of the minority and majority parties? Even allowing for the absence of solid data on the Speaker, these questions cannot all be answered with assurance, but they must be examined if a complete estimate of the legislative party and its leadership is to be arrived at.

As the tables of bloc structure in Chapter 5 indicate, the seniority leaders in both parties were distributed over the entire range of the voting pattern.[49] As far as these data go they provide no evidence

---

[47] The *Congressional Government* was written before the full flowering of the Speakership under Reed, Crisp, and Cannon. Lecturing at Columbia University in 1907, in the heyday of Cannon, Wilson—following the briefer reinterpretation of 1900 (see note 4)—markedly altered his early view of leadership in the House. (*Constitutional Government in the United States*, New York: Columbia University Press, 1908, pp. 91–107.) It is interesting that since the revolt against Cannon in 1910 commentators have usually relied on the authority of the earlier view, as if the House leadership had since that event returned to the state it was in during the Speakership of Carlisle or even of Keifer.

[48] Wilson, *Congressional Government*, p. 58.

[49] See Tables 30A and B, 31A and B, 34, and 35 for the positions of the seniority leaders on the low- and intermediate-cohesion sets.

that the seniority leaders were acting in concert with any regularity. The data in Table 44, showing the mean scores and number of agreements of the seniority leaders in the two parties, have the same implication. In comparison with the Democrats, the Republican seniority leaders were more cohesive and voted more regularly with the ma-

Table 44

RELATIVE COHESION AND PARTY ORTHODOXY OF THE DEMOCRATIC AND REPUBLICAN SENIORITY LEADERS, 81ST CONGRESS, HOUSE OF REPRESENTATIVES

	Democrats	Republicans
Low-cohesion votes		
Second Session		
Mean score	26.7	35.1
Number of complete agreements	0	1
Intermediate-cohesion votes		
First Session		
Mean score	32.8	34.2
Number of complete agreements	1	8
High-cohesion votes		
Second Session*		
Mean score	33.8	45.4
Number of complete agreements	22	29
Mean party orthodoxy index		
First Session	3.92	4.11
Second Session	3.83	4.17

* In the high-cohesion sets there were 66 Republican and 62 Democratic votes; in all other sets there were 74 roll calls.

LEGEND: *Mean score:* The mean of the number of agreements between each member of the group and each other member. *Complete agreements:* Number of votes on which all members of the group were unanimous or on which less than half the members were unrecorded and the remainder were unanimous. A *mean party orthodoxy index* of 5.00 would mean support of the party majority on all votes in the session, an index of 1.00 would mean equally consistent opposition.

jority of their party. However, the differences between the two parties, although not entirely traceable to variations in "absence" rates, are probably not of major importance, since the number of agreements among the seniority leaders of both parties was negligible except on the high-cohesion sets. It is evident that the seniority leaders as groups merely reflected the unity of the parties when this occurred but did not anticipate and almost certainly did not produce it. The substance of the agreements points to the same conclusion. For example, on the intermediate- and high-cohesion sets the Republican seniority leaders' agreements included almost no votes (3 out of the 37 agreements) dealing with agriculture or with foreign policy, the issues that were most likely to divide the party.

Since the relations among the seniority leaders, as indicated by these roll calls, were simply those of rank-and-file members of the two parties, those between the principal elective leaders and the seniority leaders must have been, in the House as in the Senate, specialized ones, if they had any significance at all. That is, if the seniority leaders had any role in a coherent party program and if the Floor Leaders were in any sense functioning as sponsors of such a program, they must have worked together as individuals on the matters of concern to the seniority leader's own committee and on virtually no others.

Specialization seems generally to be more characteristic of life in the House than it is in the Senate. Size is once again probably the basic reason for this, since, in a relatively fluid body of 435 or even in a party of 200 or so whose cohesion is not remarkably high, only a few are likely to be able to acquire and maintain relations that will permit them to be influential on more than one or two subjects. The more homogeneous character of the normally smaller House constituencies may also be a factor. In any event, the lore of the Senate permits, even encourages, a member to be a generalist, while that of the House discourages any such tendencies. Sam Rayburn's usual advice to the freshman representative, the wisdom of which is attested to by many informants, is not to wait for any specified time before making his maiden speech to the House but to delay participation in debate until the House is considering something on which he is especially well informed; not to avail himself of every opportunity to become involved in the affairs of committees to which he does not belong but to stay close to those to which he has been assigned.

Among the indications that such specialization carries over into the relations between the Floor Leaders and the ranking committee members in the House is the infrequency with which seniority leaders were "absent" on votes concerning matters dealt with by their committees, despite the tendency, especially on the Democratic side, for the seniority leaders to be unrecorded much more often than the remainder of the party on the whole range of roll calls. More important for purposes of the present analysis, however, is the evidence that the Floor Leader and the individual seniority leaders were much more likely to agree on votes concerning measures reported by their committees than on votes dealing with other matters. These data are presented in summary form in Tables 45 and 46.[50]

Comparisons between the parties on this matter are risky principally because of differences in "absence" rates. Unquestionably the sharper contrasts on the Democratic side (Table 45) are in part a function of

Table 45

AGREEMENTS BETWEEN HOUSE MAJORITY LEADER AND DEMOCRATIC SEN-
IORITY LEADERS ON VOTES CONCERNING MEASURES REPORTED BY THEIR
COMMITTEES AND ON ALL OTHER VOTES, 81ST CONGRESS

	Votes on Committee Measures			Other Votes		
	Total*	Agree-ments	Per Cent	Total	Agree-ments	Per Cent
Low-cohesion votes Second Session	55	37	72.7	1203	496	41.2
Intermediate-cohesion votes First Session	73	62	85.0	1037	575	55.4
High-cohesion votes Second Session	61	49	80.3	993	638	64.2

* The numbers of committee measures do not equal the total votes in the sets for the following reasons: in the low-cohesion set 12 tactical votes dealing with the F.E.P.C. issue could not properly be assigned to any committee; 7 additional votes concerning the Committee on Education and Labor were omitted because they were taken while it was chaired by Representative Lesinski of Michigan, whose death in May, 1950, permitted him to have cast too few votes to be included in the general analysis of the second session. In each of the other two sets one roll call could not properly be assigned to any committee.

the observed tendency for the Democratic seniority leaders to be un-recorded rarely on votes dealing with their committee's measures but fairly frequently on other votes. Since the Republican seniority leaders were less likely to be so selective in their voting behavior, the smaller differences shown in the Republican data (Table 46) were to be expected. These extraneous factors do not entirely account for the differences between the two parties, however, as is shown by the figures on actual oppositions between the Floor Leaders and the seniority leaders, to be discussed shortly. The fluidity of the minority party, repeatedly noticed in the analysis of both House and Senate, seems to have been reflected in a lower rate of agreement between Martin

---

[50] The data in these tables correspond to those in the equivalent tables dealing with the Senate (Tables 23 and 24).

Table 46

AGREEMENTS BETWEEN HOUSE MINORITY LEADER AND REPUBLICAN SEN-
IORITY LEADERS ON VOTES CONCERNING MEASURES REPORTED BY THEIR
COMMITTEES AND ON ALL OTHER VOTES, 81ST CONGRESS

	Votes on Committee Measures			Other Votes		
	Total*	Agree-ments	Per Cent	Total	Agree-ments	Per Cent
Low-cohesion votes Second Session	71	37	52.1	1113	608	54.6
Intermediate-cohesion votes First Session	73	42	57.5	1171	656	56.0
High-cohesion votes Second Session	56	44	78.6	1127	824	73.1

* The numbers of committee measures do not equal the total votes in the sets for the following reasons: in the low-cohesion set 3 tactical votes on the F.E.P.C. issue could not properly be assigned to any committee; in the intermediate-cohesion set one vote could not be attributed to a committee; and in the high-cohesion set there were 10 such votes, 9 of them tactical votes on F.E.P.C. and the other the Minority Leader's move to adjourn in order to delay action on the resolution to repeal the 21-day rule.

and the ranking Republican committee members on measures concerning their committees.

The details underlying Table 45 support the hypothesis concerning selective agreement between the Floor Leader and the seniority leaders a good deal more strongly than in the case of the Senate. There were almost no cases, even among committee chairmen on the extreme "right" of the party, in which the rate of agreement with McCormack on committee measures was not higher than that on other votes. This is particularly evident if McCormack's "absences" are discounted, that is, if his "absences" are omitted from the tally of committee measures; among the "right" Democrats, only Doughton of Ways and Means on the low-cohesion set and Rankin of Veterans on the intermediate-cohesion set would be inconsistent with the hypothesis if this discount were applied. Since discounting McCormack's absences on committee votes significantly alters the ratios for Rankin of Veterans and Wood of Un-American Activities on both the low- and the high-cohesion sets, it is possible to assume that these "absences" had some significance, that McCormack was avoiding open disagreement with these chairmen. The substance of the votes, however, suggests that avoidance of open opposition to the President is the more likely explanation, since most of them (four out of five) dealt with vetoes and with legislation such as the Internal Security Act on which the Administration view was rejected by a large bipartisan majority.

As would be expected, the detailed pattern underlying the Republican data (Table 46) is less consistent, but more so than was the equivalent one in the Senate. Even allowing for Martin's absences, there were four seniority leaders in the low-cohesion set and two in each of the others whose records were counter to what would be expected. Some, such as Reed of Ways and Means, Rees of Post Office and Civil Service, and LeCompte of House Administration, were in an extreme position in the party structure, but several of them were not. In any event, the pattern, though generally consistent with the hypothesis of selective agreement, seems to reflect a lower degree of program coherence on the minority side.

When the Floor Leader and a seniority leader disagreed on a vote bearing on the concerns of the latter's committee, who was more likely to be with the party majority? As in the Senate, this question must be answered before one can assume, even tentatively, that the Floor Leader was performing some sort of coordinative role and was not rather "going along" with each seniority leader in turn and having no important impact upon the voting of the legislative party. As in the Senate, it can be expected that a Floor Leader who was acting effectively as, in some sense, the voice of his party would normally have the majority of the party with him in such cases, would be on the prevailing side in the House if he were Majority Leader, and would even carry with him a majority of his party's membership on the affected committee.

Because the rates of disagreement between the Floor Leaders in the House and the several seniority leaders were quite low, as compared with the Senate, the data on the outcomes of these votes on all three sets have been consolidated in Table 47. McCormack's record was highly consistent with the expectation, though the number of votes involved was low. He was on the side of the party majority on two-thirds of the disagreed votes, on the prevaling side in the House on better than three-quarters, and in only one case out of the nine did a majority of the Democrats on the committee back the chairman rather than him. Martin's record with his party was even stronger than McCormack's, the majority voting as he did on over 90 per cent of the disputed roll calls, and he was on the prevailing side in the House more frequently than might have been expected of a Minority Leader. With the Republican rank and file on the committees, however, he did some-

Table 47

FREQUENCY WITH WHICH MAJORITY AND MINORITY LEADERS WERE ON PREVAILING SIDE IN THEIR PARTIES, IN THE HOUSE, AND AMONG THEIR PARTY'S COMMITTEE MEMBERS WHEN THEY AND THE SENIORITY LEADERS DISAGREED ON VOTES CONCERNING MEASURES REPORTED BY THE COMMITTEES, 81ST CONGRESS

	Number of Disagreed Votes	Majority of Party with Floor Leader on:	Majority of House with Floor Leader on:	Majority of Party Committee Members		
				with Floor Leader on:	with Seniority Leader on:	"Absent"* or Evenly Divided on:
Majority Leader and Committee Chairmen†	9	6	7	4	1	4
Minority Leader and Republican Seniority Leaders‡	39	36	22	21	17	1

* "Absent" means those votes on which half or more of the party committee members were not recorded.

† The roll calls considered here were the same as those on Table 45. See the explanation on that table. The 9 disagreements were distributed among 6 committee chairmen.

‡ The roll calls considered here were the same as those on Table 46. See the explanation on that table. The 39 disagreements were distributed among 15 Republican seniority leaders.

what less well; a majority of them sided with the chairman on over two-fifths of the disputed votes.[51]

In general the records of the Majority and Minority Leaders in relation to the seniority leaders are similar and are consistent with the proposition that they were both in some measure acting as spokesmen of their legislative parties. There was, however, between the two records a sharp contrast that requires discussion, namely, that Martin's rate of disagreement with his seniority leaders was markedly higher than McCormack's, nearly 20 per cent as against slightly under 5 per

[51] The details on this point are of some interest. With a seniority leader fairly far to the "right" of the party, such as Taber of Appropriations or Rees of Post Office and Civil Service, the rank and file were regularly with Martin. In the case of a moderate dealing with a subject peculiarly close to the Administration, as Eaton of Foreign Affairs, the rank and file broke with Martin and with the party majority to go along with the seniority leader.

cent, although Martin was unrecorded on more of these votes than was McCormack. What does this contrast imply? Was this a reflection of Martin's performance of his role? Or was it rather a consequence of some characteristic of the minority party?

If this high disagreement rate was a peculiarity of Martin, it was one he shared with the principal alternative leader, Representative Halleck. The range and rate of Halleck's disagreements with the seniority leaders were almost as marked, although he was unrecorded even more frequently than Martin. Since roughly half of their disagreements were in common, one might infer that the differential between them and McCormack signified a joint inability or disinclination of the Republican leadership to reach agreement with the seniority leaders on the measures emerging from the committees. Whether this interpretation is valid or not, the discrepancy argues again the point that the minority party was less coherent, displayed a less programmed appearance than did the majority.[52] Examination of the comparable tables on the Senate will show a similar discrepancy there and with similar implications.[53]

---

[52] An alternative explanation, that McCormack's lower rate of disagreement represented merely a greater inclination on his part than on Martin's or Halleck's to let the seniority leaders have their heads, is, of course, possible. It, however, does not seem consistent with the other indications, both in the House and in the Senate, of fluidity on the minority side.

[53] Compare pp. 140 through 143. It will also be evident that both leaders in the Senate had higher rates of disagreement with the seniority leaders than did their counterparts in the House. This is one of those points at which comparisons between the two chambers must be made with caution. Aside from the generally lower "absence" rates of the Senate leaders, which afforded them more opportunity to dissent from the views of the ranking committee members, the lack of the Committee of the Whole procedure in the Senate much increases the possibility that such disagreement will appear on the formal record there, since the great bulk of the voting in the House is done in Committee of the Whole, where "yea-and-nay" votes are not in order. There are other procedural and contextual factors that, together with those mentioned, will adequately explain the differences noted. It is tempting, however, to suggest, though the point cannot be verified, that the Senate Floor Leaders may have dissented more frequently from the views of their seniority leaders because in the smaller body it is easier for the Leader to go over the head of the ranking committee member to the rank and file of both the Senate and its committees. The literature is silent on this point, and the judgments of informants are conflicting, but there is some logic in the suspicion that the greater size of the House makes its elective leaders as well as the ordinary members more dependent upon, more the captives of, the machinery of the chamber, including its committees.

SUMMARY

The principal inferences from this analysis of House leadership roles can now be drawn together. The data of the preceding pages argue strongly the pivotal character, in the House as in the Senate, of the roles of Minority Leader and Majority Leader, the latter as the Speaker's adjutant, in their respective legislative parties. Except for the assumed relations between the Majority Leader and the Speaker, the party leadership, on the evidence of the record votes, shows little or no collegial character. The individual elective leaders, the four or five in each party, were somewhat more unified than the other collective leadership elements, but even the relations of the Whips with the Floor Leaders, especially on the minority side, showed less than complete collaboration.

The power of the Floor Leaders appears, even more clearly than in the Senate, as interstitial and personal rather than formal and authorized. Among the Democrats this may have been accentuated by the basic cleavage in the party, but it was evident among the Republicans as well. Despite the obvious importance of formal machinery in the House, the leaders on both sides of the aisle apparently were obliged to find supplements to their formal powers in whatever likely places were available to them. The limits on their formal influence are persuasively summarized in the differential character of the "followings" of the Majority and Minority Leaders, the former relying disproportionately upon the juniors and the political marginals within his party and the latter upon the seniors and those entering the House after the midterm elections.

The behavior of both Floor Leaders reflected the imperatives of the mediate group in that both, even more than their principal associates, stood midway in the voting structure of their parties. The performances of McCormack and Martin indicated further—and also in keeping with the mediate character of the legislative party—that in the House, as in the Senate, the discretionary aspects of the Floor Leader's role were very wide. Within broad limits his skills and inclinations defined the meaning of the position. But, judging from the evidence on the minority party, it also seems apparent that the role was an integral one. If, from choice or necessity, its occupant defined it narrowly, there was little likelihood that another would take over the excluded functions. The facts normally may be somewhat different on the majority side, especially if the President is of the same party, but if the Majority Leadership and the Speakership can be properly regarded as closely interdependent roles, the presumption is strong that jointly they too have this integral character.

Despite the flexibility of the Floor Leader's role and the informal nature of much of his influence, little basis is evident in these data for the charge that the legislative party in the House is voiceless, or that it is heard only through the cacophony of the multitude of seniority leaders. The power of the principal elective leaders is not unlimited, and evidence of independent leadership by individual seniority leaders can be seen in the voting patterns of the parties. But it seems equally clear that the behavior of the Floor Leaders in considerable measure bore out the implications of the purely institutional fact that theirs has become a full-time job. They were not at the mercy of the seniority leaders and they did, with varying degrees of effectiveness, act as if they were the trustees of the party's record.[54]

Variations were evident, however. In these materials, as in other portions of this book, the Republican minority—in its voting structure, in the instability of the Minority Leader's "following," and at other points—especially on those votes on which its cohesion was relatively low, showed an unprogrammed, almost kaleidoscopic fluidity. Despite the minority party's generally higher indexes of cohesion, not the case in the Senate, its majorities on the low- and intermediate-cohesion sets had a less stable composition than did the Democrats', as was also the case in the Senate. Fluidity was seen in both parties, but it was more evident on the Republican side.

From these comments emerge two questions that will be the chief concern of the following two chapters. If the members of neither party consistently found the cues for their own voting choices in the activities of the principal elective leaders, where did they find them? What features of the majority party's situation gave it, in both houses, a less fluid, more coherent appearance?

---

[54] Here as elsewhere, of course, it is necessary on the majority side to think of the Floor Leader and the Speaker together.

chapter seven

INTRAPARTY GROUPS

AND

VOTING STRUCTURE IN THE HOUSE:

The State Delegations
and the Standing Committees

The evidences of instability in the voting structures that have been examined in the four preceding chapters, more evident in the House of Representatives than in the Senate and more marked within the minority than among the majority, are of the sort upon which critics of the American parties have relied in reaching the judgment that these parties, especially in their legislative phase, are not "responsible." [1] Whatever view one may take of the these criticisms, the symptoms of disunity and fluidity within the legislative party signify that, although the party label evidently is the single most reliable indicator of congressional voting behavior, the individual representative may fairly often dissent from the views of his party colleagues, not only on matters of local or minor significance but also on issues of national or even global import.

The representative's "independence" is most commonly, and in a

---

[1] For an admirable summary and critical analysis of this position see Austin Ranney, *The Doctrine of Responsible Party Government: Its Origins and Present State,* Urbana: University of Illinois Press, 1954.

good many cases accurately, ascribed to peculiarities of his constituency. These, it is assumed, generate organized or unorganized demands for a nonconforming vote or, perhaps more frequently, are the source of recriminations and penalties if he does not display independence of his party colleagues on certain types of issues. But the member of Congress is by no means always able to predict the electoral consequences of his choices even though he is sure that they may produce repercussions in his district. This unpredictability contributes to the unstructured character of his position. The political intelligence supplied by interest groups and individual petitioners and advisers, valuable though it may be in helping to resolve doubts, is neither so complete nor so accurate as to eliminate the uncertainties and risks associated with the representative's response to a call for the "yeas and nays." It can rarely provide him with a reliable estimate of his vote's effects upon the drawing-power of the party label, on which, as earlier chapters have suggested, he is in some measure dependent for re-election.

To the ambiguities of the cues the legislator receives from or perceives in his constituency may be added doubts concerning the preferences and intentions of the formal party leadership on any given vote. On those matters in which the leaders are genuinely interested, means are available for communicating the "party" position to the rank and file and even, after a fashion, for enforcing it. But on a probably larger number of votes no such communication may be available, and the ordinary representative, especially if he is a relatively junior member of the House, has no notion of how the party leaders want him to vote.[2] The reasons for this state of affairs may include a prudent nonfeasance or a tacit reliance on the probability that most representatives will vote with the party majority if they feel that they can, or, rarely, a deliberate abdication by the leadership. As earlier comments on the discretionary breadth and the middleman character of the elective leaders' roles have indicated, the stable requirements of these roles in both House and Senate may impose this lack of explicit guidance, or it may merely reflect the personality of the man occupying one of these roles. But, whatever the precise causes, the fact of uncertainty on the part of the rank and file is unmistakable.

In the absence of well-defined, institutionalized, and continuously operative cue-giving mechanisms within the legislative party, one would anticipate that a variety of informal, only partly conscious, but

---

[2] These statements are based on a number of interviews with members of Congress from both parties. They do not reflect a systematic sampling. Confidence in them rests rather upon the consistency with which these views were reported.

not entirely haphazard devices would be employed by representatives in arriving at their voting decisions. Moreover, within a body as large as the House or one of the parties in the House these substitute sources of voting cues would be expected to grow up around familiar associations and relationships serving alternative functions. These would include personal friendships not necessarily political in character and even contacts created or reinforced by the proximity of offices or residences in Washington. They would certainly include the almost ready-made relationships within the state party delegation and probably the relations of confidence developed through joint service on standing legislative committees. The latter two will be examined in the present chapter.

As these remarks imply, the problem of voting cues and their sources is located primarily in the House. Although in later paragraphs some parallels between the House and Senate on this score will be noted, the smaller body involves fewer ambiguities, and the positions of its members consequently are in this respect more structured. The Senate's complexities, though great, are more nearly within the perceptual range of the ordinary legislator, so that uncertainties reflecting the internal structure of the chamber are less frequent. Moreover, because senators are both more visible as individuals and less hounded by the recurrent urgencies of re-election they are less dependent on minor and temporary reactions within their generally heterogeneous constituencies. In short, a senator has more chance of knowing and of influencing what is going on and, in consequence, is less in need of supplementary cue-giving mechanisms than his colleague in the House.

THE STATE PARTY DELEGATIONS

Under certain fairly obvious conditions, voting agreement within the state party delegations is likely to be high. The issues in a given set of roll calls may be of particular importance to organized statewide interests. They may be of special concern to more localized interests strategically associated with the party organization in the state. Similar voting behavior within the delegation may reflect a tendency of the state party to elect members of Congress from districts roughly similar in socio-economic composition or to recruit candidates with closely comparable backgrounds and attitudes. If the legislative party splits into two opposing wings on certain kinds of issues, moreover, high intrastate agreement would accompany increased regional solidarity in the House. Finally, if the voting within the legislative party approaches unanimity, it must also, of course, do so within most state delegations.

In addition, however, it seems likely that the delegation as a group affects the voting decisions of its members and, under appropriate circumstances, produces marked agreement among them. Some of the factors mentioned in the preceding paragraph, added to the intradelegation relationships arising from joint concern with matters of legislative party organization, such as assignments to the standing committees, or from purely social considerations, make it easy and natural for members of a delegation to consult one another on a variety of legislative questions. Moreover, a mutual dependence upon a limited number of agencies for disseminating news may often counsel the wisdom of agreement. The press, and especially the metropolitan press, may without intent turn intradelegation agreement to the advantage of all members.

The delegation thus tends to constitute a communication structure whose repeated use results in a heightened consensus and similarity of voting among its members. In short, the state party delegation in the House may be a significant alternative cue-giving mechanism within the legislative party, especially on matters whose political implications are ambiguous. Uncertainty is misery and misery loves company.

In order to perform an adequate but manageable test of this hypothesis, 10 Republican delegations and 13 Democratic delegations were selected, representing various regions of the country.[3] The data for the analysis were each party's three sets of roll calls and the number of agreements between each member of these delegations and each other member of his party in the House, as in the analysis of voting structure. By limiting the number of cases, however, it was feasible to consider a wider range of agreements than in the construction of the House matrixes, 38 or more in the low- and intermediate-cohesion sets, 34 and 32 for the Republican and Democratic high-cohesion sets, respectively.

---

[3] The largest state party delegation was chosen from each of 8 regions if it amounted to at least 3 men, and the second largest party delegation if it amounted to more than 3. In addition, one extra Democratic delegation was selected from the South (Alabama) and one extra Republican delegation from the East North Central region (Wisconsin). The regions used were New England, Middle Atlantic, East North Central, West North Central, Border, South, Mountain, and Pacific. No Republican delegations qualified from the Border, South, and Mountain states. The states selected were, for the Republicans: Massachusetts, New York, Pennsylvania, Michigan, Illinois, Wisconsin, Iowa, Kansas, Oregon, and California; for the Democrats: Massachusetts, New York, Pennsylvania, Ohio, Illinois, Minnesota, Missouri, Oklahoma, North Carolina, Alabama, Texas, Colorado, and California.

How frequently did the members of these delegations agree with one another? That is, how cohesive were they and what variations were there among the delegations on this score? To answer these questions it was necessary to determine how nearly the number of agreements within a state delegation approached the number theoretically possible if the group were perfectly cohesive. The first step was to list, for each member of each selected delegation, the number of scores, beginning with his highest, equal to one less than the number of legislators in the delegation. For example, there were four men in the Democratic delegation from Minnesota, so the three highest scores of each were listed. Representative Wier's three highest agreements on the roll calls of the intermediate-cohesion set were with Representatives McCarthy of Minnesota, Blatnik of Minnesota, and Jacobs of Indiana. He thus had two intradelegation scores among his top three. The same procedure was followed for the three other men in the delegation, and the number of these intrastate scores in the delegation was then totaled for each of the three sets of roll calls.[4]

If a delegation were perfectly cohesive, "absences" excluded, the number of intrastate scores in this summation would be equal to the number of men in the delegation multiplied by one less than that number. That is, in the four-man Minnesota Democratic delegation the highest scores of each man would be with his three state colleagues, giving a possible total of 12. The ratio of the actual number of scores to this theoretically possible number is an indicator of the frequency of intrastate agreements, a rough measure of the group's cohesion, and a basis of comparison with other delegations in the party.[5] On the intermediate-cohesion set of the first session there were 3 actual intrastate scores in the Minnesota Democratic delegation, or 25 per cent of the theoretically possible figure. Tables 48 and 49 list these percentages on each set of roll calls for the 13 Democratic and the 10 Republican delegations, respectively.[6]

---

[4] In counting the number of scores with others from the same state, 2 or more tie scores in the lowest position were counted as only one.

[5] For the technically minded reader, the formula for the number of possible pairs of items in a group of N size, $N(N-1)/2$, could not be used in this case because of the wide discrepancies possible between the top scores of two men in a delegation. For example, in a delegation of 10, one would be interested in the first 9 scores of each man in the group. If, on 74 votes, the top score of man A is with man B of the same delegation and they vote the same way on 45 of the roll calls, but this 45 represents B's fifteenth-ranking score and A's third, A will not appear among B's intrastate agreements, although B's name will appear on A's list.

[6] The effect of ignoring the lower scores (37 and below on the low- and intermediate-cohesion sets, 33 or lower on the Republican high-cohesion set and 31

Table 48

RATIOS OF ACTUAL TO POSSIBLE AGREEMENT SCORES WITHIN SELECTED
STATE DEMOCRATIC DELEGATIONS TO THE HOUSE OF REPRESENTATIVES,
81ST CONGRESS

State	First Session Intermediate Cohesion, 74 Roll Calls, per cent	Second Session	
		Low Cohesion, 74 Roll Calls, per cent	High Cohesion, 62 Roll Calls, per cent
Alabama	36.1	18.1	11.1
California	7.8	24.5	4.5
Colorado	33.3	33.3	16.7
Illinois	24.2	24.5	12.7
Massachusetts	6.7	6.7	3.3
Minnesota	25.0	0.0	0.0
Missouri	34.8	15.9	22.7
New York	10.7	26.1	10.9
North Carolina	7.6	7.3	10.0
Ohio	6.8	15.2	4.5
Oklahoma	23.2	37.5	1.8
Pennsylvania	11.0	26.7	15.2
Texas	30.0	26.6	13.5
13 states	18.0	23.1	11.5

Given the variety of factors that might affect the votes of a state
party delegation, one would not expect to find perfect consistency in
a set of results such as those listed in the tables. Yet a sufficiently
stable pattern emerges from the data to provide a basis for speculation
and cautious inference. The diversity of factors affecting the delegations' choices is reflected in the variations among the groups and in
one group from one set of roll calls to another.[7] Nevertheless, the ratios in these tables are high enough in most instances to support the

on the Democratic) is to understate the cohesion of the delegations listed in
Tables 48 and 49. For example, this convention would treat as if he had not
voted at all a New York City representative who might have spent so much time
in Manhattan and might have been so indifferent about inserting in the *Record*
an indication of how he would have voted that he was recorded as agreeing with
no member of his party on as many as 38 of the 74 votes on the low-cohesion set.
He would be treated as contributing nothing to his delegation's solidarity, even
though he might have indicated his preference on 35 of the votes and agreed with
7 other New Yorkers on all 35.

[7] The Spearman rank-correlation coefficients, comparing the rankings of the
delegations two sets at a time, were in no case higher than plus .5.

Table 49

RATIOS OF ACTUAL TO POSSIBLE AGREEMENT SCORES WITHIN SELECTED
STATE REPUBLICAN DELEGATIONS TO THE HOUSE OF REPRESENTATIVES, 81ST
CONGRESS

State	First Session Intermediate Cohesion, 74 Roll Calls, per cent	Second Session Low Cohesion, 74 Roll Calls, per cent	Second Session High Cohesion, 74 Roll Calls, per cent
California	15.4	25.0	12.1
Illinois	18.1	15.4	12.8
Iowa	21.4	46.4	1.8
Kansas	26.7	16.7	3.3
Massachusetts	28.6	33.9	12.5
Michigan	15.2	10.6	10.6
New York	7.9	18.9	10.3
Oregon	0.0	0.0	8.3
Pennsylvania	23.5	23.2	16.7
Wisconsin	14.3	23.2	3.6
10 states	16.1	21.0	11.6

proposition that the state delegation, in both parties, is a factor in the process of voting decision. (It is well, of course, that these ratios fall considerably short of 100 per cent since, if the latter situation existed, it would almost certainly reflect a condition of party disintegration or chaos in the House and in the country, with each state's representatives functioning as ambassadors to, rather than officials of, a national government.)

The composite ratios which summarize the data in Tables 48 and 49, indicate a pattern that may help to explain the place of the state delegation within the legislative party.[8] Taken together, the delegations in each party show a higher cohesion on those sets of votes that divided the party and a lower degree of unity on the roll calls on which the party was relatively unified. Among the individual delegations the pattern is not consistently in this direction, but examination of the tables shows that in half or more of the cases the cohesion of the delegations was highest on the party's low-cohesion sets. Moreover, if the low- and intermediate-cohesion sets are examined together, it is ap-

[8] These composite ratios are based on the sum of the actual agreement scores in the delegations divided by the sum of the theoretically possible scores. The means of the ratios in the tables are not appreciably different.

parent that all but two state delegations, the North Carolina Democrats and the Oregon Republicans, were most cohesive on one of the two sets of votes characterized by relatively low party cohesion. The strength and consistency of the general pattern appears with special clarity when the composite delegation ratios are arrayed against the median indexes of party cohesion for the several sets of roll calls, as in Table 50.

Table 50

REDUCED PARTY COHESION ACCENTUATES THE COHESION OF STATE DELE-
GATIONS: MEDIAN INDEXES OF PARTY COHESION AND COMPOSITE RATIOS OF
ACTUAL TO POSSIBLE INTRADELEGATION AGREEMENT SCORES ON SIX SETS
OF ROLL CALLS, HOUSE OF REPRESENTATIVES, 81ST CONGRESS

Party and Set	Median Index of Cohesion	Composite Ratios Democrats: 13 Delegations Republicans: 10 Delegations
Democrats, 81:2, low-cohesion set	34.6	23.1
Republicans, 81:2, low-cohesion set	45.05	21.0
Democrats, 81:1, intermediate set	47.45	18.0
Republicans, 81:1, intermediate set	57.05	16.1
Republicans, 81:2, high-cohesion set	87.95	11.6
Democrats, 81:2, high-cohesion set	89.3	11.5

The composite ratios are those shown at the bottom of Tables 48 and 49.

What this seems to reveal is that a property of lowered cohesion of the legislative party is not merely a bipolarization but a fractionation of the party, or a tendency in that direction, out of which the state delegations emerge as one of the elements of residual significance. Clearly they are not the only such elements, nor would one expect them to be. The considerable variations among the states in Tables 48 and 49 suggest the influence of factors other than delegation ties. Moreover, the relatively low ratios, even for comparatively cohesive groups such as the Missouri Democrats or the Massachusetts Republicans, testify to less than complete dominance by the state grouping. Nevertheless, the data in general support the proposition that the issues that most sharply divided the legislative parties in the House of Representatives did not set up comparable cleavages within the state delegations, with the result that the cohesiveness of the latter tended to rise as that of the party declined.

This pattern holds in both parties, which indicates that its explanation probably does not lie in the substance of the issues in the Demo-

cratic or Republican sets but rather in more general factors.[9] Before
turning to possible explanations of the pattern, however, it is necessary
to deal with the possibility that chance factors may largely account for
the regularities noted.

Since the data do not readily lend themselves to precise probability
calculations, the simplest appropriate assumption to make is that, if
the relationships within the state delegations were of no significance
and were due entirely to chance, the ratio of intradelegation agreements to the total scores in a sample (here the number of high scores
corresponding to one less than the number of legislators in a delegation) should be equal to the ratio of the delegation to the party as a
whole. Thus, in a legislative party of 100 and a state delegation of 10,
one would expect that on a purely chance basis one (actually .9) of
the top 9 scores of any member of the delegation would be an intrastate
score. Any number of intrastate scores in excess of this, in this example 2 or more, could be regarded as reflecting the influence of intradelegation relationships.

For each of the legislators in the selected delegations the top scores
in each of the sets of roll calls were analyzed in this fashion.[10] The
results for each party and for each of the delegations are summarized
in Tables 51 and 52 so as to show the total number of men considered,
the number having intradelegation scores in excess of expectation, and
the average number of such excess scores for those recorded as having
them. Conventions adopted in this analysis understate the frequency
of agreement within the delegations composed of only 3 or 4 men and,
on the low-cohesion set, within the Democratic delegations.[11] Never-

---

[9] In this connection it is important to bear in mind that the votes in the Democratic and Republican sets are not identical, since the issues that divided the one
party were not necessarily those that split the other. In the intermediate-cohesion
sets 50 roll calls appear among the 74 votes of both parties. In the low-cohesion
sets the overlap is 43 out of 74, and in the high-cohesion sets it is 29 out of 66
Republican and 62 Democratic votes. It is also true, of course, that, even if a
vote appears in the equivalent set in both parties, it may occur at the upper end
of the distribution in one and at the lower end in the other.

[10] In the 23 delegations there were 256 legislators in the first session and 254 in
the second. The number of "top scores," as elsewhere in the analysis, is equal to
the number in the delegation less one.

[11] In the first place, a single intradelegation score was never treated as significant, no matter how small the delegation; hence the low ratings in Tables 51
and 52 for the delegations from Colorado, Minnesota, and Oregon. In the second
place, in the low-cohesion Democratic votes, where the North-South cleavage
was particularly sharp, the denominator in the ratio of the state delegation to
the party as a whole was reduced. For the Southern delegations the ratio was
based on the 137 Democrats from the South and the Border rather than on the

theless the results indicate that, with minor exceptions, the rates of intradelegation agreement were higher than would be expected by chance on the low- and intermediate-cohesion sets. On the high-cohesion sets, on the other hand, these rates were in most cases little, if any, higher than they would have been on a chance basis. In only one delegation of the 23, the North Carolina Democrats, was the proportion of the delegation having a significant number of scores in excess of chance higher on the high-cohesion votes than on the sets where the party was relatively disunited. Moreover, in both the Democratic and the Republican delegations the highest proportion with more intrastate scores than would be expected by chance is on the low-cohesion set and *vice versa*.[12]

It thus seems clear that in both legislative parties in the House the issues that divided the party as a whole did not split the state delegations or at least did not split them as widely. Rather these votes tended to increase the relative cohesion of the delegations. In other words, agreement within the state delegations was not simply a reflection of high party cohesion. Nor, among the Democrats, was it merely a consequence of solid delegation adherence to one of two united wings of the party. Rather the intradelegation relationships seem to have had an independent connection with the voting choices of representatives on those issues that divided the party most sharply.

What was there about the diminished cohesion of the party or about the issues leading to such cleavage that should have produced this

---

whole Democratic membership of 258. (Speaker Rayburn was, of course, omitted from all calculations.) For the Northern delegations and the two from the Border, which were somewhat more closely associated with the non-Southern Democrats, it was based on the 158 Democrats from outside the 11 states of the South. By thus discounting the effect produced by a delegation's voting solidly with one of two cohesive wings of the party, the special influence of intradelegation relationships is shown more accurately, but the degree of intradelegation agreement on this set of votes is somewhat understated in relation to those of the intermediate set. For example, if the calculations for the 24-man New York delegation had been based on all 258 Democrats, the number of intradelegation scores that might have been attributed to chance would have been 2 rather than 4. Twenty-one members, rather than 19, would have had more intrastate scores than expected on a chance basis, and the mean of the excess scores would have been 4.85 rather than 2.89 (Table 51).

[12] Comparisons between the parties on the basis of the data in Tables 51 and 52 are unreliable, and the differences in any case are not great. But the fluidity of the Republican structure noted in chaps. 5 and 6 does not seem to have been closely associated with increased cohesion of these Republican delegations. Although, on the low- and intermediate-cohesion sets, the proportion of Republicans with scores in excess of chance is slightly higher than that of the Democrats in these delegations, the mean of the Republican excess scores is slightly lower.

Table 51

DISTRIBUTION OF INTRASTATE AGREEMENT SCORES IN EXCESS OF EXPECTED
INCIDENCE* WITHIN THIRTEEN SELECTED DEMOCRATIC STATE DELEGATIONS
TO THE HOUSE OF REPRESENTATIVES, 81ST CONGRESS

| | | First Session | | Second Session | | | |
| | | Intermediate Cohesion, 74 Roll Calls | | Low Cohesion 74 Roll Calls | | High Cohesion 62 Roll Calls | |
State	Number in Delegation†	Number with Excess Scores	Mean Excess Scores	Number with Excess Scores	Mean Excess Scores	Number with Excess Scores	Mean Excess Scores
Alabama	9	8	2.25	5	1.2	0	0.0
California	10–11	1	1.0	9	1.89	1	1.0
Colorado	3	0	0.0	0	0.0	0	0.0
Illinois	12–11	9	2.33	7	2.86	4	1.25
Massachusetts	6	0	0.0	0	0.0	0	0.0
Minnesota	4	1	1.0	0	0.0	0	0.0
Missouri	12	11	3.09	7	1.43	11	1.64
New York	23–24	10	2.0	19	2.89	12	1.92
No. Carolina	12–11	3	1.3	1	3.0	4	1.25
Ohio	12	2	1.0	5	1.8	1	2.0
Oklahoma	8	4	1.5	6	2.3	0	0.0
Pennsylvania	15	8	1.5	13	2.08	10	1.7
Texas	20–19	17	4.6	14	2.8	11	2.5
13 states	146–145	74	2.65	86	2.33	54	1.83
(Per cent)		(50.7)		(59.3)		(37.2)	

* *Excess scores:* Take the proportion of the number in a delegation to the number in the whole party; multiply this by one less than the number in the delegation. Any number of intradelegation "top scores" in addition to this is in excess of what would occur by chance. The number of a member's "top scores" is the number of men with whom he most frequently agreed equal to one less than the number in his delegation. In the low-cohesion set of the second session region was controlled by using the 17 Southern and Border states as equivalent to the party for the Southern delegations in the above analysis and by using the 37 states outside the South in the same fashion for the North and Border delegations.

† The size of the delegations from some states varied slightly in the two sessions. Where two numbers appear in this column they refer to the first and second sessions, respectively.

pattern? Reflection suggests that the issues that most sharply divide a party are of two broad types. First are those difficult, highly controversial questions, the representative's vote on which seems certain to produce important consequences both for the interests with which he identifies and for his own survival in public life. Although these are

Table 52

DISTRIBUTION OF INTRASTATE AGREEMENT SCORES IN EXCESS OF EXPECTED
INCIDENCE* WITHIN TEN SELECTED REPUBLICAN STATE DELEGATIONS TO THE
HOUSE OF REPRESENTATIVES, 81ST CONGRESS

| | | First Session | | Second Session | | | |
| | | Intermediate Cohesion, 74 Roll Calls | | Low Cohesion 74 Roll Calls | | High Cohesion 66 Roll Calls | |
State	Number in Dele- gation†	Number with Excess Scores	Mean Excess Scores	Number with Excess Scores	Mean Excess Scores	Number with Excess Scores	Mean Excess Scores
California	13–12	8	1.75	9	2.4	4	1.0
Illinois	14–13	11	1.91	7	2.0	6	1.5
Iowa	8	5	1.2	8	2.25	0	0.0
Kansas	6	3	1.0	1	1.0	0	0.0
Massachusetts	8	6	1.5	6	2.0	0	0.0
Michigan	12	5	1.6	4	1.5	4	1.0
New York	20	4	1.75	14	2.64	5	1.2
Oregon	4	0	0.0	0	0.0	0	0.0
Pennsylvania	17–18	12	2.58	12	3.08	11	1.5
Wisconsin	8	3	1.0	5	1.2	1	1.0
10 states	110–109	57	1.79	66	2.32	31	1.32
(Per cent)		(51.8)		(60.6)		(28.4)	

* *Excess scores:* Take the proportion of the number in a delegation to the number in the whole party; multiply this by one less than the number in the delegation. Any number of intradelegation "top scores" in addition to this is in excess of what would occur by chance. The number of a member's "top scores" is the number of men with whom he most frequently agreed equal to one less than the number in his delegation.

† The size of the delegations from some states varied slightly in the two sessions. Where two numbers appear in this column they refer to the first and second sessions, respectively.

freighted with significant effects, the certainty of the effects may be much clearer than their precise nature. The representative thus confronted with a situation both insistent and ambiguous is likely to look about him both for guidance and for reassurance. Consultation with the members of his own state delegation may serve those purposes, among other reasons because there is defensive value in legislators from the same area and party presenting a solid front on issues of high controversy.[13]

[13] Among the many informal but continuing partisan and bipartisan gatherings on Capitol Hill, many of which may be of far more consequence than their place in the literature would suggest, the ostensibly social but politically functional

On such difficult issues, moreover, the formal leadership may offer little guidance because it prudently avoids becoming identified with either faction on a hot and closely contested issue, because it cannot, in the intensity of the conflict, hope to carry more than a small majority of the party with it, or because the leaders themselves are not in agreement on the issues. Such questions are not necessarily, if this speculation is valid, "local" in their impact, in the sense that the effects of rivers and harbors legislation, a general tariff revision, or an inclusive agricultural bill are local. They may rather be "national" issues of either high or low intensity locally, as seems to be the case with many questions of foreign policy. Although the distinction here is probably more in degree than in kind, a difference does seem to exist between the locally concentrated access of national interests and the access of purely parochial interests, though legislative voting patterns on the two may be identical.

Second, the votes characterized by low party cohesion may be expected to include a number of issues of trifling importance, "free" votes on which the party leadership makes no position known because the outcome is a matter of complete indifference to them. The representative who rushes over from his office or committee room in answer to the bell announcing a roll call on such an issue may be completely ignorant of its substance and import. He may get a quick and decisive briefing from the first acquaintance he meets on his way through the lobby, from a friend on the committee handling the measure, or from

---

meetings of state and regional party delegations are common. An interesting example is discussed in Tom Connally, *My Name Is Tom Connally*, New York: Crowell, 1954, pp. 89–92. For a suggestive case of a somewhat different sort see Stephen K. Bailey and Howard D. Samuel, *Congress at Work*, New York: Henry Holt, 1952, pp. 125–6. See also Jerry Voorhis, *Confessions of a Congressman*, New York: Doubleday, 1947, pp. 66 ff. Both senators and representatives testify to the value of solidarity in state party delegations on controversial measures likely to cause difficulty in election campaigns, especially primary elections. This opinion is evidence in part of the unifying effect of an area's media of communication. Unless deep personal or political differences intervene, two senators from the same state and party may work out a common position on a set of votes about to be taken in the chamber. Much the same thing takes place, apparently, within the House delegations. On occasion such arrangements may bridge the wide gulf between the two wings of the Capitol and, of course, they may cross party lines as well. Informants within the Congress have told of a number of instances in which an entire state delegation from a given party, both senators and representatives, have agreed, in advance of the voting on a particular measure in either chamber, that, however they vote, they will vote as a unit. For further evidence on the relevance of the state delegation to House voting in this Congress see Duncan MacRae, Jr., *Dimensions of Congressional Voting*, Berkeley and Los Angeles: University of California Press, 1958, pp. 269–70, 275.

a familiar source within his state party delegation. On such votes, therefore, it is less accurate to say that the party is divided than to characterize it as not being united because the matter of party is irrelevant. But the influence of intrastate relationships may nevertheless be high.[14]

Correspondingly one would infer that the state delegation normally plays a diminished role on votes of high party cohesion because there is no need for it to be influential. The issues in this type of situation are no longer controversial, are noncontroversial—even if important in many instances—are trifling but unambiguous, or, if controversial, are by definition productive of cleavages between rather than within parties. Some of the last would include those cases in which a unified leadership commits its reserves of influence, for whatever reason, in order to assure maximum support of a "party" position.

It is one thing to allege that votes of low and high party cohesion have these characteristics but another thing to demonstrate the point. Without going into burdensome detail, however, and without attempting to eliminate the essentially subjective element in a classification of votes by these criteria, it seems clear, upon examination of these six sets of votes, that at least there are more issues of trifling importance among the low-cohesion votes of both parties than among the high-cohesion votes. For both parties roll calls such as those on authorizing daylight-saving time and changing the hours for the sale of liquor in the District of Columbia, on the omnibus rivers and harbors bill, on legislation for the benefit of limited groups of veterans, on efforts to rescind the curtailment of postal service, and on legislation authorizing library demonstrations in rural areas are much more characteristic of the low-cohesion sets than of either of the others. Minor issues, by any definition, are present in some measure on all the lists, but their distribution seems to accord with the expectation previously stated. "Important" issues of "national" consequence are also evident in all of the sets, but an assertion that they are more frequent on votes on which the party is unified can only be an inference from the more easily documented conclusion that minor matters are less common.

What of the other assumed characteristic of the low-cohesion votes, that they tend to be highly controversial? By definition these are controversial within the parties, especially when they involve issues of more than trifling import. Do they also tend to be controversial within the House? The simplest way to approach an answer to this question is by examining the margin by which a motion was carried or lost as

---

[14] For an illustration of the casual, last-minute influences on a legislator's voting, see Bailey and Samuel, *Congress at Work*, p. 132.

a percentage of the total number in the House who were voting. This is not a completely satisfactory indicator, since "the House" is a constantly changing quantity. Thus a vote on a trivial matter settled by a close margin appears as a controversial item even though as few as 218 members bother to vote on it. However, since failure to vote, as earlier comments have shown, is often an act of avoidance as much as a reflection of indifference, further refinement of the measure to take account of the number of nonvoters does not seem readily practicable or entirely necessary.

Table 53 shows the distribution of the votes in the several sets according to these plurality margins in the House.[15] In both parties the concentration of the low- and intermediate-cohesion votes toward the lower end of the distribution, where motions were carried or lost by relatively narrow margins, indicates that these issues tended to be controversial within the House as well as within the parties. The U-shaped distribution of the two high-cohesion sets, on the other hand, reflects the fact that these votes either tended to be noncontroversial or were straight party votes—controversial only between the parties—and therefore were marked by a high degree of discipline on both sides.

The conclusion thus seems warranted that the distinguishing features of the issues on which the state party delegations were most conspicuous and, presumably, most influential—the votes of relatively low cohesion—were of two sorts. Either they were tough questions, controversial both within the party and within the House, and politically ambiguous ones on which the representative felt genuinely uncertain and subject to mutually exclusive claims, or they were matters of trivial or purely local importance. On both types the familiar associations within the state delegations apparently provided guidance, reassurance, and the defensive advantages of solidarity or near solidarity among partisans exposed to the same or closely related publics.

What other factors can be identified that may help to explain the apparent connection between intradelegation relations and voting pat-

---

[15] The plurality margin in the House is a more satisfactory indicator of controversy within the House, despite the limitations mentioned, than is the incidence of "party votes," on which a majority of Democrats oppose a majority of Republicans. As the cluster of votes at the upper end of the distributions in the last two columns of Table 53 suggests, the high-cohesion votes of both parties contained a disproportionate number of nonparty votes, which testifies to the noncontroversial character of many of these roll calls. When one party or both are badly split, however, the incidence of party votes may be high, but it need not be, since controversy within the House does not necessarily follow party lines. For instance, in the Democratic low-cohesion set of the second session there were 31 votes of

Table 53

DISTRIBUTION OF ROLL CALLS BY LEVELS OF COHESION AND BY PLURALITY
MARGINS, HOUSE OF REPRESENTATIVES, 81ST CONGRESS

House Plurality (per cent)	First Session		Second Session			
	Intermediate Cohesion		Low Cohesion		High Cohesion	
	Republican	Democratic	Republican	Democratic	Republican	Democratic
0.1– 9.9	8	14	10	17	9	2
10.0–19.9	12	19	15	14	11	12
20.0–29.9	9	8	16	8	5	13
30.0–39.9	13	14	13	8	2	7
40.0–49.9	8	7	10	17	9	3
50.0–59.9	2	2	4	5	3	2
60.0–69.9	6	4	1	1	1	1
70.0–79.9	5	2	3	4	4	3
80.0–89.9	8	4	2	0	5	7
90.0–99.9	3	0	0	0	17	12
Total	74	74	74	74	66	62

terns in the House on issues that divided the legislative parties internally? In the first place, it seems possible that some of what appears in
the foregoing analysis as the influence of the state party delegations
may more accurately be attributed to more localized sources. That is,
although the term "state delegation" has been employed throughout,
the evidence of intradelegation variation in the first five tables of this
chapter suggests the possibility that what appears to be a "state" phenomenon is only an artifact of a classification that has ignored locality
factors. The latter, impinging from "outside" the House directly upon
a cluster of legislators or creating a reason for consultation in a frame-
work less inclusive than a whole state, may have constituted a more
substantial basis of cohesion than that of associations within the state
delegation as such. Since none of the delegations examined in this

the 74 on which the corresponding Republican cohesion indexes were relatively
high. When these roll calls involved a coalition between the Republicans and the
Northern wing of the Democrats, who constituted a majority of the Democratic
representatives, a nonparty vote typically resulted. However, when the votes reflected a coalition between the Republicans and the Southern wing of the Democrats, a minority of the party, the result was a party vote. Thus, though party
votes slightly outnumbered nonparty among all the low-cohesion votes of both
Republicans and Democrats, the difference—6 percentage points—was not great.

chapter reached or even approached the theoretically possible—but highly improbable—perfect unity, some clustering of agreements within them must have existed. Did such clustering characteristically reflect locality rather than state associations?

Examination of the scores within these 23 delegations reveals that only in a very few cases were the intradelegation clusterings to be accounted for primarily in locality terms. An outstanding example, however, was the Illinois Democratic delegation. Numbering 11 men in the second session, this group included 9 men from Cook County

Member and District	District Numbers											
	2	3	4	6	8	11	9	1	7	21	25	
O'Hara, 2nd		61	59	61	61	58					58	
Linehan, 3rd			63	62	63	63						
Buckley, 4th		63		60*	60*	61						
O'Brien, 6th	61	62	60		62	64						Cook County
Gordon, 8th	61	63	60	62								
Chesney, 11th		63	61	64								
Yates, 9th					56						58	
Dawson, 1st	(No scores of 38 or higher)											
Sabath, 7th	(No scores of 38 or higher)											
Mack, 21st	(None of first 10 scores from Illinois)											
Price, 25th	(None of first 10 scores from Illinois)											

Figure 13. Local organization control: agreements within the Illinois Democratic delegation, on 74 low-cohesion roll calls, House of Representatives, 81st Congress, 2nd session.

Counting only those intrastate scores included among the 10 highest scores for each man. This figure should be read horizontally. Each row indicates those of the man's 10 highest scores that are with others in the delegation.

* Only one of these scores counted in delegation total, as they were tied for 10th place on Buckley's list.

(Chicago and its close suburbs), one from a district composed of 7 "downstate" counties, including the city of Springfield, and one from a 2-county district adjacent to the preceding and including the city of East St. Louis. As is evident from Figure 13, 6 of these men made up a cohesive and all but solid bloc on the low-cohesion roll calls of the second session. Among them these 6 accounted for all but 3 of the scores on which the percentage recorded in Table 48 is based, and all of them were from Cook County.[16] Of the 3 Cook County members

---

[16] For a comment on a comparable clustering among 5 of these 6 men, see above, chap. 5, note 9.

not part of this bloc, Yates was a freshman representative from a district containing a number of high-income residential areas, and Dawson and Sabath were unrecorded on too many of these votes to have any scores of the minimum frequency.[17] What has been described as "Illinois" solidarity, therefore, was in fact primarily a closely knit portion of the Chicago delegation. Moreover, this was probably an instance of influence from "outside" more than from associations within the House, since this group is reputed to be one of the few delegations in the House over which the county leadership can and does exercise continuous and effective discipline.

A very slight degree of the same sort of localization was evident in the New York Democratic delegation, 20 of whose 24 members in the second session were from New York City districts. Although the pattern was much less clear than in Illinois, signs of some clustering along borough lines appeared, especially within the 9-man delegation from Brooklyn, a tendency that is not astonishing in view of the coalition character of the city's Democratic politics. While these signs could be seen, however, it was also clear that the pattern of agreements spread over not only the whole city but also all those parts of the state represented by Democrats. Some of the solidarity within the delegation was largely independent of locality.

In a few other Democratic delegations symptoms of intrastate localism appeared, but they were even less sharply defined. In the Alabama group, for example, there was some evidence that representatives from the northern end of the state tended to agree with one another more frequently than with their colleagues from the southern end, and *vice versa*. This, however, seems to have reflected little more than a tendency for pairs of legislators from adjoining districts to vote together with a high degree of frequency, a tendency apparent in many delegations in both parties.

Among the ten Republican delegations the only instance showing marked signs of intradelegation localism was Wisconsin (Figure 14). It was not a highly cohesive group, as a comparison of the scores in Figure 13 and Figure 14 will indicate, and the localism was apparently

---

[17] The case of Representative Price of the Illinois 25th district is an interesting illustration of the way in which influential associations may flow across state lines, perhaps aided by a common dependence on the press of a metropolitan area. Although none of Price's top scores was with other members of the Illinois delegation, on all three sets his 10 high scores included at least 2 of the 3 representatives from the city and county of St. Louis, Missouri, across the river: Representatives Karst, Karsten, and Sullivan. Price, it might be noted, attended high school and college in St. Louis and was once a correspondent for one of that city's leading newspapers.

Member and District	District Numbers								
	1	2	7	8	6	3	9	10	
Smith, 1st		51							East
Davis, 2nd	51		55						
Murray, 7th	44	48							
Byrnes, 8th		55							
Keefe, 6th	(No scores of 38 or higher)								
Withrow, 3rd							53	53	West
Hull, 9th						53		51	
O'Konski, 10th		43				53	51		

Figure 14. Geographic factions: agreements within the Wisconsin Republican delegation, on 74 low-cohesion roll calls, House of Representatives, 81st Congress, 2nd session. Counting only those intrastate scores included among the 7 highest scores for each man. This figure should be read horizontally. Each row indicates those of the man's 7 highest scores that were with others in the delegation.

of a sort different from that of the Illinois Democrats. A division between the western districts (3, 9, and 10) and those in the eastern half of the state (1, 2, 7, and 8) is apparent in Figure 14, but it was not absolute. This clustering, moreover, seems to have reflected not the sort of "outside" influence noted in connection with the Illinois Democrats but rather a fairly complex combination of ecological and strictly political or factional influences that may have fostered association within the House. The "western" districts included large portions of the cutover forest land of the state and most of the poorer farm land, and in general were less prosperous than the sections nearer Lake Michigan. Much of the area once given to strong support of the LaFollettes is included in the three "western" districts, and here were two of the three counties in the state carried by Stevenson in 1952. The cleavage between the two areas also corresponded roughly to the boundary between the western Protestant, Scandinavian districts and the Catholic, German sections in and around Milwaukee.

The case of the Wisconsin Republicans suggests that a factionalism related not at all or only very slightly to localism may in some instances have produced intrastate clustering reflected in the data on delegation cohesion. A single fairly clear example of this, especially noticeable on the intermediate-cohesion votes, was the Texas Democratic delegation. On these votes the Texans were spilt three ways, into a highly cohesive ten-man majority, a looser seven-man minority, and a three-man remainder that could not readily be classified. Though there were signs of a rough east-west cleavage between the two principal groupings, this followed no well-defined geographic or socio-economic boundary. It seems rather to have reflected a division between those Texans generally willing to accept the moderate leadership of Rayburn and the larger fraction of the delegation, which was often inclined to repudiate his initiative and to cast in with the more "typical" Southerners in the House.[18]

In a few instances it is clear that locality or persistent state factionalism restricted or even supplanted the influence of the state party delegation on voting choices in the House. Like the delegations that were unmarked by such internal clusterings, many of these probably represented patterns of association within the House rather than a common response to "outside" demands. It is impossible, however, to make this assertion categorically, not only because there are technical obstacles to separating such "internal" and "external" influences but also because the two are frequently complementary rather than alternative. An illustration is the California Democratic delegation, whose voting structure on the low-cohesion set was centered upon four men, two from San Francisco (Havenner and Shelley), one from Los Angeles (King), and one from San Diego (McKinnon). It showed no locality cleavage and no evidence of factionalism, so it is reasonable to infer that intradelegation associations were influential. Yet there is also a likelihood that the members of this nucleus (and others in the delegation) were especially accessible to the legislative claims of organized labor.[19] Supposing this to be the case, it might be argued that the statistical cohesiveness of the delegation on this set of votes was no more than a reflection of the accessibility of its individual members, as individuals, to the claims of the same national interest group. It is not necessary, that is, to conclude in this case that intradelegation relations were operative at all, but the general organizational functions of the state delegations in the legislative party and the political ad-

---

[18] In support of this point it should be noted that 6 members of the 7-man minority were on the list of McCormack's top scores on the high-cohesion votes, as were 2 of the 3 men described as not classified; all but 2 of the 10-man majority were not on this list. Five of this last grouping—Wilson, Pickett, Lucas, Burleson, and Fisher—composed the cohesive Texas nucleus noted in the discussion of Democratic voting structure on the intermediate-cohesion votes (see chap. 5, note 9). Finally, the constituencies of the "Rayburn" wing, curiously enough, contained a much higher proportion of Negroes than did the constituencies of the more "Southern" wing of the delegation. For additional detail on the Texas situation see David B. Truman, "The State Delegations and the Structure of Party Voting in the United States House of Representatives," *American Political Science Review*, Vol. 50, no. 4 (December 1956), pp. 1040–1041.

[19] Representative Shelley, for example, was president of the California Federation of Labor when he was sent to the House after a special election in 1949.

vantages of solidarity among legislators from neighboring constituencies would suggest that both influences—interest-group demands and intradelegation relationships—were operating simultaneously.[20]

The California Democratic delegation also illustrates another situation of the same sort. Those top scores for each member that were not intradelegation agreements typically were rather widely scattered, from New York to Washington. For example, the first 10 scores of Representative Helen Gahagan Douglas on the low-cohesion votes included—in addition to 4 of her fellow Californians, 3 more than would have been expected by chance—Representatives Price of Illinois, Karsten and Sullivan of Missouri, Jackson of Washington, O'Sullivan of Nebraska, and Feighan of Ohio. Much the same sort of pattern occurred in the Pennsylvania, Illinois, and other Northern delegations. Since intradelegation agreement apparently increased on the low-cohesion votes, on which the party was most sharply divided between North and South, may it not be possible that the apparent increase in delegation unity was in fact partly caused by a tendency for representatives from the larger urban areas to vote the same way on this kind of issue? This did not seem to be the case in California nor in the other delegations examined,[21] but the problem illustrates the complex of factors involved in these voting patterns.

[20] Informants have supplied occasional bits of direct evidence on the political and organizational functions of the delegations. For example, the 12-man Missouri delegation in the 81st Congress, 7 of whom were newcomers to the House in 1949, reportedly made a special effort at delegation solidarity as a way of supporting their fellow Missourian in the White House. (This incidentally may account for some of the peculiarities in the Missouri data in Tables 48 and 51.) Other delegations make a practice of attempting to work as a team, with a pre-arranged division of labor and frequent conferences. By always holding a place on the Appropriations Committee and on the Committee on Committees, among others, they can both look after the state interests of their members and impose sanctions on recalcitrants within the delegation.

[21] This conclusion is based on comparisons of the scores in the several sets. For example, while the proportion of "big city" scores within the California delegation was higher on the low-cohesion votes than on the high (by 12.9 percentage points), the proportion of intrastate scores was still higher (by 16.9 percentage points). On the low-cohesion votes the incidence of intrastate scores was higher than on the intermediate-cohesion set (by 13.8 percentage points), but the proportion of "big city" scores was smaller (by 3.5 percentage points). Since almost all Northern Democrats represent "urban" districts, devising a test appropriate to this problem involves difficulties. "Big city" districts were here defined as ones which (1) were in or contained a Standard Metropolitan Area and (2) were in or contained a city of 100,000 or more, or (3) contained a county of 100,000 or more. The percentages cited in the California example are not identical with those in Table 48, since all tie scores were included in these calculations, there being no defensible way of discriminating among out-of-state scores.

The evidence of this analysis of the delegations is consistent with the proposition that the face-to-face relationships within the state groupings were indeed an independent factor making for solidarity, but it is clear that they were not the only or consistently the most important influence. The indications of increased delegation unity on the low-cohesion votes apparently were not merely an artifact of the procedures employed in the analysis, but they do not warrant a single-factor explanation of voting within the House.

Given the apparent relevance of the face-to-face relationships within the state party delegations for the voting choices of their members on the issues that tended to split their parties most sharply, were there characteristics that particularly strongly disposed some representatives toward solidarity with their delegation colleagues? Since the incidence of intradelegation agreement was decidedly uneven, some such factors presumably were operating, but apparently they were not of the more obvious political sort, such as seniority and political marginality. In the delegations of both parties the men whose intradelegation scores exceeded the number that could be accounted for by chance were analyzed in terms of their length of service in the House. On general grounds and because of the curious relations between seniority and rate of agreement with the Floor Leaders, discussed in Chapter 6, this seemed a particularly appropriate variable to examine. The results indicated no reliable relationship. Less experienced representatives in both parties were neither more nor less likely to tie to others in the delegation than were those of more senior status. Analysis of these same men in terms of the size of their 1948 electoral majorities yielded equally inconclusive results. In neither party was there any stable connection between electoral marginality and the proportion of intradelegation scores.[22] Apparently the unevenness in the incidence of intradelegation scores reflected either less directly political similarities between constituencies or, as seems more likely, personal characteristics of the individuals involved.

The phenomenon of solidarity in the state party delegations has been examined in this chapter in an effort to account for some of the instabilities in the voting structures and to identify alternative sources of voting cues. Fluidity in the bloc structures was not entirely lacking in the Senate, however, especially among the Republicans, and it is

---

[22] For the Republican delegations and the 10 Northern and Border Democratic delegations the 1948 election results were analyzed in three categories: those who won by less than 55 per cent of the two-party vote; those with from 55 to 60 per cent; and those with over 60 per cent. In the Southern Democratic delegations similar categories were applied to the primary elections.

therefore worth noting that intrastate solidarity also had some place in the Senate party structures. The tendency is less easily analyzed in quantitative terms because of the smaller numbers in the Senate, but it is only necessary to examine the tables of bloc structure in Chapter 3 to discover a strong tendency for senators from the same state to turn up in the same bloc and to rank very close to one another in that bloc.[23] It seems unlikely that sources of voting cues within the upper chamber are as ambiguous as they apparently tend to be in the House. But there is no reason to suppose that senators are completely confident of the intelligence that emerges from their constituencies or that they can be entirely certain of the consequences of their voting choices. The six-year term, their personal visibility, and a generally greater heterogeneity in their constituencies undoubtedly afford a larger measure of impunity to senators' choices, but the political advantages of solidarity with their state colleagues in the party on controversial votes apparently are not eliminated.

For example, in both Senate parties on the low-cohesion votes of the first session, of the senators whose state colleagues were of the same party (42 Democrats and 30 Republicans), approximately half included those state colleagues in their top 5 scores. As in the House, and presumably for the same reasons, the incidence was lower in the high-cohesion sets.

In the Senate regional or sectional groupings in some respects seem to have functioned as the state delegations did in the House, as the discussion in Chapter 3 has already indicated. Except possibly for the Southern Democrats, however, it is doubtful that such association was as closely articulated with the organization and operation of the party as was the state delegation in the House. There is in the Senate no formal equivalent of the meetings of state party delegations in the House because one is not needed. Regional voting patterns in the Senate, in other words, probably reflect similarity of constituency demand more often than the mediating influence of a continuing association within the chamber.

THE STANDING COMMITTEE DELEGATIONS

The standing legislative committees of the House, traditionally the whipping-boy of Congress's critics, logically must also be considered as sources of voting cues for representatives. A member of the House

---

[23] See Tables 3, 4, 6, 7, 10, 11, 13, and 14 in chap. 3.

who desires to accomplish anything through legislation normally must concentrate upon working through the committees. Since the traditions of the House and the attitudes of the party leaders discourage intervention by a rank-and-file representative in the affairs of a committee of which he is not a member, this means that he is almost obliged to confine his energies to matters within the jurisdiction of the particular committee to which he has been assigned. He may, of course, in order to improve his political standing, aspire to membership on a different committee, thereby augmenting somewhat the sanctions in the hands of leaders in a position to satisfy or thwart such ambitions, but the frequency of such reassignment is apparently not very great. The pressure on the representative is thus toward becoming a specialist in legislative matters, and, even if he is not unusually conscientious, the ordinary member is likely to spend a considerable proportion of his time meeting with his committee colleagues and otherwise carrying on the concerns of the "little legislature" to which he belongs.

Given the ambiguities of the House, the apparent imperfections of communication within it, and the place of the standing committees in that setting, one might reasonably expect that associations within the committees would resemble those in the state delegations and that as a result there would be a tendency toward similarity of voting among the members of each party on a committee. To be of major significance as a source of voting cues, however, such similarity would have to extend beyond those roll calls dealing with measures handled by the respective committees and would have to include the full range of votes in the House, as in the case of the state delegations. That is, if the voting patterns represented something more than conscious agreement within the committee on its affairs and developed into a somewhat unconscious, generalized use of the party group on the committee as a source of voting cues, this should appear in a wide assortment of issues and not merely in those of special concern to the committee.

To test these expectations and to permit fruitful comparison, the standing committees were analyzed by the same procedures used in connection with the state delegations. For the Democrats all 19 standing committees (excluding the House membership on the Joint Committee on Atomic Energy) were examined. In the interests of simplicity only the 9 major committees whose reports were responsible for the bulk of the record votes in the House were analyzed in the case of the Republicans. In the following pages, therefore, comment will be focused primarily upon these 9 in both parties.

Tables 54 and 55, which should be compared with Tables 48 and 49,

Table 54

RATIOS OF ACTUAL TO POSSIBLE AGREEMENT SCORES AMONG DEMOCRATIC
MEMBERS OF SELECTED STANDING COMMITTEES OF THE HOUSE, 81ST
CONGRESS

Committee	First Session Intermediate Cohesion, 74 Roll Calls, per cent	Second Session	
		Low Cohesion, 74 Roll Calls, per cent	High Cohesion, 62 Roll Calls, per cent
Agriculture	7.7	11.0	7.7
Appropriations	12.3	12.0	6.6
Banking and Currency	8.8	11.7	17.1
Education and Labor	7.9	1.9	1.0
Foreign Affairs	1.6	3.3	1.6
Interstate and Foreign Commerce	6.3	10.0	13.3
Judiciary	7.0	8.5	5.1
Rules	7.1	1.8	1.8
Ways and Means	10.5	9.0	13.8
9 committees	8.7	9.2	7.9

Table 55

RATIOS OF ACTUAL TO POSSIBLE AGREEMENT SCORES AMONG REPUBLICAN
MEMBERS OF SELECTED STANDING COMMITTEES OF THE HOUSE, 81ST
CONGRESS

Committee	First Session Intermediate Cohesion, 74 Roll Calls, per cent	Second Session	
		Low Cohesion, 74 Roll Calls, per cent	High Cohesion, 66 Roll Calls, per cent
Agriculture	8.9	5.6	7.8
Appropriations	9.2	13.1	16.7
Banking and Currency	8.2	0.0	14.5
Education and Labor	2.8	1.4	0.0
Foreign Affairs	5.5	7.3	0.9
Interstate and Foreign Commerce	9.1	6.4	2.7
Judiciary	12.2	12.2	7.8
Rules	0.0	0.0	0.0
Ways and Means	10.0	4.4	3.3
9 committees	8.4	7.7	8.9

show the degree to which, respectively, the Democratic and Republican contingents on the committees approached a theoretically perfect cohesion on the votes of the three sets. There are several important implications in these tables. In the first place, it is obvious that the cohesion of these committee groupings was generally a good deal lower than that of the state party delegations. Second, no clear pattern emerges in the composite ratios at the bottom of the two tables, such as there was in the case of the state delegations. The Democratic ratios (Table 54) resemble those in Table 48, in that they show a slight tendency toward an inverse relation between the cohesion of the party and that of these committees, but the differences are small. The pattern is reversed among the Republicans (Table 55), and, if the table covered all 19 committees, the Democratic pattern would approximate the Republican. There thus seems to have been no reliable tendency for the committee contingents to become unified when the party was split. Third, despite the absence of a general pattern, there were instances, as among both parties' members of the Judiciary Committee, in which the cohesion of the committee contingent varied as did that in most of the state delegations. The differences were generally fairly small, however, and, as will shortly be evident, confidence in them is not increased by other features of the data.

When, again following the procedure applied in the analysis of the state delegations, account is taken of the chance element in the rates of agreement within the committee groupings (Tables 56 and 57), the generally lower importance of these groups as sources of cues in comparison with the state delegations (Tables 51 and 52) is evident. It is also apparent that no pattern among the committee groupings reliably parallels that among the state delegations. To be sure, the mean excess scores among the nine Republican committees (Table 57) were lowest on the high-cohesion roll calls, but this is not significant. The differences were not great, the number of Republicans showing such excess scores was small, and the Democratic committee members, among whom there were many more with such excess scores, showed no tendency of this sort. Moreover, in both parties the proportion of committee members with excess scores was at its peak on the high-cohesion sets, just the reverse of the pattern among the state delegations.[24]

The tendency thus was for the rate of agreement within the committee contingents to increase as the cohesion of the parties increased,

---

[24] Among the Democrats an equal proportion had such scores on the low- and high-cohesion sets, but among all 19 of the Democratic committees the proportion was clearly higher on the votes with the greatest party cohesion.

Table 56

DISTRIBUTION OF AGREEMENT SCORES IN EXCESS OF EXPECTED INCIDENCE*
AMONG DEMOCRATIC MEMBERS OF SELECTED STANDING COMMITTEES OF THE
HOUSE, 81ST CONGRESS

| | | First Session | | Second Session | | | |
| | | Intermediate Cohesion, 74 Roll Calls | | Low Cohesion, 74 Roll Calls | | High Cohesion, 62 Roll Calls | |
Committee	Number on Committee†	Number with Excess Scores	Mean Excess Scores	Number with Excess Scores	Mean Excess Scores	Number with Excess Scores	Mean Excess Scores
Agriculture	17	6	1.17	11	1.55	7	1.29
Appropriations	27	8	2.13	10	1.50	3	1.33
Banking and Currency	16	6	1.33	8	1.75	14	1.79
Education and Labor	16–15	6	1.17	0	0.0	0	0.0
Foreign Affairs	14	1	1.0	0	0.0	0	0.0
Interstate and Foreign Commerce	17–16	2	2.0	7	1.42	11	1.55
Judiciary	17	5	1.2	6	1.67	4	1.0
Rules	8	1	1.0	0	0.0	0	0.0
Ways and Means	15	7	1.29	7	1.0	10	1.5
9 committees	147–145	42	1.43	49	1.29	49	1.51
(Per cent)		(28.6)		(33.8)		(33.8)	

* *Excess scores:* Take the proportion of the number in a party committee contingent to the number in the whole party; multiply this by one less than the number in the committee contingent. Any number of intra-contingent "top scores" in addition to this is in excess of what could be expected by chance. The number of a representative's "top scores" is the number with whom he most frequently agreed equal to one less than the number in the committee contingent.

† The party contingents on some committees varied slightly in size from one session to another. When two numbers appear in this column they refer to the first and second sessions, respectively.

which means that the importance of these groupings as sources of cues was at most not conspicuous. Even more than among the state delegations, however, variations existed among the several committee contingents in this respect. Note, for example, the contrast in both parties between the members of Appropriations and those belonging to Foreign Affairs. The explanation for this kind of contrast is not entirely clear. Length of service on the committee apparently was not a factor. This being the case, one suspects that a complex of causes was responsible, including the relative skill with which the committees' affairs were conducted.

Neither the number of votes dealing with measures reported by the several committees nor the rate of agreement within these contingents on such votes seems to explain the variations in Tables 56 and 57. The frequency of agreement within the committees on votes concerning their own measures in most cases fluctuated directly with the cohesion of the parties, as Tables 58 and 59 demonstrate. Moreover, neither the

Table 57

DISTRIBUTION OF AGREEMENT SCORES IN EXCESS OF EXPECTED INCIDENCE*
AMONG REPUBLICAN MEMBERS OF SELECTED STANDING COMMITTEES OF THE
HOUSE, 81ST CONGRESS

| | | First Session | | Second Session | | | |
| | | Intermediate Cohesion, 74 Roll Calls | | Low Cohesion, 74 Roll Calls | | High Cohesion, 66 Roll Calls | |
Committee	Number on Committee	Number with Excess Scores	Mean Excess Scores	Number with Excess Scores	Mean Excess Scores	Number with Excess Scores	Mean Excess Scores
Agriculture	10	1	2.0	1	2.0	2	1.0
Appropriations	18	5	1.2	9	1.7	14	1.4
Banking and Currency	11	1	1.0	0	0.0	5	1.2
Education and Labor	9	0	0.0	0	0.0	0	0.0
Foreign Affairs	11	1	1.0	2	1.0	0	0.0
Interstate and Foreign Commerce	11	2	1.5	1	1.0	0	0.0
Judiciary	10	2	1.0	4	1.25	1	2.0
Rules	4	0	0.0	0	0.0	0	0.0
Ways and Means	10	1	2.0	0	0.0	1	1.0
9 committees	94	13	1.42	17	1.39	23	1.35
(Per cent)		(13.8)		(18.1)		(24.4)	

* *Excess scores:* Take the proportion of the number in a party committee contingent to the number in the whole party; multiply this by one less than the number in the committee contingent. Any number of intra-contingent "top scores" in addition to this is in excess of what could be expected by chance. The number of a representative's "top scores" is the number with whom he most frequently agreed equal to one less than the number in the committee contingent.

number of such votes nor the degree of solidarity on these votes among the committee contingents seems to have borne any consistent relation to the agreement rates of the committee members on the whole range of roll calls. Take the Republican Rules contingent, for example. In the three sets there were 18 votes dealing with matters from this committee, and these 4 men were in complete agreement on two-thirds of them (Table 59). Yet none of the 4 appeared among the top scores of any of the others. Or note the Democratic group on Foreign Affairs. These men agreed on 18 of the 20 votes dealing with their committee's measures in the three Democratic sets. Nevertheless, their general cohesion was low (Table 54) and they had almost no scores above the number that might have been expected by chance (Table 56). Both parties' contingents on the Appropriations Committee showed a reverse tendency. Each was agreed on less than one-third of the votes bearing on the committee's measures (among the Democrats, considerably less than one-third), as Tables 58 and 59 indicate, yet the general rates of agreement among them tended to be fairly high (Tables 54–57).

Table 58

AGREEMENTS AMONG DEMOCRATIC MEMBERS OF SELECTED STANDING COMMITTEES OF THE HOUSE ON VOTES DEALING WITH MEASURES REPORTED BY THEIR COMMITTEES, 81ST CONGRESS

| | First Session | | Second Session | | | |
| | Intermediate-Cohesion Set | | Low-Cohesion Set | | High-Cohesion Set | |
Committee	Votes	Agreements	Votes	Agreements	Votes	Agreements
Agriculture	4	1	2	1	4	3
Appropriations	11	1	5	0	4	3
Banking and Currency	11	7	6	2	8	7
Education and Labor	4	0	7	0	0	- - -
Foreign Affairs	9	7	5	5	6	6
Interstate and Foreign Commerce	3	0	7	0	3	1
Judiciary	3	1	6	2	8	7
Rules	5	2	3	0	5	2
Ways and Means	0	- - -	2	0	5	5
9 committees	50	19	43	10	43	34
(Per cent)		(38.0)		(23.3)		(79.1)

Agreements include those roll calls on which all members of the committee contingent were unanimous plus all those on which less than half the contingent were unrecorded and the remainder were unanimous.

The conclusion thus seems inescapable that, as compared with the state party delegations, the party contingents on the standing committees of the House did not exercise a primary influence upon the general voting choices of their members. These associations apparently did not provide the setting or the motivations by which they could be used significantly to structure their members' voting decisions and to reduce the ambiguities attendant upon the representative's position.

Although this was the general tendency, there were isolated exceptions, such as the Democrats on the Committee on Agriculture (Table 56). Comparatively few of these cases appeared, however, especially among the Republicans, and with the available data it is impossible to determine why the exceptions occurred, to what extent they reflect a set of entirely fortuitous factors, and, therefore, in what measure they might warrant a modification of the general conclusion.

This comparison with the state party delegations does not mean,

Table 59

AGREEMENTS AMONG REPUBLICAN MEMBERS OF SELECTED STANDING COMMITTEES OF THE HOUSE ON VOTES DEALING WITH MEASURES REPORTED BY THEIR COMMITTEES, 81ST CONGRESS

| | First Session | | Second Session | | | |
| | Intermediate-Cohesion Set | | Low-Cohesion Set | | High-Cohesion Set | |
Committee	Votes	Agreements	Votes	Agreements	Votes	Agreements
Agriculture	4	1	6	0	0	- - -
Appropriations	7	0	4	0	6	5
Banking and Currency	9	0	8	0	8	2
Education and Labor	4	3	5	0	2	0
Foreign Affairs	7	3	9	0	2	0
Interstate and Foreign Commerce	4	0	7	0	3	0
Judiciary	2	1	2	0	11	3
Rules	10	8	6	2	2	2
Ways and Means	3	1	3	1	6	2
9 committees	50	17	50	3	40	14
(Per cent)		(34.0)		(6.0)		(35.0)

Agreements include those roll calls on which all members of the committee contingent were unanimous plus all those on which less than half the contingent were unrecorded and the remainder were unanimous.

certainly, that the associations within the committee contingents were entirely without impact on individual voting decisions. Both the general run of the data and the occasional exceptions among the committees indicate that these groupings have some importance, not only on their own measures but also on other House votes, even though they may not be dominant or major. The behavior of individual pairs of legislators, moreover, in a number of instances carries the same implication. For example, a case that illustrates this point and also suggests the random sources of voting cues among the ambiguities in the House setting is that of two Republicans, Representative Golden of the ninth district in southeastern Kentucky and Representative Gross of the third district in north-central Iowa. These men, whose constituencies bore no striking resemblance, were first-term members of the Congress in 1949–1950. On the 74 low-cohesion roll calls of the second session they agreed 55 times. This was Golden's highest score in the set and Gross's second highest. These two men were the only Republican freshmen on the Committee on Post Office and Civil Service. On this set of votes, which contained 9 roll calls on measures emerging from this committee, no other member of the committee appeared among the top scores of either man. They occupied neighboring suites in the House Office Building. Unless one is prepared to give extraordinary weight to coincidence, the presumption is strong that one or both of these men found in their association on the committee, possibly in their common position as neophytes, a source of guidance that is reflected in these scores.

It may be, of course, that one reason for the minor importance of the *party* contingents on the standing committees is that the effects of associations within these bodies were bipartisan. That is, as Woodrow Wilson and others have argued, it may be that membership on the committees, composed as they are of both majority and minority elements, dissolves the lines of party and sets up patterns of association and influence that negate the party structure.[25]

Inferences from the data of this study would not support an extreme version of this interpretation. That is, it seems most improbable that the differences between the parties, evident, for example, in the Administration support indexes, could have been regularly and generally dissolved by committee membership. Some individual cases, however, illustrate what appear to be bipartisan influences. An example is Representative (later Senator) Case of New Jersey. In the high-cohesion set Case was the only Republican member of the Judiciary Committee to dissent from the majority of the House Republicans on four party votes dealing with the creation of additional judicial positions (none of them in New Jersey), the bills on which had been reported by this committee. The reasons for Case's voting with the Democrats on these measures may have been many, but it seems entirely possible that, for a man who carried the demands of party somewhat lightly anyhow (Table 34), bipartisan associations on the committee may have been influential.

Whether or not the bipartisan composition of the committees was responsible, it is evident that the committee contingents were a good deal less significant in Republican voting than in Democratic. With the exception of the two high-cohesion sets, the Republican groupings were generally less unified than the Democratic (Tables 54 and 55); a smaller proportion of their members had more intracommittee scores than would have been expected by chance (Tables 56 and 57); and,

---

[25] Compare Woodrow Wilson, *Congressional Government*, New York, Meridian Edition, 1956, pp. 78–79.

with isolated exceptions, they were agreed on a smaller proportion of the votes dealing with measures reported by their committees (Tables 58 and 59). These differences suggest that in general the committee contingents in the House, unlike the state party delegations, affect the voting behavior of their members more strongly if they are of the majority party. The point is illustrated by accounts of the steps followed in the first session of the Eighty-fourth Congress in connection with a revision of individual income taxes proposed by the Democrats. The notion apparently had its origin in discussions between one of the ranking Democrats on the Committee on Ways and Means and Speaker Rayburn. It was elaborated and refined by the staff of the committee, but, before it was presented to the Republican members or formally introduced in the House, its sponsors went over it with the Democrats on the committee and reached agreement with them on its substantive provisions. Apparently, within the committees as within the House itself, the minority was characterized by fluidity and the lack of a stable consensus. This is particularly evident in the data of Tables 58 and 59, which were unaffected by differences in the "absence" rates within the two parties.

Fluidity and lack of cohesion within the minority's committee contingent does not necessarily imply that the stronger influence of the majority groupings and the higher rate of agreement within them on votes dealing with committee matters reflected adherence to a program sponsored by the legislative party as a whole and concurred in by the majority contingents on the committees. Obviously unity within a committee can disintegrate a leadership program or it may signify, as in Wilson's classic argument, the substitution of committee leadership for party leadership. Nevertheless, the indications that within the majority contingents on the committees there were tendencies toward agreement, not consistently controlling but stronger than in the minority, suggest again the possibility that the majority party had a basis for coherence that the minority lacked. This possibility, since it has emerged repeatedly in these pages and since, if substantial, it has real significance for understanding the Congressional parties, will be examined directly in the following chapter.

chapter eight

FUNCTIONAL INTERDEPENDENCE:

The Elective Leaders,

the White House,

and the Congressional Party

To discern stable patterns of behavior among the complexities of the Congressional parties is a matter of the utmost difficulty. Members of the Congress are not automatons but reasoning men and women acting in a setting in which they are subject to a bewildering barrage of conflicting, or at the least inconsistent, demands—from within their constituencies, from organized and unorganized interests both narrower and more extensive than their electoral districts, from within the government, from within the Congress itself, and from their own conceptions of what is required for the strength and survival of the polity of which they are among the most important trustees. The actions of these men and women are not to be accounted for by any simple ascription of motive or intent, and this injunction applies with special force when these actions are manifest primarily in the form of a series of record votes. And yet, because the members of the Congress

279

are reasoning beings and because the array of claims upon any one of them is not unique, one must expect to find, even through the roll calls, regularities in their behavior, however complex and qualified. To assume the contrary is either to deny this rationality or to assert that so little correspondence exists among the demands to which the various legislators are subject that the parties, if not the chambers and the Congress itself, are almost meaningless except as convenient labels for a chaotic jungle of hopelessly unpredictable individual actions.

Few observers would accept as anything but caricature the proposition that the Congress or even the legislative parties are so lacking in pattern as to be meaningless. For the skeptical the data in the foregoing pages should demonstrate at least that in the Eighty-first Congress many identifiable and persistent modes of behavior were common to clusters of senators and representatives. The question is not whether these exist but whether among them there is any central tendency, any system that will permit a coherent explanation of the congressional parties, of the roles of their leaders, and of their place in the inclusive scheme of national government.

EMERGENT PATTERNS AND THEIR IMPLICATIONS

Running through the preceding five chapters are three threads of evidence that suggest consistencies leading in turn toward an integrated conception of the congressional party.[1] In the first place, differences existed between the majority and minority parties with respect to fluidity of voting structure. Second, in both parties, though again with differences between them, the relations between the principal elective leaders and the seniority leaders showed a tendency toward specialization. Third, the data revealed, despite differences within the parties, a clear tendency toward partisanship in both House and Senate that distinguished most members of the majority parties from most of those in the minority.

---

[1] "Threads" may be too confident a term, since they are more accurately categories of fragmentary evidence. The items in these categories have no clear meaning in isolation from one another, and even in combination they do not speak with perfect clarity, since they have appeared in terms of more or less, of perceptible but not striking differences, and only rarely in those of unmistakable contrast. In so complex a set of institutions as the Congress and its component elements this was to be expected, and yet the fragments that have appeared have shown sufficient similarity and they have recurred frequently enough so that they suggest consistent threads of tendency in a discernible, if not tightly woven, fabric.

The first of these inferences, differential fluidity in the parties' voting structures, must be asserted with caution, for the data on which it is based are fragmentary, not perfectly consistent, and not entirely free of the effects of troublesome factors such as differences in absence rates. Yet in both House and Senate the minority party recurrently appeared to be more fluid, almost regardless of its relative cohesion and regardless of the frequency with which its members' preferences were recorded. The minority's voting structure, more than the majority's, tended to shift, not quite from issue to issue, but from one cluster of votes to another. In both chambers there were generally more Republican blocs than Democratic; these were wings and splinters of the principal aggregations, which could only reflect more varied lines of cleavage within the party. Only on the high-cohesion votes of the second session in the House, where the unity of the Republicans reached a peak, was this not evident. On the other two House sets the Republican structure showed not only a multiplicity of blocs, as on the Senate side, but also a lack of close correspondence between the bloc structures on the two sets that was not evident among the majority. In addition, the blocs were proportionately smaller, and a lower percentage of the Republicans belonged to blocs—allowing for differences in "absence" rates—presumably because more of them shifted their allegiances with changes in the substance of the issues.

In both Senate and House, though more strikingly in the upper chamber, the data showed less correspondence between the votes of the Floor Leaders and of the Whips on the minority side. Possibly this was an indication of a difference in party practice; to some extent, certainly in the Senate, it was a reflection of personal differences in attitude; but presumably this kind of disagreement was also less awkward, less embarrassing for the leadership of the minority. And the same inference seems to follow from the disagreements between the House Minority Leader and the ranking Republican on the Rules Committee. The minority elective leaders in both chambers, despite the higher Republican party cohesion in the House, were collectively less united than were their majority equivalents. On the minority side the evidence indicated much less accommodation between the Floor Leaders and the individual seniority leaders than existed among the majority, and this was the case also in the relations between the ranking committee members and men who might be regarded as alternative leaders on the minority side, such as Senator Taft and Representative Halleck.

In the House, fluidity in the minority structure was also suggested by the lack of correspondence between the list of men who scored high with the Minority Leader on the low-cohesion votes and his "following" on the intermediate-cohesion votes, by the smaller proportion of the minority party who appeared on these lists, and by the curious composition of those lists on the low- and intermediate-cohesion votes.

These indications of fluidity in the voting structure of the minority are important because they signify a relative lack of program, a comparatively unstable policy posture. This may be characteristic of the minority Congressional party. It is consistent with other fragments of the data, such as the indications that the committee contingents in the House were more influential among the majority than among the minority.

The second "thread" of evidence indicates that, although the seniority leaders of neither party operated as a collegial body, as individuals they and the Floor Leaders tended to agree on votes concerning measures reported by the seniority leaders' committees. That is, their relations as leaders apparently were specialized along particular substantive lines rather than generalized over the whole range of matters voted upon in the chambers.[2] Especially on the majority side, these data pointed to a disposition toward a selective accommodation between the Floor Leader and the ranking member of a standing committee, not on all affairs of the chamber, but at those points of peculiar consequence to the performance of the legislative party: the legislation assigned to the seniority leader's committee.

Since the relations between Floor Leaders and seniority leaders were close to the heart of any approximation of a legislative party program, they inevitably reflected the more coherent voting structure of the majority and the looser corresponding pattern among the minority. In both Senate and House the Minority Leaders displayed much less disposition than the Majority Leaders toward accommodation of seniority leaders from opposing wings of the voting structure on roll calls growing out of the projects of their committees. The rates of disagreement between the minority's Floor Leaders and seniority leaders on these votes were consistently higher than those on the majority side. Though these contrasts of course in part reflected personal characteristics of the Minority Leaders, especially in the case of the Senate

---

[2] See, on the Senate, Tables 23 and 24 and, on the House, Tables 45 and 46. This specialization may help to explain the ambiguity surrounding the term "the leadership." A former representative says: "The 'Leadership' is a term constantly used in conversations among House members. It can mean the Speaker alone or the Speaker and the majority leader or these two gentlemen plus their unofficial advisers among the older members." (Jerry Voorhis, *Confessions of a Congressman*, New York: Doubleday, 1947, p. 254.)

Minority Leader, they were so nearly duplicated by likely alternative leaders such as Senator Taft and Representative Halleck that obviously more was involved than these individual peculiarities.[3] The Minority Leader's role in this setting either did not require or did not permit the degree of accommodation evident on the majority side.

Despite divisions within the legislative parties and differences in the leaders' behavior, the third "thread" evident throughout these chapters points to a clear divergence in the central tendencies of the parties on matters of substantive policy. Above divisions and coalitions a cleavage persisted between the parties that distinguished the policy preferences of most Republicans from those of most Democrats. This interparty difference was revealed primarily in behavior on the roll calls that were classified as Administration support votes and in the indexes that were based on them. The latter clearly indicated that with few exceptions the blocs in the Democratic structures in the House and Senate were composed of men who supported the Administration position on these votes more frequently than did the members of the corresponding Republican blocs. Even the Republican blocs whose mean Administration support indexes deviated from this norm agreed with the Administration view less often than did most of the Democratic groupings, and the deviant Democratic blocs were less hostile to the Administration than all but the extreme "left" Republican formations.[4]

These differences between the parties are illustrated in somewhat different fashion for the Senate in Figure 15 and for the House in Figure 16. The figures show the distribution of Republican and Democratic senators and representatives, regardless of their bloc memberships, according to their mean Administration support indexes in the second session. (The curves for the first session, not shown here, are essentially identical to those of the second.) The overlapping areas at the center of each of the figures testify to the prevalence of bipartisan or coalition voting in both houses, but each of the distributions indicates clearly that the centers of gravity of the two parties were not only distinguishable but consistently different.[5] In the Senate the most anti-

---

[3] See Tables 25 through 27 and 47.

[4] For the Senate see Figures 3 and 7 and Table 9 in chap. 3; for the House, Figure 12 in chap. 5.

[5] Indications of the same kind of differences in the House in this Congress are reported in Duncan MacRae, Jr., *Dimensions of Congressional Voting*, Berkeley & Los Angeles: University of California Press, 1958, pp. 295–296, 310, and *passim*. For comparable data on the first two sessions of Congress under the Eisenhower Administration, see V. O. Key, Jr., *Politics, Parties, and Pressure Groups*, 4th edition, New York: Crowell, 1958, pp. 729 ff.

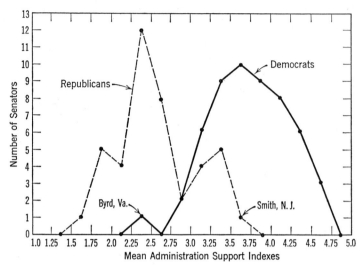

Figure 15. Interparty differences: distribution of Republican and Democratic senators according to mean Administration support indexes, 81st Congress, second session.

Administration Democrat (Byrd of Virginia) had a mean Administration support index approximately equal to the most characteristic index value among the Republicans. Correspondingly, the Republican Senator who in the 1950 session most strongly supported the Administration

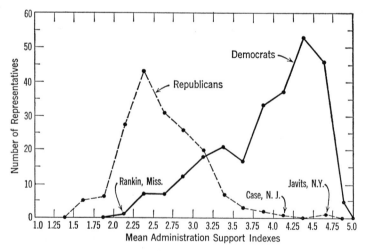

Figure 16. Interparty differences: distribution of Republican and Democratic representatives according to mean Administration of support indexes, 81st Congress, second session.

position (Smith of New Jersey) had a mean index equivalent to the one most commonly registered among the Democrats.

These indications of partisanship, though based entirely upon votes involving an express or clearly implied Administration preference, are consistent with less precise evidence supplied by informants. Leaders and informed staff people in both House and Senate volunteered the impression that most members of the Congress dislike recording themselves in opposition to the leadership and to the majority of the party. Psychologically the pressure toward party regularity apparently is felt even though frequently it may be effectively resisted.

One major implication of these three "threads" of evidence is that the persistent voting structure of both legislative parties was focused upon one or a pair of positions: the Floor Leaders, joined at times, particularly on the Democratic side, by the Whips and, among the House Democrats, impliedly by the Speaker. Other men in both houses may, for limited periods and for restricted purposes, have exercised initiative in matters of policy and almost certainly were dominant from time to time, but no other identifiable role was as continuously pivotal. Challenges, as expected, seem to have come most typically from the seniority leaders, but, as the data on the disagreements between the latter and the Floor Leaders testify, when the Leader and the ranking committee member were opposed, a majority of the party and a majority of the party's contingent on the affected committee more often than not went along with the Floor Leader.[6] Formal and informal leadership were not always identical, but if the Congressional party had a focus at all, it was upon the Floor Leader.

But there were differences between the majority and minority parties in the degree to which these roles were central and pivotal. Although, like the Majority Leaders, they voted like middlemen in the party, the Floor Leaders on the minority side were more frequently opposed to the seniority leaders and they were somewhat less likely to carry with them a majority of their associates in the party or on the affected committee. Their initiatives on the floor were, on the whole, less effective within their parties than were those of the Majority Leaders, and in general they seem to have been less consistently a source of voting cues for their party associates, both of the rank and file and among the other elective leaders. The Minority Leaders' roles, in short, showed fewer consistent program characteristics.

The chief implication of these data, however, lies in an answer to the question, why, given the pivotal character of the Leaders' roles on

---

[6] For the Senate see Tables 25 and 26; for the House, Table 47.

both sides of the aisle, should these differences between the parties have appeared so consistently? What was there about the majority party that made its structure more coherent and its leaders more central in the party's performance? No single answer is perfectly satisfactory, and none can be offered without qualification or without concern for the fortuitous effects of setting, skill, and personality. Nevertheless, one cannot escape the inference that without the initiatives and the known program preferences of a President from the same electoral party the distinctive features of the majority Congressional party that have appeared here would not have existed or would have emerged greatly modified from the complexities of the legislative scene.

Analysis of the relations between the Majority Leaders and the individual seniority leaders has identified a tendency, even when the chairman normally was associated with a dissident wing of the party, toward accommodation on votes concerning measures handled by a chairman's committee. This has implied the probability that such adjustment occurred along the lines of a program, one of special consequence to the performance of the legislative party.

Whence the program? If it was indeed the case that the initiatives and known preferences of the President produced the distinguishing characteristics of the majority Congressional party, then those preferences must have formed the core of the selective agreements between the Majority Leaders and the committee chairmen. The data in Tables 60 and 61 indicate beyond much doubt that the Administration support votes in both House and Senate revealed the principal basis for agree-

Table 60

PRESIDENTIAL PREFERENCES AND MAJORITY COHERENCE IN THE SENATE: AGREEMENTS BETWEEN MAJORITY LEADER AND COMMITTEE CHAIRMEN ON ADMINISTRATION SUPPORT VOTES AND ON OTHER VOTES CONCERNING MEASURES REPORTED BY THEIR COMMITTEES, 81ST CONGRESS

	Agreements on Administration Support Votes, per cent	Agreements on Other Votes, per cent
Low-cohesion votes		
First Session	64.3	43.6
Second Session	46.9	26.8
High-cohesion votes		
First Session	91.4	94.6
Second Session	85.7	57.8

Table 61

PRESIDENTIAL PREFERENCES AND MAJORITY COHERENCE IN THE HOUSE: AGREEMENTS BETWEEN MAJORITY LEADER AND COMMITTEE CHAIRMEN ON ADMINISTRATION SUPPORT VOTES AND ON OTHER VOTES CONCERNING MEASURES REPORTED BY THEIR COMMITTEES, 81ST CONGRESS

	Agreements on Administration Support Votes, per cent	Agreements on Other Votes, per cent
Low-cohesion votes		
Second Session	75.0	67.6
Intermediate-cohesion Votes		
First Session	97.1	73.7
High-cohesion votes		
Second Session	82.1	78.8

ment between the Majority Leaders and the individual committee chairmen. Although the rate of Leader-chairman agreement was fairly high on all votes concerning measures reported by the several committees, it was higher on those that carried the Administration support designation on each of the seven sets of votes in the two houses, with one minor exception. This, as Table 60 indicates, was the high-cohesion set in the Senate's first session, when the rate of agreement on all votes was so high, paralleling the very high mean cohesion of the Senate party, that the slightly lower agreement rate on the Administration votes need not be regarded as significant.[7]

The number of cases underlying these tables is too small to permit a confident analysis of each committee chairman individually, but some of the tendencies in the material should be noted. The general pattern did not apply uniformly to all of the chairmen, of course. But in the Senate it was apparently the case that if agreement occurred between the Majority Leader and a chairman from the dissenting wing of the party, such as George (Finance), Johnston of South Carolina (Post Office and Civil Service), McCarran (Judiciary), or McClellan (Expenditures in the Executive Departments), it was most likely to involve a vote that could be designated as an Administration issue. Similarly, a chairman such as Thomas of Utah (Labor and Public

---

[7] Since neither the validity nor the reliability of the list of Administration support votes can be established beyond question, one may wish to accept this conclusion cautiously, but the consistency of the data in these tables is a source of confidence. See, in this connection, the discussion of the Administration support index in the Appendix. These tables take no account of "absences," but the essential pattern would not be changed if these were omitted from the calculations.

Welfare), who belonged to the Majority Leader's wing of the party and tended to agree with him on most committee votes, was still more likely to agree on the committee votes that involved an Administration preference. In the House the details are less revealing, since the oppositions between the Majority Leader and the chairmen on committee votes were few, but it may be worth noting that of the nine disagreements of this sort, only two could be classified as Administration support votes.[8]

The voting relations of the Majority Leader and the seniority leaders on the roll calls dealing with measures reported by their committees thus help to confirm the inference that the element of program that tended to give coherence to the majority party and meaning to the roles of the Majority Leaders could be traced to the initiatives and preferences of the President. What of the minority? Did this same "program" draw together, either in opposition or in support, the principal elective leaders and the individual seniority leaders on the minority side? As the data in Tables 62 and 63 indicate, the answer is not entirely clear, but it is evident that the effect of the President's initiatives was, to say the least, slighter than on the majority side.

Table 62

PRESIDENTIAL PREFERENCES AND MINORITY COHERENCE IN THE SENATE: AGREEMENTS BETWEEN SELECTED REPUBLICAN ELECTIVE LEADERS AND SENIORITY LEADERS ON ADMINISTRATION SUPPORT VOTES AND ON OTHER VOTES CONCERNING MEASURES REPORTED BY THEIR COMMITTEES, 81ST CONGRESS

	Minority Leader, Wherry		Chairman of Minority Policy Committee, Taft	
	Agreements on Administration Support Votes, per cent	Agreements on Other Votes, per cent	Agreements on Administration Support Votes, per cent	Agreements on Other Votes, per cent
Low-cohesion votes				
First Session	35.7	40.7	39.5	46.2
Second Session	25.0	28.1	50.0	51.8
High-cohesion votes				
First Session	37.1	63.9	48.3	72.2
Second Session	50.0	53.7	50.0	48.4

[8] See above, Table 47. One of these disagreements was with Rankin (Veterans) and the other with Doughton (Ways and Means).

Table 63

PRESIDENTIAL PREFERENCES AND MINORITY COHERENCE IN THE HOUSE: AGREEMENTS BETWEEN MINORITY LEADER AND REPUBLICAN SENIORITY LEADERS ON ADMINISTRATION SUPPORT VOTES AND ON OTHER VOTES CONCERNING MEASURES REPORTED BY THEIR COMMITTEES, 81ST CONGRESS

	Agreements on Administration Support Votes, per cent	Agreements on Other Votes, per cent
Low-cohesion votes		
Second Session	69.7	36.8
Intermediate-cohesion votes		
First Session	53.7	62.5
High-cohesion votes		
Second Session	85.7	71.4

In the Senate (Table 62) the Minority Leader was less likely to agree with the seniority leaders on Administration support votes with which their committees were concerned than on other votes on committee measures. The pattern thus was the reverse of that between the Majority Leader and the chairmen. This was in part a reflection of Senator Wherry's personal peculiarities, but not entirely, for, when the same analysis was made, substituting Senator Taft for the Minority Leader, the pattern was essentially unchanged, though it was somewhat modified on the high-cohesion set of the second session.

Table 63 indicates that the Administration's preferences afforded more basis for coherence among the minority leaders in the House than in the Senate. That is, in two of the three sets the distribution of agreements resembled that among the Democratic leaders, but the level was generally lower. The preferences of a majority President thus seem to have supplied no reliable basis for coherence among the leaders of the legislative minority. Their responses to his initiatives, as reflected in the Administration support votes, had no consistent programmatic character.

LEADERSHIP OF THE PRESIDENT'S MAJORITY

Generalized in the baldest terms these data demonstrate that the "program" of the President had a centripetal effect upon the majority Congressional parties that gave coherence to their leadership structures and meaning to the roles of the leaders, especially those in the principal "elective" positions. In other words, and somewhat more extreme ones, the Democratic majority parties in the Congress worked as groups because of and in response to the initiatives of a Democratic Administration.

This conclusion, given the complexity and the crudity of the underlying data, calls for some qualification. What, precisely, is the nature of the relations implied by the data? Do they mean more, for example, than the familiar characterization of the Presidency as involving the role of "Chief Legislator"? This term has no very explicit or precise meaning, but it usually denotes an aspect of the President's relations with the Congress as an inclusive institution and hence does not make the point that is here intended.[9] The response of interest here is not that from the Congress as a whole but rather the response from the Congressional party. Nor is the same sense conveyed by the notion of the President as "party leader," since this ascription normally implies no distinction between the electoral party and the Congressional party or, more accurately, parties. It is not even very helpful to refer to the President as the "leader" of the House and Senate parties. These groups have their own leaders, whose roles, as the data on the Eighty-first Congress have shown, are real ones. These roles are not, however, independent of the Presidency, and their occupants do not have resources of power equal to those of the President.

What is needed to describe the relations between the President and the leaders of his Congressional majority that are pointed to in these data is perhaps a slightly modified conception of leadership in the context of the Congressional party. In contemporary social science precise notions of leadership have grown primarily from the close observation of relatively small groups, in which the leader is defined operationally as one who characteristically initiates action for the other members of the group. These studies, for understandable reasons of research manageability, have tended to treat the small group—committee, neighborhood clique, trade union local, factory work-group—in isolation rather than as a unit in a more inclusive system or organization. In consequence they do not throw much light on more complex situations in which initiative does not have its origins within the membership of the group.[10]

---

[9] See, for example, Edward S. Corwin, *The President: Office and Powers*, 3d Edition, New York: New York University Press, 1948, chap. 7, and Clinton Rossiter, *The American Presidency*, New York: Harcourt, Brace, 1956, p. 14 and *passim*.

[10] For critical comments on the shortcomings of observation of small groups *in vacuo* and on the distortions resulting from projecting inferences about small groups

For it is a commonplace that the President is not a member of the Congressional party. Without attempting to draw a sketch that is more precise than the materials warrant, one may surmise that in the complexities of the Presidency and the Congressional parties one is dealing with mutually dependent sets of relations, the Congressional party leaders with their rank-and-file members and the President with his more inclusive audience going beyond the Congress and the executive branch to the nation and the world. The relations of the President with the leaders of the Congressional party at the convergence of these sets are typically not symmetrical, since the power resources of the President generally exceed those of the Congressional party leaders, but they are mutually dependent because the initiatives of the President are necessary for his performance of his role in his larger constituency and are also essential in the Congressional leaders' performance of their roles within the legislative party.

An analogy that implies a clear hierarchy in this pattern is not entirely fortunate, but one may think of the President as resembling, not the leader in the small group, but a plant manager who may lead a work-group through its foreman. The parallel is not close, but it suggests the essential point that the President's initiatives, though indispensable to the effective functioning of the legislative party, are not normally equivalent to the direct leadership of that group.[11] The analogy to the plant manager is also helpful in its suggestion that the common enterprise of the electoral party, though possibly less completely absorbing than an industrial enterprise, encourages a convergence of view that otherwise would not occur.

The President, as these comments suggest, does something more than merely provide an agenda for the Congress or even for the legislative parties. If that were all he did, the policy differences between the two parties and between their respective elective leaders, which have been identified here, would not be accounted for. The minority parties and their leaders would not have diverged so consistently from the majority. The President's initiatives and preferences do set an agenda, to be sure. This has become one of the unwritten components of his role, regardless of whether his party is in the majority in the

---

upon large and complex systems, see William F. Whyte, *Patterns for Industrial Peace*, New York: Harper and Brothers, 1951.

[11] The Woodrow Wilson of 1907 made a number of the distinctions indicated here, though the points were not elaborated and, in a sense, they could not be until after his Administration. (In Woodrow Wilson, *Constitutional Government in the United States*, New York: Columbia University Press, 1908, see, for example, pp. 72 ff. and 107 ff. Compare also Arthur N. Holcombe, *Our More Perfect Union*, Cambridge: Harvard University Press, 1950, pp. 236–283.)

Congress and almost regardless of his personal conceptions of the position. But, especially if his is the majority party in the legislature, his preferences also provide leverage useful if not absolutely essential to the principal elective leaders of the legislative party in the performance of their roles.

This distinction between setting an agenda for the Congress as a whole and providing leverage for the elective leaders of the President's legislative party permits some clarification of the different senses of the term "program" in these pages. The word appeared first in Chapters 3 through 6 as a means of characterizing the tendency toward a voting pattern in the majority party that showed elements of coherence along substantive policy lines. This tendency was treated as evidence of the "program" of the majority legislative party, and the data in this chapter indicate that it had more than a little to do with both the initiatives and the agenda of the President. But the agenda of the President, composed of his public requests to the Congress, clearly is not identical with the program of the legislative party or even with the President's own program. Some occupants of the White House demand much of the Congress and some relatively little, but none, with the possible exception of Franklin Roosevelt in the first months of his first term, is granted all that he asks for. (No Congress, however compliant, could reasonably be expected even to act on, to say nothing of granting, the range of requests making up Harry Truman's agenda for the Eighty-first.) The actions he most wants the legislature to take, his program, presumably fill a considerably shorter list, approximating the items he judges he can or must get, and the program of the Congressional party is likely to be still less comprehensive. The principal elective leaders, on the basis of their own preferences and their estimates of what they in turn can expect from the committees and from their chambers, arrive at what the legislative schedule and the voting indicate as the program of the Congressional party. But the emergence of this program of the legislative party is a function of the mutual dependence of the President and the principal leaders of the Congressional party, in which the leverage provided by the President's preferences is crucial.

The importance for the principal elective leaders of their relations with the President, especially if the Congressional party is in the majority, is fundamentally traceable to the peculiar characteristics of these groups. As earlier chapters have argued, the legislative parties are marked by a paradoxical set of attributes: fractionation and, in some instances, structural fluidity, but also a tendency toward shared attitudes and expectations, even in substantive policy matters, and an apparent interdependence of role among the members, both of which testify to their persistence as groups. These attributes have been summarily described in these pages by designating the Congressional parties as "mediate" groups, meaning that the relations constituting the groups are distinctively affected but not wholly determined by their members' affiliations with and dependence upon other groups.[12] The latter would include primarily interest groups and constituency parties but would of course not be confined to these.

One of the implications of the mediate character of the Congressional party is that the risks to which its members are subject are not fully integrated into the shared attitudes and goals of the group, as they would be in an immediate group such as a militant labor union, a military combat group, or even a well-managed business firm. Its members' fortunes are not identical with those of the legislative party, but at the same time they are not completely independent of it. The degree of independence, as has been suggested earlier, is probably less in the House than in the Senate. In addition, the degree of independence is not a fixed quantity but is subject to fluctuation with various circumstances—the nature of emergent issues, the timing and imminence of the re-election contest, the vigor and popular standing of the President, and the like. These fluctuations usually are not highly predictable or subject to precise ranking. Hence the distribution of risks as between those produced by the performance and fortunes of the legislative party and those more closely related to "outside" groups is often decidedly unclear and ambiguous.

This ambiguity of risk and the mediate function of the legislative party seem to be the keys to the roles of the principal elective leaders. Ambiguity may help to support the demands of the Floor Leader if he is able, unconsciously or by design, so to define the context in which the party's members make their choices that the apparent risks

---

[12] The implication desired here is that of a relation that is dependent upon "outside" influences and hence is derivative and supplementary rather than direct and inclusive. As applied to a group, "mediate" obviously must be a term of degree. In justification of this excursion into the coining of labels, note that neither the sociologists nor the social psychologists concerned with "group dynamics" have developed a satisfactory typology of groups and that, in particular, they have paid relatively little attention to identifying variations in the characteristics of groups dependent on differences in their settings and their functional relations with other groups in the society. Robert K. Merton (*Social Theory and Social Structure,* revised edition, Glencoe, Illinois: The Free Press, 1957, pp. 308–326) has developed a suggestive "provisional list of group-properties." Most relevant to the concept of the mediate group are those he labels as "degree of engagement of members in the group," "degree of expected conformity to norms of group," and "autonomy or dependence of the group."

involved in opposing the leadership are emphasized. The ambiguity of risk also places a premium on being close to the centers of communication within the legislative party, for to be "in the know" concerning impending events in and outside the Congress is to be better prepared to minimize the risks they may imply. In consequence, the influence of one who, like the Floor Leader, occupies a position at the center of such communication can hardly fail to be enhanced.[13]

Given the mediate function of the Congressional party, the powers of its leaders, especially its principal elective leaders, cannot be expected, except in very small measure, to be formalized, codified, and at all times fully adequate for meeting the vicissitudes of their roles. Rather they are for the most part informal, personal, interstitial, and—somewhat like those of the President—often less extensive than the range of expectations they must meet. For reasons that have already been discussed, there appear to be differences in this respect between the House and Senate party leaders, but in both chambers the influence of the principal leaders depends heavily upon their recurrently improvising effective combinations among fragments of power of the most varied sorts.

A former leader, commenting upon this aspect of the role, reported that he had on occasion persuaded a "lobbyist" whom he knew to be close to a wavering member of his party to influence the latter to vote with the party and its leadership. This testimony illustrates both the mediate character of the party and the kinds of fragments of power on which the elective leader must often rely. The fragment in this instance was formally outside the party group. It thus resembled the kind of leverage with which a President's initiatives may provide a Majority Leader, for clearly the leader of a mediate group, who almost by definition ranks little above his colleagues, must, if he chooses to perform his role with maximum effectiveness, avail himself of any outside resources that may be converted into influence within the legislative party.

This potential of presidential initiatives as leverage for the leadership of the Congressional party has already been referred to in discussing the relations of the President and the leaders of his Congressional party in terms of convergence of interdependent sets of

---

[13] Presumably much the same inference is to be drawn from the apparent value of belonging to what William S. White calls "the Inner Club" in the Senate (*Citadel*, New York: Harper, 1957, chap. 7). Voorhis makes the same point in discussing the "select circle" in the House. "I confess," he says, "to having had a deep desire to have the friendship and understanding—if not the agreement—of certain of these men." (Voorhis, *Confessions of a Congressman*, pp. 31–32.)

leader-follower relations. The basic point is that the imperatives of the Presidency and the peculiarities of leadership in a Congressional party with the characteristics of a mediate group make collaborative relations between the President and the principal elective leaders of his legislative party functionally useful for both participants.

Illustrations of this utility are not hard to find. A key leader in the House, who has been Majority Leader both when the President was of his party and when he was not, described his efforts under the latter circumstances to negotiate with the standing committee chairmen, individually, in order to develop an agreed program for a Congressional session. When asked whether the President's being of his party made any difference in the performance of this task, the immediate reply was, "Much easier, much easier." [14] A respected and experienced member of the Senate's staff, commenting on his own observation of the relations of Floor Leader and President, noted their tendency toward collaboration and emphasized particularly the inclination of Senate elective leaders not only to acquiesce in but to encourage presidential initiatives. He cited the case of a Floor Leader, not publicly known for his dependence on his party's President, who increasingly during his tenure solicited White House intervention with wavering senators in aid of agreed legislative projects.

The utility of the collaborative relation between the President and the leaders of his legislative party is further suggested by the fact that the regular White House meetings of the President and the "Big Four" or "Big Six" of the Congressional parties, meetings which in the past two decades have become a normal feature of governmental operation, provide the most regular contact between President and Congress and the only institutionalized point of meeting for the leaders of the parties in the Senate and House. Other communication between them takes place, of course, but apparently more casually and in a more restricted context. The White House meetings are not highly formalized, their results normally are not recorded except in the limited replies to inquiries from the press or in accounts of later discussions in the policy committees, and there is in the public domain little information concerning precisely how they operate. Some former participants have stated in interviews that at least occasionally the meetings involve considerable give and take and some effort to achieve common ground.

From the standpoint of their value for the performance of the elec-

---

[14] Programming is not equivalent to implementation, as Neustadt has pointed out, but in this context the two may be regarded as closely related. See Richard E. Neustadt, "Presidency and Legislation: Planning the President's Program," *American Political Science Review*, Vol. 49, no. 4 (December 1955), p. 1016.

tive leader's role, however, the precise character of the meetings is probably less important than their regular occurrence and the comparative privacy surrounding them. Some reporting of the discussions is usually made in the meetings of the policy committees and other sessions of the legislative party leaders, but if all that occurred in them immediately transpired, their utility would be considerably reduced, both as a locus of genuine negotiation and as a source of leverage for the Congressional party's leaders. The mere fact of the meetings, uniquely composed as they are and normally conducted without even the presence of staff, presumptively gives the Congressional participants "inside" intelligence concerning both the President and the other chamber that, whether communicated subsequently or not, in the context of the mediate group can be a source of influence.[15]

These comments should not be interpreted as suggesting that the elective leaders of the Congressional party do or can have a monopoly of information, especially concerning the President's intentions. Individual seniority leaders, perhaps especially in areas where the President's prerogatives and responsibilities are large, such as foreign policy, may enjoy a high degree of intimacy. But these are inevitably single areas, however important, and the data on the seniority leaders and the principal elective leaders would support the inference that they probably do not extend very far over the interconnections among all the parts of the legislative program. Moreover, the suspicion is strong that if these relations with the committee chairmen do not supplement but steadily bypass the elective leaders, they may reduce rather than augment the President's influence. Given the tremendous range of demands on his time and energies, to say nothing of the obstacles inherent in the Congressional institution, the President probably cannot successfully attempt to become regularly the direct leader of the Congressional party, working exclusively through the committee chairmen or directly with the rank and file. If this interpretation is correct, Franklin Roosevelt's reliance upon the leaders of the Congressional party and his refusal to bypass them by creating an alternative structure of communication with the Congress showed more wisdom than

---

[15] Informants report a more formalized arrangement during most of the Eisenhower Administration, with attendance at the meetings by the Assistant to the President and the Deputy Assistant to the President, and apparently with minutes taken at least concerning the agreements reached. The effect of this formalization, especially the presence of presidential staff, may be to reduce the utility of the meetings for participants on both sides. One suspects that such alterations would not be acceptable to some Democratic leaders, such as Speaker Sam Rayburn.

some of his critics are willing to grant.[16] He could and did attempt to influence the legislative party's choice of elective leaders, but had he not relied upon them, once they were chosen and regardless of whether they were his favored candidates, his effectiveness almost certainly would have been reduced.

Experienced members of both parties testify to the desirability of being "in on things," of knowing what is going on, and the importance of such information is suggested by the regular, but frequently unsatisfied, demands of the more junior members of the rank and file on both sides of the aisle for more meetings of party members. In Chapter 4 essentially this point was offered in explanation of the functions of the policy committees in the Senate. Those who stand at major junction points in an important communication network may acquire power from that fact alone. Even the appearance of being on the inside, however little it corresponds to reality, may have value for the leadership of a mediate group.

Other things being equal, therefore, the elective leaders of the President's legislative party have a stake in their regular meetings at the White House and a corollary interest in the President's political standing. As leaders, they lose if he loses. Other things, of course, may not be equal. Attachment to the role of elective leader may be less than that to other opportunities and aspirations. Personal and political animosities may be too strong to be submerged in even the semblance of a collaborative effort. Participants on either side may be insensitive to the subtleties of the relation. Or a President's missteps and misfortunes may make association with him an embarrassment rather than a reliance. Proximity to the White House is not the only fragment of power available to the leaders of the Congressional party, and circumstances may reduce it to unimportance despite a general tendency in the other direction.

The benefits of a fruitful collaboration, however, are not all on one side. They accrue also to the President's account. In the thundering crises that are the normal lot of Presidents in times when "normalcy" exists only in the past, the clock provides no hours for the cultivation of rank-and-file legislators which direct leadership of the Congress would require. But in addition the President is dependent upon the principal elective leaders of the Congressional party in much the same way, if not to the same degree, as are their colleagues on the Hill. If the agenda he sets is to emerge in a product he favors, he must have

---

[16] See James M. Burns, *Roosevelt: The Lion and the Fox*, New York: Harcourt, Brace, 1956, pp. 348–350 and *passim*.

the information and the means for day-to-day assessment, if not actual guidance, of Congressional activity. The elective leaders wield no monopoly here, but, standing at strategic communication points, they are, for the President much as for their legislative associates, an important source of intelligence, entirely aside from their capabilities as facilitators or obstructors of his program. And on the score of obstruction, the lengths to which as adroit a tactician as Franklin Roosevelt went in 1937 to forestall the selection of an uncongenial Senate Majority Leader are illustrative enough of this aspect of the mutually dependent relation.[17] But the President, save in exceptional instances, must rely on the leaders of the Congressional party. If means exist by which he can do without them on a continuous, day-by-day basis, the record does not reveal what they are. Relations with the leaders of the Congressional party can be supplemented, as they often have been, but no substitutes have appeared on which he can rely with equal confidence. To the degree that the mechanism of the Congressional party is relied upon, however, it must be taken as it is, with the leaders it has produced. For a President to attempt to act directly as the leader of the Congressional party almost certainly would be to destroy, for the time being, this valuable, if variable, governing instrument.

To call the relations between the President and the leaders of his Congressional party collaborative and mutually useful is to raise the problem of whether occupants of these legislative positions are to be viewed primarily as "his" or as the leaders of their respective houses and Congressional parties. The formal answer, that their principal loyalties must be toward those whose suffrage they hold, their colleagues in the Congressional party, is not very helpful since it avoids the underlying realities. The question itself would lack point, in fact, if an answer were given categorically either way.

The fundamental complexity and subtlety of the role lie in the fact that the elective leaders are, and probably must be, both the President's leaders and the party's leaders. However, if the analysis developed in these pages is valid, it follows that, in order to be fully effective as leaders of the Congressional parties, they must above all be effective spokesmen for the President; or at least, excepting the most unusual circumstances, they must appear to be his spokesmen. The data on the Floor Leaders in the Eighty-first Congress clearly point in this direction. Senator Lucas, it will be remembered, appeared somewhat to the "left" of the center of his party largely because of his position on the Administration support votes, and Representative McCormack

---

[17] *Ibid.*, pp. 309, 361–362.

apparently went to considerable lengths to avoid being recorded in opposition to the President, even when the overwhelming majority of the House Democrats were opposing the White House.[18] Open opposition to the President—as distinguished, perhaps, from covert failure to press his programs aggressively—apparently was something to be avoided.

The position that support for the President is a pivotal element in the roles of the principal elective leaders of the President's Congressional party is not accepted by some observers, especially as it applies to the Senate. William S. White, whose discerning observations on the upper chamber cannot be dismissed lightly, places chief emphasis on the requirement of loyalty to the views of legislative colleagues. Noting that in the Senate there is little agreement on what a Floor Leader ought to do but a broad consensus on what he ought not to do, White argues that "in all but those rare and comparatively brief periods when it is thrust into the background by extraordinary circumstances" the Senate "expects" that the Floor Leader of the party holding the White House "will not so much represent the President as the Senate itself." At the height of Franklin Roosevelt's prestige, White observes, "there arose a highly oversimplified public notion of the duties of Senate leadership based on the assumption that a leader of Democrats in the Senate *necessarily* owed obedience to a Democratic President. The compulsive actions of the Senate itself . . . for a time had the effect of promoting what the Senate felt to be a profound heresy." [19]

In these comments White correctly calls attention to the element of variability in the role of the Senate leader. The broad discretionary range implied in the expectations composing it, inevitably reflecting changes in the external setting of the legislative party, is unquestionable. The data in these pages amply demonstrate that in attempting to reach an understanding of leadership in the Congressional party one must beware of beguiling absolutes. One must seek central tendencies, not constants. Nor can one quarrel with the proposition that a Leader not in sympathetic communion with his legislative colleagues will in most circumstances fail to perform his functions effectively.

One must acknowledge also a reality of structure and of attitude in the separation of Senate from House and especially of both from the President.[20] The patterns of risk are not the same. They do converge,

---

[18] See chaps. 4 and 6 of this book.

[19] White, *Citadel,* pp. 96–98. Italics in the original.

[20] The restraining impact of this reality is suggested by President Truman in a comment on relations between a President, on the one hand, and the Speaker and Vice President, on the other. "The President cannot afford to have his confidential

but convergence does not produce identity. Nevertheless, if the findings of this study are in any degree representative, the imperatives of presidential politics produce more than an echo in the Congressional party, and the partisan responses at either end of Pennsylvania Avenue have a detectable mutual resemblance.

Within the Congress the contrasts between the Senate and the House, rooted in differences of risk and in the related factor of the size of the two bodies, are real and perceptible. They supply additional reason for the elective leaders to avoid too open emphasis upon their ties to the President. These contrasts are reflected in the rules of the two chambers, in the relative "visibility" of senators and representatives, in the attitudes of the members and even of the professional staff in one house toward the other, and in a variety of other ways. The two chambers are not totally unlike, but they are quite different groups. In consequence, the legislative parties within them do not impose the same requirements on their leaders, and preservation of the leaders' base of influence assumes sensitivity to these differences in demand.

The disposition of the elective leaders to play down their spokesmanship for the President also follows from the fact that the Congressional party as a mediate group affords its leaders little opportunity for command, in the strict sense. Their influence in either house is only slightly the product of hierarchy and, because the limits on their influence are ambiguous, their power may in fact be more extensive than any of their followers would be willing to grant in a formal delegation of authority. Actions propose definitions, and in a loosely integrated structure—perhaps in any structure—action that explicitly proposes to invoke the outer limits of implied power is likely to fail, and the resulting definition to fall short of what had previously received *de facto* acknowledgment.[21] If the elective leaders only rarely can command, they also can publicly commit their followers to a given action only after elaborate preparation.

An instance that can be interpreted as illustrating the caution imposed on the leaders of the legislative party by the requirements of their roles was provided by the events surrounding the creation of a

---

matters discussed in Senate cloakrooms. A leak from the White House to the Senators and Representatives is always worth a headline, and that compels a President always to be on guard when he is being interviewed by members of Congress. That is also one of the reasons why it is very difficult for a President to take the Vice President completely into his confidence." (Harry S. Truman, *Memoirs*, Vol. I, *Year of Decisions*, New York: Doubleday, 1955, p. 54.)

[21] This appears to be the real significance of the "overthrow" of Speaker Joseph Cannon in 1910–1911.

Democratic advisory committee following the election of 1956. Meeting shortly after the election, in which the Democrats retained control of the Congress despite a landslide victory for President Eisenhower that included marked gains in most of the large metropolitan areas, the executive committee of the Democratic National Committee decided to create an advisory committee to develop a legislative program for the party. Early in December Chairman Paul Butler named twenty members to the group, including the seven principal elective leaders in both houses: from the Senate, Majority Leader Lyndon Johnson, Whip Mike Mansfield, and Chairman of the Campaign Committee George Smathers; from the House, Speaker Sam Rayburn, Majority Leader John McCormack, Whip Carl Albert, and Campaign Committee Chairman Michael Kirwan. Despite some press reports that Butler's invitations were merely a formality and that acceptance had been assured before the list was announced, within ten days all seven of these leaders declined to serve. Since the movement for the committee was known to have been sponsored by the national committeemen from California, Pennsylvania, and Illinois, and since some of its proponents presented it as an effort to produce a "liberal" legislative program and, at least by implication, to bypass the Congressional leadership, interpretations of Mr. Butler's somewhat comic embarrassment almost inevitably talked about "liberals" against "conservatives" in the party and about challenges to the Congressional leaders.

Although party factions and the status of the Congressional leaders obviously were relevant, the debacle can be interpreted in quite different terms. Even if the seven leaders of the Congressional party were in sympathy with the substantive objectives of the movement, which is well within the realm of the possible, and even if the preliminary arrangements had been made more adroitly so that the announcement could have come as the result of negotiations between the National Committee and the Congressional leaders rather than as a proposal from the Committee to the legislative leaders, Messrs. Johnson and Rayburn and their associates would have been ill advised to enter the group.

For if its decisions were made public, as the proposals of the subsequently reconstituted committee have been, the leaders of the Congressional party would have assumed a position of command that they may have by implication and after maneuver and negotiation but that they can rarely announce in open forum. Even after conferences with the President the leaders of his legislative party, though they may head a majority, normally avoid specific public commitments about what the Congressional party will do. Rather they report what the President wants and indicate an intent to help get it for him if they can. What they do not do as spokesmen for the White House they clearly cannot appear to do as members of a group created by the National Committee.

Matters would not be much different if the decisions of such an advisory committee were not made public. In their negotiations within the Capitol the principal elective leaders would not seem to be speaking in the comfortably ambiguous name of an unspecified "party" majority composed of colleagues similarly situated and with equivalent political risks, nor would they be speaking for a President with at least contingent claims upon their support. Rather they would appear to be acting for an "outside" agency without status or legitimacy.[22]

In either case, with or without publicity, the party leaders recurrently would be placed in a position, whether justifiably or not, of asking or commanding without success. Given the mediate character of the legislative party and its attendant factionalism, commitment of the party by the elective leaders normally must follow internal negotiation, not precede it, and, if negotiation fails, the leaders will be better off in most cases if they are not too frequently and openly identified with the losing side. In his dealings with the Congress, a President may be able without net loss to make public demands that are repeatedly denied by the legislature, if he makes compensating gains within the electorate. The leaders of the Congressional party are not situated in the same way. Repeated failure of their public initiatives, even if enunciated in the name of the President, is more likely to destroy them entirely. They can, as Senator Johnson did in declining membership on the advisory committee, invite the views of an "outside" group, but if these views commit the leaders, the implied initiatives are likely to produce a restricted rather than a broadened definition of their power.[23]

The two requirements, that the principal elective leaders of the

---

[22] Even when acting on behalf of the President, a Congressional leader cannot afford to appear to be speaking exclusively to rather than from his colleagues. Thus after the Eighty-third Congress (1953–1954) the view was common on Capitol Hill that Representative Martin was stronger in the House than Representative Halleck, who, as Majority Leader, had become so completely and so dogmatically a spokesman for the Administration that he had lost some of his effectiveness in the House.

[23] This account is based on the reports and interpretations published in the *New York Times* for November 28, December 6, 13, 14, 19, and 23, 1956, and January 16, 1957. It should not be construed as a negative assessment of the utility of the reconstituted committee, but only of the original plan to include the Congressional party leaders.

Congressional party support a President of their own party and that they function as the spokesmen for their colleagues in the Congress, are not always cleanly compatible. At the same time it seems clear that they are generally interdependent, in the sense that representing the President provides a focus and part of the leverage for leadership of the Congressional party, and sympathetic reflection of the problems of legislative colleagues is an essential in advancing the President's program. One or the other element may be more conspicuous from time to time. Apparently, moreover, the Congressional base is generally nearer the surface; it is more openly expressed. But the element of support for the Administration is normally present, if only implicitly and though often reflected in ambivalent terms.

The implicitly acknowledged interdependence of these two features of the role and the resulting ambivalence concerning them, especially in the case of the Floor Leader, can be easily illustrated. They are evident, for example, in estimates of the special hazards associated with the position. When a number of senators, representatives, and staff people were asked whether they felt a Floor Leader ran any special risks, the almost unanimous response was in the affirmative, the normal explanation being that as Leader he was obliged to act and to vote as he would not act and would not vote if he were an ordinary member of the Congress.

The typical illustrations for this reply were the cases of Majority Leader Lucas and Majority Whip Myers, both of whom failed to be re-elected in 1950, and the case of Majority Leader McFarland, who was defeated in the election of 1952. There may well be doubt whether holding these positions and being identified with the Administration in fact contributed significantly to the defeat of these men. The important point is that in and around the Congress a strong belief persists that this was the case. There is evidence that Senator Lister Hill for just this reason was persuaded, after the departure of Lucas, not to become Majority Leader, as he might easily have done. The choice of McFarland, although undoubtedly it owed much to the sponsorship of Senator Russell, can be traced in part to the reluctance of more vigorous members of the party to accept a post that would inevitably involve representation of an Administration increasingly regarded as a political liability.

The criticism of McFarland as Senate Majority Leader in the Eighty-second Congress and even some of the explanations of his shortcomings illustrate the ambivalence concerning the dual aspects of the role.[24] The Arizona Senator, though personally popular, was regarded

---

[24] Compare White, *Citadel*, p. 106.

as insufficiently aggressive, as unable to be "tough" with his colleagues. But in extenuation it is said that, even had he chosen to be less complacent, McFarland could not have been much more effective because of the declining prestige of President Truman. In other words, he was expected to be aggressive, and the basis for such behavior normally would be the White House program.

The conflicts, ambiguities, and ambivalences in the role of the Senate Majority Leader are particularly well illustrated by the case of Senator Knowland in the Eighty-third Congress and especially in 1954. In February, 1954, Knowland spoke and voted against President Eisenhower's position on the so-called Bricker amendment to the Constitution, which proposed to place restrictions on the treaty power. During the summer he advocated a declaration that the United States would withdraw from the United Nations if the Communist government of China were admitted to membership and also called for breaking diplomatic relations with the Soviet Union. Finally, in November he called for a Congressional review of the Administration's entire policy in the "cold war." [25]

These actions provoked a good deal of comment. The press carried reports of intense resentment in the White House, of suggestions that Knowland should resign as the Republican Leader, and even of rumors that he would resign.[26] Commenting on these responses, White says that ". . . men very high in the Eisenhower Administration honestly felt that Senator Knowland of California simply had no *right* as the Republican leader to denounce Administration policy on China. The Senate itself has been wholly unimpressed; . . . Knowland, . . . far from overextending his credit in the Institution as Republican leader, became in a way ever more acceptable to it during the Eisenhower years." [27]

Criticisms of Knowland were not confined to "outsiders," however. In an interview some time later a former Senate Majority Leader, albeit a Democrat, stated flatly that he would have resigned as Floor Leader if he felt that he could not go along with a President of his own party, especially on a matter of foreign policy. Knowland himself, moreover, said that he would resign his post if the Administration ever granted diplomatic recognition to the Communist government of China.

---

[25] A good summary of these events and the text of Senator Knowland's speech demanding a review of foreign policy appeared in the *New York Times*, November 16, 1954.

[26] *New York Times*, July 1, November 17 and 21, and December 2 and 3, 1954.

[27] White, *Citadel*, p. 98.

By this statement, as Arthur Krock noted in the *New York Times*, the Republican Senate Floor Leader conceded implicitly "that there are limits to the usefulness of a party leader in Congress who opposes a major policy of a President of that party." [28]

More significant than this implied acknowledgment by Knowland of the dual character of his role was the dramatically explicit gesture that the Republican Leader made early in this series of events. This came after the Bricker amendment had been altered by the Senate's adopting changes proposed by Senator Ferguson and acceptable to the President and by its passage of alterations sponsored by Senator George that were not approved by the White House. Just as the final roll call was about to be taken on the modified Bricker resolution, when, after five weeks of debate, senators were calling for a vote, Mr. Knowland exchanged desks with Senator Saltonstall, the Republican Whip, and addressed the chair:

> Mr. President, I know the hour is growing late, and I do not wish to detain the Senate. . . .
>
> I have left the desk of the majority leader because I wish to make it very clear that what I say is not said as majority leader, but is said in my capacity as an individual Senator of the United States. . . .
>
> So far as I know, the President of the United States has not changed his view that the only amendments acceptable to the administration were those which were presented by the distinguished Senator from Michigan [Mr. Ferguson]. . . . I say that in order that there may be a clear understanding that there has been no change in the situation, and in order that no Senator may vote under a misapprehension.
>
> I have left the desk of the majority leader because I feel that I have an obligation, while speaking in my individual capacity, to make that very clear.[29]

He then went on to an account of his prolonged efforts at reaching a compromise satisfactory to the President and to the sponsors of the measure, explained his concern over the issue, and announced that he would vote for the resolution.

Although Senator Knowland did not repeat this gesture in his later estrangements from the President—when no votes were involved—he here clearly demonstrated the point that, subject to some variations in the conceptions of individual incumbents, the role required him to be

---

[28] *New York Times,* May 3, 1955. Krock added that the chief difference between Knowland and his critics was that they thought these limits had already been passed.

[29] *Congressional Record,* 83d Cong., 2d sess., 100:2 (February 26, 1954), 2371.

also the President's leader if he was to be the Senate party's leader.[30]

These are requirements of the Leader's role, but the precise definition of those requirements lies within the discretion of the man performing it at the time. His background, his skills, his energy level, and his own policy preferences will determine his conception of the role and, in general, his effectiveness in performing it. He may easily be satisfied with exploiting the potentialities of the role at a minimal level, especially if the President's own skills in this realm are not an inducement to vigorous activity.

It is also possible that practice, resting on convention alone rather than on a full appreciation of possibilities, encourages performance at levels well below the full potential. Thus the data on the importance of the state delegations in the House, which were examined in Chapter 7, raise the question whether the influence of these intradelegation relations reflects a sort of power vacuum within the party or rather an inevitable restriction on the influence of the leaders. The data of the present study will not permit an adequate answer to this question, but, to the extent that the unity of the delegations is a response to ambiguity in the House rather than to claims from the constituency— and some of the evidence points in the former direction—it may indicate a failure of the leaders to realize the full potential of their roles.[31]

Some circumstantial evidence carries the same implication. Inter-

---

[30] The Knowland example sharpens the implications of Senator Barkley's resignation as Majority Leader following Franklin Roosevelt's veto of the 1944 tax bill, for the implied relations were not clear on the face of that incident. Barkley's vigorous speech of denunciation was in response to what he regarded as a gratuitous insult to the Congress, yet in discussing the case later he referred to himself as "the Administration's floor leader" and expressed his conviction that he was obliged to resign in the event of a "fundamental and irreconcilable disagreement with the President." (Alben W. Barkley, *That Reminds Me*, New York: Doubleday, 1954, p. 173.) Roosevelt's action undermined Barkley's value as the Administration's leader by treating him, implicitly, as exclusively that. Barkley's resignation and immediate re-election as Majority Leader restored the emphasis on his ties to his colleagues and re-established the dual relationship, though not, apparently, in identical form. Illustrations such as these occur more readily in the Senate than in the House in part because of the circumstances that make the Leader's behavior in the upper chamber more conspicuous. Since in the House the Speaker does not vote and neither he nor the Majority Leader takes as open and prominent a part on the floor as does the Senate Leader, their positions are less obvious and their apparent commitments more ambiguous. There is every reason to assume, however, that duality is as central to a definition of their roles as it is in the Senate.

[31] H. Bradford Westerfield, *Foreign Policy and Party Politics: Pearl Harbor to Korea*, New Haven: Yale University Press, 1955, pp. 92 and *passim*, offers the opinion that House Democratic leaders did not utilize the full resources of their positions.

views with representatives in both parties indicate that communication of the policy preferences of the party leaders is frequently badly timed, inadequate, and ambiguous. Representatives on one side of the aisle, moreover, many of whom have served several terms in the House, support this point implicitly by exaggerating the quality of performance on the other. Though an adequate sample has not been taken, scattered testimony indicates that many Republican legislators regard the Democrats as better organized and more aware of their leaders' policy views than are those on their own side, and many Democratic legislators have a similar view of the Republicans. These symptoms are hardly conclusive, but, if they are reliable, they suggest the possibility that the roles of the elective leaders may one day, as a result of the skill and imagination of a single incumbent, break with existing practice and move to a new level of effectiveness. Such a level, once achieved, would likely remain the norm, even for less talented successors, as long as the underlying conditions remained unchanged. A Lyndon Johnson, under whom the office of Floor Leader apparently became a clearance point for the whole Senate party to an unprecedented degree, might, after long occupancy of the position, bequeath to his successor a role whose dimensions had been materially altered.

Whatever the extent of the gap between performance and potentiality, it is important to emphasize that these inferences concerning the role of the principal elective leaders, especially in their relations with the White House, do not and almost certainly could not span the whole range of the legislative agenda. Inevitably they refer to major items and to leading proposals. Most of what is routine, uncontested, or only narrowly controversial—probably the bulk of Congressional business—and some of what is highly explosive is left to the committees, their chairmen, the executive departments and agencies, and the relevant interest groups, except as one of the elective leaders may have a personal stake in them. Within these circles, of course, commitments and prerogatives become established, and, as in almost any complex organization, intervention from unaccustomed quarters in matters that have suddenly been projected from the obscurity of custom into the center of controversy may provoke resistance that places restrictions on any leadership, even if it has the prestige of presidential endorsement.

The Congressional party, in the form of the President's majority, is a governing instrument of great, possibly growing, value, but it is important to remember that it is not the only mechanism for determining legislative action. The structure described and analyzed in these pages demonstrates that the Congressional party has meaning as a system of relations extending over a wide range of the voting behavior in both Senate and House. But, as the cleavages on the low-cohesion votes indicate and as the material in Chapter 7 on the state delegations testifies, there are other patterns of Congressional action in which the mechanism of the legislative party plays no part or only a minor one. Coalitions and alliances, operating *ad hoc* or more or less continuously through the leadership of particular committee chairmen, along lines of sectional and interest-group affiliation, are a normal feature of the Washington scene, and they may provide patterns of action entirely outside those of the legislative party on matters of grave importance.[32] The Congressional party, however, is a system of relations at least as important as these and probably more lasting than any of them.

PERPLEXED MINORITIES AND TRUNCATED MAJORITIES

The explanatory comments offered in the preceding pages have dealt with the majority Congressional party whose presidential candidate occupied the White House. What can be said of the minority? What, further, can be conjectured about a "truncated" Congressional majority, one without partisan ties to the President? And what about the legislative party that is in the minority on Capitol Hill but is "in power" in the White House? The data of the Eighty-first Congress, of course, bear on only the first of these questions, but, assuming the validity of the broad scheme of explanation offered in this chapter, it should be possible to suggest answers to the others.

The conspicuous characteristics of the minority Congressional party in the Eighty-first Congress have been described in earlier chapters and need not be repeated in detail here. In general the Republican structure in both houses was more fluid, at times almost kaleidoscopic, in appearance. This fluidity was paralleled by a lower rate of agreement among the principal elective leaders of the minority and by much less evidence of accommodation between the Republican Floor Leaders and the several seniority leaders than appeared on the Democratic side. The latter peculiarities may have been primarily a consequence of the personalities and skills of the Minority Leaders, but the similar behavior of Senator Taft and Representative Halleck suggests, among other things, that, though personal differences were not wholly irrelevant, if accommodation were to occur it had to be through the

---

[32] David B. Truman, *The Governmental Process,* New York: Knopf, 1951, chaps. 11, 13, and *passim.*

Floor Leader. Its absence reflected less urgency among the minority and less opportunity to effect agreement.

In other words, the minority Congressional party, out of power in the White House, seems to have encountered special obstructions to coherent and programmed voting behavior. Since the minority were limited in their influence upon the agenda, program—as distinguished from isolated efforts on a small number of issues—was of little or no relevance for them. This conjecture is consistent with the apparent fact that the minority party in the Senate was able to function without conspicuous evidences of internal conflict although its Floor Leader, Senator Wherry, inadequately satisfied what would seem to be one of the basic requirements of the role, a middle position in the voting structure of the party. It also helps in interpreting the kinds of disagreements that occurred between the House Minority Leader and, respectively, the Whip and the ranking member of the Rules Committee. These would not be remarkable if there was in the minority a general unconcern with a coherent program.

The suspicion is strong that perhaps the major reason for these Republican peculiarities in the Eighty-first Congress was that the minority Congressional party and its principal leaders reflected, but not precisely in reverse, the importance of the White House for the effective working of the legislative group.[33] Given the presidential program, they did not mirror in opposition the pattern of the majority. (Had they done so, the peaks of the Republican curves in Figures 15 and 16 would have been nearer the low end of the Administration support indexes.) Presidential initiatives distinguished minority from majority, but not in exact opposition presumably in part because the Minority Leaders lacked the leverage supplied by partisan association with the President, though they shared with their colleagues of the majority the agenda provided by the White House.

The nature of the Presidency itself probably contributes to the awkward position of the minority leaders. For the President of the United States is not, and is expected not to be, merely a partisan figure. Some Presidents more and some less, but all to a degree, speak for and to the nation as a whole. When they do, they increase the relative

---

[33] It is worth noting that in these respects the minority wing of the majority party bore a resemblance to the minority party. Especially in the House, its structure showed similar symptoms of fluidity and presumably for comparable reasons. Except in policy areas such as those involving race relations, it seems to have lacked a legitimizing focus for opposition, with the result that variously composed splinters of the wing broke off from it, and the remaining segment of the wing showed a changing membership from one issue to another.

strength of their own Congressional leaders and threaten that of the opposition leaders, who normally lack not only most of the means of developing an alternative program but also the leverage of an alternative "outside" source of legitimacy. In a substantive area, notably foreign affairs, in which the propriety of presidential initiative is generally conceded, this predicament of the minority is particularly evident, as others have noted.[34] This view of the minority helps to explain as well both the frequency with which the seniority leaders on the Foreign Affairs and Foreign Relations Committees disagreed with the Minority Leaders and also the frequency with which the rank-and-file Republican members of those committees supported the seniority leaders on those disagreements.[35]

The effect of the President's position on the Minority Leader's ability or inclination to establish a successful alternative program makes understandable the curious pattern of Representative Martin's top scores, as noted in Chapter 6.[36] Apparently Martin's kind of "middle" position was acceptable to a fair proportion of the more senior members of the minority and those elected at the midpoint of a Democratic President's term—or at least his preferences resembled theirs—but it was less acceptable to those elected for the first time in recent presidential years. The latter stood a good deal to the "left" or "right" of the Minority Leader in their voting on Administration issues. Unlike their Democratic counterparts, they could not respond to the structuring influence of a known President and a known program bearing their partisan label. Lacking the leverage of the White House, Martin was unable, or disinclined, to develop a substitute focus within the minority party.

These tendencies of the Republican minority probably were accentuated by the circumstances of the Eighty-first Congress. Had these been different, this particular minority's behavior might not have shown the assumed general tendencies so conspicuously. In the first place, the relative size of the Congressional minority almost certainly was a matter of some importance. A tiny minority, confined to a few constituencies in which it held unchallenged supremacy, would be likely to show a somewhat more structured voting pattern. In the

---

[34] For example, George L. Grassmuck, *Sectional Biases in Congress on Foreign Policy*, Baltimore: The Johns Hopkins Press, 1951, pp. 134–136, 172 and *passim*, demonstrates the tendency for a Congressional party without a President in the White House to shift its position on foreign policy matters when it becomes the President's party, and he argues that the minority lacks the focus provided by the President's foreign policy program.

[35] See Tables 26 and 47.

[36] See Table 41 and accompanying text.

Eighty-first Congress, the Republican contingent in the House was not remarkably small, and in the Senate it held more seats than in the last Congress in which it had been a minority (1945–1946).[37]

Second, though there are apparent limits to what can be accomplished by a minority leadership deprived of the political assets of the White House, a dedicated and skilled leadership acceptable to almost all factions of a party plainly can do much toward checking looseness in the voting structure, and its absence can have the opposite effect. In the Eighty-first Congress the Republicans, especially in the Senate, were not blessed with great skill on the part of their principal elective leaders.

Third, the immediate political conditions and the issues confronting a particular Congress clearly make a difference in the performance of any legislative party. A minority demoralized by an unexpected electoral defeat, as the Republicans apparently were after 1948, and confronted with a series of issues that are controversial within the party because they are connected with disputed explanations of the defeat, is certainly likely to show more fluidity in its voting structure than a party that is assured and confident that the issues are working in its favor.

Finally, the way in which the majority's President and his associates exploit the issues and influence the legislative program may contribute to the fractionation and fluidity of the minority while at the same time favorably affecting the structure and coherence of the majority. Whatever may be said of its skill, the Administration during 1949 and 1950 was unmistakably aggressive in its demands upon the Congress, and many of the issues it raised, not only in the realm of foreign policy, but on the domestic front as well—public housing, social security extension, minimum wage increases—scarcely contributed to the coherence of the minority.

It seems likely, however, that the tendencies of the minority Congressional party are considerably altered when its candidate has successfully gained the White House. At any rate, the logic of the general explanation offered in these pages suggests that inference. Provided that it has not been temporarily discredited and that its occupant does not entirely neglect the opportunity to set the legislative program, the Presidency should be a source of leverage to the minority's leaders even though their position does not permit exercising control over the

---

[37] There had been more House Republicans in the 78th, 79th, and, of course, the 80th Congresses, but the number elected in 1948 was larger by 9 seats than the number chosen in 1940 (77th Congress). In the Senate there were 9 fewer Republicans than there had been in the 80th Congress, but 4 more than in the 79th.

precise schedule of the Congress or influence upon the timing of reports from committees and the form in which bills are reported. Depending on the skill of the leadership in both legislative parties, as well as on that in the White House, the responses of the minority in these circumstances would be expected to resemble those of a party in the majority at both ends of Pennsylvania Avenue. Testing this expectation lies outside the scope of the present study, but, as comments in earlier chapters have suggested, there were signs of behavior in the Eighty-fourth Congress (1955–1956) consistent with the hypothesis. For example, the frequent meetings of the Republican Policy Committees in both houses and their evident importance as centers of communication testified to President Eisenhower's role as a focus for the Congressional minority.

By the same token, a truncated legislative majority, nominally dominant in the Congress but facing a President of the other party, should display much the same unprogrammed, fluid appearance identified here in the case of the Congressional minority. During the 1948 campaign President Truman vigorously denounced the Republican Eightieth Congress for its alleged "do-nothing" record. The charge was, of course, exaggerated, but it was not wholly unwarranted. If, moreover, the line of analysis pursued in this chapter is valid, any Congress situated as the Eightieth was, that is, any Congress in which the majority is truncated, is likely to appear as a "do-nothing" body. Between 1930 and 1959 there were four such Congresses: the Seventy-second (1931–1933), in which the Republicans had a nominal Senate majority but were in a clear minority in the House, the Eightieth, the Eighty-fourth (1955–1956), and the Eighty-fifth. The political situation confronting the majority in each of these was, of course, somewhat different, but they all seem to have shared the dual characteristic of being unable to make use of the President's initiatives and being unable, or at least disinclined, to develop a coherent alternative program. Ineffectiveness rather than unified opposition is likely to characterize a truncated majority. The Seventy-second Congress suffered from the special peculiarity that party control was not the same in both houses. Its record, moreover, was written in another era of American government; and its closing months were those of a "lame-duck" legislature, unresponsive to the President and as yet not guided by the President-elect. In the absence of compelling initiatives from the White House, it produced many proposals, but no program.[38]

The Republican majority in the Eightieth Congress, the first since

---

[38] Arthur M. Schlesinger, Jr., gives an excellent account of these years in *The Crisis of the Old Order,* Boston: Houghton Mifflin, 1957, chaps. 25, 26, 34, and 35.

the Hoover landslide of 1928, was supremely confident, as its Democratic counterpart had been in 1931. The election of 1946 was regarded generally in the country as a repudiation of the Administration. President Truman was a mere place holder for the Republican who would surely occupy the White House in January, 1949. His initiatives thus could be ignored with impunity, though in fact they were not entirely passed over, even in the domestic sphere. This was the Congress that supported the so-called Truman Doctrine, designed to keep Greece and Turkey from falling into the Soviet sphere, and gave effect to the Marshall Plan for European economic recovery. In the domestic field it is usually associated with the passage of the Taft-Hartley Act over a presidential veto, but it also voted a token anti-inflation measure in response to the President's demand for a strong program which included selective wage and price controls. During its critical second year, however, the Eightieth Congress was bombarded, both in its regular second session and in the special session convened after the two national party conventions, with a steady succession of demands dealing with both foreign and domestic policy. It was the limited response to these that became the target of the President in the 1948 campaign.

Though the response was limited, the important point in the present context is that there were efforts within the Congressional majority to develop and enact an alternative program. In particular, Senator Taft, as Chairman of the Senate Majority Policy Committee, sponsored and secured Senate passage of a comprehensive housing bill and one extending Federal aid to education. Neither, however, was passed in the House. As one perceptive observer has noted, ". . . the cumulative impact of these messages [from the White House]—indeed of the whole Truman offensive—would have been very considerably diluted had not the House leadership frustrated Senator Taft's own program for Congressional achievement. . . ."[39] The fact of the Ohio Senator's aspirations to the Republican nomination in 1948 complicates but does not otherwise alter the inference that a truncated Congressional majority lacked an effective focus, an "outside" point of leverage sufficient to produce a coherent, programmed performance.[40]

The Democratic majority that took over in January, 1955, was in a

---

[39] Richard E. Neustadt, "Congress and the Fair Deal," *Public Policy*, Vol. 5, Cambridge: Harvard University Press, 1954, p. 364, n. 20.

[40] In an interview, one of the key leaders in the House volunteered the judgment that, lacking the advantages of the White House, the inability of the Republican leaders to develop a program for the Eightieth Congress was a major factor in the debacle of 1948.

highly ambiguous position, since the midterm elections of 1954 by no means indicated a diminution in President Eisenhower's prestige. It had in the House the familiar leadership of Rayburn and McCormack and in the Senate Lyndon Johnson, one of the new virtuosos of legislative maneuver. Almost at once, however, and particularly in the House, an absence of policy guidance was noted by members of the majority whose service dated back six years or more but who were not yet high in the formal hierarchy of the party. By comparison with their experience in earlier Congresses in which the Democrats had been in the majority, they received little communication on what the "party program" was. Several of them were inclined in interviews to attribute this to the leaders' having grown accustomed to a Democrat in the White House, but to an outsider the parallel to other truncated Congressional majorities is more impressive.

In the Senate, Majority Leader Johnson exerted his energies toward an accommodation among the dissident Democratic elements. As White describes the effort, Johnson's ". . . first necessity was to find *some* areas upon which all could agree, and these areas when found, were necessarily somewhat thin, sometimes rather dusty with age, and always deeply traditional." [41] Noting that as these efforts at unifying the Senate Democrats succeeded, members of the party outside the Senate began to complain of the unaggressive performance of the Senate majority and of its apparent reluctance to do battle with the Administration, White continues:

> The non-Senatorial Democrats began to make complaint that Democratic unity in the Senate was all very well; but what of the millions of non-Senatorial Democrats as against the few in the Institution? What of the national, the state, the county and city and ward organizations? What sort of record was being made in the Senate for these sinews, these repositories of the blood and guts, of the party? Who could win a campaign in '56 on co-operation? [42]

White's principal explanation of this performance, which he thinks involved a more than ordinary amount of bipartisan accommodation, is that Johnson, partly unconsciously but partly by design, was reestablishing and even extending the Senate's "historic claim" to an "independent political life." [43] There is no reason to quarrel with this explanation. The reality of the Senate as a group and as an object of loyalty is clear. But, granting this point, one may yet inquire whether

---

[41] White, *Citadel*, p. 103.
[42] *Ibid.*, pp. 103–104.
[43] *Ibid.*, pp. 101 ff.

it was the only or even the major factor, especially as the House majority presented much the same appearance. Many motives could be assigned to Johnson in the situation and many undoubtedly were guiding him, but, although he was probably not guilty of an excess of zeal for the national party record, it is clear that his range of alternatives was narrow. A new Majority Leader, relatively junior in Senate service, working with a divided party and the narrowest of majorities, yet ambitious to make a record, would not have been very impressive in a policy of relentless attack upon a popular Administration. But, given the nature of the Senate party and particularly, perhaps, the Democratic party, any Leader of a truncated majority who was more disposed toward positive action than toward obstruction or inaction would have been pushed toward a moderate position because he lacked the outside leverage that would permit his doing otherwise. Even a popular President of the other party could not, except in the most extreme sort of crisis, adequately provide such leverage. The main stream of politics in the United States is presidential politics, from Washington to the whistle stops. A legislative leader may not play this game very consciously or with great effectiveness, but he can rarely ignore it to the extent of calling for unity in the Congressional party on the grounds of loyalty to a President who belongs to the other side.[44]

Johnson's "resources," therefore, were concentrated on Capitol Hill. There, even had he not had political and personal ties to the Southern wing of the party, he could hardly have avoided being drawn toward the Southerners in any effort to develop the semblance of a program likely to be acceptable to most Senate Democrats. The weakness of even this sort of effort at avoiding a "do-nothing" appearance was evident, however, when, in November, 1955, shortly before the opening of the second session of the Eighty-fourth Congress, Johnson an-

---

[44] Rarely can an opposition leader say, as did the Republican Floor Leader during the House "debate" on emergency banking legislation in March, 1933: "The house is burning down, and the President of the United States says this is the way to put out the fire." (Quoted in Pendleton Herring, *Presidential Leadership*, New York: Farrar and Rinehart, 1940, pp. 57–58.) Moreover, if this analysis of the dilemma of a truncated majority is valid, more than partisan advocacy may be cited in justification of Eisenhower's pleas for a Republican Congress in the elections after 1952. Without a majority of his own persuasion the President lacked a valuable instrument of governing. In this connection it is worth noting that no public or journalistic protests greeted Eisenhower's requests in these campaigns. Since the days of the allegedly widespread criticism of Wilson for the same action in 1918, attitudes apparently have altered. The continuance of truncated majorities in successive elections from 1958 onward, however, would suggest that popular appreciation of the handicaps imposed on a President by a party distribution of this type is still inadequate.

nounced a thirteen-point "program." Although he apparently felt sufficiently sure of his position in the Senate to make such an announcement, his reach did not go much beyond the north wing of the Capitol. In the House Speaker Rayburn indicated that he had not been
consulted about the "program" proclaimed by his Senate colleague.[45]
The actors were different, and the setting was not identical, but the
situation was reminiscent of the Taft debacle of 1948. These events,
moreover, were of a piece with the initial miscarriage of the Democratic National Committee's proposal at the opening of the Eighty-
fifth Congress to include the leaders of the Congressional party in an
advisory committee created to develop a party program. The negative
response from Speaker Rayburn, Senator Johnson, and their immediate
associates had its roots in 1957 in the dilemma of the truncated majority; the divergence of Johnson and Rayburn two years earlier had
essentially the same source.

CASES AND TRENDS

The interpretations offered in the preceding paragraphs go well beyond the data of the Eighty-first Congress. Though they are con-
jectural and must therefore be treated as subject to change or total
rejection on the basis of further research, they are presented quite deliberately, on the assumption that the value of a single case lies not in
its uniqueness but in the light it may throw on underlying patterns
and general tendencies.

In the simplest terms the argument of these pages has been that the
Congressional party has reality as a group, has a determinate behavioral structure; that within the limitations of its peculiar characteristics
suggested by the notion of the mediate group, this structure in both
houses is focused chiefly upon the roles of the principal elective leaders;
that these leaders and hence also the parties in the two houses achieve
their full function when they are based on majorities in the Congress
of the same persuasion as the President; that there is a functional interdependence between the majority leaders in Congress and a President of the same party; and that the Congressional parties and their
leaders are of limited significance—within each of the chambers and

---

[45] *New York Times*, November 22 and 23, 1955. In the Eighty-fifth Congress
the deepening foreign policy crisis after October, 1957, and the onset of economic
recession seemed to provide enough leverage to the Democratic Leaders, enough
centripetal pressure, to permit the development of a fairly coherent program, but
many of the characteristic earmarks of the truncated majority were still evident.

in the relations between the two houses—when the President is tied to a Congressional minority, or when the majority on Capitol Hill is truncated, or when the Congressional party is "out of power" at both ends of Pennsylvania Avenue.

It may be, of course, that this argument is valid at most for the Eighty-first Congress, that the pattern would not hold for subsequent sessions of the national legislature. The tendencies identified here could have been entirely a product of the conditions prevailing in the years 1949 and 1950, of the personalities in both parties and in the White House, and of a variety of entirely accidental factors. They may not have been a set of responses to continuing and compelling features of contemporary national affairs, responses affected only in detail by the unique aspects of this Congress. However, reasons lying outside the events of 1949 and 1950 permit the assumption that the pattern sketched in these pages is not unique. These can be reduced to the proposition that in general outline the pattern is consistent with the most fundamental trend of the American political system in the twentieth century, the emergence of the Presidency as the pivot of the whole enterprise.

At the turn of the century Woodrow Wilson saw in the consequences of the Spanish-American War the re-emergence of the President.[46] Writing seven years later, he expressed himself even more confidently. "The President," he said, "can never again be the mere domestic figure he has been throughout so large a part of our history. . . . Our President must always, henceforth, be one of the great powers of the world, whether he act greatly and wisely or not. . . . We have but begun to see the presidential office in this light; but it is the light which will more and more beat upon it, and more and more determine its character and its effect upon the politics of the nation." [47] No more perceptive insight into the future has come from the pen of an observer of our politics. Though Wilson did not then anticipate the impact of domestic changes upon the Presidency, his projections for the new importance of foreign policy were uncannily accurate. What is more, he saw that changes in the Presidency would of necessity produce far-reaching effects upon the whole system.

The relevant point here is that, given this trend, it is reasonable to assume that there have been consequent changes in the functioning of the Congress, in the Congressional party, and in its leadership roles. As controversies such as that over the so-called Bricker amendment

---

[46] Woodrow Wilson, *Congressional Government*, New York: Meridian Edition, 1956, pp. 22–23.

[47] Wilson, *Constitutional Government in the United States*, p. 78.

demonstrate, the trend with respect to the Presidency is not completely understood or, if understood, not fully accepted. Moreover, a number of men who had long been participants in Congressional affairs indicated in interviews that they saw no major changes in the leaders' roles over the past three or four decades. Though their judgments must command respect, their views are not astonishing. If the more obvious changes in the Presidency are recent and their acceptance even more so, small wonder that subtler and more grudging alterations in the legislature should not be fully recognized.

For the currently accepted practices of the Presidency, especially in relation to the Congress, are very new. It is not only, as Corwin has observed, that "The present-day role of the President as policy determiner in the legislative field is largely the creation of the two Roosevelts and Woodrow Wilson. . . ." [48] The scale, the methods, and, above all, the structure of expectations have changed even more recently. Commenting on the view that President Eisenhower was resuming a "customary" practice when, early in 1954, he presented the Congress with a comprehensive, detailed legislative agenda, Richard Neustadt pointed out that this "custom" was less than a decade old. [49] Scope, detail, and open acknowledgment distinguish the current practices from precedents that can be found as far back as Jefferson.

These changes have their recognized counterparts in the Congress, especially the scope of legislative preoccupations. Three of the top elective leaders in the House, both Republican and Democratic, in interviews pointed to the magnitude of the problems confronting it as the most basic change in the Congress over the past 30 years and added that this had vastly complicated the tasks they were called upon to perform. Such an increase in scope and growing recognition of the complexity of the consequences following upon Congressional action understandably have led to readier acceptance by all participants of a coordinated view of both program and results. In consequence, the kinds of interdependencies that have been emphasized in these pages, while not eliminating conflict, have yet had a wide acceptance in fact. Presidential initiatives that a few years ago would have stirred up a tempest of protest like that created by a Jacksonian veto today not only are taken for granted but also are expected. Specification and advocacy of a legislative program, once the distinguishing mark of "strong"

---

[48] Corwin, *The President*, p. 321.

[49] Neustadt, "Presidency and Legislation: Planning the President's Program," p. 981.

Presidents, has become an institutionalized activity. As Neustadt has pointed out in comment on these developments,

> . . . from the congressional point of view, 'service,' not domination is the reality behind these presidential undertakings. In practical effect, they represent a means whereby Congress can gain from the outside what comes hard from within: a handy and official guide to the wants of its biggest customer; an advance formulation of main issues at each session; a work-load ready-to-hand for every legislative committee; a borrowing of presidential prestige for most major bills—and thus a boosting of publicity-potentials in both sponsorship and opposition.[50]

These are the sorts of factors that have contributed importance to the leaders' roles as centers of communication and have both complicated and augmented their positions by emphasizing the expectation that those of the President's party will be his spokesmen.[51] As long as the relations between legislative party leaders and the President carry mutual advantages, these expectations are likely to persist undiminished. The longer they continue, the more likely they are to become accepted, institutionalized fact.[52]

The consistency between these trends and the data on the Eighty-first Congress does not give to the inferences here proposed a validity beyond the period that they cover. It does, however, lend strength to the presumption that the patterns they describe are not unique. Granting this point, they still indicate central tendencies rather than completely conforming behavior, as the evidence in many of the tables amply shows. Nor do they mean that Americans will awake some morning to find that they have inherited a system of party government on the British model. They reveal important tendencies, indigenous to American constitutional and political practice, tendencies subject to a continuous evolution the limits of which have surely not been reached.

---

[50] *Ibid.*, p. 1014.

[51] During the Eighty-first Congress the Majority Leaders of both Senate and House, as well as the chairmen of a number of standing committees, including the House Committee on Rules, regularly checked with staff in the Budget Bureau or the White House for the current Administration stand on pending bills. Richard E. Neustadt, "Presidency and Legislation: The Growth of Central Clearance," *American Political Science Review*, Vol. 48, no. 3 (September 1954), p. 662.

[52] One should perhaps note the possibility, however, that a prolonged hiatus might delay this development. Between 1946 and 1958 three of the six Congresses were of the truncated-majority type. Two of these, the Eighty-fourth and Eighty-fifth, may have reflected no more than the skewing effect of a presidential personality not conspicuously identified with partisanship. But their consequences for the governing process might be the same.

appendix

THE ANALYSIS PROCEDURE

The structural analysis. The procedure followed in identifying and analyzing the bloc structures of the two parties was essentially that developed by Stuart A. Rice for political bodies of 25 to 30 members.[1] The elements of that method are tabulating the frequency of voting agreement between all possible pairs of members of a legislative body and identifying by inspection those clusters or blocs of at least a designated minimum size, but including less than the whole number of legislators, among all of whom, pair by pair, the rate of agreement is equal to or greater than some designated minimum figure. Attributes of the blocs can then be determined from data on the personal characteristics of the members and on their constituencies. A bloc is thus defined as a cluster of interrelated pairs. This is the definition underlying the present study.

Four years after the appearance of Rice's ingenious analysis Herman C. Beyle published a report in which he attempted to refine Rice's method and to improve upon its techniques.[2] Beyle's criticism of Rice's method was twofold. First, he objected to the arbitrarily designated minimum frequency of agreement between pairs of legislators

---

[1] Stuart A. Rice, "The Identification of Blocs in Small Political Bodies," *American Political Science Review,* Vol. 21, no. 3 (August 1927), pp. 619–627; reprinted in *Quantitative Methods in Politics,* New York: Knopf, 1928, chap. 16.

[2] Herman C. Beyle, *Identification and Analysis of Attribute-Cluster-Blocs,* Chicago: University of Chicago Press, 1931.

as the basis for admitting them to bloc membership. Second, he deplored the failure to retain a record of the substance of the voting agreements within blocs and the consequent exclusive reliance upon external data for identifying the basis of the clustering. This latter objection was a reasonable one, and supplying the deficiency it implied was not a matter of great difficulty. The present study followed Beyle in retaining these data on the substance of intrabloc agreement, although the procedure here was slightly different.

In attempting to avoid an arbitrary minimum rate of agreement as the criterion for bloc membership, Beyle devised an "index of significant cohesion of pairs" on the basis of a probability argument.[3] Unhappily, as a number of critics demonstrated, the assumptions underlying this argument were untenable, and the index was essentially spurious.[4] It is not used in the present investigation, and no use was made of a series of related "indexes" designed to measure the attributes of blocs, since these were based on the original invalid measure.

At the level of technique, however, Beyle improved on Rice's inspection procedure for identifying clusters by introducing the matrix for arraying frequencies.[5] His matrix is essentially like that in Figure 1, except that in some applications he separated prevailing from nonprevailing agreements. In the present study it seemed more appropriate to deal with this attribute at the stage of describing the bloc rather than at the pair level. Beyle also retained a number of structural data by distinguishing a bloc from its nucleus or nuclei (the highly cohesive small cluster or clusters of interrelated pairs around which a bloc develops), by identifying the fringe (legislators having a minimum rate of agreement with some but not all the members of a bloc), and by taking note of overlapping blocs.

Stripped of Beyle's spurious probability calculations, the Rice-Beyle method is essentially descriptive, involving no complicated assumptions and no highly refined statistical manipulations. It stays close to the original data. In following it, however, one is obliged to pay a price, namely, forgoing most of the refined techniques of statistical in-

---

[3] *Ibid.*, pp. 29–32, 53–55.

[4] The most effective criticism of this aspect of Beyle's work is Samuel P. Hayes, Jr., "Probability and Beyle's 'Index of Cohesion,'" *Journal of Social Psychology*, Vol. 9, no. 2 (May 1938), pp. 161–167. An insightful discussion of Beyle and some features of Rice's work can be found in Warren E. Miller, "A Study of Some Statistical Techniques for Investigating Legislative Voting Behavior," unpublished M.A. thesis, University of Oregon, 1950.

[5] Beyle also proposed a graphic device for identifying blocs which was not found useful for handling large numbers of cases and which is unnecessary when the number of legislators is small.

ference that are at least theoretically possible with more elaborate methods, some of which will be discussed shortly. In the present investigation avoidance of over-abstraction from the basic voting data was considered more important than statistical elegance.

The first step in the analysis was to prepare for each roll call in the Congress an index card showing its date, session, location in the *Record*, substance, and the vote in the chamber as a whole and within each party. Other classificatory notations were added to these as the study progressed, such as the party indexes of cohesion and the subject-matter classifications, and the cards were used for basic reference at all stages of the work.

The machine procedure developed for the bloc analysis could not efficiently handle simultaneously more than 74 roll calls.[6] It was thus necessary to adopt a means of selecting from among the total roll calls. What was required was an objective criterion that would also be relevant to the purposes of the study. Subject-matter categories were rejected on the ground that classification on these lines was almost certain to be unreliable and subjective. Since the immediate concern was with variations in structure and since the voting structure of the two legislative parties in each chamber was the principal focus of curiosity, the decision was made to use level of party unity, measured by the Rice index of cohesion, as the criterion for selection.[7] Adoption of this procedure meant, of course, that no bipartisan blocs would be identified, though it would be possible to identify blocs in each party that were conspicuously engaged in coalition voting across party lines.

When the indexes of cohesion were calculated for all roll calls, excepting quorum calls, votes on private bills, and a handful of votes in

---

[6] The machine employed was the I.B.M. Card-Programmed Electronic Calculator, or C.P.C., consisting of four individual but integrated machine units, an accounting machine or tabulator, an electronic calculating unit, an auxiliary storage unit, and a gang summary punch. Machines that have appeared more recently, notably the I.B.M. 650, would be more versatile. The equipment was made available through the courtesy of the Watson Scientific Computing Laboratory operated at Columbia University in collaboration with International Business Machines Corporation.

[7] The index is described in *Quantitative Methods in Politics*, pp. 208–209. Arithmetically it is the difference between the per cent for and the per cent against a given motion, a 50–50 split giving an index of zero and unanimity an index of 100. The probability assumptions underlying this index are not beyond challenge. (Compare Miller, "A Study of Some Statistical Techniques for Investigating Legislative Voting Behavior," pp. 29–32.) However, since it has become a conventionally accepted measure and since no alternative of equal simplicity was available, the index was adopted.

each chamber which the whole body subsequently reversed,[8] the roll calls of each party were listed by session in order from the lowest to the highest index of cohesion. Successive sets of votes were then drawn from each list to form the bases for the several bloc analyses. In the Senate in each session a low-cohesion set of 74 votes was drawn for each party, and a set next higher in cohesion, with one exception also numbering 74, was subsequently drawn. (The exception was in the Democratic votes of the second session; only 73 "high-cohesion" votes were used because the next two higher indexes were identical.) Because there were fewer votes in the House from which to choose, a single set of 74 votes of lowest cohesion was drawn from the roll calls of each party in the first session. In the second session a low-cohesion set of 74 votes was designated in each party and smaller high-cohesion sets covering 62 Democratic and 66 Republican votes, that is, all the remaining votes on which the party was not unanimous. In both chambers the votes of highest cohesion were thus excluded. Alternatively it would have been possible to build the high-cohesion sets downward from the unanimous votes, excluding those in the middle. Though this would have accentuated the contrasts between sets, it would have revealed little about the internal structure of the parties on the high-cohesion votes, since the sets would have been composed preponderantly of votes on which the party was unanimous or nearly so.

In coding the responses of the senators and representatives on these roll calls an effort was made to minimize the factor of absences by recording all announced preferences as if they were votes. An "absence" thus meant that the *Congressional Record* contained no indication of the nonvoting member's preferences on the motion. The coded responses were then punched on cards, one for each man in each set, that is four cards for each senator seated throughout the Congress and three for each representative.

Each of the sets of cards was then processed through the machine. The responses on the first card in the deck were stored on counters, and these were compared, column by column, with each of the remaining cards. The agreements between each pair of cards were totaled and printed. When the first card had been compared with each of the others, it was removed from the machine and the responses on the second card were entered in the storage counters and compared with those on each of the remaining cards. The process was repeated until every card in the deck had been compared with each of the others.

---

[8] There were 10 votes in the Senate excluded on the basis of subsequent reversal and 3 in the House.

The clerical labor involved in manual handling of this stage of the Rice method, determining the number of agreements between all pairs of legislators, was the principal reason for his restricting the procedure to "small political bodies" of not more than 25 or 30 members, and Beyle described this as "the one laborious step in the procedure." Both contemplated the use of mechanical sorting equipment as a short cut, but of course neither anticipated the advantages to be had from handling the whole process by electronic computation.[9] When one is dealing with a body of the size of the Senate or one of its parties, Beyle's characterization of this as the most laborious step in the analysis is sound. However, in analyzing a group as large as the House or one of its parties, the identification of blocs by developing and inspecting a matrix becomes almost equally tedious, though it remains manageable.

Once the paired agreements were tabulated, those scores that were too low to be considered in constructing the matrix were eliminated. As noted earlier, the choice of this cut-off point is an arbitrary one. Beyle's attempt to base it on a calculation of significance cannot be accepted. Nevertheless, the choice need not be haphazard. If it is set high, the blocs will be relatively small and fewer members of the body will have scores of the minimum magnitude, but the number of votes on which all members of a bloc are agreed will be relatively high. If it is set low, the blocs will be larger and the matrix system more inclusive, but the number of unanimous votes within blocs will be smaller. The logic of the method assumes that these unanimous votes are in some degree indicative of concerted action by the members of the bloc, but it permits no precise determination of a point at which the number of these complete agreements is to be regarded as adventitious. Caution therefore dictates that the cut-off point not be set so low as to deny even common-sense meaning to the agreed votes. Rice used minimum paired agreement rates of 60 and 80 per cent in his study of the New Jersey Senate. Varying cut-off points were chosen in the present study. In the Senate sets agreements on more than half of the roll calls were considered. In the House agreements on 46 or more in the sets containing 74 votes were retained; in the two high-cohesion sets of the second session scores of 52 or higher on the 62 Democratic votes and scores of 56 or higher on the 66 Republican votes were used. The higher cut-off points on the House sets reduced somewhat the labor involved in constructing the matrixes without misrepresenting the essential voting structures of the parties.

---

[9] Rice, *Quantitative Methods in Politics*, p. 238; Beyle, *Identification and Analysis of Attribute-Cluster-Blocs*, p. 167.

For each set the scores of at least the minimum magnitude were listed on the tabulating machine in descending order, and the construction of the matrixes was begun. After some experimentation it was found that the procedure most likely to reveal all of the blocs as they appeared was to enter the highest pair score in the appropriate cells at the upper left corner of the matrix, on either side of the diagonal (Figure 1), and to postpone the insertion of subsequent pair scores unless they occurred with one of the men already listed on the matrix. (The code numbers of legislators were, of course, entered only when their first scores were posted.) This involved continual review of the postponed scores as additional pairs were entered, but it reduced the labor required for inspecting the matrix at each score level to detect the emergence of blocs. This inspection cannot be made wholly effortless. In bodies as small as the Senate parties it is comparatively simple. The parties in the House, however, are large enough to make this part of the operation increasingly time-consuming as the matrix is enlarged. A series of notes was maintained at each score level on the appearance of the matrix, on the size and composition of the blocs and nuclei, and on any peculiarities of the bloc development that were observed. These permitted quick reconstruction of the blocs at various stages of their growth and checks on the accuracy of the clerical work.

With high-speed computational equipment it may be possible to perform the operation of matrix construction by machine. If this were done, however, some loss probably would occur, since the process of constructing the matrix manually is likely to produce fruitful insights and suggestive questions for further analysis. If the purposes of the inquiry can tolerate loss of this sort, automatic identification of the blocs might save considerable labor. However, if the investigator feels that he can afford to separate himself so far from his data, he may find it even more appropriate to drop the essential Rice method in favor of one of the more rigorous techniques, such as factor analysis.

When the various blocs had been identified, it was a simple matter to list the votes of each member by running the original I.B.M. cards through a tabulator. From these listings the agreements common to all members of a bloc could be determined easily by inspection. As noted in the text, at this stage these agreements were defined to include not only votes on which the bloc was unanimous but also all those on which less than half the members were unrecorded and the remainder were unanimous, thus reducing the effect of "absences" while providing a fuller indication of the voting tendencies of the bloc. Personal and constituency characteristics of the bloc members were determined by the same kind of procedure. Reference to the cards descriptive of the various votes permitted calculating the number of common agreements on the prevailing side of the chamber, on the side of the party majority, and similar descriptive information.

Although the Rice method as used in this study does not permit much in the way of rigorous statistical inference, it was found useful to set up a few summary figures for use in describing the blocs and their members. The rank of each member in a bloc was determined by taking the mean of his scores with all other members of the bloc. To describe the relative cohesion of the bloc as a whole, the simplest figure seemed to be the mean of the paired agreements of all members. Since there was no intention to base further calculations on the mean, measures of dispersion were not regularly calculated. However, the mean score of a bloc was not used in the description when inspection indicated that it seriously misrepresented the distribution. These distributions characteristically were skewed in the same direction, of course, because uniformly the blocs grew at an accelerating rate at the lower score levels regardless of the pattern of their growth at the early stages.

Given the availability of the paired agreement scores, it was possible to perform a number of specialized analyses for particular subgroups within the parties. Matrixes corresponding to those constructed for the party as a whole were set up for designated groupings, such as the seniority leaders, the elective leaders, the policy committees, and the like. The data were also used for analyzing the voting behavior of particular pairs of legislators, such as the Floor Leaders and individual seniority leaders; for examining the relations of a single role, such as the Floor Leader's, with a large number of rank-and-file legislators; and for identifying a number of special voting patterns, such as those of the state delegations and the party committee contingents in the House.

The party orthodoxy index. In order to characterize the degree to which individual legislators showed a general tendency to adhere to party majorities outside of the sets used for the bloc analyses, an index of party orthodoxy was set up for each session. Based on all the "yea and nay" votes of the session, excluding those on private bills, regardless of whether majorities of the two parties were opposed, the index was designed to take systematic account of "absences" and to assign different weights to votes and to the preferences of nonvoting members.[10] The votes of each legislator on each roll call were scored ac-

---

[10] The familiar "party unity" score developed by the *Congressional Quarterly* is based entirely on votes on which majorities of the two parties are opposed and takes no account of "absences" or of the recorded preferences of nonvoting members.

cording to the following weights: Voted with the party majority, 5; paired or announced on the side of the party majority, 4; no preference recorded ("absent"), 3; paired or announced against the party majority, 2; voted against the party majority, one.[11] The mean of these scores for each man was used as his index of party orthodoxy for the session. The party voting tendencies of blocs or other groupings in the parties were determined by computing the means of the indexes of their members for the session.

The Administration support index. The tendency of each senator and representative to vote with or against the Administration was characterized by a similar index. Weighting was done in exactly the same way as in the case of the party orthodoxy index, but constructing this measure presented special problems, since it required making a selection from among the total roll calls on some defensibly objective basis. The criteria of selection were as follows: automatically included were votes on overriding presidential vetoes, votes on presidential reorganization plans, and, in the Senate, votes on the confirmation of presidential nominations and on the ratification of treaties; other votes were included if the public record revealed an express presidential preference concerning the precise content at stake in the vote. For this purpose the *Congressional Record,* the *Congressional Quarterly Almanac,* and the *New York Times* were examined for indications of presidential preferences in messages to Congress, in communications to individual members of the legislature, in public speeches, in press conferences, and in reports of conferences with Congressional leaders. Using these criteria the following numbers of roll calls were designated as Administration support votes: In the Senate, 100 in the first session and 90 in the second; in the House, 56 in the first session and 73 in the second. (For some purposes, noted in the text, the second session total in the House was reduced to 59 by eliminating 14 highly repetitive tactical votes dealing with the F.E.P.C. bill.)

The chief problem with an index of this sort is that the observer cannot validly distinguish between publicly expressed preferences that the President intends to be taken seriously and those that are merely gestures. Presumably any chief executive at any level of government asks the legislature for some things that he not only doesn't expect to get but would be distressed to have granted. In addition, it is almost

---

[11] A system of weights from 4 to 0 might have had a slightly better empirical "feel" but for the fact that the "absence" was felt to be the neutral point of the index and assigning it a weight of 2 would have given the appearance of two "zero" points. Giving a score of 0 to "absences" and using positive and negative numbers for the other positions would have increased the likelihood of error in computing.

impossible to assign weights among those presidential requests that one is fairly confident are matters of serious concern to the Administration.

Under these circumstances it was a matter of great good fortune that late in the research an opportunity arose to examine a list of roll calls that was maintained by the White House staff during the Eighty-first Congress. This list, whose objective was essentially the same as that of the index, covered all of the first session and the first six months of the second. The list had been used for the purpose of scoring every member of Congress. The scoring system employed differed from that on the index, in that no distinction was made between votes and paired or announced positions and some votes were weighted more heavily than others. "Absences" were handled essentially as they were in the index. As would have been expected, the index list was a good deal longer than the "inside" one, even in the first session, but the longer list contained all but a few of the roll calls included on the shorter one.

The availability of this material offered an unusual opportunity for a rough validation of the index. Accordingly, the rankings of the elective and seniority leaders of both parties in both chambers and in both sessions were arrived at on the basis of each list and scoring system, and the sets of rankings were compared by means of the Spearman rank order correlation coefficient. As Table 64 indicates, the rankings

Table 64

CORRELATIONS OF RANKINGS OF HOUSE AND SENATE LEADERS ON TWO MEASURES OF ADMINISTRATION SUPPORT, 81ST CONGRESS

	Democratic Leaders	Republican Leaders
Senate		
First Session	+.83	+.91
Second Session	+.88	+.95
House		
First Session	+.86	+.68
Second Session	+.90	+.81

based on the two lists of votes were closely similar. Although the coefficient for the Republican leaders in the first session is considerably lower than the others, it is reasonable to infer that the two ranking systems were getting at the same basic tendencies. Of course, the validity of neither is beyond question. The White House list, though it was based on better information than an outsider would have available, was not constructed by the President himself, and staff members inevitably are not perfectly informed on presidential strategies and intentions. Nevertheless, the results of these comparisons afford a basis for confidence that the Administration support index used in this study is not seriously misleading. They also lend encouragement to the possibility that the same procedure as was used in constructing the index could be applied in the study of other Congresses. An Administration that was less explicit in stating its preferences might provide fewer reliable clues to the investigator, but this should not completely invalidate the technique.

Alternative methods. The modified Rice-Beyle method on which this study was based has the considerable advantages of keeping close to the data and of requiring few assumptions in manipulating them. As noted earlier, however, it is less elegant and permits little in the way of technical statistical inference. Under some circumstances and for investigations with somewhat different requirements a method involving greater statistical flexibility and rigor might be more useful.[12]

The method of factor analysis has much to recommend it, especially as it permits using an explicit and sophisticated model of legislative voting. The method has been little used, however. Perhaps the chief reason for this is that it is not readily adapted to handling large masses of data.[13] With high-speed computational equipment it may be possible to overcome this handicap. As in all methods of this sort, however, one might still have a serious problem of assigning concrete meaning to the principal factors after they were identified.

Closely related is the technique of "orthometric" analysis, developed by Tryon as an improvement on factor analysis for the identification of clusters emerging from batteries of psychological tests. The method was later applied by him to the analysis of data of the census type.[14] As in the case of more conventional methods of factor analysis, it is a matter of question whether the gains in rigor possible through this technique would be accompanied by equal gains in relevance.

A clearly significant and useful alternative method is that of cumu-

---

[12] A good discussion of several of these approaches is contained in Duncan MacRae, Jr., *Dimensions of Congressional Voting,* Berkeley & Los Angeles: University of California Press, 1958, pp. 300–308.

[13] Chester W. Harris, "A Factor Analysis of Selected Senate Roll Calls, 80th Congress," *Educational and Psychological Measurement,* Vol. 8, no. 4 (Winter 1948), pp. 582–591, based his study on only 10 votes.

[14] Robert C. Tryon, *Cluster Analysis,* Ann Arbor: Edwards Brothers, 1939, and *Identification of Social Areas by Cluster Analysis,* Berkeley and Los Angeles: University of California Press, 1955.

lative scales.[15] This procedure shares with the method of bloc analysis the virtue of keeping close to the data and, as applied by MacRae and others, rests on similar sorts of assumptions, since votes that will not scale almost certainly will not produce sizable blocs with any degree of cohesion. The results of this method, as it was applied by MacRae to selected roll calls of the House in the Eighty-first Congress, at many points resemble those of the present study. Intercorrelations of scales such as these may permit better summary descriptions of blocs than does direct reference to common agreements, as in this study. It is not clear, however, whether scaling will independently identify a structure built around a bloc or nucleus at the intersection of a number of choice dimensions as clearly as will bloc analysis. Scaling, moreover, does not seem to carry with it many of the byproduct values of paired agreements, by means of which more restricted relationships can be examined. On the basis of existing experience it may be wise to regard these two approaches as complementary rather than as alternative. Further use of both may reveal more clearly the particular strengths and limitations of each and may permit more conclusive judgment concerning the circumstances under which one should be used to supplement the other.

---

[15] In addition to MacRae, *Dimensions of Congressional Voting*, and the literature cited there, see Hugh D. Price, "Are Southern Democrats Different? An Application of Scale Analysis to Senate Voting Patterns," paper delivered at the 53rd annual meeting of the American Political Science Association, New York City, September 1957.

INDEX

Absence rate, definition of, 53f., 323
  leaders', 107f., 169, 188, 205ff., 209,
  215f., 219f., 223, 225, 239f., 241
Acheson, Dean, 133n
Administration, support of, 61f., 71, 81,
  86, 88, 91, 110f., 118f., 160, 163,
  184, 191, 205, 208f., 218, 224, 241,
  283ff., 298, 303
  support index, 60, 327ff.
  see also President
Agreement, definition of, 58n, 325
Agriculture, 24, 27, 88, 180, 229, 239
Aiken, George, 86, 138
Albert, Carl, 150, 301
Alexander, De Alva S., 202n
Allen, Leo, 235
American Medical Association, 23, 25,
  34
Anderson, Clinton, 102
Anderson, William, 6
Appropriations, 21f., 34, 36f.
Arends, Leslie, 17, 199, 208, 228–230

Bailey, Stephen K., 28n, 97n, 120n,
  172n, 259n, 260n
Bales, Robert F., 43n
Barkley, Alben, 17, 306n
Barth, Alan, 8n
Basing-point prices, 27f., 34
Beyle, Herman C., 45n, 320ff.
Bloc, definition of, 47
  types of, 54
Blocs, House Democratic, agreements
  in, 157ff., 164ff., 167ff.
  House Republican, agreements in,
  179f., 188ff.
  numbering of, 57n
  procedures for analyzing, 320ff.
  Senate Democratic, agreements in,
  58f., 68ff., 90f.
  Senate Republican, agreements in,
  78f., 80f., 87ff., 90f.
Boggs, Hale, 165
Bone, Hugh A., 102n, 133n
Bonner, Herbert, 169

331

Border-state legislators, 57n, 67n, 163f.
Borgotta, Edgar F., 44n
Brewster, Owen, 70, 76, 102
Bricker, John, 20, 31, 70, 78
  Amendment, 4, 304ff., 317f.
Bridge voter, 162, 164
Bridges, Styles, 33, 112ff., 139
Burns, James M., 8n, 297n, 298n
Butler, Hugh, 101, 124f.
Butler, Paul, 301
Byrd, Harry, 34, 284

Cain, Harry, 20, 34, 70
Campaign Committees, Congressional,
    199, 231, 301
  Senatorial, 102, 125, 301
Cannon, Clarence, 34
Capehart, Homer, 20, 70, 78, 127
Case, Clifford, 189, 277
Caucus, House, 199
  Senate, 17, 40, 101
Chavez, Dennis, 137, 141
Clayton Act, 40
Cloture, see Filibuster
Coalition voting, 18, 31, 35, 37, 61f.,
    66f., 70f., 76f., 80, 86, 89, 148,
    161, 171, 182f., 188, 229, 277, 283,
    322
Cohesion, classification of votes by, 48
  fluidity and, 178n
  index of, 48f., 322f.
  in House committees, 270ff.
  in state delegations, 251ff.
Committee of the Whole, House, 204,
    208
Committees, Congressional, 12–13,
    133ff., 140ff., 200f., 249, 269–278,
    310
  on committees, House, 199, 200, 203,
    231ff.
  on committees, Senate, 101
Commodity Credit Corporation, 22
Conference, see Caucus
Congress, methods for studying, 10–13,
    44f., 320–330
  role of, 1–7, 9, 318f.
Connally, Tom, 137, 259n
Constituency, influence of, 69, 71, 91,
    109, 119, 164, 166, 171, 180, 191,
    196, 210f., 217, 218f.

Constitutional reform, 8
Corwin, Edward S., 8, 290n, 318
Cox, Eugene, 24, 30, 160

Dahl, Robert A., 108n
Davis, James, 165
Dawson, William, 264
Defense, Department of, 22
  Production Act, 37f.
Democratic Advisory Committee (Coun-
    cil), 300ff., 316
Democratic National Committee, 301
Democratic party, divisions in, 17–18,
    49f., 147f., 205
  House, voting structure of, 150–172
  Senate, voting structure of, 50–72
Displaced persons, 28, 32
Donnell, Forrest, 77f., 114
Doughton, Robert, 241
Douglas, Helen G., 267
Douglas, Paul H., 28, 32, 37, 135

Eberharter, Herman, 18
Education, aid to, 21
Eisenhower, Dwight D., 296n, 304ff.,
    312, 314, 318
Election, 1946, 16, 313
  1948, 16–18, 22, 311f.
  1950, 38f., 303
  1952, 303
  margin, voting and, 211ff., 216ff.,
    219ff., 225, 268
Elective leaders, House, 198ff., 204,
    230ff., 248, 259, 289ff., 300ff.
  Senate, 99ff., 122ff., 289ff., 300ff.
  see also Floor Leader, Whip, Speaker
Electoral college, 30
Elliott, William Y., 8n
Executive branch, functions of, 2–7

Factor analysis, 329
Fair Employment Practices Commission,
    29f., 33, 131, 159, 160, 163, 180,
    188, 229
Federalism, 5, 9
Ferguson, Homer, 114, 305
Festinger, Leon, 44n
Filibuster, 18, 33, 34, 131
Finletter, Thomas K., 8n
Fisher, O. C., 165

Floor Leader, House, 17, 198f., 202–227, 237–246, 281f., 285ff., 293, 300ff.
  Senate, 17, 74n, 94, 98, 101, 104–117, 118ff., 126, 130, 132, 135ff., 144, 281f., 285ff., 293, 299ff., 304ff.
Follett, Mary P., 232n
Foreign aid, 20, 26, 33, 35f., 40, 88
Foreign policy, Republican disunity on, 78f., 88, 120, 150, 179f., 229, 239, 310
Fringe, definition of, 47

George, Walter, 26, 36, 137, 141, 287, 305
Golden, James, 276
Gossett, Ed, 30, 165
Grassmuck, George L., 310n
Griffith, Ernest S., 7n
Gross, H. R., 179, 276
Gurney, Chan, 41, 86

Hall, Leonard, 199
Halleck, Charles, 17, 199, 207f., 227, 233, 235, 244, 281f., 308
Hardy, Porter, Jr., 169
Harlow, Ralph V., 202n
Harris, Chester W., 329n
Hasbrouck, P. D., 195n
Havenner, Franck, 214, 266
Hayden, Carl, 102, 137, 141
Hayes, Samuel P., 321n
Haynes, George H., 103n, 117n
Hazlitt, Henry, 8n
Health insurance, 22f.
Herring, Pendleton, 315n
Hickenlooper, Bourke, 76
Hill, Lister, 303
Hoffman, Clare, 189
Holcombe, Arthur N., 98n, 291n
Homans, George C., 95n
Housing, 20, 23f., 31, 70
Huber, Walter, 171f.
Huitt, Ralph K., 44n
Hull, Merlin, 189
Humphrey, Hubert, 107

Interest groups, 6, 69, 71, 171, 196, 249, 266, 294
Internal Security Act, 38, 158

Isolates, definition of, 47, 54n
  House, 147, 185
  Senate Democrats, 54–57, 66f.
  Senate Republicans, 76f., 86f.
Ives, Irving, 16

Jenner, William, 38, 70, 78
Jennings, Helen H., 44n
Johnson, Edwin, 70, 137, 141
Johnson, Lyndon, 112f., 301f., 307, 314ff.
Johnston, Olin, 137, 287

Kefauver, Estes, 33
Kelley, Harold H., 95n
Kem, James, 40
Key, V. O., Jr., 6n, 9n, 59, 150n, 165n, 283n
Kilburn, Clarence, 189
Kilgore, Harley, 32, 69
King, Cecil, 266
Kirwan, Michael, 199, 301
Knowland, William, 17, 26, 35, 40, 77, 113ff., 304ff.
Korean War, 35ff., 38f.
Krock, Arthur, 305

Langer, William, 70, 86
Lapham, Lewis J., 18n, 197n, 198n
LeCompte, Karl, 242
Lesinski, John, 30
Lindzey, Gardner, 44n
Lippmann, Walter, 8
Lodge, Henry Cabot, 17, 30
Lucas, Scott, 17, 18, 28, 31, 33, 39, 40, 101, 106ff., 116, 118f., 123, 130f., 137, 140f., 298, 303

McCarran, Pat, 28, 32, 137, 287
McCarthy, Joseph, 31, 33, 76, 86
McClellan, John, 137, 287
McCormack, John, 17, 169, 198f., 203, 205–219, 225f., 228f., 233f., 236, 241ff., 298, 301, 314
McFarland, Ernest, 112f., 117, 303f.
McKellar, Kenneth, 102, 122, 125, 137, 141
McKinnon, Clinton, 226
Macmahon, Arthur W., 6n

MacRae, Duncan, Jr., 44n, 165n, 186n, 205n, 219n, 259n, 283n, 329n, 330
Magnuson, Warren, 70
Majority party, peculiarities of, 93, 148, 226, 278, 282, 286ff., 289ff.
 truncated, 308, 312ff.
Mansfield, Mike, 301
March, James G., 108n
Martin, Joseph, 17, 23, 29f., 188, 198f., 203, 205–208, 219–227, 228ff., 235, 240ff., 310
Maybank, Burnet, 137
Mediate group, 95ff., 115ff., 130, 193ff., 205, 217, 225, 292ff., 297, 300ff.
Merton, Robert K., 293n
Miller, Warren E., 321n, 322n
Millikin, Eugene, 17, 70, 101, 122, 125, 139, 142
Minimum wages, 25f.
Minority party, peculiarities of, 76, 85, 93, 110, 121, 126, 143, 148, 185f., 192, 226, 232, 246, 281f., 286ff., 308ff.
Morse, Wayne, 77, 86
Murdock, John, 199
Myers, Francis, 17, 39, 101, 117ff., 303

Nasatir, David, 108n
National Science Foundation, 31
Natural gas, 25, 31f., 107f., 180
Neely, Matthew, 69, 107
Neustadt, Richard E., 22n, 37n, 295n, 313, 318f.
Newcomb, Theodore M., 44n
Nicholson, Donald, 189
Nixon, Richard M., 39
North Atlantic Treaty, 25, 88
Nucleus, definition of, 47

Olds, Leland, 25
O'Mahoney, Joseph, 28, 36

Parties, Congressional, policy differences, 81, 91ff., 184, 191, 283ff., 291
Party, Congressional, 8–10, 42f., 81, 95ff., 193ff., 217, 247, 280ff., 292ff., 300ff., 316ff.
 size of house and, 96, 145ff., 194ff., 249

Party, see also Majority party, Minority party, Democratic party, Republican party
Party, electoral, 6, 8, 196, 290f.
Party orthodoxy, Democratic, 61, 69, 71, 107, 118f., 123f., 160ff., 206, 230f., 233f., 238
 Republican, 80f., 89, 107, 118f., 122ff., 181f., 206, 230f., 233f., 238
 index, 60, 326f.
Patronage committee, Senate, 102f., 125
Pickett, Tom, 165
Polanyi, Karl, 3n
Policy committee, House, 39, 199f., 231ff.
 Senate, 17, 101, 103f., 126–132, 297
Poll taxes, 24, 159, 165, 180, 229
President, role of, 3–4, 8, 9, 50, 81, 93, 99, 104, 131, 186, 226, 232, 286ff., 289–319
 see also Administration
President pro tempore, 102f.
Price, Hugh D., 330n
Price, Melvin, 263, 267
Priest, Percy, 17, 150, 165, 199, 228–230
Public works, 32, 137, 141

Railway labor, 40
Rankin, John, 241
Ranney, Austin, 247n
Rayburn, Sam, 17, 18, 23, 24, 25, 27, 30, 32, 33, 197f., 203, 233, 236, 266, 278, 296n, 301, 314, 316
Reciprocal trade, 19, 26
Rent control, 19, 20, 34f., 39, 88, 179f., 229
Reorganization, executive, 19, 25, 33f.
Republican party, divisions in, 16–17, 49f., 150, 205, 224
 House, structural fluidity in, 172ff., 184ff., 188, 190, 220, 225ff., 228, 230, 240f., 278, 281f.
 voting structure of, 172–190
 Senate, structural fluidity in, 74ff., 81, 82ff., 86, 91ff., 121, 126, 137f., 244, 281f.
 voting structure of, 72–89
Rice, Stuart A., 45n, 48n, 320ff.
Riddick, Floyd M., 98n, 117n, 195n

Riecken, Henry W., 95n
Rogers, Lindsay, 195n
Roll calls, as data, 12–13, 44, 146
Roosevelt, Franklin D., 292, 296f., 298, 299, 306n
Rossiter, Clinton, 290n
Rules Committee, House, 18, 23f., 27, 40, 197, 201, 231ff.
  see also Twenty-one-day rule
Russell, Richard, 97, 113, 117, 303

Sabath, Adolph, 18, 23, 264
Saltonstall, Leverett, 17, 41, 102, 117ff., 122, 125, 305
Samuel, Howard D., 28n, 120n, 172n, 259n, 260n
Scaling, cumulative, 329f.
Scheduling function, 105, 129, 131f., 203, 229
Schlesinger, Arthur M., Jr., 312n
Score, definition of, 45f.
Secrest, Robert, 171
Sectional cleavages, 57f., 72, 77f., 91, 150ff., 179, 191
Selective Service, 35
Seniority, voting and, 211ff., 215ff., 219ff., 268, 273, 277
Seniority leaders, House, 201, 237–244, 282, 287f., 296, 307
  Senate, 99f., 133–144, 282, 286ff., 296, 307
Shelley, John, 266
Sherif, Muzafer, 44n
Simmel, Georg, 97n
Smathers, George, 301
Smith, H. Alexander, 285
Smith, Margaret Chase, 41
Social security, 27, 35, 179f.
Southern Democrats, House, 158ff., 162, 164ff., 170f., 207, 211
  Senate, 58f., 61ff., 66, 70, 91, 315
Speaker of the House, 17, 197f., 202, 204, 232
Specialization, in House, 239f., 270
State delegations, House, 158n, 178, 225, 236, 247–269, 272, 275f.
  Alabama Democrats, 264
  California Democrats, 266f.
  Illinois Democrats, 263f.
  New York Democrats, 264

State delegations, House, Texas Democrats, 265f.
  Wisconsin Republicans, 264f.
  Senate, 47f., 69f., 268f.

Taber, John, 189
Taft, Robert A., 16, 17, 20, 23, 25, 26, 29, 30, 39, 76, 97, 101, 110, 113ff., 117, 122, 125, 139, 142ff., 281f., 289, 308, 313, 316
Taft-Hartley Act, 20f., 23, 30, 34, 88
Tax bills, 29, 36, 39, 180, 278
Thibaut, John W., 95n
Thomas, Elbert, 23, 39, 137, 287
Thomas, Elmer, 137
Thye, Edward, 77
Tobey, Charles, 86, 139
Truman, David B., 6n, 131n, 266n, 308n
Truman, Harry S., 16, 17, 19, 22, 28f., 30, 32, 33f., 36, 37, 38, 39, 40f., 292, 300n, 304, 312f.
Tryon, Robert C., 329
Turner, Julius, 9n, 165n
Twenty-one-day rule, 18, 23, 24, 27, 29f., 31, 32, 159, 160, 180, 197, 233f.
Tydings, Millard, 31, 33, 39, 137

Udall, Stewart L., 194n
United Mine Workers, 69

Vandenberg, Arthur, 25, 33, 139
Vetoes, presidential, 32, 34, 38, 209, 242
Voorhis, Jerry, 6, 259n, 282n, 294n

Walter, Francis, 199
Wechsler, Herbert, 6n
Weiss, Robert S., 44n
Westerfield, H. Bradford, 306n
Wherry, Kenneth, 17, 18, 25, 70, 101, 106ff., 116, 118ff., 122, 124f., 135, 138f., 141f., 289, 309
Whip, House, 17, 227–230, 281, 301
  Senate, 17, 101f., 117–122, 281, 301
White, William S., 4n, 97n, 104n, 108n, 115n, 117, 132n, 141n, 294n, 299, 303n, 304n, 314
Whyte, William F., 43n, 291n

Wiley, Alexander, 86, 139
Williams, John, 78
Williams, Philip, 9n
Wilson, Woodrow, 98f., 133f., 196, 237, 277f., 291n, 317
Wolcott, Jesse, 31

Wolff, Kurt H., 97n
Wood, John, 241
Woodruff, Roy, 199

Yates, Sidney, 264
Young, Milton, 76, 86